FACTORY PRODUCTION IN NINETEENTH-CENTURY BRITAIN

THE VICTORIAN ARCHIVES SERIES
General Editor: Mary Poovey

THE FINANCIAL SYSTEM IN NINETEENTH-CENTURY BRITAIN
Mary Poovey, *New York University*

FACTORY PRODUCTION IN NINETEENTH-CENTURY BRITAIN
Elaine Freedgood, *New York University*

Send us your comments on this card or online (http://www.oup-usa.org/highered/subject).

My comments on

Author/Editor _____ Title _____

_____

_____

_____

_____

_____ Date _____

May we quote you? ☐ yes ☐ no

Course name _____ Level ☐ Fresh. ☐ Soph. ☐ Sen. ☐ Grad.

Will you adopt? ☐ Definitely ☐ Possibly ☐ No   For use as: ☐ Required text ☐ Recommended reading

Decision date _____ Approximate enrollment _____

Current text _____

Name (please print) _____

Department _____ Position _____

Institution _____

City _____ State _____ Zip code _____

E-mail address _____

Telephone number _____

FACTORY PRODUCTION IN NINETEENTH-CENTURY BRITAIN

Edited by
Elaine Freedgood
New York University

New York   Oxford
OXFORD UNIVERSITY PRESS
2003

Oxford University Press

Oxford New York
Auckland Bangkok Buenos Aires Cape Town Chennai
Dar es Salaam Delhi Hong Kong Istanbul Karachi Kolkata
Kuala Lumpur Madrid Melbourne Mexico City Mumbai
Nairobi São Paulo Shanghai Taipei Tokyo Toronto

Copyright © 2003 by Oxford University Press, Inc.

Published by Oxford University Press, Inc.
198 Madison Avenue, New York, New York, 10016
http://www.oup-usa.org

Oxford is a registered trademark of Oxford University Press

Library of Congress Cataloging-in-Publication Data

Factory production in nineteenth-century Britain / edited by Elaine Freedgood.
        p. cm. — (The Victorian archives series ; 2)
     ISBN 0-19-516101-7 (cloth) — ISBN 0-19-514872-X (pbk. : alk. paper)
        1. Production management—Great Britain—History—19th century. 2. Factory
management—Great Britain—History—19th century. I. Freedgood, Elaine. II. Series.

TS155 .F4855 2003
670.42′0941′09034—dc21

                                                                        2002025781
Printing number: 9 8 7 6 5 4 3 2 1

Printed in the United States of America
on acid-free paper

For my students

Contents

Preface

The primary texts on factory production collected in this volume are intended for use by undergraduate and graduate students studying the literature and history of Victorian Britain. The first factories are the subject of these works, and for this reason the works may also be valuable to students of industrial development, of the history of economics, of urbanization, of women's work, and of the history of childhood, to name just a few of the topics and issues that intersect with industrialization and the factory in its most obvious material effect. The factory system is central to any conception of modernity; the documents collected here suggest how unsystematic that system was in its origins and early development.

Factory Production in Nineteenth-Century Britain brings together a small number of texts that might be easily found in any library with many others that have become obscure, having fallen outside the purview of academic disciplines as they now exist. These texts suggest that industrial development in Britain generated new genres along with new modes of production and that each of these new genres reflects a mode of understanding, and often of critiquing, the nascent system it confronts. These works also helped to write into existence a reality that was taking shape unevenly and unpredictably. Written descriptions of the "factory system" follow so closely on the heels of its establishment that we need to consider the extent to which such accounts explained and indeed invented a system before it was completely up and running, let alone intelligible to its observers.

Anthologizing any writing is inherently destructive and reconstructive, as the recent work of Leah Price has so cogently argued: The anthologist necessarily prescribes or proscribes the reading of others.[1] So let me acknowledge this problem straight out, not to dispose of it but rather to explore the possibilities it creates. I have chosen texts that I think are central to the discursive

---

1. Leah Price, *The Anthology and the Rise of the Novel* (Cambridge: Cambridge Univ. Press, 2000), 12.

construction of the factory system, and I have also included texts that I think are quirky and interesting, texts that won't easily be found by the average curious student without some help. These texts were crucial to the discursive construction of the factory system; our neglect of them has served to homogenize our sense of the changes in production that led to this new way of making things. These texts make it impossible to divide Victorians into discrete groups of supporters and critics of industrialization. They also make it impossible to put together a coherent narrative of industrial change. Rather, they suggest that the instantiation of the factory system was a messy business, going forward in one industry toward greater automation while looping backward in another to hand and home production. Written responses to this very bumpy series of developments and regressions reflect the confusion, ambivalence, hope, excitement, and fear that such unpredictable change wrought.

I hope that the well-known, little-known and unknown works collected here will illuminate one another in interesting ways and enhance our sense of the complexity of the Victorian reaction to the advent of the factory system. Together with the suggestions for further reading that appear at the end of the book, they will complicate and enlarge the ways we continue to think about the development of mass production and the social relations that attend it, including the social relations that lead to the production of what we think of as knowledge. The Victorian intellectuals who addressed both the history of painting and the politics of the economy, the wealth of nations and the wallpaper of rooms seem very far away from us now. We might imagine, as we read their work, what it would be like to undivide some labors and reunite what now seem like hopelessly disparate realms of thought and of action.

ACKNOWLEDGMENTS

The School of Arts and Sciences at the University of Pennsylvania and an American Fellowship from the American Association of University Women provided the time and money to make work on this project possible. April Fletcher and Joanna Holzman did impeccable research: They have my gratitude and admiration. Joanna also wrote most of the biographies of the authors that appear at the end of this volume. Mary Poovey has been a wonderful editor, interlocutor, and friend throughout. Nancy Bentley's friendship and advice were indispensable during the researching of this book. I wish to thank Gina Dent, Rob Held, Carolyn Lesjak, Trish Loughran, Talia Schaffer, Gauri Viswanathan, Jamie Wasserman, Caroline Weber, and Patricia White for their support and friendship. Jenna Mormelo was a pillar of strength. Debra Roth inspires all the work I do.

This book is dedicated to my students. Rachel Buurma has been influencing my ideas for a long time now; she not only did significant research for this book, through our discussions she improved my conception of it considerably. Many other graduate students at the University of Pennsylvania have inspired me: I hope that Laura Heffernan, Carmen Higgins, Michelle Karnes, Carolyn Lesnick, Damien Keane, Matthew Merlino, and Deborah Shapple in particular will accept this book as a token of my admiration. I have a great debt to my undergraduates at New York University in the fall semester of 2001, who, in the wake of September 11, continued to read, think, complain, and learn with style, verve, and tenacity. I have been truly lucky to finish this book in their fine company.

Chronology

1733	John Kay invents the flying shuttle, speeding the process of hand-loom weaving.
1759	Josiah Wedgwood's pottery opens in Burslem.
1766	Grand Trunk Canal opens.
1769	Richard Arkwright and John Kay take out a patent for a spinning frame which makes it possible for warp threads to be made of cotton rather than linen. This is the origin of calico in Britain (it has long been produced in Calicut, in India). James Watt patents his first steam engine.
1770	James Hargreaves patents the spinning jenny.
1775	Matthew Boulton and James Watt establish engineering firm.
1776	American war of independence begins.
	Adam Smith's *Wealth of Nations.*
1779	Samuel Crompton invents the spinning mule.
1782	Slubbing billy invented.
1784	Henry Cort invents "puddling" process for iron production.
1787	Power loom patented by Edmund Cartwright.
1788	French Revolution begins.
1793	Eli Whitney invents the cotton gin.
	Beginning of Napoleonic Wars.
1798	Thomas Malthus's *Essay on the Principle of Population.*
1799	The Combination Act passed, forbidding collective action and bargaining.
1880	Second Combination Act passed.
1801	Union of England and Ireland.
	First English census.
	Robert Owen establishes model factory and factory village at New Lanark, Scotland.
1802	Factory Act limits the hours of "apprentices" (usually indigent children).
	Requires mill owners to provide some education, have workers

sleep no more than two to a bed, and attend church once per month. Also requires that mills be whitewashed and ventilated.

1807   Slave trade outlawed; slave-holding continues.

1809   John Heathcoat invents lace-making machine.

1812   Luddite riots.

1814   *London Times* printed by a steam-powered press.

1819   Factory Act prohibits labor in cotton mills by children under nine. There is no way to enforce this law since there are as yet no factory inspectors; additionally, there are no birth certificates or other means to prove age.

Peterloo Massacre.

1822   Charles Babbage begins building his calculating machine, a proto-computer.

1830   Opening of Liverpool and Manchester railway.

1831   Cholera epidemic.

1832   Harriet Martineau's *Illustrations of Political Economy* published.

Reform Bill, doubling male suffrage in Britain.

1833   Parliamentary Commission of Inquiry into the condition of child laborers.

Staff of full-time factory inspectors appointed. Nightwork forbidden to all children under eighteen; no child under eleven could work more than nine hours a day; children under eleven had to be provided with twelve hours a week of school.

1834   New Poor Law, requiring that anyone in need of government assistance enter a workhouse rather than receive "outdoor" assistance.

Abolition of slavery in the British Empire.

1838   Great Western Railway opens.

1839   Charles Goodyear vulcanizes rubber.

Carlyle's *Chartism* published.

1840   Penny post established.

1841   Parliamentary Commission of Inquiry into the conditions of child laborers.

1842   Edwin Chadwick's *Sanitary Condition of the Labouring Population of Great Britain* published.

1843   Factory Act limits women and children to a twelve-hour work day.

1844   "Fencing in" of machinery required and all factory accidents to be reported to inspectors.

The Railway Act.

The Banking Act.

1845   Great Famine of Ireland begins.

1846	Corn Laws repealed.
1847	Ten Hours Act passes: women and children limited to ten hours a day of work in textile factories.
1848	Revolutionary upheavals throughout Europe.
	Great Chartist Demonstration in London.
	John Stuart Mill's *Principles of Political Economy* published.
	Elizabeth Gaskell's *Mary Barton* published.
	Karl Marx's *Communist Manifesto* published.
	Cholera epidemic.
1850	Factories can only be open for twelve hours a day—either from 6 AM to 6 PM or from 7 AM to 7 PM.
1851	Crystal Palace Exhibition.
1854	Charles Dickens's *Hard Times* published.
1867	Second Reform Bill, reducing property qualifications for the vote (for men only).
	Marx's *Capital* published (in German; first English translation 1886).
1868	Suez Canal opens.
1871	Trade Unions legalized.
1884	Third Reform Bill extends franchise to all male householders.
1889	London Dock Strike, first major strike to succeed by male unskilled workers.

INTRODUCTION

The Great Exhibition of 1851 displayed nothing less than the "Works of Industry of All Nations." It celebrated "industry" in the widest possible sense. Any goods produced, extracted, or cultivated by human labor were included, and the most unlikely items rub shoulders in its displays: sculptures of mythic figures and bushels of wheat; Jacquard looms and handmade lace; railway carriages and hand-carved tooth brushes. In page after page of the quirky and seemingly fantastic lists that make up the *Catalogue*,[1] we can find things like "a portable self-supporting pulpit" contributed by an individual inventor; a "carved book-tray, executed by a ploughman, in the evening, by candle light . . . solely with a pen knife"; "a variety of miscellaneous articles" by Mary Jane Cannings, who, it is noted, is "blind, deaf and dumb."

These "modes" of production were clearly important in the social imagination of mid-Victorian Britain. The quirky inventor; the ploughman working at night with only a penknife to aid him; the blind and deaf handicraft worker who had only the sense of touch to guide her work: These contributors to the Exhibition are emblems of innovation and resourcefulness and are as significant as the machines and the many machine-made goods on display. These kinds of work were important enough and, even more critically, still *representative* enough of British industry (in 1851) to deserve notice in the Exhibition along with the newer forms of production, forms that caused, unbeknownst to the general public in 1851, an industrial revolution.

Yet the fact remains that in 1850, less than half of British textile workers were employed in factories.[2] The production of clothing (other than hosiery), shoes, building materials, and household furniture continued to be produced

---

1. *Official Catalogue of the Great Exhibition of the Works of Industry of All Nations,* 2nd ed. (London: W. Clowes and Sons, 1851).
2. Deborah Valenze, *The First Industrial Woman* (Oxford: Oxford Univ. Press, 1995), 98.

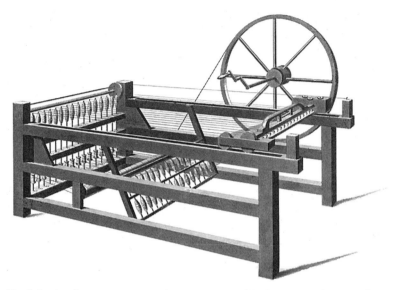

The Spinning Jenny.   (Edward Baines, Jr., *History of the Cotton Manufacture in Great Britain.* London: Fisher, Fisher and Jackson, 1835.)

in "traditional" ways.[3] The power loom, the steam engine, the spinning frame, the sewing machine: These agents of revolutionary change are on display at the Great Exhibition, but they had not achieved the dominance in mid-Victorian imaginations that we might expect in part because they had not achieved that dominance in production. Factory production was correctly understood, at the midcentury mark, as only *one* form of production. Indeed the Crystal Palace itself was made of a representative combination of machine-turned mahogany and handblown glass panes. Most significantly, at the mid-century mark, "industry" still meant "work"; it has yet to take on its later meaning of mechanized production on a large scale.

The products of industry on display at the Great Exhibition also suggest that in 1851, certain categories had not yet taken shape. An improved rolling barley chumper, a barrel of Kildrummie oats, pieces of Cornish slate, single-milled kerseymire, a "colossal" statue of the Duke of Wellington, drain pipes manufactured by machinery, elder-flower toilet soap: These items would simply not belong together in the same exhibition today. Indeed, this kind of in-

3. Eric Hobsbawm, *Industry and Empire: The Birth of the Industrial Revolution* (New York: New Press, 1999), 49.

clusive and extensive collection has come to seem particularly and peculiarly Victorian, not unlike the exuberant catalogues we find in a Dickens novel or the vertiginously additive agglomerations in one of J. R. McCulloch's dictionaries or statistical accounts. The lists of items displayed at the Exhibition suggest that we have to imagine a different epistemological model in which the categories that now seem natural and inevitable to us, if they existed at all, were still, for the mid-Victorians, in an extremely elastic state. Certainly, the idea of the "commodity" is not yet firm, and what counted as "industrial" was a much more capacious category than it will eventually become when it is used to describe the revolution in manufacture that occurred in Britain between 1750 and 1850.

Today, an "industrial" exhibition would feature factory-made goods simply because industrial production now *means* factory production; factory production, in turn, is the form of production we expect to be the source of almost everything we use. Goods made "by hand" have become rare and special. They have also been subdivided into the hierarchy of (fine) art and (rougher) craft. Neither art nor craft can usually compete with factory-made goods—in price, availability, and sometimes even in quality. And we don't expect them to do so. Factory production has become unquestionably predominant; today, questions about production are more likely to center on where it will take place rather than how.

Many modes of production were still in active coexistence in the mid-nineteenth century, and some modes of mechanical production actually engendered handicraft and small scale production: Machine-made lace required "finishing" by hand; refineries produced so much sugar that the small-scale home production of sweets increased to take advantage of this new abundance.[4] But it is nonetheless the factory and the kinds of work and ways of life it produced that became the focus of an extensive and energetic debate: The social, psychological, environmental, and economic impact of the factory system was celebrated, analyzed, criticized, and derided from all quarters. This intense debate produced thousands of pages of industrial writing, and this writing helped to write into existence a "system" that was still taking shape through the middle of the nineteenth century, the factory system. In other words, the texts of industrialization created and constructed a social reality for their readers as much as they represented or tried to reflect a reality that was already in existence. Readers of these texts could then "find" an increasingly dominant factory system out there in the world around them, although such a system was really in the process of taking hold throughout the first half of the

---

4. Raphael Samuel, "Mechanization and Hand Labour in Industrializing Britain." In *The Industrial Revolution and Work in Nineteenth-Century Europe,* ed. Lenard R. Berlanstein. (London: Routledge, 1992).

Carding, Drawing, and Roving. (Edward Baines, Jr., *History of the Cotton Manufacture in Great Britain.* London: Fisher, Fisher and Jackson, 1835.)

century, and it was only one among several active and thriving modes of production.[5]

What got written and built and worked into existence over more than one hundred years is nothing less than the process that was dubbed the "Industrial Revolution" by the Victorian historian and Oxford don Arnold Toynbee in a series of popular lectures given in 1884. Toynbee's description of the main components of this "revolution" has held up very well. He notes first of all a sudden upsurge in population growth in the mid-eighteenth century, followed by improvements in equipment used in the manufacture of cotton, the development of better and safer steam engines, and the expansion of communication and transportation networks, especially railroads. Factories became concentrated in the new phenomenon of the "great town," where once, in the form of mills, they had occupied largely rural locations because of their need for the power derived from the swift currents of streams or rivers. Factories employed a newly enormous number of workers, including women and children.

---

5. Andrew Zimmerman has pointed out that we have been unduly influenced by Marx's reading of classical political economy as an apology for a system that fully existed at the time it was described. Instead, we should understand that "the all-encompassing system of industrial manufacture that [Charles] Babbage and [Andrew] Ure allegedly justified and Marx took to be real, in fact probably did not exist at the time of their apologies" ("The Ideology of the Machine and the Spirit of the Factory: Remarx on Babbage and Ure." *Cultural Critique* #37 (Fall 1997), 5).

Technological innovation occurred at a quickened pace, and new developments—the spinning jenny, the power loom, the puddling of iron, improvements in the steam engine—made for greater productivity, and often greater social unrest, as they caused waves of unemployment, underemployment, or changes of employment. Toynbee sums up the greatest change between the domestic system of production and the factory system as a loss of independence on the part of the worker, who no longer owned the tools of his or her trade and who became subject to "the regular recurrence of periods of overproduction and depression. . . ."[6]

To Toynbee's rather staid description of the phenomenon for which he coined such a dramatic phrase, let me add the more momentous prose of the historian Eric Hobsbawm, writing at the very end of the twentieth century:

> The Industrial Revolution marks the most fundamental transformation of human life in the history of the world recorded in written documents. For a brief period it coincided with the history of a single country, Great Britain. An entire world economy was thus built on, or rather around, Britain, and this country therefore temporarily rose to a position of global influence and power unparalleled by any state of its relative size before or since, and unlikely to be paralleled by any state in the foreseeable future. There was a moment in the world's history when Britain can be described . . . as its only workshop, its only massive importer and exporter, its only carrier, its only imperialist, almost its only foreign investor; and for that reason its only naval power and the only one which had a genuine world policy.[7]

In the century between the writing of Toynbee and Hobsbawm, historians have repeatedly altered accounts of the speed, the nature, and the effects of the change that is still called the Industrial Revolution. This massive historiography shifts and changes often, as David Cannadine has pointed out, depending on the economic features of the moment in which it is written: The 1950s, for example, saw historians writing with an optimistic attitude toward growth; the 1970s found historians in more pessimistic and reserved frames of mind, declaring that the very slow pace of the changes that are called a revolution make the word a serious misnomer.[8] But for our purposes, the significant feature of the history of history writing about the changes in production

---

6. Arnold Toynbee, *Lectures on the Industrial Revolution of the Eighteenth Century in England: Popular Addresses, Notes and Other Fragments*. (New York: The Humboldt Publishing Co.), 91–2.

7. Eric Hobsbawm, *Industry and Empire: The Birth of the Industrial Revolution* (New York: The New Press, 1999), xi.

8. David Cannadine, "The Present and the Past in the English Industrial Revolution 1880–1980." *Past and Present* (No. 103): 131–172.

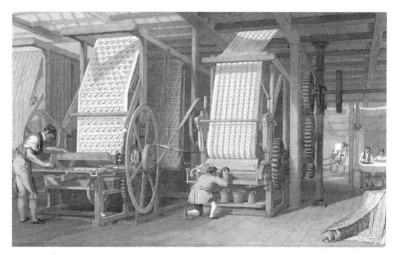

Calico Printing.   (Edward Baines, Jr., *History of the Cotton Manufacture in Great Britain.* London: Fisher, Fisher and Jackson, 1835.)

of the late eighteenth and early nineteenth centuries is that the term Industrial Revolution has stuck.

The dates of this Revolution have also been a subject of great debate. The beginning is located somewhere in the second half of the eighteenth century; the end may not yet have occurred. The "peak" or end point of the takeoff process is often cited as 1850, the year before the Great Exhibition. My texts span the seventy or so years before and after the midcentury mark: 1776 to 1921, or Adam Smith to Mahatma Gandhi. I have included Smith because of his classic theorization of the beneficial division of labor in an often-revisited pin factory; I have included Gandhi because of his classic theorization of the devastation wrought on India by the global division of labor brought about by the industrialization of cotton production.

Smith and Gandhi are also emblematic of the range of opinion that industrialization entailed and continues to entail. Even among those who supported the idea of the factory system, or saw it as inevitable, the specifics of how industrialization ought to proceed were controversial. Ideas that came to form the core concepts of industrial capitalism, for example that factory production itself is inevitable, were contested with energy and insight from every political direction. This issue brought together conservatives like Thomas Carlyle and John Ruskin, in rough ideological terms, with Luddite machine-breakers and the utopian socialist William Morris: All ferociously disputed the idea that the growth of technology should never be impeded. Machines and machine work were dehumanizing and impoverishing in the view of these writers and activists, and for them it was clear that sometimes a technological improvement should be foregone for the sake of higher human interests. Morris specifically rejected the concept that previously unheard-of quantities of uniform goods were an unmixed blessing; he argued instead for producing fewer things that were better made, preferably by hand.

Those who did support factory technology also formed a motley group. Marx and Engels believed that machinery could save time and effort that could be used by workers for more fulfilling activities, as did the utopian capitalist and factory owner Robert Owen, but all three held that the highly mechanized factory would only be socially beneficial if the right economic and social structures were in place. David Ricardo, the most important political economist of the first half of the nineteenth century, came to support the extensive use of machinery because he saw it as the only way that Britain could remain competitive in world markets. Otherwise, he was in sympathy with the workers who were breaking machines and conceded that machinery was not in their interests except in the very long term.

We can readily see that opposition to the factory system made for unlikely agreements among politically heterogeneous thinkers. It also made for outright allies in unlikely combinations. Maxine Berg has pointed out that Tory (the conservative political party) opponents of the system became enthusiastic articulators of "working class grievances, which gave them another way of expressing their own deep-seated emotional values."[9] Perhaps the most famous document of this kind is Richard Oastler's "Yorkshire Slavery" (1830), originally a letter to the editor of the *Leeds Mercury,* in which he declares that the "miserable inhabitants of a Yorkshire town . . . are this very moment existing in a state of slavery, more horrid than are the victims of that hellish system—'colonial slavery.' "[10]

A strange feature of Victorian political and economic thinking of this period is the frequent similarity of conservative and radical political, economic, and social positions. Conservatives, as their name suggests, tended to want to conserve traditional, or what Carlyle called "organic," forms of production and social organization; radicals often ended up taking similar positions in an attempt to hold back the negative effects on workers of industrial and economic "progress." For both of these groups, there was a sense that "the purpose and definition of political economy should not be confined to the narrow sphere of wealth and increasing wealth, but should concern itself with creating social happiness."[11]

---

9. Maxine Berg, *The Machinery Question and the Making of Political Economy* (Cambridge: Cambridge Univ. Press, 1980), 250.

10. Qtd in "Alfred," *The History of the Factory Movement* (London: Simpkin, Marshall, and Co, 1857), 99.

11. Berg, 272.

7 stories high—158 yds. long—18 yds. broad—660 windows—32,500 panes of glass. (Edward Baines, Jr., *History of the Cotton Manufacture in Great Britain*. London: Fisher, Fisher and Jackson, 1835.)

The defenders of the factory system were a small but obviously quite effective group: They were liberals (who are closest to today's conservatives) who believed in unimpeded technological progress and unfettered competition at every level of the economy. Some members of this group—like David Ricardo—are well-known and much-studied; in this volume I've also included writers whose work has fallen through the disciplinary cracks and has therefore been largely forgotten. Writers as various as George Dodd, a factory tourist, Andrew Ure, a philosopher of manufacture, and Edward Baines, an historian of the cotton industry, substantially contributed to the efforts of the liberal defenders of industrialization through, respectively, their celebrations of technology, their apologies for and explanations of the apparent horrors of the factory system, and their comprehensive understanding of the development of the specific processes of particular manufactures. These writers helped the factory system surmount any and all opposition largely through developing or contributing to the naturalization of mass production, that is to say, the sense that this form of production had come to stay, and that it was no longer, *pace* the Luddites, Carlyle, Ruskin, and Morris alike, optional.

The divisions of labor that multiplied at a precipitous pace within industrial production also took place in the production of knowledge. Carlyle, Ruskin, and Morris, for example, saw themselves, and indeed were seen by their contemporaries, as perfectly able to comment on political economy as

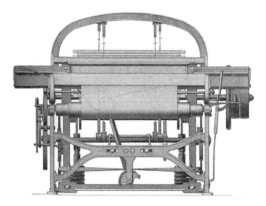

Power Loom. (Edward Baines, Jr., *History of the Cotton Manufacture in Great Britain.* London: Fisher, Fisher and Jackson, 1835.)

well as on art, literature, and culture generally. But this kind of polymathic intellectual participation changed in the nineteenth century: One of the effects of the industrial revolution was to split off economic thought from cultural criticism. Accordingly, Carlyle, Ruskin, and Morris are scarcely if ever read by economists today; their work is now preserved in the domain of literature, where much of the critique of industrialization resides. Indeed, literature became the place from which the political, economic, and social domains would be criticized, and those criticisms could and did achieve canonical status. They became unthreatening for the very reason that they were and are read as "literary" works and not as works of political economy or sociology. The Coketown of *Hard Times* and the Darkshire of *North and South* refer their readers to real places and problems, but they do so within the reassuring frame of the fictional. Similarly, when Ruskin rejects the value of machine production and attempts to rehabilitate the handcraftsmanship of the workers who built Gothic cathedrals in the Middle Ages, his recommendations are literary and therefore nontransferable in some sense: There is no threat that they will be considered as policy initiatives in the real world. The anti-industrialism of Victorian "literary" works did not threaten the spread of the factory system; rather, it provided a helpful site of harmless critique.

The literature of industrialization brought forth many new genres, some of which, like the industrial novel, are quite well known. Other genres have not received much attention; many belong to no discipline or specialty. The "condition of the laboring population" book is a work of social investigation in which workers are scrutinized physically and morally, and suggestions for their improvement are made. The most well-known "condition of the laboring population" texts are those written by Friedrich Engels, Edwin Chadwick,

James Phillips Kay-Shuttleworth and Peter Gaskell. Although these writers differ politically, ranging from the revolutionary (Engels) to the reformist (Kay-Shuttleworth, Chadwick, and Gaskell), they tend to identify the same kinds of problems. The absolute physical immiserization of the laboring classes in the jerry-built housing of the great towns is rendered in page after page of description of the rows of back-to-back buildings and the ordure that inevitably surrounds them. Here is Engels describing Little Ireland, "the most horrible spot" in Manchester:

> In a rather deep hole, in a curve of the Medlock [river] and surrounded on all four sides by tall factories and high embankments, covered with buildings, stand two groups of about 200 cottages, built chiefly back to back, in which live about 4,000 human beings, most of them Irish. The cottages are old, dirty, and of the smallest sort, the streets uneven, fallen into ruts and in part without drains or pavement; masses of refuse, offal, and sickening filth lie among standing pools in all directions; the atmosphere is poisoned by the effluvia from these, and laden and darkened by the smoke of a dozen tall factory chimneys. A horde of ragged women and children swarm about here, as filthy as the swine that thrive upon the garbage heaps and in the puddles.[12]

The physical degradation Engels describes is implicitly linked to the moral degradation implied by the fact of swarming and filthy women and children. The absence of proper domesticity is attributed by all of these writers to the long hours worked by women in factories and their consequent loss of what are problematically figured as the inherently feminine skills of homemaking.

The bad influence of the Irish is cited all too regularly. They are routinely accused of helping the English to get used to the most inhuman level of poverty:

> The Irish have taught the labouring classes of this country a pernicious lesson. . . . Debased alike by ignorance and pauperism, they have discovered, with the savage, what is the minimum means of life, by which existence may be prolonged. The paucity of the amount of means and comforts *necessary for the mere support of life,* is not known by a more civilized population, and this secret has been taught the labourers of this country by the Irish.[13]

In this extraordinary logic, poverty becomes a learned habit rather than a condition brought about by low wages and regular unemployment. And this kind of logic recurs regularly in the works of authors who are criticizing the effects of industrialization but not seeking to stop its growth.

---

12. Friedrich Engels, *The Condition of the Working Class in England.* David McLellan, ed. (Oxford: Oxford Univ. Press, 1993), 72.
13. James Phillips Kay-Shuttleworth, *The Moral and Physical Condition of the Working Classes,* 2nd ed. (London: J. Ridgway, 1832), 21.

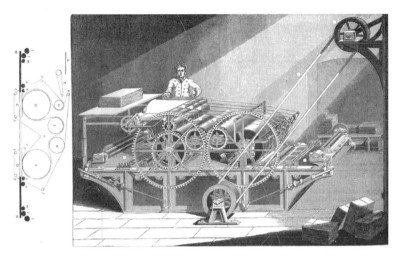

Printing Machine. (George Dodd, *Days at the Factories*. London: Charles Knight, 1843.)

The key point about this genre is that each author offers solutions for industrial problems that leave industrialization itself intact. Peter Gaskell advises that "much should be done—and done vigorously and resolutely." Otherwise "it is to be feared that an explosion will be permitted to take place, undirected by the guiding hand of any patriotic and sagacious spirit. . . ."[14] Kay-Shuttleworth assures his readers that "the evils here unreservedly exposed, so far from being the necessary consequences of the manufacturing system, have a remote and accidental origin, and might, by *judicious management,* be entirely removed."[15]

The book of factory abuses is usually a compilation of evidence, much of it from parliamentary hearings, that suggests the unmitigated horrors of the factory system. In this genre, the evil consequences of the factory system require radical reform, or the end of the system altogether. In *Evils of the Factory System,* Charles Wing, a surgeon at the Royal Metropolitan Hospital for Children, gathered together a magisterial mass of parliamentary evidence about child labor. Wing sets himself up in opposition to "the clamours of political economists" who had tried to defend a "system which has disgraced us

---

14. Peter Gaskell, *Artisans and Machinery: The Moral and Physical Condition of the Manufacturing Population* (London: John W. Parker, 1836), 362.
15. James Phillips Kay-Shuttleworth, *The Moral and Physical Condition of the Working Classes* (London: James Ridgway, 1832), 15. (emphasis in the original).

Roan-binding Shop.—Messrs. Westleys and Clark's Factory. (George Dodd, *Days at the Factories*. London: Charles Knight, 1843.)

as a nation. . . ."[16] Unlike the "condition of the working class" text, these works tend to suggest that there is something inherently and ineradicably damaging about factory work.

On a much lighter note, the factory tourist tale, a kind of travel writing of industrial production, is a highly entertaining form of industrial literature. A major work of this genre is George Dodd's *Days at the Factories* (1843). Dodd points out that "the bulk of the inhabitants of a great city, such as London, have very indistinct notions of the means whereby the necessaries, the comforts, or the luxuries of life are furnished." Dodd, in a proto-Marxian moment, accuses money of acting as a "veil which hides the producer from the consumer."[17] Dodd would remove the veil by taking us on a tour of factories and workshops in London. We learn about production in painstaking and vivid detail. We see finishers pressing beaver bonnets into shape at a hat factory; men and boys trimming types at a printing office; key-cutters preparing ivory at a pianoforte factory; curriers beating tanned skins with a mace at a leather factory; workers cutting cotton into wicks at a candle factory. Dodd's tales made it possible for curious Victorians to "see" inside factories and to understand processes of production.

---

16. Charles Wing, *Evils of the Factory System* (London: Saunders and Otley, 1837), front matter.
17. George Dodd, *Days at the Factories* (London: Charles Knight & Co., 1843), 1.

Harriet Martineau wrote a series of articles, in the mid-1850s, for Dickens's magazine *Household Words,* chronicling the making of a delightful array of consumer goods, including buttons, umbrellas, screws, and dolls. She encourages her readers to see the complexities of production hiding in each consumer good, showing us that even the smallest among them is the result of a detailed system of labor: "'I don't care a button,' we say: but little as a button may be worth to us, one single specimen may be worth to the manufacturer long days of toil and nights of care, and the gain or loss of thousands of pounds." Martineau guides us through the engraving, punching, drilling, stamping, and polishing processes involved in button manufacture until we realize that, if we are going to be analogically precise, to care a button might be to care quite a bit and with an unexpected range of feelings.

Histories of particular industries were also popular: Edward Baines, for example, wrote a history of cotton manufacture that remains a standard text on the subject to this day. He chronicles the changes in production that have occurred in the industry, charts its origins in India, and offers minute descriptions of carding, spinning, weaving, and dying. The popularity of his work, and the numerous Victorian histories of industries and industrialists, suggests the extent to which the new processes of production fascinated Victorians. Herbert Sussman has suggested that Victorians were the first "technotourists";[18] they were also great readers about technology. Mechanical reproduction was, for its early audience, an exciting, dangerous, and attractive phenomenon. It is hard for us to imagine that the minutiae of factory equipment held considerable allure for its nineteenth-century audience, but its considerable attractions did generate an entirely new occupation—that of the machine illustrator.[19] Perhaps only the Hershey's Chocolate Factory in Pennsylvania, which now offers a tour of a simulated version of its actual factory, can still inspire in us the kind of fascination and delight many Victorians experienced in seeing or reading about the production processes of everything from cotton fabrics and pins to umbrellas, hats and pianofortes.

For those who were pessimistic about the vicissitudes of factory production, machines seemed like a juggernaut throwing people into and out of employment, with both liberating and devastating results. The factory system of cotton cloth production, for example, replaced a domestic system in which the family rather than the individual was the unit of production. The father/

18. Herbert Sussman, "Machine Dreams: The Culture of Technology." *Victorian Literature and Culture* (28:1): 197–204.
19. "Even if the readers of the *Edinburgh Review* had never been inside a textile mill, they had almost surely seen pictures of the stationary engine and spinning machinery; for the demand for knowledge of the new technology was so great in the century as to call into being the new profession of machine illustrator." Herbert Sussman, *Victorians and the Machine: The Literary Response to Technology* (Cambridge, MA: Harvard Univ. Press, 1968), 17.

"Sending-out Warehouse."—Beaufoy's Vinegar Works. (George Dodd, *Days at the Factories.* London: Charles Knight, 1843.)

husband did the weaving, the wife the spinning, and the children prepared the raw cotton. In this system, the man of the family contracted and controlled the work of his wife and children. With the advent of the factory, women and children became independent contractors in a sense—liberated from husbands and fathers but indentured to a new and impersonal form of authority.

Child labor was of course one of the most controversial issues of industrialization. Liberal apologists for the new form of production maintained that children were better off in factories than in the streets. Moreover, they argued, factories sometimes provided meals, and eventually they were required to have schools and provide a few hours of education a day at a time when there was no education for the poor outside of the occasional charity school. The missionary and explorer David Livingstone grew up working as a piecer in a cotton factory outside Glasgow; he studied in the factory school for two hours each night and was, as a result of this apparently meager course of study, able to qualify for medical school. His life became an emblem for the defenders of child labor: it seemed to prove that any motivated laborer might go to medical school. Versions of his biography were widely reprinted in cheap editions as inspirational literature: in one such work, *The Weaver Boy who Became a Missionary,* we learn that "with his first week's wages [Livingstone] pur-

Type-Foundry.   (George Dodd, *Days at the Factories*. London: Charles Knight, 1843.)

chased 'Ruddiman's Rudiments of Latin,' which language he studies for several years at an evening school which met between the hours of eight and ten."[20]

William Cook Taylor, a Victorian factory inspector and defender of the system, argued that "infant labour . . . was at its worst before anybody thought of a factory. Spinning was so profitable, that every child in the cottage was forced to help in the process—picking the cotton, winding the yarn, and arranging the card-ends. . . . The tasks imposed upon the children were most onerous."[21] At least in the factory system, children were paid wages and could avail themselves of limited educational benefits. Peter Gaskell, a would-be reformer of the factory system, pointed out that the fact of children receiving wages gave them too much authority within the family: "Each child ceases to view itself as a subordinate agent in the household; so far indeed loses the character and bearing of a child, that it pays over to its natural protector a stated sum for food and lodging; thus detaching itself from parental

20. H. G. Adams, *The Weaver Boy Who Became a Missionary* (New York: Robert Carter and Brother, 1882), 10.
21. Quoted in Neil Smelser, *Change in the Industrial Revolution: An application of theory to the British Cotton Industry* (Chicago: Univ. of Chicago Press, 1959), 78.

subjection and control. . . . Parents are thus become the keepers of lodging-houses for their offspring."[22] The debate between these two positions raged on to little effect, and meanwhile "it took twenty-five years of legislation to restrict a child of nine to a sixty-nine hour work week, and that only in cotton mills."[23]

Improvements in machinery made it possible for women to spin vastly increased quantities of yarn, or to become weavers instead of spinners because less strength was required to work a power loom than a hand loom. As a result, women began to participate more profitably in the making of wool and cotton. Indeed, technological innovations caused extensive and disruptive redivisions of labor along gender lines: Men became spinners when the "mule" was introduced; women became weavers when the power loom came to prevail in textile production.

Feminist historians argue that although gender was largely ignored in early accounts of the industrial revolution, it "profoundly shaped the making of the British working class," not least because "employers continually sought to substitute cheaper female and child labor for skilled men, whether in sweated workshops or in factories."[24] Historians have long been debating whether this employment made for more independence for women workers or more drudgery, while nineteenth-century commentators like James Phillips Kay-Shuttleworth, Friedrich Engels, and Peter Gaskell uniformly bemoaned the factory woman's loss of domestic skill and the decline of the quality of domesticity in laboring class homes. In his study of the laboring class of Manchester, Engels argues that the condition of greater employment for women and the resulting decrease in employment for men "unsexes the man and takes from the woman all womanliness without being able to bestow upon the man true womanliness, or the woman true manliness". Although Engels seems on the verge here of making a radical critique of the social construction of gender, a few pages later he resumes a more conventional view of the gendered division of labor when he mourns the fact that "female operatives prove wholly inexperienced and unfit as housekeepers."[25]

The British factory system had global connections and implications from the beginning. The cotton industry relied on raw material from the United States, and therefore on slavery, and during the Civil War, the north of England suffered a "cotton famine." In the autobiography of a weaver, John Ward O'Neil, we find him chronicling that war in as much detail as he can

22. Gaskell, 93–94.
23. Spencer Walpole, qtd. in Clara D. Rackham, *Factory Law* (London: Thomas Nelson and Sons, Ltd., 1938): 21.
24. Anna Clark, *The Struggle for the Breeches: Gender and the Making of the British Working Class* (Berkeley: Univ. of California Press, 1995), 164, 166.
25. Engels, 155, 157.

Packing Warehouse.—Day and Martin's Blacking Factory.   (George Dodd, *Days at the Factories*. London: Charles Knight, 1843.)

gather from news reports, and it becomes evident that the outcome of each battle had profound implications for British cotton workers.

Prior to the advent of the fine quality made available by British mule-spun yarn, Indian muslins were the finest cottons available and were imported to Britain, and to Europe, in large quantities. In his history of cotton, Edward

Baines points out the origin of cotton weaving in India and makes clear the extent to which the British have borrowed Indian techniques. The consequences of this borrowing were devastating for the Indian cotton industry: In the midcentury, cheaper British cotton virtually destroyed Indian cotton production. In Gandhi's vision of independence (*swaraj*), home spinning of cotton was critical in solving Lancashire-wrought poverty and dependence in India. The charka, or spinning wheel, became a symbol of the possibilities for economic revival and political independence in Indian nationalism; wearing indigenous handloomed fabric became a patriotic act in the early twentieth century. The spinning wheel of the Indian nationalist imagination brings us full circle: The British factory system had not only prevailed by the end of the nineteenth century, it became a symbolic target of resistance and rebellion for an entire subcontinent.

O N E

LOOKING INSIDE

The texts collected in this section all involve a curious activity: industrial spectatorship. From Babbage's directions for how to observe "manufactories" to Harriet Martineau's celebration of button production, these works suggest the interest and indeed the awe with which new methods of production were regarded by their Victorian audience. In the detailed history of the cotton manufacture written by Edward Baines, we get a sense of the excitement surrounding the highly profitable inventions of various textile-manufacturing improvements. Hargreaves, we learn, although "illiterate and humble" was also "one of the greatest inventors and improvers in the cotton manufacture": his invention, the spinning jenny, became the emblem of the beginning of the factory system (although early jennies were actually small and could be used in home production). Baines also makes clear the global implications and reverberations of improved cotton manufacturing: He chronicles the efforts of silk and woolen producers to prohibit or heavily tax the import of Indian calicoes promoted by British silk and woolen producers in the late eighteenth century. This calico was often printed or dyed in England, so that the fabric, like today's Toyotas and Hondas, was neither entirely foreign nor strictly domestic. The pressures to heavily tax this cloth continued until the introduction of the spinning mule, which made English calico fine enough to compete with the Indian-handmade variety.

This sense of the globalism of the manufacturing endeavor is exuberantly represented by George Dodd whose engaging chronicle of a visit to a hat factory celebrates the importation of beaver from North America, of neutria furs from South America, and of "gums, resins, and dyes from almost every part of the globe!" By the end of Dodd's essay, we have become conversant with every moment of beaver-hat production and can appreciate the complexity and the massive international division of labor its making requires.

Iron, the stuff out of which so much machinery for factories was and is made, was made almost entirely by hand in the nineteenth century. Lady Bell, whose husband owned an iron works, describes the labor of iron making with dispassionate precision until she comes to the issue of the heat and the cold that the ironworkers must endure as "they pass from the almost unbearable heat of their immediate surroundings to the biting cold a few yards off." Yet even after her compassionate and vivid description of the severe hardships of iron production, she maintains that iron workers, in their security of constant employment and decent wages, are as happy or unhappy as other workers even given the considerable exigencies of their labor.

Finally, Lady Emilia Dilke is anything but dispassionate: Her description of the industrial position of women is that of the muckraking reformer of industrial organization, a group that appeared initially the 1830s and 1840s and then reemerged in the 1890s. Even if they are skilled workers, Dilke argues, women are plagued by the discontinuities of their labor: They work until they marry, yet after marriage are very often "thrown back on the market, forming a fluctuating mass which seeks occasional or partial employment." What from some points of view would be the improvement of the lot of laboring class women, as manifested in their ability to withdraw at least temporarily from constant work, also provides another possibility for exploitation. And exploitation, like mechanical production and its wondrous processes, formed a significant site for spectatorship in the nineteenth century.

CHAPTER ONE

TOURISTS

GEORGE DODD
∞∞∞

A DAY AT A HAT-FACTORY

The early history of our manufactures frequently excites a smile at the quaint and energetic manner in which some of the old writers denounce the fashions of their times; but while we are often disposed to agree with them in ridiculing the strange forms of dress which have been adopted at different periods, we must withhold our assent to the principles of their commercial economy, which are often lamentably short-sighted.

Philip Stubbs, a writer of the Elizabethan age, published, in 1585, his "Anatomie of Abuses," in which, among other things, the costume of the time is made the subject of censure. After anatomizing ladies' dresses, and discoursing on the iniquities of ruffs and furbelows, he visits the wardrobes of the other sex for a similar purpose, and thus speaks of the then fashionable hats:—"Sometimes they use them sharp on the crown, peaking up like the spear or shaft of a steeple, standing a quarter of a yard above the crown of their heads, some more, some less, as please the fancies of their inconstant minds. Some others are flat and broad on the crown, like the battlements of a house. Another sort have round crowns, sometimes with one kind of band, sometimes with another, now black, now white, now russet, now red, now green, now yellow; now this, now that, never content with one colour or fashion two days to an end. And thus in vanity they spend the Lord's treasure, consuming their golden years and silver days in wickedness and sin." But the ma-

From *Days at the Factories: Manufacturing in the Nineteenth Century.* London: Charles Knight & Co., 1843.

terial pleases him as little as the form and colour:—"And as the fashions be rare and strange, so is the stuff whereof their hats be made divers also; for some are of silk, some of velvet, some of taffetie, some of sarcenet, some of wool; and, which is more curious, some of a certain kind of fine hair. These they call *Bever Hats,* of twenty, thirty, or forty shillings price, fetched from beyond the seas, from whence a great sort of other vanities do come beside."

What would be the surprise of Philip Stubbs if he could now witness the extent to which the "vanity" of "Bever Hats" influences the commercial arrangements of England;—the importation of beaver and musquash furs from North America, of neutria furs from South America, of wools from various parts of Continental Europe, of gums, resins, and dyes from almost every part of the globe! If he found, too, that one single firm gives employment to fifteen hundred persons in making hats of various kinds, and that the value of all the hats made in Great Britain in one year is probably not much less than three millions sterling, he would perhaps cease to include "bever hats" in his list of abuses.

It will serve to mark the advance made in this respect, since the time of Stubbs, if we glance through a vast hat-factory now existing in Bermondsey, and reputed to be the largest in the world. This establishment, the property of Messrs. Christy, occupies two extensive ranges of buildings on opposite sides of Bermondsey Street, Southwark. These we will term the east and west ranges, each of which is approached by a gateway leading from the street. On entering the gateway to the east range, the first object seen at the end of a long avenue is a lofty chimney connected with a steam-engine, and rising to the height of one hundred and sixty feet. Over the gateway is a range of warehouses for wool and other articles; and from thence, proceeding onwards, is seen on the left a pile of buildings, occupied by cloth cap makers, hat-trimmers, and packers. On the right of the same avenue is another range of buildings, consisting of a fire-proof varnish storeroom, silk-hat workshops, and shops wherein the early stages of beaver hatting are carried on. At the left of the great chimney is a building wherein common black-glazed or japanned hats are made; and near it is an archway leading northward to another avenue surrounded by buildings. These consist of a turner's shop, where blocks for shaping hats are made; a shell-lac store, where the lac is bruised, ground, and prepared for use; a blacksmith's shop, for the repair of iron-work used in various parts of the factory; a saw-mill and sawing-room, where machine-worked saws cut up timbers into boards for packing-cases required in the export department; a logwood warehouse, wherein a powerful machine cuts the logs into fine shreds; a fur-room, in which the beaver and other furs are cut from the skins by machinery; rooms wherein the coarse hairs are pulled from the skins; the steam-engine with its boiler, furnace, &c.; a carding-room, for disentangling the locks and fibres of wool; a blowing-room, for separating two qualities of beaver-fur, or hair; together with various warehouses, store-rooms, carpenter's shops, timber yard, &c. This brings us to the northern extremity of the range; on returning from which we pass wool-warehouses and sorting rooms, wool and fur washing-houses, stoving-rooms, fur-hat workshops, "picking" rooms, clerks' offices, &c.

Crossing Bermondsey Street to the western range, we find a "beaver store-room," the dye-house, stoving-rooms, shaping and finishing rooms, &c.; the whole being, however, much less extensive than the east range.

It may excite surprise to hear of saw-mills, and blacksmiths', turners', and carpenters' shops, on the premises of a hat-maker; but this is only one among many instances which might be adduced, in the economy of English manufactures, of centralization, combined with division of labour, within the walls of one factory.

The nature of the operations carried on in the greater number of these buildings will perhaps be best explained by tracing the history of a beaver hat from the time when the crude materials enter the factory, till the hat, in a finished state, is warehoused.

If a dozen individuals to whom the subject is new were asked "How is a beaver hat made?" it is not improbable that we should receive a dozen different answers. One would think it is cast in a mould; another that the beaver's fur, skin and all, is stiffened and shaped; a third, that the fur is in some way woven into a kind of cloth, and put on a stiff foundation; but perhaps not one would have an idea of the beautiful process of *felting,* which is the groundwork of the whole theory of hat-making. A beaver hat consists mainly of two parts,—the *body* and the *covering;* the former of which is made of fine wool and coarse fur, mixed, felted, stiffened, and shaped; and the latter of beaver fur, made to adhere to the body by the process of felting. Wool and fur constitute therefore the main ingredients employed. For hats of inferior quality, coarse wool is employed for the body, and coarser fur, or sometimes fine wool, for the covering.

The wool is brought to the factory in a dirty and greasy state, retaining much of the moisture derived from the animal whence it was sheared. It is carried to a large washing-house, on a level with the ground, where the steam rising from immense boilers and tubs indicates the great scale on which the process is conducted. The wool is soaked and washed until the greasiness is removed, and is then subjected to the action of a screw-press, whereby all the water is expelled and the wool left in a clean state. From the washing-house the wool is conveyed to a drying-room; and when required for use, it undergoes the process of *carding* in the carding-room. This carding is analogous to one of the early operations in the cotton manufacture:—a machine worked by the same steam-engine which sets so many other parts of the working apparatus in motion, combs out the fibres of wool, and presents them in a light and tolerably disentangled state. The wool is then ready for the hatter; and we will trace the preparation of the fur up to the same point.

The term *fur,* in a general sense, refers to the hairy coating of such animals as the beaver, bear, marten, minx, hare, and rabbit. The skins of these animals, when merely dried after being stripped from the body, are called *peltry;* when the skin of the inner side has been converted into a sort of leather, by a peculiar process of tanning, the skins obtain the name of *furs,* in a restricted sense; and the term is still more restricted when applied to the hairy coating cut from the skin, and presented in the form of delicate filaments.

Now it is in the last-named form that fur is useful to the hatter; and the furs to which he gives the preference are those of the beaver, the musquash, the neutria, the hare, and the rabbit, of which the first is by far the most valuable. The beaver inhabits the districts of North-West America, where its peculiar habits of life have given rise to many marvellous tales, the truth of which is now more than doubted. The romantic details often presented in the lives of beaver-hunters, as well as the mode of dealing between them and the fur-dealers, have formed the subjects of many interesting narratives, with which the reader may be more or less familiar. The skins, as received at the factory, from the Hudson's Bay Company, are tolerably flat and stiff, measuring, generally, about three feet by two. The hairy surface is of a brownish colour, but is not that to which the hatter attaches value; for this animal has two kinds of hair on his skin, the innermost of which is short, implicated, and as fine as down, and the outermost thicker, longer, and more sparing. Of the separation of these two kinds we shall speak presently.

Neutria is the fur of a small animal called the *coypou,* the *quoiya,* or the *Myopotamus Bonariensis,* found in various parts of South America. The long or coarse hairs are generally of a reddish colour; and the inner or soft hairs brownish ash colour. It was not until about thirty years ago that hatters, influenced by the high price of beaver fur (which within a century has risen from 20*s.* to 80*s.* per pound), began to use neutria fur; but since that time the employment of them has become so extensive, that one million neutria skins have sometimes been imported in one year. This animal is yet little known to naturalists, but certain peculiarities in the skin beneath the fur have led to much conjecture among those who have frequent opportunities of inspecting the skins, concerning the structure and habits of the animal.

The *Musquash,* or *Mus Zibethicus,* is a North American animal, about the size of the common rabbit, and covered, like the beaver and the coypou, with two kinds of hair or fur, having different degrees of fineness. The name *musk rat* is sometimes given to this animal, on account of its secretion of a peculiar fluid having the odour of musk.

The fur of *hares* and *rabbits* is so well known as to render few words of description necessary. The rabbits fed on the wolds of Yorkshire are said to yield fur much exceeding in value that of the rabbits bred near London, by reason of the superior length and strength of the hairy filaments.

We have digressed a little in order to show the nature of the furs employed by the hatter. The skins, or pelts, on being conveyed to the factory, are rather greasy and dirty, and are therefore cleansed with soap and water: this is effected in the same large washing-house where the wool is cleansed. When the pelts are dried and required for further processes, they are carried to the "pulling-room," where a number of women, seated on stools, are employed in pulling out the coarse outer hairs from the skins: these coarse hairs are utterly useless to the hatter, and, if preserved at all, are sold for stuffing cushions and such-like purposes. Each woman lays a pelt on her lap, or on a low bench, and, by means of a knife acting against the thumb, tears out the larger hairs; her fingers and thumb being guarded by a stout leather shield.

We next trace the progress of the pelt into a room where, to one unused to the din of machinery, everything seems noise and confusion. This is the "cutting" or "cropping" room, in which six or eight machines are actively at work, each attended by a female. We Englishmen, happily, know very little of the guillotine, or we should probably find some resemblance between its action and that of the cropping-machine. A long, broad, and sharp blade, having the edge downwards, works very rapidly, with a chopping action; and the pelt being introduced between the blade and a support beneath, the fur is cut from it with a precision that nothing can exceed. The impression on the mind of a visitor is that the pelt must inevitably be chopped to shreds; but, by some admirable adjustment of mechanism, the fur is removed without the skin being cut. The female who attends the machine puts it in or out of work when required, guides the pelt through it, collects the filaments of fur, &c. Such outer fragments or small pieces of the pelt as do not lose their fur by the action of the machine are laid on a table, and women, by the aid of small instruments shaped somewhat like a cheese-cutter, remove the remaining fur. The denuded skins are useless to the hatter, and are sold at a small price to sisemakers in the north of England.

We have said that the women in the "pulling" room cut, tear, or pull out the long coarse hairs from the pelts, and that these hairs are useless to the hatter. But it is impossible completely to separate the coarse from the fine fur by this means; and, therefore, the fur, when cropped from the pelt by the machines, is conveyed to the "blowing-room," finally to effect the separation. This room is probably the largest in the factory, and presents a remarkable appearance. It is of small height, but measures, perhaps, fifty feet by forty, having eight hollow boxes or trunks extending nearly the whole length of the room. The action of these hollow machines is exceedingly beautiful, and may, perhaps, be understood without a minute detail of mechanism. A quantity of beaver or other fur is introduced at one end, near a compartment in which a vane or fly is revolving with a velocity of nearly two thousand rotations in a minute. We all know, even from the simple example of a lady's fan, that a body in motion gives rise to a wind or draught; and when the motion is so rapid as is here indicated, the current becomes very powerful. This current of air propels the fur along a hollow trunk to the other end of the machine, and, in so doing, produces an effect which is as remarkable as it is valuable. All the coarse and comparatively valueless fur is deposited on a cloth stretched along the trunk, while the more delicate filaments are blown to a receptacle at the other end. Nothing but a very ingenious arrangement of mechanism could produce a separation so complete as is here effected; but the principle of action is not difficult to understand. If there were no atmosphere, or if an enclosed place were exhausted of air, a guinea and a feather, however unequal in weight, would fall to the ground with equal velocity; but in ordinary circumstances, the guinea would obviously fall more quickly than the feather, because the resistance of the air bears a much larger ratio to the weight of the feather than to that of the guinea. As the resistance of air to a moving body acts more forcibly on a light than on a heavy substance, so likewise does air, when in motion, and acting as a moving force. When particles of sand and gravel are driven by the wind, the lightest particles go to the greatest distance. So it is with the two kinds of fur in the "blowing machine"; those fibres which are finest and lightest being driven to the remote end of the machine.

We have thus visited those parts of the factory in which the crude materials are prepared for the hatter, and will now, therefore, take our materials to the "body-makers," and witness the processes of forming them into a hat.

In one corner of the factory is a dark dingy room, where, around a steaming "kettle," we see six or eight men busily employed at some operation, the nature of which can scarcely be divined through the clouds of steam. We pass by them, however, and visit some upper rooms, where the fur and wool are worked up together. The "body," or "foundation," of a good beaver hat is now generally made of eight parts rabbits' fur, three parts Saxony wool, and one part of lama, vicunia, or "red" wool. A sufficient quantity of these for one hat (about $2\frac{1}{2}$ ounces) is weighed out and placed in the hands of the "bower." On entering the "bowing-room," a peculiar twanging noise indicates to the visitor that a stretched cord is in rapid vibration; and the management of this cord by the workman is seen to be one of the many operations in hatting wherein success depends exclusively on skilful manipulation. A bench extends along the front of the room beneath a range of windows, and each "bower" has a little compartment appropriated to himself. The bow is an ashen staff, from five to seven feet in length, having a strong cord of catgut stretched over bridges at the two ends. The bow is suspended in the middle by a string from the ceiling, whereby it hangs nearly on a level with the workbench, and the workman thus proceeds:—The wool and coarse fur, first separately and afterwards together, are laid on the bench, and the bower, grasping the staff of the bow with his left hand, and plucking the cord with his right by means of a small piece of wood, causes the cord to vibrate rapidly against the wool and fur. By repeating this process for a certain time, all the original clots or assemblages of filaments are perfectly opened and dilated, and the fibres, flying upwards when struck, are by the dexterity of the workman made to fall in nearly equable thickness on the bench, presenting a very light and soft layer of material. Simple as this operation appears to a stranger, years of practice are required for the attainment of proficiency in it.

The point in the routine of processes at which we have now arrived requires a brief consideration of the operation of felting, on which the whole manufacture of a beaver hat depends. Felting is a process whereby animal fibres are made to cohere and to form a kind of cloth, without the aid of weaving, plaiting, knitting, sewing, or any analogous operation—warmth, moisture, and friction being the means by which it is effected. There is reason to believe that the process of felting was known in early times, and that the tents of the Tartars, as well as some articles of clothing, were produced by these means; but the evidence on this point is rather indistinct. At what time felted wool was first employed for making hats it would be difficult now to say; but there is a legend current among some of the continental hatters which gives the honour to St. Clement, fourth bishop of Rome. Most fraternities love to have a patron saint, when they can find one; and those hatters who regard St. Clement in this light inform us that this holy man, being forced to flee from persecutors, found his feet to be so blistered by long-continued travel, that he was induced to put a little wool between his sandals and the soles of his feet. On continuing his journey, the warmth, moisture, motion, and pressure of the feet worked the wool into a uniformly compact substance. Finally, the wanderer, observing the useful nature of this substance, caused it to be introduced in the manufacture of various articles of apparel.

But leaving St. Clement and his felted "inner soles," we may remark that the philosophy of felting was not understood until the microscope was applied to the examination of animal fibres. It was then found that the fibre, whether of wool or fur, is surrounded by a vast number of minute teeth projecting obliquely from the central stem. As these teeth are very sharp and are turned in one direction, they present an obstacle to the motion of the fibre in that direction, but enable it to glide easily in the opposite one; just as an ear of barley, when placed stalk uppermost within the cuff of the coat-sleeve, will soon work its way up to the shoulder by the motion of the arm. In some woolly fibres the irregularities appear like concentric cups, rather than sharp teeth.

When a heap of such fibres is rubbed and pressed, and the fibres made to curl slightly by the action of warmth and moisture, they twist around each other, and the teeth interlace so tightly as not to separate. So complete, indeed, is the entanglement of fibres thus produced, that a coat made from cloth manufactured solely by the felting process has been known to last in wear ten years.

The purpose which the serrated structure of hair or fur is intended to answer is matter for conjecture. With respect to the double fur of such animals as the beaver, the following opinion has been offered:—that, as the beaver passes much of its time in the water, the little projections from the filaments of the inner fur may serve as receptacles whereby the water is prevented from reaching the skin; and that the outer fibres may perhaps act like valves, which, when closed, shield the animal from cold, and when open permit the evaporation of water from the inner fur, and likewise permit respiration to go on from the pores of the skin.

But whatever be the purpose which these arrangements answer in the animal economy, it is evident that the minute serrations on the fibres of fur and wool are the primary source of the felting property. This being understood, we shall be able to comprehend how the fur and wool are worked up into the form of a hat; and we therefore return to the "bowing" room. The bowed materials for one hat are divided into two portions, each of which is separately pressed with a light wicker frame, and afterwards with a piece of oil-cloth or leather, called a "hardening-skin," until, by the pressure of the hands backwards and forwards all over the skin, the fibres are brought closer together, the points of contact multiplied, the serrations made to link together, and a slightly coherent fabric formed. These two halves, or "batts," are then formed into a hollow cap by a singular contrivance. One of the "batts," nearly triangular in shape, and measuring about half a yard in each direction, being laid flat, a triangular piece of paper, smaller in size than the batt, is laid upon it, and the edges of the batt, being folded over the paper, meet at the upper surface, and thus form a complete envelope to the paper. The two meeting edges are soon made to combine by gentle pressure and friction; and the other batt is laid over the first in a similar way, but having the meeting edges on the opposite side of the paper. The doubled layer, with the enclosed paper, are then folded up in a damp cloth and worked by hand; the workman pressing and bending, rolling and unrolling, until the fibres of the inner layer have incorporated with those of the outer. It is evident that, were there not a piece of paper interposed, the whole of the fibres would be worked together into a mass by the opposite sides felting together; but the paper maintains a vacancy within, and when withdrawn at the edge which is to form the opening of the cap, it leaves the felted material in such a form as to constitute, when stretched open, a hollow cone.

Our visit to this part of the factory has been somewhat lengthy; but the process of transforming the "bowed" materials into a conical cap is so important, as illustrative of felting, that if this be clearly understood, all that follows will be tolerably plain.

Few "kettles" are the scene of such busy operations as the hatter's "kettle," and few would be so uninviting to a person fastidious as to cleanliness. Imagine a large kettle or boiler open at the top, having a fire beneath it, and eight planks ascending obliquely from the margin, so as to form a sort of octagonal work-bench, five or six feet in diameter, at which eight men may work. The planks are made of lead near the kettle, and of mahogany at the outer part; and at each plank a workman operates on a conical cap, until the process of felting or "planking" is completed. The "kettle" contains hot water slightly acidulated with sulphuric acid; and, as far as words can do so, the following may convey an idea of the process:—The cap is dipped into the hot liquor, laid on one of the planks, and subjected to a long felting process: it is rolled and unrolled, twisted, pressed, and rubbed with a piece of leather or wood tied to the palm of the workman's hand, and rolled with a rolling-pin. From time to time the cap is examined, to ascertain whether the thickness of the material is sufficient in every part; and if any defective places appear, they are wetted with a brush dipped in the hot liquor, and a few additional fibres are worked in. Considerable skill is required in order to preserve such an additional thickness of material at one part as shall suffice for the brim of the hat. When this felting process has been continued for about two hours, it is found that the heat, moisture, pressure, and friction have reduced the cap to one half of its former dimensions, the thickness being increased in a proportionate degree.

In many parts of the factory are "stoving" rooms, in which, by the judicious arrangement of flues, a high temperature is maintained. To such a room the felted or "planked" cap is taken, and, when dried, it presents the appearance of a fine, stout, and very strong kerseymere, having a drab or greyish colour. There can be little doubt that such a fabric is well calculated to serve the purposes of common broadcloth, provided the means of manufacturing it of large dimensions were ensured.

Is not the reader still puzzled to know how or when the *hat* will make its appearance? We have described numerous materials, and have visited many departments of the factory, but have still produced only a drab-coloured, flexible, conical cap, about fifteen inches wide and fourteen high, as here represented, and without a particle of beaver on its surface. The surface, colour, and form are, however, now about to be changed.

In the first place, the cap is taken to the "water-proofing" room, where the odour of gums, resins, and spirits gives some intimation of the materials employed. Gum-lac, gum-sandrach, gum-mastic, resin, frankincense, copal, caoutchouc, spirits of wine, and spirits of turpentine, are the ingredients (all of a very inflammable nature) of which the water-proofing composition is made. This is laid on the cap by means of a brush, and the workman exercises his skill in regulating the quantity at different parts, since the strength of the future brim and crown depends much on this process.

After another "stoving," by which the spirit is evaporated, the exterior of the cap is scoured with a weak alkali, to remove a portion of the gummy coating, and thereby enable the beaver fur afterwards to cling to the woolly fibres of the cap.

Now, for the first time, we have to direct our attention to the fine beaver fur, the purchase and preparation of which are so costly. The washing, plucking, cropping, and blowing departments we have already visited, and have seen the fibres of fur divided into two qualities, of which the finer is that to which the hatter attaches value. This finer quality, which appears to have been formerly known by the name of "fix," was, in bygone times, used not only for hats, but also for hosiery purposes—in allusion to which Dyer, in his poem of the "Fleece," has these lines:—

> The beaver's flix
> Gives kindliest warmth to weak, enervate limbs,
> When the pale blood slow rises through the veins.

The fur, being bowed very carefully by a smaller bow than that employed for wool, is spread out into a layer, and by means of the "hardening-skin" is pressed and worked into a very delicate and light felt, just coherent enough to hold together. This layer, which is called a "ruffing," or "roughing," is a little larger than the cap body; and, to unite the two, another visit to the "kettle" is necessary. The cap being softened by submersion in the hot liquor, the "ruffing" is laid on it, and patted down with a wet brush, a narrow strip of beaver being laid round the inside of the cap, to form the underside of the future brim. The beavered cap is then wrapped in a woollen cloth, submersed frequently in the hot liquor, and rolled on the plank for the space of two hours. The effect of this rubbing and rolling is very curious, and may be illustrated in a simple manner:—If a few fibres of beaver-fur be laid on a piece of broad-cloth, covered with tissue-paper, and rubbed gently with the finger, they will penetrate through the cloth and appear at the opposite side. So, likewise, in the process of "ruffing," each fibre of fur is set in motion from root to point, and enters the substance of the felt cap. The hairs proceed in a pretty straight course, and just enter the felt, with the substance of which they form an intimate union. But if the rolling and pressing were continued too long, the hairs would actually pass through the felt, and be seen on the inside instead of the out: the workman, therefore, exercises his judgment in continuing the process only so long as is sufficient to secure the hairs in the felt firm enough to bear the action of the hat-brush in after-days. Eighty or a hundred years ago, when beaver fur was cheap, an "old English gentleman" was wont to have his hat so well beavered, that as much nap felted through it to the inside as remained on the exterior; and when the hat showed symptoms of decay and old age, it was sent to the maker, who turned it inside out, and gave it nearly the pristine freshness of a newly-made hat.

At length the cap is to assume somewhat the shape of a hat, before it finally leaves the "kettle." The workman first turns up the edge of the cap to the depth of about an inch and a half; and then draws the peak of the cap back through the centre or axis, so far as not to take out the first fold, but to produce an inner fold of the same depth. The point being turned back again, produces a third fold; and thus the workman proceeds, till the whole has acquired the appearance of a flattish circular piece, consisting of a number of concentric folds or rings, with the peak in the centre. This is laid on the "plank," where the workman, keeping the substance hot and wet, pulls, presses, and rubs the centre until he has formed a smooth flat portion equal to the intended crown of the hat. He then takes a cylindrical block, on the flat end of which he applies the flattened central portion of the felt; and by forcing a string down the curved sides of the block, he causes the surrounding portion of the felt to assume the figure of the block. The part which is to form the brim now appears as a puckered appendage round the edge of the hat; but this puckered edge is soon brought to a tolerably flat shape by pulling and pressing.

We here terminate our visit to the "blocking-shop." The conical cap has been converted into a hat with a flat brim; and we take leave of the "kettle," with its hot acid liquor, its wet planks, its clouds of steam, and its ingenious attendants. We will suppose the hat to have been dried in a stoving-room near the great chimney, and will then place it in the hands of the "shearer." In an appropriate room, this workman raises and opens the nap of the hats, by means of a peculiar sort of comb; and then shears the hairs to any required length. Connoisseurs in these matters are learned as to the respective merits of "short naps" and "long naps;" and by the shearer's dexterity these are regulated. The visitor recognises nothing difficult in this operation; yet years of practice are necessary for the attainment of skill therein; since the workman determines the length of the nap by the peculiar position in which the long light shears are held. A nap or pile as fine as that of velvet can be produced by this operation.

The routine of processes now requires that we should visit the western range of buildings, on the opposite side of Bermondsey Street. At the remote end of the court-yard we see a dark and dismal-looking building, having very little light, and that little received through unglazed windows,—large boiling cauldrons, which it requires some nerve to look into,—a spacious brass cage or frame,—cranes and tackle for raising weights, and a party of workmen whose persons and garments denote the staining effect of the hot dye to which they are exposed. This is the "dye-house," where the hats exchange their drab or grey hue for a black one. The dyeing ingredients are logwood and some metallic salts, boiled in certain proportions in soft water. The logwood is imported from Campeachy in logs five or six feet long, and from five to ten inches thick; and a room in this extensive factory is appropriated to the cutting of these logs into fine shreds. For this purpose a powerful revolving wheel, provided with four cutting-blades inserted radially in one of its faces, is employed; the ends of the logs being applied to these blades, the wood is cut into shreds with astonishing force and quickness.

The cauldron with the dyeing ingredients being ready, a number of hats are fixed upon blocks, and the blocks, by means of a hole at one end of each, are fixed to brass pegs inserted in a large skeleton frame, so that the hats shall not touch each other. The frame is then lowered into the cauldron, and turned in such a manner as to allow all the hats to be submerged in the dye; after which the frame is hauled up, and the hats allowed to drain for thirty or forty minutes. This alternate submersion and partial drying is repeated twelve or fifteen times, until every fibre of the hat—felt as well as nap—is thoroughly dyed. This is followed by soaking and washing, which frees the surface from impurities; and the hat is then again "stoved." A few subsequent processes remove certain irregularities of shape, which the hat has acquired by repeated submersions in the dye-liquor.

We next visit a department of the building where "finishers" are employed. A boiler is so arranged as to yield a jet of steam, over which the hat is held until thoroughly softened; and having a block shaped in every part nearly as the hat is intended to be, the "finisher" pulls, rubs, and presses the hat, until it assumes the form of the block; after which the nap is stretched, turned in any required direction, and smoothed, by various sets of brushes, small cushions of velvet, and heated irons. Fig. 10 [not included] shows three successive stages in the shaping of the hats, from the first rough "blocking" to the production of a flat and smooth-edged brim while on the finishing block; likewise a beaver bonnet on the block by which it is shaped.

Once again we cross to the east range, and visit the first story of a large pile of buildings on the left hand. Here the busy hum of lively voices soon indicates to the visitor the sex of the inmates. We enter a large square room, full of litter and bustle, and find fifty or sixty young females employed in "trimming" hats, that is, putting on the lining, the leather, the binding, &c. Some are sitting at long tables,—some standing,—others seated round a fire, with their work in their laps; but all plying the industrious needle, and earning an honourable subsistence.

A word or two respecting the employment of females in factories. The texture of English society is such, that the number of reputable employments for females in the middle and humble ranks is very small. Most fathers and brothers are well aware of this; and women themselves, however desirous of contributing to their means of support, are cramped in their efforts by the limited range of avocations left open to them. The effect of this is such as never fails to result when the vineyard is too small for the labourers; the number of employments being few, so many females embark in them that the supply greatly exceeds the demand, and the value of female labour is thereby brought to a very low level. Under such circumstances it is important to inquire how far female labour may be available in factories where the subdivision of employments is carried out on a complete scale; and the factory now under consideration may afford some valuable hints on this point. The number of females employed here is not far short of two hundred, whose earnings vary from eight to fourteen shillings per week. The degree of ingenuity required varies considerably, so as to give scope for different degrees of talent. Among the processes by which a beaver hat is produced, women and girls are employed in the following:—plucking the beaver skins; cropping off the fur; sorting various kinds of wool; plucking and cutting rabbit's wool; shearing the nap of the blocked hat (in some cases); picking out defective fibres of fur; and trimming. Other departments of the factory, unconnected with the manufacture of beaver hats, also give employment to numerous females. Where a uniform system of supervision and of kindness on the part of the proprietors is acted on, no unfavourable effects are to be feared from such an employment of females in a factory. We cannot dwell longer on this matter; but in endeavouring to solve the important problem, "How can all live—and live honestly?" the nature and extent of female employments becomes a prominent subject for thought.

But we have not yet finished our hat. However carefully the process of "blowing" may be performed, in order to separate the coarse fibres of the fur from the more delicate, there are always a few of the former left mingled with the latter; and these are worked up during the whole of the subsequent processes. Women are employed, therefore, after the hats have left the "finishers," in picking out, with small tweezers, such defective fibres as may present themselves at the surface of the hats.

Lastly, the hat is placed in the hands of a workman whose employment requires an accurate eye, and a fertile taste in matters of shape and form: this is the "shaper." He has to study the style and fashion of the day, as well as the wishes of individual purchasers, by giving to the brim of the hat such curvatures in various directions as may be needed. Simple as this may appear, the workman who possesses the requisite skill can command a high rate of wages. Fortunate is the "shaper" who, during a ramble to any place of fashionable resort, can espy a new form of brim,—a curl here, a depression there,—and can imitate it at his work-bench: he will please his employer, and profit himself.

Thus we arrive at the finished state of the beaver hat; and may now leave it to run its career through all weathers,—wet and dry,—cold and heat,—till it is destined to be replaced by a new one. Whether we are contented with the "shocking bad hat" of street phraseology, or have to endure the uneasy pressure of the stiff and glossy new one with fortitude, we must assuredly acknowledge that a beaver hat, considered with reference both to the peculiar processes by which it is produced, and to the number of distinct sets of workpeople (from twenty to twenty-five) through whose hands it passes, occupies an interesting and important place in the manufacturing history of this country.

In tracing the progress of a beaver hat, from the time when the materials are brought into the factory, till the hat is made, trimmed, and shaped, we have carried the reader through the greater part of this large establishment, and have shown the purposes to which the different departments are appropriated. It will, however, be desirable to say a few words respecting the silk-hat department.

As the number of beavers caught annually in America has greatly declined, the price of beaver-fur has of late years increased; and this circumstance has led to the production of a kind of hat which presents some resemblance to beaver, and yet may be produced at a low rate. This is the *silk* hat, the manufacture of which has gone through several stages of improvement, by which even a humble "gossamer" now presents a neat and glossy exterior.

Silk is wholly incapable of the process of felting, and therefore cannot be employed in the same manner as fur and wool. The body of the silk hat is made either of coarse felted wool, or of some light material, such as willow or stiffened cambric; and on this is placed a covering or hood of silk plush, sewn to the proper size for the hat. The Messrs. Christy weave their own plush at a factory in Lancashire, and send it to London in the form of a soft glossy material, which is cut and sewn by women to the requisite shape of the hats.

The bodies are made in a very rough way, by shaping the willow, cotton, or felted wool round blocks, and using a substance of extra thickness for the brim. A varnish cement is used to join the various parts; and a resinous stiffening composition is laid over the outer surface. Some time before the plush hood is laid on, the body is coated with a peculiar varnish, which, being softened by a heated iron after the hood is laid in its proper position, causes the plush to adhere to the foundation. This process is the most difficult in the silk-hat manufacture; for not only must the plush be made to adhere in every part, but the seam or joining up the side of the hat must be made as little visible as possible. No sewing is here employed; but the two meeting edges are brought precisely together, pressed down with a heated iron, and the silk shag brushed over the joint.

The minuter details of the silk-hat department we must pass over; for, so far as they differ from beaver hatting, they are of much less interest. Beaver hatters look down with some little scorn on the operations of silk hatting; and certainly, so far as regards manipulative skill acquired by long practice, the former branch of handicraft is by far the most remarkable; but still the silk hatter appeals with such moderation to the purse of the purchaser, that we cannot afford to lose sight of him.

The silk hatters, instead of occupying different parts of the factory, are congregated in one building along the southern side of the avenue leading to the great chimney, the building being divided into numerous small apartments. On the left of the chimney is a range of shops wherein are made common black glazed hats, such as are worn by sailors and persons much exposed to the weather. The bodies of these hats are made of common felted, wool, and the outer covering is a thick coating of black varnish or japan, presenting a glossy surface. A high temperature is required for this purpose, and the situation and arrangement of the shops are such as to insure this temperature.

There is a distinct range of apartments in which seal-skin and other skin or fur caps are made. In these, unlike beaver hats, the fur is not cut from the pelt and then felted; but the pelt, with the fur remaining on it, is dressed into leather, and is cut up into such pieces as may, by subsequent processes, be formed into caps of various shapes.

Another department entirely distinct from the rest, is that in which cloth caps of various kinds are made. This, generally speaking, is effected by needlework, and wholly differs from the processes of hatmaking.

Here we terminate our visit to an establishment which presents so considerable a number of interesting processes. We have selected that of Messrs. Christy, because, from the completeness and systematic arrangement of the details, it well illustrates the economy of a large factory,—the concentration of many departments within the walls of one establishment, the division of labour, the exercise of delegated authority by foremen to each department, and a general supervision of the whole by the proprietors. It is difficult to estimate the area of ground covered by all the workshops; but the reader may, from the foregoing details, form some idea of the numerous piles of building constituting the factory. There are many establishments in and near London, such as water-works, gas-works, ship-yards, tan-yards, brewhouses, distilleries, glass-works, &c., the extent of which would excite no little surprise in those who for the first time visited them. Indeed the densely packed masses of building forming the eastern districts of the metropolis, on both sides of the river, include individual establishments which, although they would appear like little towns if isolated, scarcely meet the eye of a passenger through the crowded streets.

We may here remark, as a completion of this notice of the hat manufacture generally, that the making of straw hats, so much worn in country places, is in the hands of a class of persons altogether different from those engaged in the other branches of hatting. The finer qualities of straw, as well as white whalebone and white chip, are used for bonnets rather than for hats; but the mode of manufacture is nearly the same in all. There are delicate planing-machines in use, by which any soft kind of wood can be cut into thin shavings, and the shavings, at the same time, cut into very narrow strips with great precision. Such is the case with willow, and also with whalebone. The willow of which the foundations of silk hats are frequently made is prepared in some such way as this; the narrow strips of willow being plaited, or perhaps we might say woven, into a square sheet sufficiently large for three hats. A slight glance at the willow foundation of a silk hat will show the nature of the material, and will also show that the mode in which the narrow strips are linked together resembles weaving rather than plaiting. It is not difficult to imagine, from these few details, that a hat or bonnet may be made from any such materials as whalebone, wood, straw, cane, rush, or others wherein a longitudinal fibrous structure is found; and the reader will readily call to mind numerous examples of such an application of fibrous materials.

HARRIET MARTINEAU

WHAT THERE IS IN A BUTTON

It is a serious thing to attempt to learn about buttons at Birmingham. What buttons are we thinking of? we are asked, if we venture an inquiry. Do we want to see gilt, or silvered buttons? or electro-plated? or silk, or Florentine buttons? or mother-of—pearl, or steel, or wood, or bone, or horn buttons? All these are made here. Before we have made up our minds what to see first, we hear somebody say that button-dies are among the highest objects of the die-sinkers, and medallists' art. This not only suddenly raises our estimate of buttons, but decides us to follow the production of the button from the earliest stage,—if Messrs. Allen and Moore will kindly permit us to see what their artists and workmen are doing. This is not the first time that we have had a hankering after this spectacle. When we saw electro-plating—when we saw the making of pencil cases and trinkets—we observed and handled many steel dies, and wondered how they were made. Now we are to learn.

It was not a little surprising to see, in other manufactories, ranges of shelves, or pigeon-holes, covering whole sides of rooms, filled with dies, worth from ten shillings to twenty-four shillings each. It was rather sad, too,

----

From *Household Words,* No. 138. November 13, 1852: 106–112.

to be told that a large proportion of these might never again be of any use—the fashion of a few weeks, or even days, having passed away. Much more surprising is the sight of the dies arranged along the shelves of the makers of this curious article. Messrs. Allen and Moore have made three thousand dies within the last three years: and upon each one, what thought has been spent—what ingenuity—what knowledge—what taste—what skill of eye and hand! A single die will occupy one man a month, with all his faculties in exercise; while another, with more natural aptitude, or courage, or experience, will do the same thing in two or three days. To think of one thousand in a year, produced with this effort and ability, and then to remember that button dies are among the highest productions of the art, cannot but elevate our respect for buttons very remarkably.

First, what is this steel die, which is so much heard of, and so seldom seen, except by those who go to seek it? It is a block of metal, round or square, as may happen, about four or five inches in height, and rather smaller at the top than the bottom. It consists of a piece of soft steel in the centre, surrounded by iron, to prevent its cracking by expansion, under the treatment it is to be subjected to. The bar of iron is wound round the steel when hot, and welded to it; and thus it comes from the forge, rough and dirty. The steel surface at the top is then polished; and if it is intended for a medal, it is turned in the lathe. The artist sketches his subject upon it, from the drawing before him, with a pencil. When he has satisfied himself with his drawing, he begins to engrave. He rests his graver (a sharp point of steel) across another graver, and cuts away—very gently; for it is always easy to cut away more, but impossible to restore the minutest chip when the stroke has gone too deep. He keeps beside him a lump of red clay, which he now and then lays upon his work, knocking it down smartly through a frame, which keeps it in shape; and thus he has presented to him his work in relief, and can judge of its effect so far. Little brushes in frames are also at hand, wherewith to brush away particles of steel, oil, and all dirt. When the engraving is done, the most anxious process of all succeeds. The steel must be hardened. All has been done that could be done to prevent fracture by the original surrounding of the steel with iron; but cracks will happen sometimes, and they spoil the work completely. The block is heated to a crimson heat—not to "a scaly heat," but a more moderate degree; and then a dash of cold water hardens the steel. This dash of cold water is the nervous part of the business. In medals representing heads, there is usually only a narrow line left between the top of the concave head and the edge of the steel; and this is where the fracture is to be first looked for. When the Jenny Lind medal was to be struck at this house, no less than four dies were spoiled in succession. It was vexatious; but the artists went to work again, and succeeded. The Queen's head is less mischievous than Jenny Lind's, as the shallow work about the top of the crown intervenes between the deeper concavity and the rim. If the steel stands the hardening, the die is ready for use, except only that the plain surface must be well polished before the medal or button is struck.

Before we go to the medal press, we must look round this room a little. Ranged on shelves, and suspended from nails, are casts of limbs, of whole figures, of draperies, of foliage,—of everything that is pretty. This art comes next to that of the sculptor; and it requires much of the same training. When partially-draped figures are to be represented, the artist engraves the naked figure first, and the drapery afterwards; and to do this well, he must have the sculptor's knowledge of anatomy. He must be familiar with the best works of art, because something of a classical air is required in such an article as a medal. The personifications of virtues, arts, sciences,—of all abstract conceptions which can thus be presented,—must be of the old classical types, or in close harmony with them. And then, how much else is required! Think of the skill in perspective required to engrave the Crystal Palace in the space of two or three inches! Think of the architectural drawing that an artist must be capable of who engraves public buildings by the score;—endowed grammar-schools, old castles, noblemen's seats, market houses, and so forth! Think of the skill in animal drawing required for the whole series of sporting buttons—from the red deer to the snipe! Think of the varieties of horses and dogs, besides the game! For crest buttons, the lions and other animals are odd and untrue enough; but, out of the range of heraldry, all must be perfect pictures. And then, the word "pictures" reminds us of the exquisite copies of paintings which the die-sinker makes. Here is the "Christus Consolator" of Scheffer reproduced, with admirable spirit and fidelity, within a space so small, that no justice can be done to the work unless it is viewed through a magnifying glass.

So much for the execution. We have also not a little curiosity about the designing. The greater number of the designs are sent hither to be executed;—coats of arms; livery buttons; club buttons; service buttons;—buttons for this or that hunt; foreign buttons—the Spanish one sort, the French another. Sometimes a suggestion comes, or a rough sketch, which the artist has to work out. But much is originated on the premises. There is a venerable man living at Birmingham, who has seen four generations, and watched their progress in art; and he it is, we are told,—Mr. Lines, now above eighty, who has "furnished" (that is, discovered and trained) more designers than anybody else. It must be pleasant to him to see what Birmingham has arrived at since lamps were made with a leopard's foot at the bottom, expanding into a leaf at the top, and so on, through a narrow circle of grotesque absurdities. Now, one cannot enter a manufactory, or pass along the streets of this wonderful town, without being impressed and gratified by the affluence of beauty, with good sense at the bottom of it, which everywhere abounds: and, to one who has helped on the change, as Mr. Lines has done, the gratification ought to be something enviable.

The variety of dies is amusing enough. Here is a prize medal for the Queen's College at Cork: on one side, the Queen's head, of course; on the other, Science—a kneeling figure, feeding a lamp; very pretty. Next, we see General Tom Thumb;—his mighty self on one side, and his carriage on the other. This medal he bought here at a penny apiece; and he sold it again, with a kiss into the bargain, to an admiring female world, at the low price of a shilling. Then, we have the Duke of Cambridge, and the Governesses' Institution; and Prince Albert, and the Crystal Palace; and, on the same shelf, the late Archbishop of Paris, on the barricade; and, again, the medal of the Eisteddfod—the eagle among clouds, above which rises the mountain peak: on the other side, Cardiff Castle; and for the border, the leek. But we must not linger among these dies, or we shall fill pages with accounts of whom and what we saw there;—the Peels and the Louis Napoleons; the Schillers and the Tom Thumbs; the private school and public market medals; royal families, free trade, charities, public solemnities, and private vanities, out of number. We will mention only one more fact in this connection. We saw a broken medal press—a press which was worth one hundred pounds, and which broke under the strain of striking off seventy thousand medals for the school-children who welcomed the Queen to Manchester last autumn. Yes, there is another fact that we must give. Many thousands of "national boxes" are required for exportation, especially to Germany. These boxes contain four counters, intended for the whist table. These counters are little medals, containing the portraits of the Queen, of Prince Albert, of the Prince of Wales, and of the other royal children. The Germans decline all invitations to suggest other subjects. They prefer these, which are interesting to all, and which can cause no jealousy among the various states of Germany. So these medals are struck everlastingly.

The medal-press is partly sunk in the earth, to avoid the shock and vibration which would take place above-ground, and injure the impression from the die. Its weight is three tons; the screw and wheel alone weighing fifteen hundred-weight. The screw is of an extraordinary size, being six inches in diameter. One die is fixed to the block, which rises from the ground; and the other is fastened to the end of the screw, which is to meet it from above. Of course the medal must lie between them. This medal, called a "blank," is (if not of gold, silver, or copper) of pure tin, cut out by one machine, cleaned and polished by another, and now brought here to be stamped by a third, and the greatest. This "blank" is laid on the lower die, and kept in its place, and preserved from expansion, when struck, by the collar, a stout circle of metal which embraces the die and blank. As the heavy horizontal wheel at the top revolves, the screw descends; so two or three men whirl the wheel round, with all their force; down goes the screw, with its die at its lower end, and stamps smartly upon the blank. A second stroke is given, and the impression is made. The edges are rough; but they are trimmed off in a lathe, and then the medal is finished. Button blanks are stamped in a smaller machine; some on these premises, but many in the manufactories of the button-makers. To those manufactories we must now pass on.

When little children are shown old portraits, they are pretty sure to notice the large buttons on the coats of our forefathers. Those buttons were, no doubt, made at Birmingham; for few were, in old days, made anywhere else in the kingdom. Those buttons were covered by women, and by the slow process of the needle. Women and girls sat round tables, in a cosey way, having no machinery to manage; and there was no clatter, or grinding, or stamping of machinery to prevent their gossiping as much as they liked. Before the workwomen lay moulds of horn or wood, of various shapes, but most commonly round, and always with a hole in the middle. These moulds were covered with gold or silver thread, or with sewing silk, by means of the needle. One would like to know how many women were required to supply, at this rate, the tailors who clothed the gentlemen of England? At last, the tailors made quicker work, by covering the moulds with the material of the dress. So obvious a convenience and saving as this might have been expected to take its place, as a matter of course, among new arrangements; but there were plenty of people who thought they could put down such buttons by applying to Parliament. A doleful petition was sent up, showing how needle-wrought buttons had been again and again protected by Parliament, and requesting the interposition of the Legislature once more against the tailoring practice of covering moulds with the same material as the coat or other dress. What would the petitioners have said, if they had been told that, in a century or so, one establishment would use metal for the manufacture of buttons to the amount of thirty-seven tons, six hundred-weight, two quarters, and one pound weight in one year! Yet this is actually the state of things now in Birmingham. And this is exclusive of the sort of button which, a few years ago, we should have called the commonest—the familiar gilt button, flat and plain.

As for the variety of kinds, William Hutton wrote about it as being great in his day; but it was nothing to what it is now. He says, "We well remember the long coats of our grandfathers, covered with half a gross of high-tops; and the cloaks of our grandmothers, ornamented with a horn button, nearly the size of a crown-piece, a watch, or John-apple, curiously wrought, as having passed through the Birmingham press. Though the common round button keeps in with the pace of the day, yet we sometimes find the oval, the square, the pea, the pyramid, flash into existence. In some branches of traffic the wearer calls loudly for new fashions; but in this, fashions tread upon each other, and crowd upon the wearer." We do not see the square at present; but the others, with a long list of new devices, are still familiar to us.

Some grandmother, who reads this, may remember the days when she bought horn button moulds by the string, to be covered at home. Some middle-aged ladies may remember the anxieties of the first attempts to cover such moulds—one of the most important lessons given to the infant needle-woman. How many stitches went to the business of covering one mould! what coaxing to stretch the cover smooth! what danger of ravelling out at one point or another! what ruin if the thread broke! what deep stitches were necessary to make all secure! And now, by two turns of a handle, the covering is done to such perfection, that the button will last twice as long as of old, and dozens can be covered in a minute by one woman. The one house we have mentioned sends out two thousand gross of shirt buttons per week; the gross consisting of twelve dozens.

"But what of metal?" the reader may ask. "Have shirt buttons anything to do with metal? except, indeed, the wire rim of those shirt buttons which are covered with thread and which wear out in no time? When you talk of thirty-seven tons of metal, do you include wire?" No, we do not. We speak of sheet iron, and copper, and brass, used to make shirt-buttons, and silk, and satin, and acorn, and sugar-loaf, and waistcoat buttons, and many more, besides those which show themselves to be metal.

Here are long rooms, large rooms, many rooms, devoted to the making an article so small as to be a very name for nothingness. "I don't care a button," we say: but, little as a button may be worth to us, one single specimen may be worth to the manufacturer long days of toil and nights of care, and the gain or loss of thousands of pounds. We can the better believe it for having gone through those rooms. There we see range beyond range of machines—the punching, drilling, stamping machines, the polishing wheels, and all the bright and compact, and never-tiring apparatus which is so familiar a specta-cle in Birmingham work-rooms. We see hundreds of women, scores of chil-dren, and a few men; and piles of the most desultory material that can be found anywhere, one would think—metal plates, coarse brown pasteboard, Irish linen, silk fringes, and figured silks of many colours and patterns.

First, rows of women sit, each at her machine, with its handle in her right hand, and a sheet of thin iron, brass, or copper, in the other. Shifting the sheet, she punches out circles many times faster than the cook cuts out shapes from a sheet of pastry. The number cut out and pushed aside in a minute is beyond belief to those who have not seen it done. By the same method, the rough pasteboard is cut; and linen (double, coarse and fine) for shirt buttons; and silk and satin;—in short, all the round parts of all buttons. The remains are sold—to the foundries, and the ragman, and the paper-makers. Very young children gather up the cut circles. Little boys, "just out of the cradle," range the pasteboard circles, and pack them close, on edge, in boxes or trays; and girls, as young, arrange on a table the linen circles, small and larger. Meantime, the machines are busily at work. Some are punching out the middle of the round bits of iron, or copper, or pasteboard, to allow the cloth or linen within to protrude, so as to be laid hold of by the needle which is to sew on the button. This makes the back or underpart of the button. Another machine wraps the metal top of the button in cloth, turns down the edges, fixes in the pasteboard mould, and the prepared back, and closes all the rims, so as to complete the putting together of the five parts that compose the common Florentine button which may be seen on any gentleman's coat. It is truly a wonderful and beautiful apparatus; but its operation cannot well be described to those who have not seen it. Black satin waistcoat buttons, and flat and conical buttons covered with figured silks, are composed of similar parts, and stuck together, with all edges turned in, by the same curious process. Shirt-buttons are nearly of the same make; but, instead of two pieces of metal, for the back and front, there is only one; and that is a rim, with both edges turned down, so as to leave a hollow for the reception of the edges of all the three pieces of linen which cover the button. A piece of fine linen, lined with a piece very stout and coarse, covers the visible part of the button, and goes over the rim. A piece of middling quality is laid on behind: and, by the machine, all the edges are shut fast into the hollow of the rim—the edges of which are, by the same movement, closed down nicely upon their contents, leaving the button so round, smooth, compact, and complete, that it is as great a mystery where the edges are all put away, as how the apple gets into the dumpling. No one would guess how neat the inside of the button is, that did not see it made. The rims are silvered as carefully as if they were for show. When struck from the brass or copper, and bent, they are carried to the yard, where an earnest elderly man, dressed in an odd suit of green baize, stands at a stone table, with a bucket of stone ware, pierced with holes, in his hand, and troughs before him, containing—the first, diluted aquafortis, and the others, water. The bucket, half full of button rims, is dipped in the aquafortis bath, well shaken there, and then passed through successive waterings, finishing at the pump. The rims, now clean and bright, must be silvered. They are shaken and boulted (as a miller would say), covered with a mysterious silvering powder, the constitution of which we were not to inquire into; and out they come, as white as so many teaspoons. Thus it is, too, with the brace-buttons, on which the machines are at work all this time. Each has to be pierced with four holes; necessary, as we all know, for sewing on buttons which have to bear such a strain as these have. This piercing with four holes can be inflicted, by one woman, on fifteen gross per hour. The forming the little cup in the middle of the button, where the holes are, in order to raise the rim of the button from the surface of the dress, is called counter-sinking; and that process has a machine to itself; one of the long row of little engines which look almost alike, but which discharge various offices in this manufacture, at once so small and so great. These buttons go down to the burnisher's department in company with some which make a prodigious show at a very small cost—the stage ornaments which are professionally called "spangles." Let no novice suppose that these are the little scales of excessively thin metal which are called spangles on doll's dresses and our grandmothers' embroidered shoes. These stage spangles are nearly an inch in diameter, cut out in the middle, and bent into a rim, to reflect light the better. In the Hippodrome they cover the boddices of princesses, and stud the trappings of horses at a tournament; and in stage processions they make up a great part of the glitter. Of these, twenty-five thousand gross in a year are sent out by this house alone; a fact which gives an overwhelming impression of the amount of stage decoration which must always be exhibiting itself in England.

In our opinion, it was prettier to see these "spangles" burnished here than glittering on the stage; and, certainly, the brace-buttons we had been tracing out would never more be so admired as when they were brightening up at the wheel. The burnisher works his lathe with a treadle. The stone he uses is a sort of bloodstone, found in Derbyshire, which lasts a lifetime in use. Each button is picked up and applied: a pleasant twanging, vibrating tune—very like a Jew's harp—comes from the flying wheel; the button is dropped—polished in half, a second; and another is in its place, almost before the eye can follow. Six or eight gross can thus be burnished in an hour by one workman. If the brace-buttons are to have rims, or to be milled, or in any way ornamented, now is the time; and here are the lathes in which it is done. The workmen need to have good heads, as well as practised hands; for, even in an article like this, society is full of fancies, and there may be a hundred fashions in a very short time;—a new one almost every week. These harping lathes, in a row, about their clean and rapid work, are perhaps the prettiest part of the whole show. At the further end of the apartment sits a woman with heaps of buttons and spangles, and piles of square pieces of paper before her. With nimble fingers she ranges the finished articles in rows of half-a-dozen or more, folds in each row, and makes up her packets as fast, probably, as human hands can do it. But this is a sort of work which one supposes will be done by machinery some day.

Still, all this while, the long rows of machines on the counters, above and below, and on either hand, are at work, cutting, piercing, stamping, countersinking. We must go and see more of their work. Here is one shaping in copper the nut of the acorn: another is shaping the cup. Disks of various degrees of concavity, sugar-loaves, and many other shapes, are dropping by thousands from the machines into the troughs below. And here is the covering or pressing machine again at work—here covering the nut of the acorn with green satin, and there casing the cup with green Florentine; and finally fitting and fastening them together, so that no ripening and loosening touch of time shall, as in the case of the natural acorn, cause them to drop apart. This exquisite machinery was invented about eleven years ago, and is now patented by the Messrs. Elliott, in whose premises we are becoming acquainted with it.

We have fastened upon the acorn button, because it is the prettiest; and, just now, before everybody's eyes, in shop, street, or drawing-room: but the varieties of dress-button are endless. Some carry a fringe; and the fringes come from Coventry. To ornament others, the best skill of Spitalfields is put forth. In a corner of an up-stairs room there is a pile of rich silks and other fabrics, which seem to be out of place in a button manufactory, till we observe that they are woven expressly for the covering of buttons. They have sprigs or circles, at regular distances. One woman passes the piece under a machine, which chalks out each sprig; and the next machine stamps out the chalked bit. This, again, is women's and children's work; and we find, on inquiry, that of the three or four hundred people employed on these premises, nearly all are women and children. We saw few men employed, except in the silvering and burnishing departments.

The most interesting and beautiful kind of button of all, however, depends upon the skill of men employed elsewhere—the die-sinkers, of whom we have already given some news. There is a series of stamped buttons, gilt or silvered, which one may go and see, as one would so many pictures;—that sort of badge called sporting buttons. Members of a hunt, or of any sporting association, distinguish themselves by wearing these pretty miniature pictures; here, a covey of partridges, with almost every feather indicated in the high finish;—there, a hound clearing a hedge;—now, a group of huntsman and pack;—and again, a fishing-net meshing the prey; or the listening stag or bounding fawn. In these small specimens of art, the details are as curious, the composition as skilful, the life of the living as vivid, and the aspect of the dead as faithful, as if the designer were busy on a wine-cup for a king, instead of a button for a sporting jacket. Here there must be a dead ground; there a touch of burnish; here a plain ground; there a plaided or radiating one; but everywhere the most perfect finish that talent and care can give. There is surely something charming in seeing the smallest things done so thoroughly, as if to remind the careless, that whatever is worth doing at all, is worth doing well. We no longer wonder as we did, that the button branch in one of the most advanced in the business of the die-sinker and medallist.

Pearl buttons have their style of "ornamentation" too; but the die-sinker and professional designer have nothing to do with it. There is something more in the ornamenting of pearl buttons than the delicate work done with the turning tools;—the circles, and stars, and dots, and exquisite milled edges, with which our common pearl buttons are graced. At the manufactory we are shown drawers full of patterns; and among those in favour with working men are some with pearl centres, on which are carved, with curious skill, various devices;—a dog, or a bird, or some such pretty thing. These designs are notions of the workmen's own.

The pearl button manufacture is the prettiest, after all;—the prettiest of that family of production. Perhaps the charm is in the material,—the broad shell, which we know to have been, a while ago, at the bottom of the Indian seas. The rainbow light, which gleams from the surface, seems to show to us the picture of where this shell once was, and what was done about it. This is not from the Gulf of Mexico—this shell. Many come from thence; but this is of too good a quality for those western seas. Nor is it from Manilla, though the Manilla shells are very fine. This comes from Singapore, and is or the best quality. To get it, what toil and pains, what hopes and fears, what enterprises and calculations have been undertaken and undergone! What boastful of barbarians went out, amidst the muttering and chanting of charms, to the diving for the shells for our handling! How gently were they paddled over those deep clear seas, where the moon shines with a golden light, and sends her rays far down into the green depths which the diver is about to intrude upon! As the land-breeze came from stirring the forest, and breathing over the rice-grounds, to waft the boats out to sea, the divers prepared for their plunge, each slinging his foot on the heavy stone which was to carry him down, nine fathoms deep, to where his prey was reposing below. Then there was the plunge, and the wrenching of the shells from the rocks, and putting them into the pouch at the waist; and the ascent, amidst a vast pressure of water, causing the head to seethe and roar, and the ears to ache, and the imprisoned breath to convulse the frame; and then there was the fear of sharks, and the dread spectacle of wriggling and shooting fishes, and who knows what other sights! And then, the breath hastily snatched; and the fearful plunge to be made again! And then must have followed the sale to the Singapore merchant; and the packing and shipping to England; and the laying up in London, to gather an enormous price—the article being bought up by a few rich merchants—and the journey to Birmingham, where the finest part of the shell is to be kept for buttons, and the coarser part sent on to Sheffield, to make the handles of knives, paper-cutters, and the like.

Through such adventures has this broad shell gone, which we now hold in our hand. In the middle is the seamed, imperfect part, from which the fish was torn. From that centre, all round to the thin edge, is the fine part which is to be cut into buttons. From that centre back to the joint is the ridgy portion which, with its knots will serve for knife-handles. There is, perhaps, no harder substance known; and strong must be the machine that will cut it. It is caught and held with an iron grip, while the tubular saw cuts it in circles, a quarter of an inch (or more) thick. Some of the circles are an inch and a half in diameter; others as small as the tiny buttons seen on baby-clothes. They are, one by one, clutched by a sort of pincers, and held against a revolving cylinder, to be polished with sand and oil. Then, each is fixed on a lathe, and turned, and smoothed; adorned with concentric rings, or with stars, or leaves, or dots; and then corded or milled at the edges, with streaks almost too fine to be seen by the naked eye. The figures in the middle are to mask the holes by which the button is to be sewn on. In a small depression, in the centre of the pattern, the holes are drilled by a sharp hard point which pierces the shell. The edges of the holes are sharp, as housewives well know. But for the cutting of the thread, in course of time, by these edges, pearl buttons would wear for ever. Now and then, the thin pierced bit in the middle breaks out; but, much oftener, the button is lost by the cutting of the thread. They last so long, however, as to make us wonder how there can be any need of the vast numbers that are made. Birmingham supplies almost the whole world. A very few are made at Sheffield; and that is all. In the United States, where the merchants can get almost any quantity of the shell, from their great trade with Manilla and Singapore, the buttons are not made. The Americans buy an incredible quantity from Birmingham. Many thousands of persons in this town are employed in the business; and one house alone sends out two thousand gross per week, and very steadily; for fashion has little or nothing to do with pearl buttons. The demand is steady and increasing; and it would increase much faster but for the restriction in the quantity of the material. The profit made by the manufacturer is extremely small—so dear as the shell is. The Singapore shell was sold not many years ago at sixty-five pounds per ton; now, it cannot be had under one hundred and twenty-two pounds, ten shillings, per ton. The manufacturer complains of monopoly. If this be the cause of the dearness, the evil will, in the nature of things, be lessened before long. Time will show whether the shells are becoming exhausted, like the furs of polar countries. We ventured to suggest, while looking round at the pile of shell fragments, and the heaps of white dust that accumulate under the lathes, that it seems a pity to waste all this refuse, seeing how valuable a manure it would make, if mixed with bone-dust or guano. The reply was, that it is impossible to crush a substance so hard; that there is no machine which will reduce these fragments to powder. If so, some solvent will probably be soon found, which will act like diluted sulphuric acid upon bones. While we were discussing this matter, and begging a pint or quart of the powder from under the lathes, to try a small agricultural experiment with, a workman mentioned that when he worked at Sheffield, a neighbouring farmer used to come, at any time, and at any inconvenience to himself, to purchase shell-powder, when allowed to fetch it, declaring it to be inestimable as a manure. In a place like Birmingham, where the sweepings and scrapings of the floors of manufactories are sold for the sake of the metal dust that may have fallen, we venture to predict that such heaps and masses of shell fragments as we saw, will not long be cast away as useless rubbish. If one house alone could sell two hundred and fifty tons of shell-refuse per year, what a quantity of wheat and roots might be produced from under the counters, as it were, of Birmingham workshops! And we were told that such a quantity would certainly be afforded. Such a sale may, in time, become some set-off against the extreme dearness of the imported shell. While the smallest pearl button goes through nine or ten pairs of hands before it is complete, the piece from which it is cut may hereafter be simmering in some dissolving acid; and sinking into the ground, and rising again, soft and green, as the blade of wheat, or swelling into the bulb of the turnip. Will not some one try?

While this dust was bubbling out from under the turning-tools, and flying about before it settled, we had misgivings about the lungs of the workmen. But it seems there was no need. The workman who was exhibiting his art in the dusty place, told us he had worked thus for nine-and-twenty years, and had enjoyed capital health; and truly, he looked stout and comfortable enough; and we saw no signs of ill-health among the whole number employed. The proprietor cares for them—for their health, their understandings, their feelings, and their fortunes; and he seems to be repaid by the spectacle of their welfare.

The white pearl buttons are not the only ones made of shells from the Eastern seas. There is a sort called black, which to our eyes looked quite as pretty, gleaming as it did with green and lilac colours, when moved in the light. This kind of shell comes from the islands of the Pacific. It is plentiful round Tahiti, and Hawaii, (as we now call Otaheite and Owhyhee). It is much worn by working men, in the larger forms of buttons. We remember to have often seen it; but never to have asked what it was.

The subsidiary concerns of these large manufactories strike us by their importance, when on the spot, though we take no heed to them in our daily life. When the housewife has taken into use the last of a strip of pearl buttons, she probably gives to the children the bit of gay foil on which they were tacked, without ever thinking where it came from, or how it happened to be there. The importation of this foil is a branch of trade with France. We cannot compete with the French in the manufacture of it. When we saw it in bundles—gay with all gaudy hues—we found it was an expensive article, adding notably to the cost of the buttons, though its sole use is to set off their translucent quality, to make them more tempting to the eye.

We saw a woman, in her own home, surrounded by her children, tacking the buttons on their stiff paper, for sale. There was not foil in this case between the stiff paper and the buttons, but a brilliant blue paper, which looked almost as well. This woman sews forty gross in a day. She could formerly, by excessive diligence, sew fifty or sixty gross; but forty is her number now—and a large number it is, considering that each button has to be picked up from the heap before her, ranged in its row, and tacked with two stitches.

Here we had better stop, though we have not told half that might be related on the subject of buttons. It is wonderful, is it not? that on that small pivot turns the fortune of such multitudes of men, women, and children, in so many parts of the world; that such industry, and so many fine faculties, should be brought out and exercised by so small a thing as the Button.

LADY BELL

THE PROCESS OF IRONMAKING

The brief description attempted in this chapter of the process of making iron does not profess to be anything but a crude elementary sketch, designed to give some idea of the daily work of the men employed at the ironworks, and the conditions under which it is accomplished.

The materials required are, roughly speaking, iron-stone, coke, and lime-stone, which in the district in question are all found comparatively near at hand. The town and works we are describing have the further great advantage of standing, as has been already said, on the banks of a big and navigable river, at a few miles from the place where it falls into the North Sea.

The iron ore, or ironstone, is brought to the works from the mines in the Cleveland Hills, the limestone from the quarries in the Pennine Hills, and the fuel from the coal-mines in the county of Durham, either in the form of coal or of coal already transformed into coke.

It does not come within my scheme to enter into any description of the work either of the collier, who, working underground in the narrow passage cut in the seam of coal, sometimes so low that he is not able to stand upright, loosens the coal with a pick, or of the iron-miner who, working underground in a gallery 10 feet high, drills holes for the reception of gunpowder into the ironstone, which is afterwards blown into fragments. I take up the work at the stage where the iron and coal have been already "won," according to the technical phrase, and have been brought from the mines to the works.

From *At the Works: A Study of a Manufacturing Town* (1907). London: Virago Press, 1985.

The lumps of iron ore, looking like rough pieces of ordinary greenish stone, averaging about 10 inches in diameter, are charged on trucks at the mines and conveyed to the works. Arrived at the works, these trucks, containing severally the ironstone, the coal, the coke, and the limestone, are run along the lines laid on the top of two long iron platforms called "gantries," about 60 feet high from the ground, in each of which are at intervals apertures through which, by opening the movable bottom of the trucks, the materials are emptied into their various destinations. Beneath the gantry is a series of big partitions of brick, called "bunkers," practically forming store-cupboards, open at the back and front, in which are heaped the stores of coke and limestone to use in the furnace. There is also a certain amount of ironstone stored in case the supply coming from the mines in the trucks should run short, for the furnace must not cease burning day or night, and must have its constant and continuous supply.

Underneath the other gantry, beneath which begins the actual process of the manufacture of iron, stand at certain intervals huge kilns in a row, looking like black round towers made of iron. These kilns are about 45 feet high and 21 feet in diameter, tapering to 13 feet 6 inches, joined together at the top by the gantry, in which the tops of the kilns form a series of large round openings.

In these kilns the ironstone is calcined, in order to drive off the moisture and carbonic acid contained in it. The fire in the first instance is kindled at the bottom of the kiln by the usual methods, after which the ironstone is dropped into the kiln from the gantry above through the opened bottom of the truck, brought over the hole at the top of the kiln. The kiln is fed with coal as often as necessary. The fire gradually rises. Once alight, it is not allowed to go out, but continues burning night and day unless it is necessary to extinguish it and relight it for repairs, or from some accident. All round the bottom of the kiln there are huge iron shutters, which let down, so that the ironstone, when sufficiently roasted, can be drawn out through these, taken on barrows, and wheeled away to the furnace. It is now, after having been calcined, of a dull red. These barrows, together with other barrows containing, some, coke, and others limestone (the limestone at the first cursory glance looks not unlike the ironstone before calcination, but has a more decided blue tinge, the ironstone being green), are then placed upon a lift which goes up to the top of the blast-furnace, into which the contents of the barrows are from thence emptied.

The blast-furnace is, to look at, a huge round black tower of iron, 80 feet high and 30 to 40 feet across. It is filled from the top, where there is a great circular opening like the mouth of an immense funnel, but closed by a "bell," which can be lowered, on to which the charge of the furnace is thrown. The charge put into the furnace at one time is six barrows of ironstone, six of coke, three of limestone. This charge is called a "round." The coke is put in for fuel, the limestone is put in to serve as what is called a "flux"—that is, a material which in combination with another makes a fusible compound. For the iron-stone contains silica, or sand, and alumina, or clay, which are difficult to melt: the combination with the limestone makes them fusible. The mass of heated material is constantly sinking down through the furnace, and being drawn out at the bottom in the form of pig-iron and slag.

About 6 to 8 feet from the bottom of the furnace a strong blast of air, playing the part of a gigantic bellows in fanning the flames inside the furnace, is driven in by machinery. This blast is driven in hot in order to avoid unnecessary cooling of the interior of the furnace. The gases generated by the process, including 23 per cent. of burnable gas, which can be seen blowing off at the top in a stiff whistling flame, are constantly escaping. By a skilful arrangement these gases are now conducted through a huge flue, and thence distributed to the tubes which lead them through the "stoves" (tall black cylinders about 60 feet high and 21 feet across, made of honeycombed brickwork, also like round black towers, but smaller than the furnaces) and so beneath the boilers which drive the engines propelling the blast into the furnace.

By this ingenious arrangement of circuit, therefore, the gases engendered by the furnace return to heat the blast which blows it, since the stoves become white-hot by the passage of the hot gases, and the blast blown into the furnace is heated by passing through the stoves. The gases are directed into the stoves alternately. They pass through one stove and heat it white-hot, then the gas is shut off and the air is blown through the stove in the reverse direction, cooling it and becoming heated itself—after which the blast is shut off, and the gas, which in the meantime has been heating another stove (into which the air is now again directed), again passes through and reheats the first. At the bottom of the furnace, when, a given time having been allowed, the moment has come to draw the iron out, a hole is made, and the red-hot molten iron flows out into sand-moulds prepared for it, in which it cools in the shape of short iron logs. These logs are what is called pig-iron.

The molten iron destined to make steel, instead of flowing into the sand-beds, is drawn off into a huge iron vessel called the "ladle," and of this I will only say briefly that, the impurities which make the iron too brittle and too fusible for the purposes for which steel is required having been subsequently removed by exposing it to a very high temperature, it is then cast into large blocks, called ingots, of what has now become steel. I do not propose to attempt any description of the process by which these ingots are rolled out red-hot into great bars, billets, angles, etc. From the human point of view the surroundings and the conditions of life are practically the same at the steelworks as at the ironworks.

This is a bald summary of the process of the making of iron. Let us now consider it in more detail,with the "job" of each man, as he would himself call it, and the conditions under which he works. The workmen comprise furnace-keepers, slaggers, chargers, mine-fillers, brakesmen, weighers, coke-tippers, helpers, slag-tippers, gantrymen, scarrers, metal-carriers, boiler-men, the engine-men, the men who look after the pumps, the cranes, the stoves, the labourers who help in various departments: the men who work in the "shops"—i.e., workshops—joiners, moulders, pattern-makers, who shape the various pieces of wood from which the moulder makes the moulds in which the iron will be cast for making pieces of machinery, and what is called the sailor fitter gang, practically odd men, some of whom have in reality been sailors, and who do any rigging up of anything incidental that happens to be necessary. The best paid of these men get from £2 to £3 per week, the lowest 19s. 6d. The majority are in receipt of from 25s. to 38s. per week.

The working day, since the eight-hours day was agreed upon between masters and men, is now divided into three "shifts" or spells of work of eight hours each. The first shift is from 6 a.m. to 2 p.m., the second from 2 p.m. to 10 p.m., the third from 10 p.m. to 6 a.m. On the Sunday, the odd day in each week, the men who have been during the preceding six days on the morning shift (from 6 a.m. to 2 p.m.) work sixteen hours on end—that is, from 6 a.m. to 10 p.m.—and then begin the next day at 2 p.m. and go on till 10 p.m. Every third week, therefore, they work on this long shift through the Sunday.

This distribution of work applies to those workmen whose job cannot be left for a moment—i.e., those who are concerned actually in dealing with the ironstone from the moment that it arrives at the works until, converted into iron, it is carried away. The hours of the others are not divided in the same way. The metal-carriers work from 6 a.m. until their work is done; the slag-tippers work according to the tide, at both the low tides; the crane-drivers according to the tide and the shipping. Some of the locomotive drivers have the eight-hours shift; some work from 6 a.m. to 5 p.m. The labourers work from 6 a.m. to 5 p.m.

The blast-furnaces are never allowed to go out night or day, week-days or Sundays, on account of the difficulty, trouble, damage to the furnaces, and great expense of relighting them. During the Durham coal strike in 1892, when many of the works had to be laid idle, the fires were banked up in the furnaces that they might not go out; and thus kept up on this colossal scale, they remained alight for three months. This, though better than if they had been allowed to go out and had had to be relighted, was very detrimental to the furnaces, and necessitated time, trouble, and repairs to get them into their normal condition again.

The men who work on the "gantry"—that is, the tall platform along which the trucks arrive containing the ore, the coal, the coke, and the limestone—are called "gantrymen." A gantryman has from £2 to £2 12s. 6d. a week, an income equal to that of many a curate, and that of many a junior clerk in a private, or even a Government, office. For this he works either eight hours a day or six hours a day, according to the shift, for the gantryman only has two shifts in the day, and not three, either from 6 a.m. to 2 p.m., or from 4 p.m. to 10 p.m. The daily work of the gantryman, who stands on the platform at the top of the kiln, is to superintend the calcining of the ironstone—i.e., to feed with coal the kiln into which the ironstone has been "tipped." The coal is tipped, not immediately into the kiln, but on to broad, flat sheets of iron on either side of the opening on to which the coal has been tipped from the truck. The gantryman at intervals shovels the coal into the kiln on to the top of the iron-stone, using his own judgment how much he puts in, and how often.

The shift from 6 a.m. to 2 p.m. is the hardest, as at 6 a.m. the kiln has been left since ten the night before, so that there is a great deal to do. Then by two o'clock it is so full that it can be left until four. This second shift has not so much to do as the first, as it has only two hours interval to make up. Each of the eight-hours men is supposed to have two quarters of an hour in which to have some food. This food—his "bait"—as he would himself call it—he takes up with him. It is usually something that can be carried in a can, and kept hot in the little "cabins," of which one is allotted to each particular gang of men working at the same job—comfortless little sheds enough, filled with dust and dirt and the smell of the gases. For a man working on the eight-hours shift, of course, it is possible—as far, that is, as time is concerned—whatever shift the man is on, for him to have a square meal at some reasonable hour. The men who go off at 2 p.m. can have their dinner at home in the afternoon; those who come at 2 p.m. can dine at home before leaving. A man who comes to his work in the evening has had his meal at home at suitable intervals during the day, if his wife is competent.

But none of the eight-hours men when at the works can leave their job for a square meal, although they may have short spells off in which to sit down either in the cabin or in the place where they are working and have a snack. They are not for one moment free from the need of that incessant vigilance re-quired from all the workers who share the responsibility of controlling the huge forces they are daring to use.

The gantryman, not being close to the great heat of the furnace, has not to encounter in the winter the same sudden and violent changes of temperature as those which the men standing round the foot of the furnace must endure, when they pass from the almost unbearable heat of their immediate sur-roundings to the biting cold of a few yards off. But still, the work of the gantryman is a task absolutely shelterless, and in the sharp airs of the north-east coast the winds that blow across the high platform pierce like a dagger; added to which they bring the burning fumes which blow across from the kilns and the furnaces, the choking sulphurous fumes which are constantly blowing down the throats of the men exposed to them.

And besides the fumes and the gases, every breath of wind at the ironworks carries dust with it, whirling through the air in a wind, dropping through it in a calm, covering the ground, filling the cabins, settling on the clothes of those who are within reach, filling their eyes and their mouths, covering their hands and their faces. The calcined ironstone sends forth red dust, the smoke from the chimneys and furnaces is deposited in white dust, the smoke from the steel-rolling mills falls in black dust: and, most constant difficulty of all, the gases escaping from the furnaces are charged with a fine, impalpable brownish dust, which is shed everywhere, on everything, which clogs the interior of the stoves and of the flues, and whose encroachments have to be constantly fought against. One of the most repellent phenomena at the ironworks to the onlooker is the process of expelling the dust from the stoves, for which purpose the valves of the stove are closed, the stove is filled with air at high pressure, and then one of the valves is opened and the air is forcibly expelled. A great cloud of red dust rushes out with a roar, covering everything and everybody who stands within reach, with so intolerable a noise and effluvium that it makes itself felt even amidst the incessant reverberation, the constant smells, dust, deposits, that surround the stoves and the furnaces. That strange, grim street formed by the kilns, the furnaces, and the bunkers, darkened by the iron platforms overhead between the kilns and the gantry, a street in which everything is a dull red, is the very heart of the works, the very stronghold of the making of iron, a place unceasingly filled by glare, and clanging, and vapours, from morning till night and from night till morning.

The material tipped by the gantrymen into the kilns is gradually, as it sinks down, drawn off at the bottom through the "hoppers," which can be opened or closed as required by the huge iron shutters before described. A hopper, be it said, is practically any vessel or receptacle with a hole at the bottom and sloping sides. Every now and again, if the kiln is too hot, the ironstone begins to fuse and the pieces stick together, making a lump too big to get through the inside of the kiln into the hopper. The lump is called a "scarr," and it then has to be broken into bits with an iron rod from the outside by a man called the "scarrer," who stands on a movable wooden trestle, about the height of the bottom of the hopper, and breaks up the lump by thrusting his bar into the opening until the lump is small enough to come through. The opening into the kiln above the hopper is called the "eye." The scarrer earns from 30s. to £2 a week; he spends most of the eight-hours day standing at the bottom of the kiln, the iron rod in his hand, ready to thrust it into the kiln whenever the obstacle shows itself. By him is standing another man ready to add his weight to the thrust if the strength of the first one is not enough to deal with the obstacle. For whatever operation is being carried on at the ironworks, there are always a number of men standing round in a state of watchful concentration, their attention on the alert, ready to lend a hand in a case of emergency. The spectator receives an overpowering impression of what that watchfulness needs to be, of what sudden necessities may arise, of what may be the deadly effect of some swift, dangerous variation, some unexpected development in the formidable material which the men are handling.

The "scarrs" having been broken, and the calcined ironstone, now of a dull red colour, drawn out from the hopper into shallow iron barrows, it is wheeled from the kiln to the lift of the blast-furnace, 20 to 30 yards off, by a man called a "mine-filler," who does this ten to a dozen times during the hour. On the way to the furnace he stops to have the weight of his load checked outside the "weigh cabin," a little dark, dusty shed, outside the window of which there is a platform like that used for weighing luggage at a station. The men get so well accustomed to judging the "burden" required—that is, the weight of ironstone or limestone that ought to be in the barrow—that they generally hit off almost exactly before it is weighed the required quantity of rough pieces of stone piled up in it. The mine-filler is paid 42s. a week.

The weight being ascertained to be correct, the weighman puts down a straight stroke for each barrow that passes him, and after every four draws a horizontal line through the four strokes, each of these groups of lines therefore representing five barrows. The man in the weigh-cabin receives about £1 per week. He is generally one of the older men, obliged to accept as his strength declines a lighter and less remunerative form of work. His job is to sit for the eight hours in which he is on duty in his little cabin, sheltered, at any rate, from the weather, but not from the smells, the noise, and the dust of the blast-furnaces close to which his cabin stands.

The mine-filler, the weight of his barrow being checked and found correct, then wheels it to the lift, a square, unenclosed platform which goes up and down to the top of the furnace and back again between four huge supports.

In the place we are describing there are first two furnaces and then a lift, then two furnaces again, then a lift, and so on; the same lift always serves the same pair of furnaces. The six barrows of ironstone, three of limestone, and six of coke, constituting the "round" already described, are placed on the lift and hoisted to the top of the furnace, where they are taken off by the chargers, and wheeled close to the big round aperture at the top of the blast-furnace. These men are standing on a platform about 10 feet wide that runs round this aperture, and is guarded on the outside by a railing. That aperture is closed by a huge lid, a bell and hopper in this shape: the centre edges of a hopper (which in this case is the shape of a deep saucer or shallow bowl with its middle out) rest upon the sides of a shallow cone called the "bell." The charge is lowered on to the top of the bell, on which the inner edge of the hopper is resting; the bell is then lowered, leaving, therefore, an opening, and the charge, no longer kept in place by the sides of the bell, slides down them into the furnace below.

The bell is then rehoisted into position. The sudden jet of vivid flame from the top of the furnace, so familiar to those who live in the neighbourhood of iron-works, is produced at the moment of charging. The chargers have from 30s. to £2 per week. The work of the charger is arduous and trying to the health. Men with susceptible lungs are apt to be much affected by the combination of the rapid breathing necessitated by handling the heavy barrows and the fumes inhaled with every panting step.

The temperature inside the furnace is about 3,000° F. This great mass of combustion is being perpetually fanned by the hot blast, heated, as has been before described, by passing through the stoves made hot by the passage of the gas, and incessantly driven into the furnaces at the top of the "hearth," just above the slag opening, by blowing-engines moved by machinery. The iron, being heavier, gradually sinks to the bottom, and the slag (which may be called an artificial lava, and is practically the scum or dross of the iron) rises, floating on the top of the iron, just below the place where the blast is blown in. The materials put into the furnace gradually sink down as those which pre-ceded them are consumed, and the metal is separated from the dross with which it is associated in the stone. As they sink, more material is put in above, so that the level of them at the top is always within a few feet of the bell. The heavier iron falls molten to the bottom, while the dross floats molten on its surface. As the process continues, the mass of liquid iron rises, as well as the slag or dross, until the latter flows out of the furnace through a hole provided for the purpose. Four times in the twenty-four hours the furnace is "tapped"; a hole is made at the bottom of the furnace, and the iron is allowed to run out. This is an important moment in the process of manufacture. To say that a hole is made in the furnace for the iron to run out sounds simple enough: but a stream of molten iron cannot be drawn off like water, and time after time the tapping of the furnace, accomplished by breaking by main force through the piece of fireclay, which, having been thrust cold into the red-hot aperture after the last casting, has baked and hardened in the opening to a solid mass, is a strenuous encounter with a potent and deadly enemy. To be a "furnace-keeper," and responsible for the furnace being in absolute working order, is one of the most responsible posts at the works. The keeper gets from £2 10s. to £3 per week.

A great square platform, the "pig-bed," of firm moist sand, dug from the river-bed, extends 10 feet from the ground in front of each furnace, at a level of about 1 foot below the bottom of it. In this, before each casting, the chan-nels are prepared into which the molten stream is to run, by the helpers of the furnace-keeper. These channels consist of one long main channel, 16 inches wide and 10 inches deep, at right angles to which are other channels varying in number, generally about 16 feet long; between these, parallel to the main channel, are rows of shorter channels, also varying in number according to the size of the pig-bed; there may be twenty-four, or there may be even as many as thirty-six. These shorter channels are for the pieces of iron which when cast will be known as "pigs"; the transverse and longer channels are called the "sows." The area of the sandy platform having been made tolerably smooth and level again after the last casting, the men take first of all a long piece of wood the size that the sows are to be, with an iron ring at each end of it for facility of handling, and put it across the platform where the first sow is to be. They then take a number of short oblong blocks of wood, the shape of the pigs, and drop them rapidly one after another all along at right angles to the sow, with about 3 inches of sand between them; other men standing ready with spades then throw sand into the interstices between the wooden blocks, forming a partition between each. When the row is finished, therefore, each block of wood is lying practically in a little rectangular sandy hollow. The long transverse piece, the sow, is then lifted up by two men holding the iron ring at either end and thrown across to others, who put it across at the bottom of the shorter ones, and repeat the operation. Then all the shorter wooden pieces are taken up by the ring at the end of them in the same way (except that they can be lifted by one man) and thrown across to the others standing below the next sow, who repeat the operation, as with the sow of dropping them into position and filling up the interstices with sand. Into the first row of moulds, now left empty, a man holding a wooden instrument, a thin piece of wood fastened transversely at the bottom of a long handle, like a broom ending in wood instead of bristles, goes rapidly along the channels, flattening them at the bottom; after which he is followed by another man with an instrument which has at the end of its handle a cross-piece of iron with raised letters on it, with which he in his turn goes along the channel of pigs, stamping the name of the brand at the bottom of them. And so admirably adapted is the river sand for the purpose of a mould, especially after several castings have been run over it, thoroughly drying it and burning the lime out, that this stamping by hand by a mould with raised letters, firmly pressed into each channel in turn, is enough.

To the outsider, indeed, part of the absorbing interest of watching the manufacture of iron is that in this country, at any rate, it is all done by human hands, and not by machinery. From the moment when the ironstone is lifted off the trucks, then dropped into the kilns, afterwards taken to the furnace, and then drawn out of it, it has not been handled by any other means than the arms of powerful men, whose strength and vigilance are constantly strained almost to breaking-point. It cannot be too often repeated what the risk is of dealing with a thing which you encounter only in terms of liquid fire. The path of the ironworker is literally strewn with danger, for as he walks along, the innocent-looking fragment, no longer glowing, may be a piece of hot iron of which the touch, if he stepped upon it, is enough to cripple him; one splash of the molten stream may blind him; if he were to stumble as he walks along the edge of that sandy platform where the iron is bubbling and rushing into the moulds he would never get up again. The men move about among these surroundings with the reckless—often too reckless—unconcern of long habit. You may see as you pass a man standing engaged in thickening the end of a bar of iron by leisurely twirling it round and round in a vessel full of red-hot slag, of which he will then allow a portion to cool on it, and doing it as calmly as though he were stirring round a pan of water.

When the moment comes to open the furnace for the next casting, the requisite time having elapsed since the last, a hole is drilled through the bottom of the "hearth" in the solid piece of clay with which the furnace was closed the last time it was tapped. This is done by a great iron bar, held by three men, being thrust again and again against the clay, clearing away the loose rubbish and beginning to make the hole, against which it is then held in position by two men, while two others deal alternate blows on it with big hammers. It is done as quickly and regularly as though by machinery, the top of the crowbar hit fair and square with a clang at every blow, and the men who are striking are surrounded by a group of others waiting. These last are slaggers, mine-fillers, and others, come away from their special job to help in this one. They all stand intently concentrated on the moment when the clay ɔhall finally yield. When that moment has come, the bar, with a mighty effort, is withdrawn, and the blazing stream rushes out in foaming and leaping red-hot waves through the opening, into the deep main channel prepared for it. The heat to those standing on the bank of that molten river is almost unbearable, the glare hardly to be endured. The onlooker is half blinded, half choked, as the flood rushes fiercely past him.

The men who are watching are on the alert, and with the iron bars thickened at the end by a lump of slag, the stream is controlled. It goes rushing down the whole length of the main channel to the last set of moulds, into which it is allowed to flow by having the barrier of sand which bars the access from the main channel broken down. So have we all of us in our childhood dug channels in the sand for the incoming tide, dammed them up, and then dashed one open again with our spades as the first encroaching wave came foaming along. The moment one of these sets of channels is filled, the man whose job it is, working gradually up nearer the furnace, breaks down the barrier into the one next above it, and the stream dashes into that, while at the same time the iron in the main channel is stopped from rushing below that point by having a big spade-like implement stuck across it. One channel after another becomes a quivering red mass of liquid fire as the hot iron flows into it, taking the shape of the mould as it cools. As each set of channels is filled, sand is rapidly thrown over the surface of the molten iron by men with spades, and after it has somewhat cooled cold water is thrown over it by a hose.

During this time the aperture into the furnace has been closed again by filling it with lumps of fireclay. A man, taking one of these lumps—or more, if necessary, in succession—and kneading it with his hands into a rough ball, stoops and hurls it with all his might straight into the funnel-shaped opening at the end of which the red-hot iron can be seen bubbling, the throw being instantly followed by a mighty thrust from a huge bar of iron, wielded by five men, who stand ready as each lump is thrown in to push it home. When the hole is finally filled the fireclay hardens in it, baked to a solid mass, and the aperture is sealed, to be reopened six hours later, and the whole process gone over again. Sometimes the closing of the aperture is effected in three minutes; sometimes, not often, it has taken nearly as long as an hour.

At this stage, of course, each sow is still joined to a row of pigs. As soon as they get rather cooler, but while still nearly red-hot, the little short logs, the pigs, are broken off from the main runner, the sow, which is done simply by putting an iron bar underneath them and prizing them up, for in this state the metal is very brittle. They are then lifted by pincers and put up on end leaning against one another at the top, and again watered by a hose to make them cool more rapidly. Then finally when it is possible to handle them, they are taken up and carried one at a time by the metal-carriers to the trucks which convey the metal either to the stock-yard, the place where the stores of pig-iron are kept piled one on the top of the other ready for transport by sea or land, or else directly to some ship which is going to convey the iron to the purchaser. About eighteen of these pigs go to the ton: that is, each of them weighs about 9 stone. A man lifts one of them at a time, holding it by the two ends with the middle resting on his leg. The metal-carriers do not work on the eight-hours shift: they work until the job they have in hand is done. That is, if a given quantity of pig-iron is going to be taken away on a vessel they work until it is all carried down to the bank, or if it is going first of all to stand in the stock-yard, it is carried to the stock-yard to be piled up; and the men are paid according to the amount of iron they carry.

The loading and unloading is done by "stevedores," or stowers, at the riverside. A stevedore gang gets sometimes 20s. or over per 100 tons, which is divided among the gang.

The slag—the dross of the iron, as described above—flows either into ladles or into round vessels called "bogies." The slag flowing into the latter hardens in cooling into what are commonly called slag "balls," though, of course, they are not balls, but short broad cylinders. These ladles are then taken along a railway-line to various places, where they are "tipped"—that is, emptied out on to heaps, which eventually form embankments. A frequent sight on a winter's night, one of the sights by which one "visualizes" the ironworks, is a slag ball bursting as it is tipped, and flaming up into a mass of flying fragments as it rolls down. The sides of these embankments, with the brittle jagged edges of the slag, sharp as glass, are the places where the children of the ironworkers clamber up and down, as well content, apparently, as the more fortunate children who are rolling down a grassy slope. But a slip in these jagged edges means something very different from a slide and a roll down a grassy slope; and the children playing on the slag "tip" are face to face with a daily danger, which grows more dangerous, and not less, as familiarity with it makes them more heedless.

These long grey bare headlands do at last, with the passing of time, become gradually clothed with green, but not till they have stood for many years. It is but a parody of scenery, at best, amongst which the children of the ironworks grow up. The world of the ironworks is one in which there are constant suggestions of the ordinary operations of life raised to some strange, monstrous power, in which the land runs, not with water, but with fire, where the labourer leaning on his spade is going to dig, not in fresh, moist earth, but in a channel of molten flame; where, instead of stacking the crops, he stacks iron too hot for him to handle; where the tools laid out ready for his use are huge iron bars 10 feet long or more, taking several men to wield them. The onlooker, whose centre of activity lies among surroundings different from these, walks with wonder and misgiving through the lurid, reverberating works, seeing danger at every turn, and shudders at what seems to him the lot of the worker among such grim surroundings as these. But there is many a man employed in the works to whom these surroundings are even congenial, to whom the world coloured in black and flame-colour is a world he knows and understands, and that he misses when he is away from it. And there must be hundreds and thousands of people earning their livelihood in other ways, whose actual working hours are passed in a setting that will seem to many of us still less enviable: who, adding up figures or copying letters, see nothing but the walls of one small room round them for eight hours every day. For the actual nature of the occupation of the various branches of ironmaking may appear to some of us, given the requisite strength and the requisite health, to be preferable to many other of the callings which might presumably have been open to the people engaged in it, or, indeed, to those open to other classes of society who spend their lives in sedentary anxiety.

Many of the people who have to sit in a stuffy room and pore over pages in a bad light, would probably find their nerves, physical condition, digestion, and general outlook on life entirely different if they were, for instance, making trenches in the sand, taking out moulds, and throwing them to the next man to do the same. There is, no doubt, monotony in most occupations; but it is conceivable that the monotony of the work conducted in movement is not so penetrating as that which is conducted in immobility. It has not, at any rate, the deadly uniformity of being indoors, and even in England there are many days in the year when the weather is fine, and when the vapours from molten iron, ill-smelling though they be, cannot entirely sweep away the sweet breezes from the river. There are many of the men, no doubt, who look sullen at their work, many who look discontented; but so there are in all callings. In any Government office that you can name, I believe that there is as large a proportion of sullen and discontented faces as there is at the ironworks; indeed, there are probably more, because there have been more possibilities to choose from, and the area of disappointment is therefore greater. People differ in their conceptions and their definitions of happiness. A recent paraphrase of Aristotle has defined it thus: "Happiness consists in living the best life that your powers command in the best way that your circumstances permit." The man at the ironworks, who by his character and aptitude, is safe to have regular employment, whose health is good, who has a sufficient wage to have a margin, and a wife, that he cares about, competent enough to administer it to the best advantage, who has a comfortable home and children of whom he is fond, seems to me to have as good a chance of happiness as most of his fellow-creatures—and there is fortunately many a man at the works to whom this description can apply.

CHAPTER TWO

INVESTIGATORS

CHARLES BABBAGE
❦

ON THE METHOD OF OBSERVING MANUFACTORIES

(160.) Having now reviewed the *mechanical* principles which regulate the successful application of mechanical science to great establishments for the production of manufactured goods, it remains for us to suggest a few inquiries, and to offer a few observations, to those whom an enlightened curiosity may lead to examine the factories of this or of other countries.

The remark,—that *it is important to commit to writing all information as soon as possible after it is received, especially when numbers are concerned,*—applies to almost all inquiries. It is frequently impossible to do this at the time of visiting an establishment, although not the slightest jealousy may exist; the mere act of writing information as it is communicated orally, is a great interruption to the examination of machinery. In such cases, therefore, it is advisable to have prepared beforehand the questions to be asked, and to leave blanks for the answers, which may be quickly inserted, as, in a multitude of cases, they are merely numbers. Those who have not tried this plan will be surprised at the quantity of information which may, through its means, be acquired, even by a short examination. Each manufacture requires its own list of questions, which will be better drawn up after the first visit. The following outline, which is very generally applicable, may suffice for an illustration; and to save time, it may be convenient to have it printed; and to bind

---

From *On the Economy of Machinery and Manufactures*. Philadelphia: Carey and Lea, 1832.

up, in the form of a pocket book, a hundred copies of the skeleton forms for processes, with about twenty of the general inquiries.

GENERAL INQUIRIES

Outlines of a Description of any of the Mechanical Arts ought to contain Information on the following points

Brief sketch of its history, particularly the date of its invention, and of its introduction into England.

Short reference to the previous states through which the material employed has passed; the places whence it is procured; the price of a given quantity.

[The various processes must now be described successively according to the plan which will be given in § 161; after which the following information should be given.]

Are various kinds of the same article made in one establishment, or at different ones, and are there differences in the processes?

To what defects are the goods liable?

What substitutes or adulterations are used?

What waste is allowed by the master?

What tests are there of the goodness of the manufactured articles?

The weight of a given quantity, or number, and a comparison with that of the raw material?

The wholesale price at the manufactory? £   *s.*   *d.* per

The usual retail price? £   *s.*   *d.*

Who provide tools? Master, or men? Who repair tools? Master, or men?

What is the expense of the machinery?

What is the annual wear and tear, and what its duration?

Is there any particular trade for making it? Where?

Is it made and repaired at the manufactory?

In any manufactory visited, state the number (   ) of processes; and of the persons employed in each process; and the quantity of manufactured produce.

What quantity is made annually in Great Britain?

Is the capital invested in manufactories large or small?

Mention the principal seats of this manufacture in England; and if it flourishes abroad, the places where it is established.

The duty, excise, or bounty, if any, should be stated, and any alterations in past years; and also the amount exported or imported for a series of years.

Whether the same article, but of superior, equal, or inferior make, is imported?

Does the manufacturer export, or sell, to a middleman, who supplies the merchant?

To what countries is it chiefly sent?—and in what goods are the returns made?

(161.) Each process requires a separate skeleton, and the following outline will be sufficient for many different manufactories:—

Process (   ) Manufacture (   )
Place (   ) Name (   )
       date   183

The mode of executing it, with sketches of the tools or machine if necessary.

The number of persons necessary to attend the machine.

Are the operatives men, (   ) women, (   ) or children? (   ) If mixed, what are the proportions?

What is the pay of each? (*s.*   *d.*) (*s.*   *d.*) (*s.*   *d.*) per

What number (   ) of hours do they work per day?

Is it usual, or necessary, to work night and day without stopping?

Is the labour performed by piece or by day-work?

Who provide tools? Master, or men? Who repair tools? Master, or men?

What degree of skill is required, and how many years' (   ) apprenticeship?

The number of times (   ) the operation is repeated per day or per hour?

The number of failures (   ) in a thousand?

Whether the workmen or the master loses by the broken or damaged articles?

What is done with them?

If the same process is repeated several times, state the diminution or increase of measure, and the loss, if any, at each repetition.

(162.) In this skeleton, the answers to the questions are in some cases printed, as "Who repair "the tools?—*Masters, Men;*" in order that the proper answer may be underlined with a pencil. In filling up the answers which require numbers, some care should be taken: for instance, if the observer stands with his watch in his hand before a person heading a pin, the workman will almost certainly increase his speed, and the estimate will be too large. A much better average will result from inquiring what quantity is considered a fair day's work. When this cannot be ascertained, the number of operations performed in a given time may frequently be counted when the workman is quite unconscious that any person is observing him. Thus the sound made by the motion of a loom may enable the observer to count the number of strokes per minute, even though he is outside the building in which it is contained.

EMILIA DILKE

THE INDUSTRIAL POSITION OF WOMEN

. . . I have been writing of women working in our home-industries. If we turn to those who are herded together in workshops, they are, for the most part, in almost as evil plight, and, as a rule, are far worse-off, both as to hours and sanitary conditions, than those who labour even in the least well-regulated factories. Want of publicity encourages, in their case, the growth of various anomalous abuses which would be impossible were they subject to more frequent inspection. The workers in a warehouse-workshop where sacks were made, in one of our great ports, assured me in 1890 that their hours, including the time allowed for food, were eleven daily; that their weekly earnings rarely averaged seven shillings; that their work was carried on, and their food eaten, in a room the sanitary conditions of which were an abomination; that all the workers were congregated at the top story, the only access to which was by a small iron stair, so that in case of fire not a life could be saved. The last point—that as to defective provision for egress in case of fire—can, however, now be dealt with by the local authorities, as far as regards factories, under a clause introduced into the *Factories and Workshops' Act*[1] of 1892 by my friend Mr. W. A. M'Arthur, M.P., at my request. But the clause, as finally embodied in the Bill, contains objectionable limitations, and is followed by the words, "This section shall not apply to any workshop." Workshops, therefore, are still left to take their chance.

Life, too, in factories, especially in those which are fed by a class of labour practically as unskilled as that which makes it possible to carry on, at a high profit, such trades as matchbox-making, sack-making, and the lower kinds of tailoring, has its dark chambers of horror. Though no women are employed in the chemical trades, properly so called, there are many hundreds engaged in serving ovens in factories in which white-lead is manufactured—at Newcastle-on-Tyne, Sheffield, Glasgow, and London. The conditions of their labour, as every one seems now to have begun to believe, are especially poisonous to women if it is carried on by them at such times as the pores of the skin are unusually open, and during the months which precede childbirth. In the latter case the health of the children seems to be invariably affected. The

---

From *The Fortnightly.* Vol. 60 (1893): 499–508.
1. The Factories and Workshops Act of 1892 consolidated safety and sanitary regulations and made age eleven the minimum at which children could work in factories.

complaints made to me by workers have always been of insufficient sanitary appliances, of long and uncertain hours, and extremely low pay, eleven shillings a week being the average made in some factories by sixty hours of work and waiting. In one I know the women to be subject to incredible injustice, for, whilst turning out exactly the same work as the men in the blue and white beds, stoves, and red-leads, they receive but half their wages. This Sheffield factory is managed also with what I should like to believe exceptional brutality, for the workers relate that, should a woman fall in a fit in the white beds, the manager has left her there writhing in unsolaced agony till such time as she should "come round," and has then ordered his slave to work again, and, on the fellow-workers venturing to remonstrate, he has told them that, should the like befall them, they too should lie where they fell, and should go again to work as soon as they could get up. I do not see how these poor wretches are to help themselves. In one town we called them together— names being taken under promise of strict secrecy—to discuss the possibility of remedying some of their grievances by combination, but it was soon evident that the success of such an attempt would be more than doubtful. The competition for this unhealthy and ill-paid employment in the ranks of the women and girls of the town in question was so keen, and the amount of training required for its adequate performance so small, that, supposing all the women engaged in it had been organized, and had used the extreme argument of a general strike to enforce their demands, such a course was bound to be ineffectual. "Supposing now," I said to one of the most intelligent women present, "supposing that you had good friends at your back, and all 'came out' from your 'shops,' how long would it take your foreman and his assistants to drill, say, another three or four hundred women, and make them capable of performing your duties?" "I should say," she replied, "that our places could all be filled up within a fortnight. Any smart girl might learn all there is to do in a week."

It may be urged that there are comparatively few women who are exposed to the evils of the white-lead industry, or to the perils of "dipping," i.e. plunging ware into white-lead glaze, a process which annually takes toll of our workers in the potteries. There are comparatively few, but their case is none the less monstrous, and they cannot, nor can the workers in any unskilled industry, do very much to help themselves. They stand in dire need of the protection and consideration of the State. Even in the trades which demand some measure of skill—such a measure, in fact, as would admit of our classing the workers in the ranks of our artisans—the position of women is often one of peculiar hardship, partly because they make it worse for themselves by accepting wages for which no man would perform the same amount of labour. Nor have they always the unanswerable excuse of hunger for their conduct. It is far more frequently brought about by the unspoken conviction that the woman's labour, as such, need only be paid as an extra, thrown in for a consideration by the head of the family. When the wife and girls begin to work at the father's trade this is the position taken up, but it is suicidal, for, whenever possible, employers increase the number of their women-workers at the expense of their men; and sometimes, as at Halifax a short while back, they succeed by their means in forcing the men to accept unfair conditions, or abandon their trade. The men engaged in the carpet-weaving in this Halifax mill earned 35s. a week. They struck against a threatened reduction, but the women betrayed them, and took their places at wages of 20s. per week. No one can be surprised, as long as women behave in this way, that men should endeavour to keep the higher branches of industry in their own hands. People frequently cite the file-makers of Sheffield as a delightful instance of the employment of women in a highly skilled branch of industry at the same rate of wages as men. It is true that the women and girls engaged in this industry all work from the same list of prices as the men, and most of them are connected with the union, which has protected their interests. Unfortunately, Mr. Stuart Wortley finds that, owing to the fact that the trade can be carried on in their own houses, the women practise sweating, taking in, and partially instructing, numbers of young girls, and thus shamefully abusing the rights for which the men in the trade have fought hard, and which they have generously shared with their women. File-making by hand, involving as it does a very high degree of skill, must be reckoned as an exception from the usual class of labour in which women are employed in the hardware trades, such as pen-grinding, the screwing department of the nut and bolt trade, spike-nail-making, and chain-making; but their conduct as file-makers has, naturally, inclined men working in the higher branches to close their ranks against them. All the better work in the brass-polishing trade, in Birmingham, is kept in the hands of men; the women are put on the lighter and simpler kinds, and, although their work is similar to that of the men, and they turn out about two-thirds as much in proportion to that turned out by men, they receive only half as much wages. The unfairness in this instance is partly due to a class of circumstances which have not yet been touched on, and which throw light on the worst conditions of modern industry. The whole brass industry is, unhappily, what may be termed an open industry, that is, juvenile labour is taken on without consideration as to whether the trade will afford room for the worker when the age of maturity is reached. This unchecked influx of juvenile labour (as in the case of weavers' apprentices) causes a general depreciation of wages, since there are more trained, or partially trained, workers seeking employment than the annual increase of demand for brass goods can justify. There are in each factory from three to fifty polishers; in most firms all men, in some men and women, in a few women only. The journey-man polisher is, as a rule, at day-work, and "sets on" those under him. The price of the polishing is generally fixed, although the shop is day-work, and the head man is expected to make it pay. This is a perfect example of the day-work-piece-work system which is responsible for many of the evils against which the advocates of trade-organization are fighting. Against this system the Manchester tailoresses have been not too successfully struggling; it flourishes in the sweating-shops of Cradley Heath; and the result of its application in Birmingham is that, side by side with the men-polishers, who earn from 22s. to 34s. per week, work the women, who receive but 10s. to 24s. weekly.

Even in the textile industries we find similar instances of the unfair or presumably unfair treatment of women, and it is on the labour of women that their prosperity depends. Out of a total of 933,431 persons employed in these great national industries in 1890, women, working full time, were reckoned at 521,124, nor can their labour be described as other than highly skilled labour. They are most thoroughly organized in Lancashire and the surrounding districts, where cotton is spun and woven, and there we find that women are members of the same trade unions as the men, and that, as a rule, wherever they do the same work as men, they receive the same wages. Yet even in Lancashire, when we get into the district round Manchester, where women are employed as roller-coverers, we discover that they are paid a less wage than men engaged in the same branch of the trade. Again, in the West Riding of Yorkshire, there are places where the men are all paid on a higher scale than the women, but I am told, by Mr. Allen Gee, that their number is growing less, and that he hopes, as his organization strengthens, the practice may totally disappear. In West Wilts, the original seat of the cloth-weaving, I learnt that at Trowbridge women spinners earned but 18s., whilst the men were paid at the rate of 30s. per week. There is always, in these cases, a plausible excuse forthcoming, and we are told in this instance that the work of the men on the hand-mules is three times as hard as that of the women, whom the men have also to supervise, in addition to the discharge of their own duties. This may be so; it may be that difference in work, either in quality or quantity, accounts for the unequal wages of the woolcombers in Yorkshire, of the class of spinners-piecers in and near Manchester, and of the brass-polishers of Birmingham; but my own impression is, that the difference in value between the work of the man and that of the woman is often far less than is pretended, and that a considerable amount of unfairness does exist.

The causes which appear to be at the bottom of this unfairness that prevails even in the skilled trades, are the causes which drive women everywhere into the worst, the most fluctuating, unskilled, and underpaid industries. The economic independence of women cannot become a stable factor in a renewed society, as long as the same importance is not attached to their training—either by themselves or by their families, as in the case of men—because both they and their friends look always to throwing up their industry on marriage.

They drop naturally into the lowest category of labour, and when they marry are too often thrown back on the market, forming a fluctuating mass which seeks occasional or partial employment. The bad results of these conditions are plainly shown in such trades as that of the bookbinders in London, who say they reckon from two to three thousand skilled women workers—as near as may be conjectured—but are embarrassed by "as many as five thousand of the flotsam and jetsam of the trade who are in it half the year, and who do nothing or follow some other calling throughout the other half."

It is easy to see the obvious difficulties in the way of protecting or organizing labour of this class, which is also exposed by its peculiar weakness to special dangers and hardships. In the matter of "fines," as well as in the matter of wages, women are everywhere the chief sufferers. All over the country they are enduring daily abominable injustice from this cause. Even in Yorkshire spinning-mills, within the cognisance of the active executive of a large trades union, acts of disgraceful tyranny are not uncommon. The other day a girl—a child, I should say—was observed by her young master to have one of her ends down (which as she had about two hundred to mind was no unlikely mishap); he at once took aim at her with a bobbin, which, having struck her on the head, bounded off and went through a window; for this amusement of the man, whose bread she earned, the girl at the week's end was fined 2s. 6d. "for breaking windows." Into the peculiar infamies of "favouritism" I will not, I cannot go. They are common to the lot of women's labour all over the world; they are extremely difficult to handle, and they are by no means general. It has been proposed to meet them by the substitution of women for men as overseers of women, but I do not feel certain that the women would really benefit by this change, and I am sure that these infamies will disappear as women become less dependent.

The abuses against which it is really well to cry out, are those which can be remedied either by organization, by the pressure of public opinion, or by State interference. One cannot visit any great industrial town without seeing at once that its greatness is built up out of the labour of our women and their little ones; one cannot investigate the conditions of their labour and not see in it a danger to the State. It has been said that "the secret of Belfast's prosperity is in the command of a practically unlimited supply of cheap children's fingers." In like wise, we may say that the secret of England's industrial greatness is in her command of a practically unlimited supply of the cheap labour of her women and her girls. Their lives are minted out for money. Like the vision of the king who saw a golden and silver statue, the feet of which were of iron and clay, so does this magnificent industrial prosperity of commercial England, concerning which we make our boast, dazzle the world with the radiance of its fabulous wealth, but, if we look below and seek to see that on which the costly fabric rests—behold! its foundations are laid in the sordid misery of creeping millions, in the darkness of unending toil, in the hopelessness of unavailing sorrow.

To the slaves of labour the night brings no joys of rest, and in the morning the burden of their trouble is laid upon their rising. If we shut ourselves off from the knowledge of this that lies at our very doors, and will not understand the teaching of these things, then may we fear lest their meaning be made plain to us in a lesson of wrath and ruin. As the stone that was cut with no hand smote the excellent image on the feet, so that the silver and gold were broken to pieces and became as chaff on the summer threshing-floor, even so may we fear lest our neglected ones, who fill the ranks of the army of labour, may one day shape their giant forces under the wings of an avenging angel, whose mission will not be to bring peace and prosperity to our land, but a sword.

CHAPTER THREE

HISTORIANS

EDWARD BAINES, JR.
※※※

INVENTIONS IN SPINNING MACHINES

Sir RICHARD ARKWRIGHT; his humble origin; his construction of a
machine for spinning by rollers; his settlement at Nottingham; partnership with Messrs. Strutt and Need; his first patent for the spinning
machine.—JAMES HARGREAVES invents the spinning jenny; his machine broken by a mob; riots against machinery; Hargreaves retires
to Nottingham; his subsequent history.—Effects of the spinning machines on the cotton manufacture.—Calicoes first manufactured in
England by Arkwright.—Opposition of the Lancashire manufacturers to Arkwright, and to the new manufacture.—Parliament sanc-
tions British calicoes.—Other improvements in the spinning machinery.—Carding; the old methods; the carding cylinder invented
by Lewis Paul in 1748.—Subsequent improvements in the carding
engine by Arkwright and others.—Drawing frame.—Roving
frame.—Arkwright's second patent for carding, drawing, and roving
machines.—Great extension of the manufacture.—Rise of the factory system; its advantages.—Dr. Darwin's poetical description of a
cotton mill.—Arkwright's great success stimulates envy and oppo-

From *History of the Cotton Manufacture in Great Britain.* London: H. Fisher,
R. Fisher, and P. Jackson, 1835.

sition.—His patent infringed.—Trial.—Arkwright's "Case."—Second and third trials.—The patent declared null.—Arkwright's subsequent career; he is knighted; his death; his character.

In pursuing the history of spinning by rollers, we come now to the successful introduction of that invention by sir Richard Arkwright, who, though not entitled to all the merit which has been claimed for him, possessed very high inventive talent, as well as an unrivalled sagacity in estimating at their true value the mechanical contrivances of others, in combining them together, perfecting them, arranging a complete series of machinery, and constructing the factory system—itself a vast and admirable machine, which has been the source of great wealth, both to individuals and to the nation.

Richard Arkwright rose by the force of his natural talents from a very humble condition in society. He was born at Preston on the 23d of December, 1732, of poor parents: being the youngest of thirteen children, his parents could only afford to give him an education of the humblest kind, and he was scarcely able to write. He was brought up to the trade of a barber at Kirkham and Preston, and established himself in that business at Bolton in the year 1760. Having become possessed of a chemical process for dyeing human hair which in that day (when wigs were universal) was of considerable value, he travelled about collecting hair, and again disposing of it when dyed. In 1761, he married a wife from Leigh, and the connexions he thus formed in that town are supposed to have afterwards brought him acquainted with Highs's experiments in making spinning machines. He himself manifested a strong bent for experiments in mechanics, which he is stated to have followed with so much devotedness as to have neglected his business and injured his circumstances. His natural disposition was ardent, enterprising, and stubbornly persevering: his mind was as coarse as it was bold and active, and his manners were rough and unpleasing.

In 1767, Arkwright fell in with Kay,[1] the clockmaker, at Warrington, whom he employed to bend him some wires, and turn him some pieces of brass. From this it would seem that Arkwright was then experimenting in mechanics; and it has been said, that he was endeavouring to produce perpetual motion.[2] He entered into conversation with the clockmaker, and called upon him repeatedly; and at length Kay, according to his own account, told him of Highs's scheme of spinning by rollers. Kay adds, in his evidence, that Arkwright induced him to make a model of Highs's machine, and took it away. It is certain that from this period Arkwright abandoned his former business, and devoted himself to the construction of the spinning machine; and also, that he

---

1. Kay, the clockmaker (1704–1764), was an English inventor who patented the flying shuttle. (see Glossary). [Ed.]
2. Aikin and Enfield's *General Biography*, Vol. I. p. 391.

persuaded Kay to go with him first to Preston, and afterwards to Nottingham, binding him in a bond to serve him at a certain rate of wages for a stipulated term. The particulars of what passed between Arkwright and Kay rest wholly on the evidence of the latter; but there is no doubt that Kay was thus engaged to accompany Arkwright, and that he worked for him some time at Nottingham. Those who believe in the invention of Highs find in this fact, combined with Highs's own evidence, a very strong presumption in its favour: but those who disbelieve it may adopt the conjecture, that Arkwright, not being a practical mechanic, engaged the clockmaker to construct the apparatus he had himself contrived. The statement of Arkwright, in the "Case" drawn up to be submitted to parliament, was, that "after many years' intense and painful application, he invented, about the year 1768, his present method of spinning cotton, but upon very different principles from any invention that had gone before it." It is true that Arkwright had been experimenting in mechanics, but there is no evidence to shew that he had ever thought of making a spinning machine before his interview with Kay at Warrington.

Kay appears not to have been able to make the whole machine, and therefore "he and Arkwright applied to Mr. Peter Atherton, afterwards of Liverpool," (then probably an instrument maker at Warrington,) "to make the spinning engine; but from the poverty of Arkwright's appearance, Mr. Atherton refused to undertake it, though afterwards, on the evening of the same day, he agreed to lend Kay a smith and watch-tool maker, to make the heavier part of the engine, and Kay undertook to make the clockmaker's part of it, and to instruct the workman. In this way Mr. Arkwright's first engine, for which he afterwards took out a patent, was made."[3]

Being altogether destitute of pecuniary means for prosecuting his invention, Arkwright repaired to his native place, Preston, and applied to a friend, Mr. John Smalley, a liquor-merchant and painter, for assistance. The famous contested election, at which General Burgoyne was returned, occurring during his visit, Arkwright voted; but the wardrobe of the future knight was in so tattered a condition, that a number of persons subscribed to put him into decent plight to appear at the poll-room. His spinning machine was fitted up in the parlour of the house belonging to the Free Grammar School, which was lent by the head-master to Mr. Smalley for the purpose. The latter was so well convinced of the utility of the machine, that he joined Arkwright with heart and purse.

In consequence of the riots which had taken place in the neighbourhood of Blackburn, on the invention of Hargreaves's spinning jenny in 1767, by which

---

3. Aikin and Enfield's *General Biography,* Vol. I. p. 391. The authors profess to have obtained some of these facts from private sources; and Dr. Aikin's opportunities were good, as he resided at Warrington.

many of the machines were destroyed, and the inventor was driven from his native county to Nottingham, Arkwright and Smalley, fearing similar outrages directed against their machine, went also to Nottingham, accompanied by Kay. This town, therefore, became the cradle of two of the greatest inventions in cotton spinning. Here the adventurers applied for pecuniary aid to Messrs. Wright, bankers, who made advances on condition of sharing in the profits of the invention. But as the machine was not perfected so soon as they had anticipated, the bankers requested Arkwright to obtain other assistance, and recommended him to Mr. Samuel Need, of Nottingham. This gentleman was the partner of Mr. Jedediah Strutt, of Derby,[4] the ingenious improver and patentee of the stocking-frame; and Mr. Strutt having seen Arkwright's machine, and declared it to be an admirable invention, only wanting an adaptation of some of the wheels to each other, both Mr. Need and Mr. Strutt entered into partnership with Arkwright.

Thus the pecuniary difficulties of this enterprising and persevering man were terminated. He soon made his machine practicable, and in 1769 he took out a patent. In the specification, which was enrolled on the 15th of July in that year, he stated that he "had by great study and long application invented a new piece of machinery, never before found out, practised, or used, for the making of weft or yarn from cotton, flax, and wool; which would be of great utility to a great many manufacturers, as well as to his Majesty's subjects in general, by employing a great number of poor people in working the said machinery, and by making the said weft or yarn much superior in quality to any ever heretofore manufactured or made."

The importance of this machine requires that Arkwright's own description of it in his specification should be given

> Now know ye that 1, the said Richard Arkwright, do hereby describe and ascertain the nature of my said invention, and declare that the plan thereof drawn in the margin of these presents is composed of the following particulars, (that is to say) A, the Cogg Wheel and Shaft, which receive their motion from a horse. B, the Drum or Wheel which turns C, a belt of leather, and gives motion to the whole machine. D, a lead weight, which keeps F, the small drum, steady to E, the forcing Wheel. G, the shaft of wood which gives motion to the Wheel H, and contin-

---

4. Mr. Strutt was brought up a farmer, but, having a passion for improvement and a mechanical genius, he succeeded in adapting the stocking-frame to the manufacture of *ribbed* stockings, for which improvement he obtained a patent. He established an extensive manufacture of ribbed stockings at Derby, and, after his connexion with Mr. Arkwright, he erected cotton works at Milford, near Belper: he raised his family to great wealth. Some of the circumstances connected with Arkwright's settling at Nottingham, were communicated by the late Mr. William Strutt, the highly gifted and ingenious son of Mr. Jedediah Strutt, to the editor of the *Beauties of England and Wales.* See vol. iii. pp. 518, 541.

ues it to I, four pair of Rollers, (the form of which are drawn in the margin,) which act by tooth and pinion made of brass and steel nuts fixt in two iron plates K. That part of the roller which the cotton runs through is covered with wood, the top Roller with leather, and the bottom one fluted, which lets the Cotton, &c. through it; by one pair of Rollers moving quicker than the other, draws it finer for twisting, which is performed by the spindles T. K, the two iron plates described above. L, four large Bobbins with cotton rovings on, conducted between Rollers at the back. M, the four threads carried to the Bobbins and Spindles by four small wires fixt across the frame in the slip of wood V. N, iron leavers with small lead weights hanging to the Rollers by Pulleys, which keep the Rollers close to each other. O, a cross piece of wood to which the leavers are fixed. P, the Bobbins and Spindles. Q, Flyers made of wood, with small wires on the side, which lead the thread to the bobbins, R, small worsted bands put about the whirl of the bobbins, the screwing of which tight or easy causes the bobbins to wind up the thread faster or slower. S, the four whirls of the spindles. T, the four Spindles, which run in iron plates. V, explained in letter M. W, a wooden frame of the whole machine.

Such is the original of the present water-frame and throstle. It was afterwards greatly improved by Arkwright himself; and, when horse-power was exchanged for water-power, the number of spindles in the frame was multiplied. The original machine was adapted only to perform the last operation in spinning, namely, reducing the rovings into yarn; but it was easily applicable to the process of roving itself, as will subsequently appear. It is remarkable that the inventor, in his application for a patent, described himself as "Richard Arkwright, of Nottingham, *clockmaker.*" He and his partners erected a mill at Nottingham, which was driven by horses; but this mode of turning the machinery being found too expensive, they built another mill on a much larger scale at Cromford, in Derbyshire, which was turned by a water wheel, and from this circumstance the spinning machine was called the *water-frame.*

The difficulty, delay, and expense which attended the completing of the invention, prove, at the very least, that Arkwright did not receive it from any other person a *perfect* machine. If he had seen either Wyatt's machine, or the model of that of Highs, he had still to perfect the details; and the determined assiduity and confidence with which he devoted himself to this undertaking, before the machine had ever been made to answer, show that he had sufficient mechanical capacity to appreciate its value, and sufficient talent and energy to make the invention practicable and profitable.

Having completed the history of the great invention of spinning by rollers, it will be proper, before proceeding to describe the further progress of Arkwright in combining and improving the cotton machinery, to go back in the order of time, and to mention another invention for the purpose of spinning, which came into use before the water-frame, and which, though very different in its principle, almost rivalled that machine in utility. The great demand for yarn, while the one-thread wheel was the only instrument for spinning, set other wits on contriving a substitute for it, besides those of Wyatt, Highs, and Arkwright.

We learn from the "Transactions of the Society for the Encouragement of Arts, Manufactures, and Commerce," that in 1783 the society had in its repositories models of the following spinning machines: "A Spinning Wheel, by Mr. John Webb, invented 1761. A Spinning Wheel, by Mr. Thomas Perrin, 1761. A Horizontal Spinning Wheel, by Mr. Wm. Harrison, 1764. A Spinning Wheel, by Mr. Perrin, 1765. A Spinning Wheel, by Mr. Garrat, 1766. A Spinning Wheel, by Mr. Garrat, 1767."[5] Between the establishment of the society in 1754 and the year 1783, it distributed £544. 12s. in premiums "for improving several machines used in manufactures, viz. the comb-pot, cards for wool and cotton, stocking frame, loom, machines for winding and doubling, and spinning wheels."[6] None of these inventions of spinning machines, however, succeeded. The compiler of the Transactions, writing in 1783, says, "From the best information hitherto obtained, it appears, that about the year 1764, a poor man, of the name of Hargreaves, employed in the cotton manufactory near Blackburn, in Lancashire, first made a machine in that county, which spun eleven threads; and that in the year 1770 he obtained a patent for the invention. The construction of this kind of machine, called a *Spinning Jenny,* has since been much improved, and is now at so high a degree of perfection, that one woman is thereby enabled with ease to spin a hundred threads of cotton at a time."[7]

James Hargreaves, a weaver of Stand-hill, near Blackburn, was the author of the admirable invention noticed in this extract. It has been generally supposed that the date of the invention was 1767, not 1764; and Arkwright, in his "Case," states the machine to have been made in 1767. It is, however, in the highest degree probable, that the jenny would not be at once perfected: its construction would probably occupy the author, who was a poor man, and had to work for his daily bread, some years: and as Hargreaves went to Nottingham in 1768, before which time his machine had not only been perfected, but its extraordinary powers so clearly proved, notwithstanding his efforts to keep it secret, as to expose him to persecution and the attacks of a mob, I am strongly disposed to think that the invention was conceived, and that the author began to embody it, as early as 1764.

---

5. Transactions of the Society of Arts, vol. i. pp. 314, 315.
6. Ibid. vol. i. p. 26.
7. Ibid. vol. i. pp. 33, 34.

Hargreaves, though illiterate and humble, must be regarded as one of the greatest inventors and improvers in the cotton manufacture. His principal invention, and one which shewed high mechanical genius, was the jenny. The date of this invention was some years before Arkwright obtained the patent for his water-frame; and it differs so completely from that machine, and from Wyatt's, that there can be no suspicion of its being other than a perfectly original invention.

It may be necessary to explain to some readers, that the cotton was formerly, and is still, reduced from the state of the fleecy roll called a carding, into the state of spun thread, by repeated, though similar operations: the first draws out the carding, and gives it a very slight twist, so as to make it into a loose thread, about the thickness of a candle-wick, in which state it is called a roving or slubbin; the subsequent processes draw out the roving much finer, and at length reduce it into yarn. Hargreaves's jenny, like Arkwright's machine, was intended to spin the roving into yarn; but it was not, like Arkwright's, capable of being applied to the preparation of the roving itself. Hargreaves is said to have received the original idea of his machine from seeing a one-thread wheel overturned upon the floor, when both the wheel and the spindle continued to revolve.[8] The spindle was thus thrown from a horizontal into an upright position; and the thought seems to have struck him, that if a number of spindles were placed upright, and side by side, several threads might be spun at once. He contrived a frame, in one part of which he placed eight rovings in a row, and in another part a row of eight spindles. The rovings, when extended to the spindles, passed between two horizontal bars of wood, forming a clasp, which opened and shut somewhat like a parallel ruler; when pressed together, this clasp held the threads fast. A certain portion of roving being extended from the spindles to the wooden clasp, the clasp was closed, and was then drawn along the horizontal frame to a considerable distance from the spindles, by which the threads were lengthened out, and reduced to the proper tenuity; this was done with the spinner's left hand, and his right hand at the same time turned a wheel, which caused the spindles to revolve rapidly, and thus the roving was spun into yarn. By returning the clasp to its first situation, and letting down a presser wire, the yarn was wound upon the spindle.

With this admirable machine, though at first rudely constructed, Hargreaves and his family spun weft for his own weaving. Aware of the value of the invention, but not extending his ambition to a patent, he kept it as secret as possible for a time, and used it merely in his own business. A machine of such powers could not, however, be long concealed; but when it became the subject of rumour, instead of gaining for its author admiration and gratitude,

---

8. Rees's *Cyclopædia,* and *Encyclopædia Britannica,* art. "Cotton Manufacture."

the spinners raised an outcry that it would throw multitudes out of employment, and a mob broke into Hargreaves's house, and destroyed his jenny. So
great was the persecution he suffered, and the danger in which he was placed,
that this victim of popular ignorance was compelled to flee his native county,
as the inventor of the fly-shuttle had been before him. Thus the neighbourhood where the machine was invented, lost the benefit of it, yet without preventing its general adoption;—the common and appropriate punishment of
the ignorance and selfishness which oppose mechanical improvements.

Hargreaves retired to Nottingham in 1768, where he entered into partnership with Mr. Thomas James, a joiner, who raised sufficient money to enable
them to erect a small mill. He took out a patent for the jenny in 1770, the year
after Arkwright had obtained his patent at the same place. The patent was "for
a method of making a wheel or engine of an entire new construction, and
never before made use of, in order for spinning, drawing, and twisting of cotton, and to be managed by one person only, and that the wheel or engine will
spin, draw, and twist *sixteen* or more threads at one time, by a turn or motion
of one hand, and a draw of the other." The following is the inventor's description of the process,—"One person, with his or her right hand turns the
wheel, and with the left hand takes hold of the clasps, and therewith draws out
the cotton from the slubbin box; and, being twisted by the turn of the wheel
in the drawing out, then a piece of wood is lifted up by the toe, which lets
down a presser wire, so as to press the threads so drawn out and twisted, in
order to wind or put the same regularly upon bobbins which are placed on the
spindles." The number of spindles in the jenny was at first eight; when the
patent was obtained, it was sixteen; it soon came to be twenty or thirty; and
no less than one hundred and twenty have since been used.

Before quitting Lancashire, Hargreaves had made a few jennies for sale;
and the importance of the invention being universally appreciated, the interests of the manufacturers and weavers brought it into general use, in spite of
all opposition. A desperate effort was, however, made in 1779—probably in a
period of temporary distress—to put down the machine. A mob rose, and
scoured the country for several miles round Blackburn, demolishing the jennies, and with them all the carding engines, water-frames, and every machine
turned by water or horses. It is said that the rioters spared the jennies which
had only twenty spindles, as these were by this time admitted to be useful; but
those with a greater number, being considered mischievous, were destroyed,
or cut down to the prescribed dimensions. It may seem strange, that not
merely the working classes, but even the middle and upper classes, entertained a great dread of machinery. Not perceiving the tendency of any invention which improved and cheapened the manufacture, to cause an extended
demand for its products, and thereby to give employment to more hands than
it superseded, those classes were alarmed lest the poor-rates should be bur-

dened with workmen thrown idle. They therefore connived at, and even actually joined in, the opposition to machinery, and did all in their power to screen the rioters from punishment. This devastating outrage left effects more permanent than have usually resulted from such commotions. Spinners, and other capitalists, were driven from the neighbourhood of Blackburn to Manchester and other places, and it was many years before cotton-spinning was resumed at Blackburn. Mr. Peel, the grandfather of the present Sir Robert Peel, a skilful and enterprising spinner and calico printer, having had his machinery at Altham thrown into the river, and been in personal danger from the fury of the mob, retired in disgust to Burton, in Staffordshire, where he built a cotton-mill on the banks of the Trent, and remained there some years. A large mill, built by Arkwright, at Birkacre, near Chorley, was destroyed by a mob in the presence of a powerful body of police and military, without any of the civil authorities requiring their interference to prevent the outrage.[9]

The subsequent history of Hargreaves has been very erroneously represented. The following is Arkwright's notice of this ingenious man:—"About the year 1767, one Hargreaves, of Blackburn, in Lancashire, constructed an engine that would at once spin twenty or thirty threads of cotton into yarn for the fustian manufacture; but because it was likely to answer in some measure the end proposed, his engines were burnt and destroyed, and himself driven out of Lancashire: he afterwards removed to Nottingham, and obtained a patent for his engine; but he did not even there long continue in the peaceable possession of it. His patent right was invaded, and he found it necessary to commence a prosecution: an association was soon formed against him; and being unable to contend against the united power of a body of men, he was obliged to give up the unjust and unequal contest. His invention was cruelly wrested from him; and he died in obscurity and great distress."[10]

In addition to this, it was stated in the *Edinburgh Review,* No. 91, that Hargreaves died in the workhouse at Nottingham.

I find, from careful inquiry, that both Arkwright's statement and that of the *Edinburgh Review* are unfounded. Mr. John James, formerly a cotton spinner, (the son of Mr. James, who was the partner of Hargreaves,) and also a grandson of Hargreaves's, are still living at Nottingham; and a gentleman of that town, well known for his extensive knowledge of local history and antiquities, has, at my request, kindly obtained from them, and from other authentic sources, the following particulars, which may be fully relied upon:—James Hargreaves went to Nottingham in 1768, and worked for a while in the em-

---

9. *Edinburgh Review,* No. xci. p. 14.
10. Arkwright's "Case."

ployment of Mr. Shipley, for whom he made some jennies secretly in his house. He was induced, by the offers of Mr. Thomas James, to enter into partnership with him; and the latter raised sufficient money, on mortgage and loan, to build a small mill in Hockley, where they spun yarn for the hosiers with the jenny. The patent was obtained in 1770. Finding that several of the Lancashire manufacturers were using the jenny, Hargreaves gave notice of actions against them: the manufacturers met, and sent a delegate to Nottingham, who offered Hargreaves £3000 for permission to use the machine; but he at first demanded £7000, and at last stood out for £4000. The negociation being broken off, the actions proceeded; but before they came to trial, Hargreaves's attorney (Mr. Evans) was informed that his client, before leaving Lancashire, had sold some jennies to obtain clothing for his children, (of whom he had six or seven;) and in consequence of this, which was true, the attorney gave up the actions, in despair of obtaining a verdict. The spinning business was carried on by the partners with moderate success, till the death of Mr. Hargreaves, which took place at his own house near the mill, in April, 1778. In his will he directed a guinea to be given to the vicar, for preaching his funeral sermon. His widow received £400 from Mr. James, for her husband's share in the business; and, having other property which her husband had accumulated, she left this sum to her children on her death.

It will be a consolation to the admirers of genius, to find that this benefactor of his country was enabled to live in comfort, though not in affluence, on the fruits of his invention. It is not difficult to account for Arkwright's misstatement of the facts regarding Hargreaves: the statement was calculated to awaken a sympathy for inventors, and therefore it answered Arkwright's purpose. The mention made by him of the invention of Hargreaves fell far below its real merits; but this again answered the purpose of Arkwright, whose object was to set off his own transcendent and incomparable talents as an inventor.

The two important inventions for spinning, of which the history has been traced, broke down the barrier which had so long obstructed the advance of the cotton manufacture. The new machines not only turned off a much greater quantity of yarn than had before been produced, but the yarn was also of a superior quality. The water-frame spun a hard and firm thread, calculated for warps; and from this time the warps of linen yarn were abandoned, and goods were, for the first time in this country, woven wholly of cotton. Manufactures of a finer and more delicate fabric were also introduced, especially calicoes, imitated from the Indian fabrics of that name. The jenny was peculiarly adapted for spinning weft; so that the two machines, instead of coming in conflict, were brought into use together. The spirit of invention and improvement, fully aroused by the proof which had now been given of the powers of mechanical combination, operated with extraordinary vigour; and amongst the numberless schemes and experiments tried in the workshops of Lancashire, not a few contrivances of real value were discovered, to perfect the various machines. This period of high intellectual excitement and successful effort would be contemplated with more pleasure, if there had not at the same time been displayed the workings of an insatiable cupidity and sordid jealousy, which remorselessly snatched from genius the fruit of its creations, and even proscribed the men to whom the manufacture was most deeply indebted. Ignorance on the one hand, and cupidity on the other, combined to rob inventors of their reward.

Arkwright, though the most successful of his class, had to encounter the animosity of his fellow-manufacturers in various forms. Those in Lancashire refused to buy his yarns, though superior to all others, and actually combined to discountenance a new branch of their own manufacture, because he was the first to introduce it. He has related the difficulties with which he had to contend in his "Case."

"It was not," he said, "till upwards of five years had elapsed after obtaining his first patent, and more than £12,000 had been expended in machinery and buildings, that any profit accrued to himself and partners." "The most excellent yarn or twist was produced; notwithstanding which, the proprietors found great difficulty to introduce it into public use. A very heavy and valuable stock, in consequence of these difficulties, lay upon their hands: inconveniences and disadvantages of no small consideration followed. Whatever were the motives which induced the rejection of it, they were thereby necessarily driven to attempt, by their own strength and ability, the manufacture of the yarn. Their first trial was in weaving it into stockings, which succeeded; and soon established the manufacture of calicoes, which promises to be one of the first manufactures in this kingdom. Another still more formidable difficulty arose; the orders for goods which they had received, being considerable, were unexpectedly countermanded, the officers of excise refusing to let them pass at the usual duty of 3d. per yard, insisting on the additional duty of 3d. per yard, as being calicoes, though manufactured in England: besides, these calicoes, when printed, were prohibited. By this unforeseen obstruction, a very considerable and very valuable stock of calicoes accumulated. An application to the commissioners of excise was attended with no success; the proprietors, therefore, had no resource but to ask relief of the legislature; which, after much money expended, and *against a strong opposition of the manufacturers in Lancashire,* they obtained."[11]

---

11. "Case" in Arkwright's Patent Trial, p. 99.

This opposition of the Lancashire manufacturers to the establishment of a new branch of their own trade, seems to have been gratuitously malicious, and, fortunately for themselves, it was unsuccessful. With somewhat more of reason, the silk and woollen manufacturers had opposed the introduction of Indian calicoes at the end of the preceding century, finding that this new and elegant fabric came into competition with their own products. They then, as has been shown, so completely prevailed, as to obtain the entire prohibition of Indian, Persian, or Chinese silks and printed calicoes, for home consumption: and when calico printing extended in this country, and great quantities of calicoes manufactured in India, but printed or dyed in England, were used for apparel and household furniture, parliament again interfered in 1720, and passed an Act (7 Geo. I. c. 7,) prohibiting altogether "the *use* or *wear* in Great Britain, in any garment or apparel whatsoever, of ANY *printed, painted, stained, or dyed calico,* under the penalty of forfeiting to the informer the sum of £5." By the same Act, the use of printed or dyed calico "in or about any bed, chair, cushion, window curtain, or any other sort of household stuff or furniture," was forbidden under a penalty of £20; and the same penalty attached to the seller of the article. And so far did the Act extend, that it forbad the use of any printed or dyed goods, of which cotton formed any part; so that the goods made of linen warp and cotton weft could not be used in the printed or dyed state. Calicoes dyed all blue, as well as muslins, neckcloths, and fustians, were excepted from the prohibitions of this act. The prohibition to use mixed goods containing cotton, in the dyed or printed state, seems not to have been strictly enforced; and as it obviously struck at the existence of the then rising cotton manufacture of England, that part of the Act of 1720 was repealed in 1736. The Act 9 Geo. II. c. 4, after reciting the 7th Geo. I. c. 7, set forth that, "Whereas great quantities of stuffs made of linen yarn and cotton wool have for several years past been manufactured, and have been printed and painted within this kingdom of Great Britain, and the said manufactures so printed or painted are a branch of the ancient fustian manufacture of this kingdom, and have been and now are used and worn in apparel and furniture: and whereas some doubts have lately arisen, whether the use and wearing of the said stuffs, when the same are so printed or painted, be prohibited by the said recited act, whereby the said manufacture is discouraged, and may be utterly lost, and great numbers of his majesty's subjects and their families, whose livelihoods entirely depend thereupon, may be ruined, and the poor greatly increased, if not timely prevented;" therefore it was enacted that it should be lawful to wear and use "any sort of stuff made of linen yarn and cotton wool manufactured and printed or painted with any colour or colours within the kingdom of Great Britain, *provided that the warp thereof be entirely linen yarn.*" So that even this Act prohibited the use of printed goods made entirely of cotton; a prohibition directed against the printing of Indian calicoes, no such goods being then made in England.

These laws, though injurious to the public, were (for the time at least) beneficial to the home manufacturer; but the prohibition of English-made calicoes was so utterly without an object, that its being prayed for by the cotton manufacturers of this country is one of the most signal instances on record of the blinding effects of commercial jealousy. The legislature did not yield to the despicable opposition offered to the reasonable demand of Mr. Arkwright and his partners, but, on the contrary, passed a law, in 1774, sanctioning the new manufacture, and rendering English calicoes subject only to a duty of 3d. per square yard on being printed.

MACHINES AND MANAGEMENT

The texts in this section imagine, in their various ways, how best to organize industrialized labor. The section begins with a selection from Adam Smith's *Wealth of Nations* (1776), which although obviously not a nineteenth-century text, influenced nineteenth-century thinking immeasurably. Smith's account of the pin factory forms the locus classicus of arguments for the benefits derived, for both producers and consumers, from increasingly fine divisions of labor. Specialization, Smith argues, leads not only to more productivity because each worker has one task that he can become more and more skilled at performing, but also because it leads to mechanical invention. Robert Owen, writing some forty years later, is concerned with the relationship between labor and larger patterns of social life: His factory at New Lanark is surrounded by a company-owned village so that both the working and domestic lives of "his" laborers are overseen by him. Owen imagines that he can contribute to a better "formation" of the characters of the working class to make for the greatest "general happiness of society." For both Smith and Owen, workers and owners—whether or not they realize it—are in a symbiotic relation of shared interests.

When it came to machinery and unemployment, the Luddites, the writer for the Chartist Circular and Francis Place, are all essentially in agreement with one another, and oddly enough, with the most influential economist of the first half of the nineteenth century, David Ricardo: All concurred that the introduction of machinery caused unemployment and therefore hurt the working class. Their solutions differed: The Luddites broke machinery at every opportunity; the Chartists protested the unemployment caused by machines; Ricardo argued that although machinery did cause unemployment, it had to be extensively used if Britain wished to remain competitive in world markets. Francis Place argued that mills are scenes not only of the degradation of workers, they are not the places to make the finest kinds of cotton, including gingham, muslin, and cambric. Handloom weaving must be preserved not only for the sake of the weavers but also for the sake of the fine fabrics that improvements in handloom weaving effected in the late eighteenth century.

Charles Babbage and Andrew Ure envisioned mechanical utopias in their work; for them, the more automation the better. Neither writer thinks much about the immediate effects of increasing automation on the laborers who are unemployed by technological development. Their views can be described as literally mechanical, focusing on machines and what they can do rather than on their social or economic impact. Babbage is delighted by the accuracy of machine production: "Nothing is more remarkable, and yet less unexpected, than the perfect identity of things manufactured by the same tool." He goes on to extol the virtues of the many kinds of "copying" made possible by machine production. Ure, too, looks forward to the elimination of all "irregularity" produced by fallible human hands. The uniformity that delights Babbage and Ure will prove horrific to the aesthetic sensibilities of many later Victorians (see Ruskin and Morris in Part 4).

Carlyle argues that the "captains of industry" must look up from their "money-bags and ledgers" and take on the social responsibility that their wealth and power confer upon them. Marx bewails the very dependence of workers on capitalists that Carlyle sees as potentially beneficial (if the capitalists assume the correct paternalistic role). Marx also reviles the capitalist use of machinery in the factory wherein the machine makes use of the worker rather than the other way around, dehumanizing even that part of the labor process that is still in human hands.

The divisions of labor worked out so elaborately and by so many different kinds of thinkers in the nineteenth century continue to haunt the twenty-first. But questions about efficiency, economy, and humanity have been split off from one another and isolated in various disciplines that have become too specialized—due to their own fine divisions of labor—to talk very much to one another. Consulting the biographies of the authors in this section reveals how little their education, training, discipline, or work experience restricted their willingness to think and write about a wide variety of subjects. This enthusiastic amateurism is gone forever; ironically this disappearance is due in large part to the divisions of labor advocated by many of the polymathic visionaries collected in this section.

CHAPTER FOUR

THEORY

ADAM SMITH
⬥⬥⬥

OF THE DIVISION OF LABOUR

Division of labour is the great cause of its increased powers,

The greatest improvement in the productive powers of labour, and the greater part of the skill, dexterity, and judgment with which it is any where directed, or applied, seem to have been the effects of the division of labour.

as may be better understood from a particular example,

The effects of the division of labour, in the general business of society, will be more easily understood, by considering in what manner it operates in some particular manufactures. It is commonly supposed to be carried furthest in some very trifling ones; not perhaps that it really is carried further in them than in others of more importance: but in those trifling manufactures which are destined to supply the small wants of but a small number of people, the whole number of workmen must necessarily be small; and those employed in every different branch of the work can often be collected into the same workhouse, and placed at once under the view of the spectator. In those great manufactures, on the contrary, which are destined to supply the great wants of the great body of the people, every different branch of the work employs so great a number of workmen, that it is impossible to collect them all into the same workhouse. We can seldom see more, at one time, than those employed in one single branch. Though in such manufactures, therefore, the work may really be divided into a much greater number of parts, than in those of a more trifling na-

From *An Inquiry into the Nature and Causes of the Wealth of Nations*. London: W. Strahan and T. Cadell, 1776.

ture, the division is not near so obvious, and has accordingly been much less observed.

such as pin-making.   To take an example, therefore, from a very trifling manufacture; but one in which the division of labour has been very often taken notice of, the trade of the pin-maker; a workman not educated to this business (which the division of labour has rendered a distinct trade), nor acquainted with the use of the machinery employed in it (to the invention of which the same division of labour has probably given occasion), could scarce, perhaps, with his utmost industry, make one pin in a day, and certainly could not make twenty. But in the way in which this business is now carried on, not only the whole work is a peculiar trade, but it is divided into a number of branches, of which the greater part are likewise peculiar trades. One man draws out the wire, another straights it, a third cuts it, a fourth points it, a fifth grinds it at the top for receiving the head; to make the head requires two or three distinct operations; to put it on, is a peculiar business, to whiten the pins is another; it is even a trade by itself to put them into the paper; and the important business of making a pin is, in this manner, divided into about eighteen distinct operations, which, in some manufactories, are all performed by distinct hands, though in others the same man will sometimes perform two or three of them. I have seen a small manufactory of this kind where ten men only were employed, and where some of them consequently performed two or three distinct operations. But though they were very poor, and therefore but indifferently accommodated with the necessary machinery, they could, when they exerted themselves, make among them about twelve pounds of pins in a day. There are in a pound upwards of four thousand pins of a middling size. Those ten persons, therefore, could make among them upwards of forty-eight thousand pins in a day. Each person, therefore, making a tenth part of forty-eight thousand pins, might be considered as making four thousand eight hundred pins in a day. But if they had all wrought separately and independently, and without any of them having been educated to this peculiar business, they certainly could not each of them have made twenty, perhaps not one pin in a day; that is, certainly, not the two hundred and fortieth, perhaps not the four thousand eight hundredth part of what they are at present capable of performing, in consequence of a proper division and combination of their different operations.

The effect is similar in all trades and also in the division of employments.   In every other art and manufacture, the effects of the division of labour are similar to what they are in this very trifling one; though, in many of them, the labour can neither be so much subdivided, nor reduced to so great a simplicity of operation. The division of labour, however, so far as it can be introduced, occasions, in every art, a proportionable increase of the productive powers of labour. The separation of different trades and employments from one another, seems to have taken place, in consequence of this advantage.

This separation too is generally carried furthest in those countries which enjoy the highest degree of industry and improvement; what is the work of one man in a rude state of society, being generally that of several in an improved one. In every improved society, the farmer is generally nothing but a farmer; the manufacturer, nothing but a manufacturer. The labour too which is necessary to produce any one complete manufacture, is almost always divided among a great number of hands. How many different trades are employed in each branch of the linen and woollen manufactures, from the growers of the flax and the wool, to the bleachers and smoothers of the linen, or to the dyers and dressers of the cloth! The nature of agriculture, indeed, does not admit of so many subdivisions of labour, nor of so complete a separation of one business from another, as manufactures. It is impossible to separate so entirely, the business of the grazier from that of the corn-farmer, as the trade of the carpenter is commonly separated from that of the smith. The spinner is almost always a distinct person from the weaver; but the ploughman, the harrower, the sower of the seed, and the reaper of the corn, are often the same. The occasions for those different sorts of labour returning with the different seasons of the year, it is impossible that one man should be constantly employed in any one of them. This impossibility of making so complete and entire a separation of all the different branches of labour employed in agriculture, is perhaps the reason why the improvement of the productive powers of labour in this art, does not always keep pace with their improvement in manufactures. The most opulent nations, indeed, generally excel all their neighbours in agriculture as well as in manufactures; but they are commonly more distinguished by their superiority in the latter than in the former. Their lands are in general better cultivated, and having more labour and expence bestowed upon them, produce more in proportion to the extent and natural fertility of the ground. But this superiority of produce is seldom much more than in proportion to the superiority of labour and expence. In agriculture, the labour of the rich country is not always much more productive than that of the poor; or, at least, it is never so much more productive, as it commonly is in manufactures. The corn of the rich country, therefore, will not always, in the same degree of goodness, come cheaper to market than that of the poor. The corn of Poland, in the same degree of goodness, is as cheap as that of France, notwithstanding the superior opulence and improvement of the latter country. The corn of France is, in the corn provinces, fully as good, and in most years nearly about the same price with the corn of England, though, in opulence and improvement, France is perhaps inferior to England. The corn-lands of England, however, are better cultivated than those of France, and the corn-lands of France are said to be much better cultivated than those of Poland. But though the poor country, notwithstanding the inferiority of its cultivation, can, in some measure, rival the rich in the cheapness and goodness of its corn, it can pretend to no such competition in its manufactures; at least if those manufactures suit the soil, climate, and situation of the rich country. The silks of France are better and cheaper than those of England, because the silk manufacture, at least under the present high duties upon the importation of raw silk, does not so well suit the climate of England as that of France. But the hard-ware and the coarse woollens of England are beyond all comparison superior to those of France, and much cheaper too in the same degree of goodness. In Poland there are said to be scarce any manufactures of any kind, a few of those coarser household manufactures excepted, without which no country can well subsist.

The advantage is due to three circumstances,   This great increase of the quantity of work which, in consequence of the division of labour, the same number of people are capable of performing is owing to three different circumstances; first to the increase of dexterity in every particular workman; secondly, to the saving of the time which is commonly lost in passing from one species of work to another; and lastly, to the invention of a great number of machines which facilitate and abridge labour, and enable one man to do the work of many.

(1) improved dexterity,   First, the improvement of the dexterity of the workman necessarily increases the quantity of the work he can perform; and the division of labour, by reducing every man's business to some one simple operation, and by making this operation the sole employment of his life, necessarily increases very much the dexterity of the workman. A common smith, who, though accustomed to handle the hammer, has never been used to make nails, if upon some particular occasion he is obliged to attempt it, will scarce, I am assured, be able to make above two or three hundred nails in a day, and those too very bad ones. A smith who has been accustomed to make nails, but whose sole or principal business has not been that of a nailer, can seldom with his utmost diligence make more than eight hundred or a thousand nails in a day. I have seen several boys under twenty years of age who had never exercised any other trade but that of making nails, and who, when they exerted themselves, could make, each of them, upwards of two thousand three hundred nails in a day. The making of a nail, however, is by no means one of the simplest operations. The same person blows the bellows, stirs or mends the fire as there is occasion, heats the iron, and forges every part of the nail: In forging the head too he is obliged to change his tools. The different operations into which the making of a pin, or of a metal button, is subdivided, are all of them much more simple, and the dexterity of the person, of whose life it has been the sole business to perform them, is usually much greater. The rapidity with which some of the operations of those manufactures are performed, exceeds what the human hand could, by those who had never seen them, be supposed capable of acquiring.

(2) saving of time,   Secondly, the advantage which is gained by saving the time commonly lost in passing from one sort of work to another, is much greater than we should at first view be apt to imagine it. It is impossible to pass very quickly from one kind of work to another; that is carried on in a different place, and with quite different tools. A country weaver, who cultivates a small farm, must lose a good deal of time in passing from his loom to the field, and from the field to his loom. When the two trades can be carried on in the same workhouse, the loss of time is no doubt much less. It is even in this case, however, very considerable. A man commonly saunters a little in turning his hand from one sort of employment to another. When he first begins the new work he is seldom very keen and hearty; his mind, as they say, does not go to it, and for some time he rather trifles than applies to good purpose. The habit of sauntering and of indolent careless application, which is naturally, or rather necessarily acquired by every country workman who is obliged to change his work and his tools every half hour, and to apply his hand in twenty different ways almost every day of his life; renders him almost always slothful and lazy, and incapable of any vigorous application even on the most pressing occasions. Independent, therefore, of his deficiency in point of dexterity, this cause alone must always reduce considerably the quantity of work which he is capable of performing.

and (3) application of machinery, invented by workmen,   Thirdly, and lastly, every body must be sensible how much labour is facilitated and abridged by the application of proper machinery. It is unnecessary to give any example. I shall only observe, therefore, that the invention of all those machines by which labour is so much facilitated and abridged, seems to have been originally owing to the division of labour. Men are much more likely to discover easier and readier methods of attaining any object, when the whole attention of their minds is directed towards that single object, than when it is dissipated among a great variety of things. But in consequence of the division of labour, the whole of every man's attention comes naturally to be directed towards some one very simple object. It is naturally to be expected, therefore, that some one or other of those who are employed in each particular branch of labour should soon find out easier and readier methods of performing their own particular work, wherever the nature of it admits of such improvement. A great part of the machines made use of in those manufactures in which labour is most subdivided, were originally the inventions of common workmen, who, being each of them employed in some very simple operation, naturally turned their thoughts towards finding out easier and readier methods of performing it. Whoever has been much accustomed to visit such manufactures, must frequently have been shewn very pretty machines, which were the inventions of such workmen, in order to facilitate and quicken their own particular part of the work. In the first fire-engines, a boy was constantly employed to open and shut alternately the communication between the boiler and the cylinder, according as the piston either ascended or descended. One of those boys, who loved to play with his companions, observed that, by tying a string from the handle of the valve which opened this communication to another part of the machine, the valve would open and shut without his assistance, and leave him at liberty to divert himself with his play-fellows. One of the greatest improvements that has been made upon this machine, since it was first invented, was in this manner the discovery of a boy who wanted to save his own labour.

or by machine-makers and philosophers.   All the improvements in machinery, however, have by no means been the inventions of those who had occasion to use the machines. Many improvements have been made by the ingenuity of the makers of the machines, when to make them became the business of a peculiar trade; and some by that of those who are called philosophers or men of speculation, whose trade it is not to do any thing, but to observe every thing; and who, upon that account, are often capable of combining together the powers of the most distant and dissimilar objects. In the progress of society, philosophy or speculation becomes, like every other employment, the principal or sole trade and occupation of a particular class of citizens. Like every other employment too, it is subdivided into a great number of different branches, each of which affords occupation to a peculiar tribe or class of philosophers; and this subdivision of employment in philosophy, as well as in every other business, improves dexterity, and saves time. Each individual becomes more expert in his own peculiar branch, more work is done upon the whole, and the quantity of science is considerably increased by it.

Hence the universal opulence of a well-governed society,   It is the great multiplication of the productions of all the different arts, in consequence of the division of labour, which occasions, in a well-governed society, that universal opulence which extends itself to the lowest ranks of the people. Every workman has a great quantity of his own work to dispose of beyond what he himself has occasion for; and every other workman being exactly in the same situation, he is enabled to exchange a great quantity of his own goods for a great quantity, or, what comes to the same thing, for the price of a great quantity of theirs. He supplies them abundantly with what they have occasion for, and they accommodate him as amply with what he has occasion for, and a general plenty diffuses itself through all the different ranks of the society.

even the day-labourer's coat being the produce of a vast number of workmen.   Observe the accommodation of the most common artificer or day-labourer in a civilized and thriving country, and you will perceive that the number of people of whose industry a part, though but a small part, has been employed in procuring him this accommodation, exceeds all computation. The woollen coat, for example, which covers the day-labourer, as coarse and rough as it may appear, is the produce of the joint labour of a great multitude of workmen. The shepherd, the sorter of the wool, the wool-comber or carder, the dyer, the scribbler, the spinner, the weaver, the fuller, the dresser, with many others, must all join their different arts in order to complete even this homely production. How many merchants and carriers, besides, must have been employed in transporting the materials from some of those workmen to others who often live in a very distant part of the country! how much commerce and navigation in particular, how many ship-builders, sailors, sail-makers, rope-makers, must have been employed in order to bring together the different drugs made use of by the dyer, which often come from the remotest corners of the world! What a variety of labour too is necessary in order to produce the tools of the meanest of those workmen! To say nothing of such complicated machines as the ship of the sailor, the mill of the fuller, or even the loom of the weaver, let us consider only what a variety of labour is requisite in order to form that very simple machine, the shears with which the shepherd clips the wool. The miner, the builder of the furnace for smelting the ore, the feller of the timber, the burner of the charcoal to be made use of in the smelting-house, the brick-maker, the brick-layer, the workmen who attend the furnace, the mill-wright, the forger, the smith, must all of them join their different arts in order to produce them. Were we to examine, in the same manner, all the different parts of his dress and household furniture, the coarse linen shirt which he wears next his skin, the shoes which cover his feet, the bed which he lies on, and all the different parts which compose it, the kitchen-grate at which he prepares his victuals, the coals which he makes use of for that purpose, dug from the bowels of the earth, and brought to him perhaps by a long sea and a long land carriage, all the other utensils of his kitchen, all the furniture of his table, the knives and forks, the earthen or pewter plates upon which he serves up and divides his victuals, the different hands employed in preparing his bread and his beer, the glass window which lets in the heat and the light, and keeps out the wind and the rain, with all the knowledge and art requisite for preparing that beautiful and happy invention, without which these northern parts of the world could scarce have afforded a very comfortable habitation, together with the tools of all the different workmen employed in producing those different conveniences; if we examine, I say, all these things, and consider what a variety of labour is employed about each of them, we shall be sensible that without the assistance and co-operation of many thousands, the very meanest person in a civilized country could not be provided, even according to what we very falsely imagine, the easy and simple manner in which he is commonly accommodated. Compared, indeed, with the more extravagant luxury of the great, his accommodation must no doubt appear extremely simple and easy; and yet it may be true, perhaps, that the accommodation of an European prince does not always so much exceed that of an industrious and frugal peasant, as the accommodation of the latter exceeds that of many an African king, the absolute master of the lives and liberties of ten thousand naked savages.

ROBERT OWEN
⬖⬖⬖

A STATEMENT REGARDING THE NEW LANARK ESTABLISHMENT

About twenty-six years ago, the late Mr DAVID DALE[1] of Glasgow, whose benevolence and philanthropy are well known, commenced an extensive spinning establishment near the Falls of the Clyde, and he founded it on the combined principles of public and private advantage.

It was continued by him for upwards of thirteen years, when, having no sons to succeed him, and being far advanced in life, he sold it to some English merchants, and myself, who married his eldest daughter.[2]

These gentlemen remained in partnership with me ten years, when some of them resold their interest in it to merchants resident in Glasgow, who still hold these shares.[3] But from the first sale by Mr Dale, until midsummer last, the management of the establishment was under my direction. At the commencement of that period, I arranged the outline of a plan, on a principle on which I had previously acted in a different part of the kingdom for several years; which was intended to unite and bring into action all the local advantages of the situation; to produce the greatest ultimate profits to the proprietors, with the greatest comfort and improvement to the numerous population to whom it afforded employment; that the latter might be a model and example to the manufacturing community, which, without some essential change in the formation

---

From *A Statement Regarding the New Lanark Establishment.* Edinburgh: John Moir, 1812.

1. David Dale (1739–1806) worked his way up from weaver to industrialist and philanthropist. He was also Owen's father-in-law. [Ed.]
2. Owen married Caroline Dale in 1799, the same year he bought New Lanark. [Ed.]
3. Owen originally bought New Lanark with two partners, John Barton and John Atkinson. This partnership was dissolved in 1809 and replaced by a new partnership with Atkinson, Robert Dennistoun, Alexander Campbell, and Colin Campbell. This formation was called The New Lanark Company. [Ed.]

of their characters, threatened, and now still more threatens, to revolutionize and ruin the empire. The plan was founded on the simple and evident principle, that any characters, from the savage to the sage or intelligent benevolent man, might be formed, by applying the proper means, and that these means are to a great extent at the command and under the controul of those who have influence in society; and, although mankind are generally unconscious of these important powers, there are few things admitting of any doubt, which are so easy as this, of full and complete demonstration. This system has been pursued at these works, without a single exception from the principle stated, for 13 years, and the result has been precisely that which was calculated. The population originally brought to the establishment was, with a few exceptions, a collection of the most ignorant and destitute from all parts of Scotland, possessing the usual characteristics of poverty and ignorance. They were generally indolent, and much addicted to theft, drunkenness, and falsehood, with all their concomitant vices, and strongly experiencing the misery which these ever produce. But by means so gradually introduced, as to be almost imperceptible to them, they have been surrounded with those circumstances which were calculated, first to check, and then to remove their inducements to retain these inclinations; and they are now become conspicuously honest, industrious, sober, and orderly; so that an idle individual, one in liquor, or a thief, is scarcely to be seen from the beginning to the end of the year; and they are become almost a new people, and quite ready to receive any fixed character which may be deemed the most advantageous for them to possess.

I was proceeding in preparing the means for accomplishing *this* object, when those gentlemen, who had lately become part proprietors with me of the Establishment, and who rather wished to employ their capital for a more immediate return of profit, objected to this system being pursued, and, alarmed at the events of the times, they would not consent to the temporary expenditure required for carrying it into execution.

I have said, temporary expenditure, because a comparatively small sum to that which had been expended; and a short period of time would have enabled me to complete the great outline of the plan; and in one year more, this latter part alone would have repaid the extra expense, besides giving important permanent advantages to the establishment.

In justice, however, to these gentlemen, it is necessary to state, that they are almost all strangers to the establishment and business; and that during the short period they have been part proprietors with me of the concern, they have not drawn any profits beyond the interest of their capital out of it; for, owing to our foreign political relations, which had created unknown difficulties in the commercial world, it had become necessary to reinvest these in the improvements, to place the concern beyond the risk of similar events, and enable it to meet them with success; and, in consequence of the profits being so expended, a permanent saving, exceeding six thousand pounds per annum, has been effected, and a considerable progress has also been made towards the reduction of a still larger annual sum. The contract of the company, however, vested the legal direction of the business in a majority of the shares, and they held a majority, although I possess a greater number of shares than any other individual; and, for the reasons previously stated, they came to a resolution of putting a stop to all those plans which I had in progress for the farther improvement of the community, and ultimate profit to the concern; and which, by the facts they would have established, had the plan been continued, would have soon created a very beneficial change in society, rendering that which now appears inconsistent and uncontroulable among the ignorant, plain, evident, and of easy direction. Under these circumstances, rather than be the active means of destroying a system which promises such important public as well as private advantages, and which had cost me many years close application and study, and much individual expense, I resigned the management; and the other proprietors are now endeavouring to conduct the establishment; but as they do not understand the principles on which it has been formed, and by which it is yet supported, I see the whole in their hands will soon become a manufacturing concern, similar to others in the kingdom; but I fear it will prove too extensive for them to manage with success on any other principles than those on which it has hitherto proceeded, as all its parts have been arranged to form a complete whole. In consequence, I have inquired if they will sell the interest they hold in the business, and have been given to understand, that they are willing to dispose of it on the same terms they purchased about two years ago; and if the system hitherto adopted shall be persevered in, those terms cannot fail to prove highly advantageous to the parties purchasing. I have, therefore, now to consider what is the best practicable plan for carrying these important objects into execution; for my own means are inadequate to so extensive an undertaking. But it may be said, that new schemes are hourly brought forward in all parts of the kingdom, and that ninety-nine of these out of every hundred prove visionary.

This is true; and, in reply to a fact so well known, I have to state, that this establishment has now existed upwards of twenty-six years; that besides the profits which the first proprietor derived from it, during thirteen years from its commencement, but which I have not the means of ascertaining, the latter proprietors have received, over and above five per cent. per annum upon all the capital employed in it, upwards of fifty thousand pounds; besides supporting above two thousand individuals, without any employment, for four months, at an expense exceeding seven thousand pounds. And in the same period, improvements have been carried on and finished out of the profits, which have now increased the powers of produce at the establishment to five times their original extent, and at an annual reduction of prime cost of nearly sixty thousand pounds, with a great improvement of quality in the material produced; and a considerable progress has also been made towards completing six times the extent, at an annual reduction of prime cost, exceeding eighty-five thousand pounds, which will be the state of the establishment at the end of next year. In the same period, also, an addition has been made to the village, forming part of the establishment, to contain from eleven to twelve hundred more inhabitants, which have been added to its population; and these, with the former occupiers of the houses, have been provided with all manner of public conveniencies and external comforts; and the most ample means were in preparation, and far advanced, to give their children the most beneficial education for their station in the community, and effectually to train them to habits which could not fail to make them valuable members of society. In consequence, likewise, of this system having been adopted and persevered in, the establishment, in a mercantile view, while supported by an adequate capital, is now put beyond the risk of ordinary circumstances; for the produce of it is of the nature of a raw material, applicable to the common purposes of male and female clothing in all ranks of life; it is of course in general demand, and will be always required; and although these improvements have cost upwards of eighty thousand pounds, it can now be produced, covering that expense, as low,—and, in a few months, when the arrangements in progress, which include the daily supply of fuel, food, clothes, and employment, for the whole population, shall be completed,—will be produced lower than it can be at any other establishment: Its success, therefore, becomes as certain as that of any mercantile or manufacturing concern in the kingdom, and so soon as peace shall again take place, very abundant profits may be reasonably expected, while an immediate return of ten per cent. on the capital to be advanced, may be confidently calculated upon. But to those who feel a deep interest in the well-being of their fellow-creatures, it will be considered of far more importance, that the slothful are become diligent, the thief honest, the drunkard sober, the licentious temperate, the wretched and diseased healthy, and comparatively happy; that poors' rates and litigation are banished from the community; and that the rising generation are now acquiring those habits and that knowledge which give the most heartfelt gratification to all who visit them. In consequence the village and works, which have been created at an expense probably of two hundred thousand pounds, have now more the appearance of a national benevolent institution, than of manufacturing works founded by an individual; and in fact it has become a national establishment of high interest to the community; for it may now be justly said to be the best model in practice of a charitable institution, which, in lieu of debasing the character of the poor, and impoverishing the rich, directs and enables the former to support themselves in comfort and independence, and, by their industry and good conduct, to add essentially to the national wealth and resources.

If, then, the principles on which this system has been founded, have already effected these beneficial changes, of which all may now satisfy themselves, allow me to say, on the credit of that which has been accomplished, that those parts of it which were in progress, and are to follow, would yet effect far more extensive and important improvements, and give the whole stability.

But it may be necessary to explain more particularly what I mean by those plans which I had in progress, for the further improvement of the community, and ultimate profit to the concern.

They were intended to *increase* the population, diminish its expense, *add* to its domestic comforts, and greatly improve its character. Towards effecting these purposes, a building has been erected, which may be termed the *"New Institution,"* situated in the centre of the establishment, with an inclosed area before it. The objects intended to be accomplished by which are, *first,* To obtain for the children, from the age of two to five, a play-ground, in which they may be easily superintended, and their young minds properly directed, while the time of the parents will be much more usefully occupied, both for themselves and the establishment. This part of the plan arose from observing, that the tempers of children among the lower orders are generally spoiled, and vicious habits strongly formed, previous to the time when they are usually sent to school; and, to create the characters desired, these must be prevented, or as much as possible counteracted. The area is also to afford a place of meeting for the children, from the age of five to ten, previous to and after school hours, and to serve the boys for a drill-ground. It likewise contains conveniences calculated to give the children such habits as will enable the master of police to keep the village in a decent, clean state; and this is no small difficulty to overcome, where other habits have always obtained.

Secondly, To procure a large store-cellar, which was much wanted, and, by this arrangement, has been placed in the most advantageous situation for both the works and village; and it will be found to be of much use to the establishment.

Thirdly, A kitchen upon a large scale, in which food may be prepared of a better quality, and at a much lower rate, than individual families can now obtain it; for, under this arrangement, two or three fires, and half a dozen attendants, will supersede the necessity of several hundred fires, and as many attendants, particularly in summer; and the provisions will be prepared of the most wholesome and nutritious materials, obtained at the cheapest rates, aided by every known conveniency, and the best information which can be collected on the subject. It is obvious, that most of the families among the working class, are unusually destitute of all these advantages.

Fourthly, An eating-room immediately adjoining the kitchen, one hundred and ten feet by forty within, in which those to whom it may be convenient may take all their regular meals. As several of the young persons employed at the works, reside at the county town of Lanark, more than a mile distant, and from which their meals are regularly sent at considerable trouble and expense; and as a still greater number *lodge* in the village, and now inconveniently board themselves, these will all find an immediate benefit from both the kitchen and eating-room, and they afford so many substantial advantages to the general inhabitants of the place, that it is to be feared the space allotted for the eating-room, ample as it may appear, will soon be found too circumscribed.

Fifthly, The eating-room, by an immediate removal of the tables to the ceiling, will afford space in which the younger part of the adults of the establishment may dance three nights in a week during winter, one hour each night; and which, under proper regulations, is expected to contribute essentially to their health. This part of the plan is considered of some importance, because, during the short days of winter, the young people have no means of enjoying exercise in the open air, and this can be obtained as a substitute, at a trifling expense; and this change of motion, from their constant occupations, will be most favourable for their spirits, and a strong source of attachment to the works.

Sixthly, Another room, the whole length of the building, being 140 feet long, 40 wide, and 20 high, which is to be the general education-room and church for the village, and those who attend the works. In this it was intended, that the boys and girls were to be taught to read well, and to understand what they read; to write expeditiously a good legible hand, and to learn correctly; so that they may comprehend and use with facility the fundamental rules of arithmetic. The girls were also to be taught to sew, cut out, and make up useful family garments; and, after becoming perfect in these, they were to attend in rotation in the kitchen and eating-room, to learn to cook cheap and nutritious food, and to clean and keep a house neat and in order. And the boys were to be taught in the drill-ground the manual exercise, and as much of the principles of military tactics as would enable them, with a little previous practice, at any future period of their lives, aided also by the sentiments they would acquire, to render the most effectual defence to their country.

Seventhly, This room was intended to be arranged, not only in the most convenient manner for the several branches of useful education enumerated, but also to serve for a lecture-room and church. The lectures were to be given in winter three nights in the week alternately with dancing, and to be familiar discourses to instruct the population in their domestic economy, particularly in the methods they should adopt in training up their children, and forming their habits from their earliest infancy, in which, at present, they are deplorably ignorant. By these lectures they were also to be taught how to expend their earnings to the most advantage, and to appropriate the surplus, which will arise to them in consequence; to create a well-regulated competency; thus relieving them from the anxious fear of want under any circumstances, or at any period, and giving them that rational independence arising from their own exertions and superior conduct, without which, consistency of character, or domestic comfort, are not to be expected. The church was intended to be a general one, so that no part of the population may be excluded from it, and open occasionally to every sect of Christians in their turn. But the great leading principles of its regular doctrines, were, to inculcate the healing of all religious differences,—a real respect for each other's sentiments, on the ground that every individual, from one cause or other, which in general may be easily explained, must conscientiously deem his own the best, and which, indeed, is the only reason why they are entertained. And, above all, to enforce that most important precept, which, when fully comprehended, will be found alone sufficient to direct all our social intercourse, which is, "That there is no other way by which mankind can obtain general and continued happiness, than by training every individual from its infancy, to exert itself in promoting, with sincerity, the happiness of every other individual within its circle of action." And, by adopting the *proper* means, this may be universally taught with ease and with certainty.

And, *lastly,* The plan also included the improvement of the road from the works and village to the old town of Lanark, which is now almost impassable for young children in winter, and in such a state as to prevent in a great measure the population of the latter from being available for the manufacturing purposes of the former, and from deriving any benefit from its institutions, which are calculated to educate the whole of the children in the neighbourhood, as well as the works are to give them employment afterwards.

Beneficial as these arrangements, connected with the *New Institution,* must be to the individuals employed at the works, they will be at least equally advantageous, in a pecuniary view, to the proprietors of the establishment; for the whole expense of these combined operations will not exceed six thousand pounds, three thousand of which have already been expended;and, so far as my former experience enables me to judge of the consequences to arise from them, they cannot save less to the establishment than as many thousand pounds per annum, but probably much more.

First, By the improvement of the road between the old and new towns of Lanark, by shortening and widening it, and forming a good foot-path, making the distance easy and pleasant even for the youngest children from the former, to attend the schools and works at the latter, and which, with the conveniency of the public kitchen and eating-room, will make the population of the old town nearly as available for the objects of the establishment as that of the new is at present; giving a double supply of operatives for the same demand, and of course, constituting a perpetual check against any sudden and great advance of labour, which, in its consequences, is usually as injurious to those employed as to their employers.

Secondly, The kitchen and eating-room will enable the proprietors to support the population of the village, now exceeding 2200 individuals, at 1s 6d. per week less than the expense at which they now feed themselves; which alone will constitute a saving of £8580 per annum, to be divided between the proprietors and population of both towns.

Thirdly, By the arrangements formed for the education of the children, they will be trained regularly for their employment, and all their habits, bodily and mental, formed to carry them to a high state of perfection; and this alone, in its consequences, will be of incalculable advantage to the concern; for to these people are entrusted the care and use of nice and valuable machinery, with a very great variety of materials requisite for the business, with all the varied operations of the manufacture of the establishment through all its processes to the annual value of two hundred thousand pounds, the cost and perfection of which depend essentially on their conduct; and a saving of one penny per lb. on the manufacture is now upwards of £6000 per annum, and in a short period, will be near £8000 per do.;—while hitherto, the works have been supplied with operatives from among strangers from all parts of the country, who have been instructed in the business at an almost incalculable loss and expense to the proprietors, besides keeping the establishment in a comparative state of inferiority.

Advantageous, however, as these arrangements will be to the individuals employed at the works, and to the proprietors of the establishment, they will yet prove of far higher importance in a national view by the principles they will establish, and the consequences which will arise from them. For now, the manufacturing population of this country is feelingly alive to its apparent interests, extremely active, and that activity encreased to the highest pitch by the present state of commerce, requiring all their exertions for their support; but they are also, with partial exceptions, so ignorant as to be easily misdirected, and their numbers exceed the half of the population of the kingdom. Can such a combination of circumstances be contemplated without a conviction, that, if they shall be permitted to continue much longer without an effectual remedy being applied, very fatal consequences must be the result?

The principles on which the arrangements which have been explained have been formed, point out that remedy, and the experience of more than 20 years on an extended scale, prove them to be practically correct; and if they shall be generally adopted, the consequences will be, that not only our manufacturing but our entire population will gradually change its character; and if the means recommended shall be persevered in, it will ultimately become so well instructed, as to distinguish clearly between its true and apparent interests, and to detect the fallacy of those who might attempt to mislead them from the former. Poor's rates, the bane of the lower orders, would cease, foresight and temperance would generally prevail, their industry would be directed by intelligence, and the happiness they would soon experience in consequence, would render them a far more efficient and powerful population for their numbers than has ever yet existed, and with the resources which this country possesses, would make it impenetrable to foreign attack, however formidable it might be. Thus, if this plan had been pursued at these works but for one year longer, a population of from two to three thousand individuals would have been placed in a more happy situation than is to be found in any manufacturing class at present known; and, from the singular success which their superior conduct must give to the establishment in a pecuniary view, permanence would be given to the system. And, that the advantages of such a system being seen upon an extended scale in practice, may not be lost to our country and the world in general.—

I propose, that an association of some of the leading and most patriotic characters in the country, should be formed, either by charter or otherwise, for the purpose of giving such weight and influence to the system, as would ensure its speedy and general adoption; for, as many of the most intelligent and enlightened men in the kingdom, of all sects and parties, who have seen it in practice, as well as several foreigners of the first distinction, who have also minutely inspected it, have, without one exception, given it their unqualified approbation, I consider it now ready to undergo the most severe scrutiny and investigation.

To conclude. I do not hesitate to say, that this experiment is the most important that has ever yet been attempted for the general happiness of society; and that, conscious of the security of the grounds on which I have proceeded, and mean to proceed, I am ready to pledge my life for its ultimate, full, and complete success.

DAVID RICARDO

ON MACHINERY

In the present chapter I shall enter into some enquiry respecting the influence of machinery on the interests of the different classes of society, a subject of great importance, and one which appears never to have been investigated in a

From *Principles of Political Economy and Taxation* (1821). London: George Bell and Sons, 1903.

manner to lead to any certain or satisfactory results. It is more incumbent on me to declare my opinion on this question, because they have, on further reflection, undergone a considerable change; and although I am not aware that I have ever published any thing respecting machinery which it is necessary for me to retract, yet I have in other ways given my support to doctrines which I now think erroneous; it, therefore, becomes a duty in me to submit my present views to examination, with my reasons for entertaining them.

Ever since I first turned my attention to questions of political economy, I have been of opinion, that such an application of machinery to any branch of production, as should have the effect of saving labour, was a general good, accompanied only with that portion of inconvenience which in most cases attends the removal of capital and labour from one employment to another. It appeared to me, that provided the landlords had the same money rents, they would be benefited by the reduction in the prices of some of the commodities on which those rents were expended, and which reduction of price could not fail to be the consequence of the employment of machinery. The capitalist, I thought, was eventually benefited precisely in the same manner. He, indeed, who made the discovery of the machine, or who first usefully applied it, would enjoy an additional advantage, by making great profits for a time; but, in proportion as the machine came into general use, the price of the commodity produced, would, from the effects of competition, sink to its cost of production, when the capitalist would get the same money profits as before, and he would only participate in the general advantage, as a consumer, by being enabled, with the same money revenue, to command an additional quantity of comforts and enjoyments. The class of labourers also, I thought, was equally benefited by the use of machinery, as they would have the means of buying more commodities with the same money wages, and I thought that no reduction of wages would take place, because the capitalist would have the power of demanding and employing the same quantity of labour as before, although he might be under the necessity of employing it in the production of a new, or at any rate of a different commodity. If, by improved machinery, with the employment of the same quantity of labour, the quantity of stockings could be quadrupled, and the demand for stockings were only doubled, some labourers would necessarily be discharged from the stocking trade; but as the capital which employed them was still in being, and as it was the interest of those who had it to employ it productively, it appeared to me that it would be employed on the production of some other commodity, useful to the society, for which there could not fail to be a demand; for I was, and am, deeply impressed with the truth of the observation of Adam Smith, that "the desire for food is limited in every man, by the narrow capacity of the human stomach, but the desire of the conveniences, and ornaments of building, dress, equipage and household furniture, seems to have no limit or certain boundary." As, then, it appeared to me that there would be the same demand for labour as before, and that wages would be no lower, I thought that the labouring class would, equally with the other classes, participate in the advantage, from the general cheapness of commodities arising from the use of machinery.

These were my opinions, and they continue unaltered, as far as regards the landlord and the capitalist; but I am convinced, that the substitution of machinery for human labour, is often very injurious to the interests of the class of labourers.

My mistake arose from the supposition, that whenever the net income of a society increased, its gross income would also increase; I now, however, see reason to be satisfied that the one fund, from which landlords and capitalists derive their revenue, may increase, while the other, that upon which the labouring class mainly depend, may diminish, and therefore it follows, if I am right, that the same cause which may increase the net revenue of the country, may at the same time render the population redundant, and deteriorate the condition of the labourer.

A capitalist we will suppose employs a capital of the value of 20,000*l.* and that he carries on the joint business of a farmer, and a manufacturer of necessaries. We will further suppose, that 7000*l.* of this capital is invested in fixed capital, viz. in buildings, implements, &c. &c. and that the remaining 13,000*l.* is employed as circulating capital in the support of labour. Let us suppose, too, that profits are 10 per cent., and consequently that the capitalist's capital is every year put into its original state of efficiency, and yields a profit of 2000*l.*

Each year the capitalist begins his operations, by having food and necessaries in his possession of the value of 13,000*l.*, all of which he sells in the course of the year to his own workmen for that sum of money, and, during the same period, he pays them the like amount of money for wages: at the end of the year they replace in his possession food and necessaries of the value of 15,000*l.*, 2000*l.* of which he consumes himself, or disposes of as may best suit his pleasure and gratification. As far as these products are concerned, the gross produce for that year is 15,000*l.*, and the net produce 2000*l.* Suppose now, that the following year the capitalist employs half his men in constructing a machine, and the other half in producing food and necessaries as usual. During that year he would pay the sum of 13,000*l.* in wages as usual, and would sell food and necessaries to the same amount to his workmen; but what would be the case the following year?

While the machine was being made, only one-half of the usual quantity of food and necessaries would be obtained, and they would be only one-half the value of the quantity which was produced before. The machine would be worth 7500*l.*, and the food and necessaries 7500*l.*, and, therefore, the capital of the capitalist would be as great as before; for he would have besides these two values, his fixed capital worth 7000*l.*, making in the whole 20,000*l.*

capital, and 2000*l*. profit. After deducting this latter sum for his own expenses, he would have a no greater circulating capital than 5500*l*. with which to carry on his subsequent operations; and, therefore, his means of employing labour, would be reduced in the proportion of 13,000*l*. to 5500*l*., and, consequently, all the labour which was before employed by 7500*l*., would become redundant.

The reduced quantity of labour which the capitalist can employ, must, indeed, with the assistance of the machine, and after deductions for its repairs, produce a value equal to 7500*l*., it must replace the circulating capital with a profit of 2000*l*. on the whole capital; but if this be done, if the net income be not diminished, of what importance is it to the capitalist, whether the gross income be of the value of 3000*l*., of 10,000*l*., or of 15,000*l*.

In this case, then, although the net produce will not be diminished in value, although its power of purchasing commodities may be greatly increased, the gross produce will have fallen from a value of 15,000*l*. to a value of 7500*l*., and as the power of supporting a population, and employing labour, depends always on the gross produce of a nation, and not on its net produce, there will necessarily be a diminution in the demand for labour, population will become redundant, and the situation of the labouring classes will be that of distress and poverty.

As, however, the power of saving from revenue to add to capital, must depend on the efficiency of the net revenue, to satisfy the wants of the capitalist, it could not fail to follow from the reduction in the price of commodities consequent on the introduction of machinery, that with the same wants he would have increased means of saving,—increased facility of transferring revenue into capital. But with every increase of capital he would employ more labourers; and, therefore, a portion of the people thrown out of work in the first instance, would be subsequently employed; and if the increased production, in consequence of the employment of the machine, was so great as to afford, in the shape of net produce, as great a quantity of food and necessaries as existed before in the form of gross produce, there would be the same ability to employ the whole population, and, therefore, there would not necessarily be any redundancy of people.

All I wish to prove, is, that the discovery and use of machinery may be attended with a diminution of gross produce; and whenever that is the case, it will be injurious to the labouring class, as some of their number will be thrown out of employment, and population will become redundant, compared with the funds which are to employ it.

The case which I have supposed, is the most simple that I could select; but it would make no difference in the result, if we supposed that the machinery was applied to the trade of any manufacturer,—that of a clothier, for example, or of a cotton manufacturer. If in the trade of a clothier, less cloth would be produced after the introduction of machinery; for a part of that quantity which is disposed of for the purpose of paying a large body of workmen, would not be required by their employer. In consequence of using the machine, it would be necessary for him to reproduce a value, only equal to the value consumed, together with the profits on the whole capital. 7500*l.* might do this as effectually as 15,000*l.* did before, the case differing in no respect from the former instance. It may be said, however, that the demand for cloth would be as great as before, and it may be asked from whence would this supply come? But by whom would the cloth be demanded? By the farmers and the other producers of necessaries, who employed their capitals in producing these necessaries as a means of obtaining cloth: they gave corn and necessaries to the clothier for cloth, and he bestowed them on his workmen for the cloth which their work afforded him.

This trade would now cease; the clothier would not want the food and clothing, having fewer men to employ and having less cloth to dispose of. The farmers and others, who only produced necessaries as means to an end, could no longer obtain cloth by such an application of their capitals, and, therefore, they would either themselves employ their capitals in producing cloth, or would lend them to others, in order that the commodity really wanted might be furnished; and that for which no one had the means of paying, or for which there was no demand, might cease to be produced. This, then, leads us to the same result; the demand for labour would diminish, and the commodities necessary to the support of labour would not be produced in the same abundance.

If these views be correct, it follows, 1st. That the discovery, and useful application of machinery, always leads to the increase of the net produce of the country, although it may not, and will not, after an inconsiderable interval, increase the value of that net produce.

2dly. That an increase of the net produce of a country is compatible with a diminution of the gross produce, and that the motives for employing machinery are always sufficient to insure its employment, if it will increase the net produce, although it may, and frequently must, diminish both the quantity of the gross produce, and its value.

3dly. That the opinion entertained by the labouring class, that the employment of machinery is frequently detrimental to their interests, is not founded on prejudice and error, but is conformable to the correct principles of political economy.

4thly. That if the improved means of production, in consequence of the use of machinery, should increase the net produce of a country in a degree so great as not to diminish the gross produce, (I mean always quantity of commodities and not value,) then the situation of all classes will be improved. The landlord and capitalist will benefit, not by an increase of rent and profit, but by the advantages resulting from the expenditure of the same rent, and profit, on commodities, very considerably reduced in value, while the situation of the labouring classes will also be considerably improved; 1st, from the increased demand for menial servants; 2dly, from the stimulus to savings from revenue, which such an abundant net produce will afford; and 3dly, from the low price of all articles of consumption on which their wages will be expended.

Independently of the consideration of the discovery and use of machinery, to which our attention has been just directed, the labouring class have no small interest in the manner in which the net income of the country is expended, although it should, in all cases, be expended for the gratification and enjoyments of those who are fairly entitled to it.

If a landlord, or a capitalist, expends his revenue in the manner of an ancient baron, in the support of a great number of retainers, or menial servants, he will give employment to much more labour, than if he expended it on fine clothes, or costly furniture; on carriages, on horses, or in the purchase of any other luxuries.

In both cases the net revenue would be the same, and so would be the gross revenue, but the former would be realised in different commodities. If my revenue were 10,000*l.*, the same quantity nearly of productive labour would be employed, whether I realised it in fine clothes and costly furniture, &c. &c. or in a quantity of food and clothing of the same value. If, however, I realised my revenue in the first set of commodities, no more labour would be *consequently* employed:—I should enjoy my furniture and my clothes, and there would be an end of them; but if I realised my revenue in food and clothing, and my desire was to employ menial servants, all those whom I could so employ with my revenue of 10,000*l.*, or with the food and clothing which it would purchase, would be to be added to the former demand for labourers, and this addition would take place only because I chose this mode of expending my revenue. As the labourers, then, are interested in the demand for labour, they must naturally desire that as much of the revenue as possible should be diverted from expenditure on luxuries, to be expended in the support of menial servants.

In the same manner, a country engaged in war, and which is under the necessity of maintaining large fleets and armies, employs a great many more men than will be employed when the war terminates, and the annual expenses which it brings with it, cease.

If I were not called upon for a tax of 500*l.* during the war, and which is expended on men in the situations of soldiers and sailors, I might probably expend that portion of my income on furniture, clothes, books, &c. &c. and whether it was expended in the one way or in the other, there would be the same quantity of labour employed in production; for the food and clothing of the soldier and sailor would require the same amount of industry to produce it as the more luxurious commodities; but in the case of the war, there would be the additional demand for men as soldiers and sailors; and, consequently, a war which is supported out of the revenue, and not from the capital of a country, is favourable to the increase of population.

At the termination of the war, when part of my revenue reverts to me, and is employed as before in the purchase of wine, furniture, or other luxuries, the population which it before supported, and which the war called into existence, will become redundant, and by its effect on the rest of the population, and its competition with it for employment, will sink the value of wages, and very materially deteriorate the condition of the labouring classes.

There is one other case that should be noticed of the possibility of an increase in the amount of the net revenue of a country, and even of its gross revenue, with a diminution of demand for labour, and that is, when the labour of horses is substituted for that of man. If I employed one hundred men on my farm, and if I found that the food bestowed on fifty of those men, could be diverted to the support of horses, and afford me a greater return of raw produce, after allowing for the interest of the capital which the purchase of the horses would absorb, it would be advantageous to me to substitute the horses for the men, and I should accordingly do so; but this would not be for the interest of the men, and unless the income I obtained, was so much increased as to enable me to employ the men as well as the horses, it is evident that the population would become redundant, and the labourers' condition would sink in the general scale. It is evident he could not, under any circumstances, be employed in agriculture; but if the produce of the land were increased by the substitution of horses for men, he might be employed in manufactures, or as a menial servant.

The statements which I have made will not, I hope, lead to the inference that machinery should not be encouraged. To elucidate the principle, I have been supposing, that improved machinery is *suddenly* discovered, and extensively used; but the truth is, that these discoveries are gradual, and rather operate in determining the employment of the capital which is saved and accumulated, than in diverting capital from its actual employment.

With every increase of capital and population, food will generally rise, on account of its being more difficult to produce. The consequence of a rise of food will be a rise of wages, and every rise of wages will have a tendency to determine the saved capital in a greater proportion than before to the employment of machinery. Machinery and labour are in constant competition, and the former can frequently not be employed until labour rises.

In America and many other countries, where the food of man is easily provided, there is not nearly such great temptation to employ machinery as in England, where food is high, and costs much labour for its production. The same cause that raises labour, does not raise the value of machines, and, therefore, with every augmentation of capital, a greater proportion of it is employed on machinery. The demand for labour will continue to increase with an increase of capital, but not in proportion to its increase; the ratio will necessarily be a diminishing ratio.

I have before observed, too, that the increase of net incomes, estimated in commodities, which is always the consequence of improved machinery, will lead to new savings and accumulations. These savings, it must be remembered are annual, and must soon create a fund, much greater than the gross revenue, originally lost by the discovery of the machine, when the demand for labour will be as great as before, and the situation of the people will be still further improved by the increased savings which the increased net revenue will still enable them to make.

The employment of machinery could never be safely discouraged in a State, for if a capital is not allowed to get the greatest net revenue that the use of machinery will afford here, it will be carried abroad, and this must be a much more serious discouragement to the demand for labour, than the most extensive employment of machinery; for, while a capital is employed in this country, it must create a demand for some labour; machinery cannot be worked without the assistance of men, it cannot be made but with the contribution of their labour. By investing part of a capital in improved machinery, there will be a diminution in the progressive demand for labour; by exporting it to another country, the demand will be wholly annihilated.

The prices of commodities, too, are regulated by their cost of production. By employing improved machinery, the cost of production of commodities is reduced, and, consequently, you can afford to sell them in foreign markets at a cheaper price. If, however, you were to reject the use of machinery, while all other countries encouraged it, you would be obliged to export your money, in exchange for foreign goods, till you sunk the natural prices of your goods to the prices of other countries. In making your exchanges with those countries, you might give a commodity which cost two days labour, here, for a commodity which cost one, abroad, and this disadvantageous exchange would be the consequence of your own act, for the commodity which you export, and which cost you two days labour, would have cost you only one if you had not rejected the use of machinery, the services of which your neighbours had more wisely appropriated to themselves.

THOMAS CARLYLE

CAPTAINS OF INDUSTRY

If I believed that Mammonism with its adjuncts was to continue henceforth the one serious principle of our existence, I should reckon it idle to solicit remedial measures from any Government, the disease being insusceptible of remedy. Government can do much, but it can in no wise do all. Government, as the most conspicuous object in Society, is called upon to give signal of what shall be done; and, in many ways, to preside over, further, and command the doing of it. But the Government cannot do, by all its signalling and commanding, what the Society is radically indisposed to do. In the long-run every Government is the exact symbol of its People, with their wisdom and unwisdom; we have to say, Like People like Government.—The main substance of this immense Problem of Organising Labour, and first of all of Managing the Working Classes, will, it is very clear, have to be solved by those who stand practically in the middle of it; by those who themselves work and preside over work. Of all that can be enacted by any Parliament in regard to it, the germs must already lie potentially extant in those two Classes, who are to obey such enactment. A Human Chaos *in* which there is no light, you vainly attempt to irradiate by light shed *on* it: order never can arise there.

But it is my firm conviction that the "Hell of England" will *cease* to be that of "not making money;" that we shall get a nobler Hell and a nobler Heaven! I anticipate light *in* the Human Chaos, glimmering, shining more and more; under manifold true signals from without That light shall shine. Our deity no longer being Mammon,—O Heavens, each man will then say to himself: "Why such deadly haste to make money? I shall not go to Hell, even if I do not make money! There is another Hell, I am told!" Competition, at railway-speed, in all branches of commerce and work will then abate:—good felt-hats for the head, in every sense, instead of seven-feet lath-and-plaster hats on wheels, will then be discoverable! Bubble-periods,[1] with their panics and commercial crises, will again become infrequent; steady modest industry will take the place of gambling speculation. To be a noble Master, among noble

---

From *Past and Present* (1843) Oxford: Oxford Univ. Press, 1909.

1. Bubble-periods are times of reckless speculation in stocks, in which they become seriously overvalued. The most famous "bubble" was the South Sea Bubble, which burst disastrously in 1720, but not before it inspired many similar ventures that also failed. [Ed.]

Workers, will again be the first ambition with some few; to be a rich Master only the second. How the Inventive Genius of England, with the whirr of its bobbins and billy-rollers shoved somewhat into the backgrounds of the brain, will contrive and devise, not cheaper produce exclusively, but fairer distribution of the produce at its present cheapness! By degrees, we shall again have a Society with something of Heroism in it, something of Heaven's Blessing on it; we shall again have, as my German friend asserts, "instead of Mammon-Feudalism with unsold cotton-shirts and Preservation of the Game, noble just Industrialism and Government by the Wisest!"

It is with the hope of awakening here and there a British man to know himself for a man and divine soul, that a few words of parting admonition, to all persons to whom the Heavenly Powers have lent power of any kind in this land, may now be addressed. And first to those same Master-Workers, Leaders of Industry; who stand nearest, and in fact powerfulest, though not most prominent, being as yet in too many senses a Virtuality rather than an Actuality.

The Leaders of Industry, if Industry is ever to be led, are virtually the Captains of the World; if there be no nobleness in them, there will never be an Aristocracy more. But let the Captains of Industry consider: once again, are they born of other clay than the old Captains of Slaughter; doomed forever to be no Chivalry, but a mere gold-plated *Doggery,*—what the French well name *Canaille,* "Doggery" with more or less gold carrion at its disposal? Captains of Industry are the true Fighters, henceforth recognisable as the only true ones: Fighters against Chaos, Necessity and the Devils and Jötuns; and lead on Mankind in that great, and alone true, and universal warfare; the stars in their courses fighting for them, and all Heaven and all Earth saying audibly, Well-done! Let the Captains of Industry retire into their own hearts, and ask solemnly, If there is nothing but vulturous hunger, for fine wines, valet reputation and gilt carriages, discoverable there? Of hearts made by the Almighty God I will not believe such a thing. Deep-hidden under wretchedest godforgetting Cants, Epicurisms, Dead-Sea Apisms; forgotten as under foulest fat Lethe mud and weeds, there is yet, in all hearts born into this God's-World, a spark of the Godlike slumbering. Awake, O nightmare sleepers; awake, arise, or be forever fallen! This is not playhouse poetry; it is sober fact. Our England, our world cannot live as it is. It will connect itself with a God again, or go down with nameless throes and fire-consummation to the Devils. Thou who feelest aught of such a Godlike stirring in thee, any faintest intimation of it as through heavy-laden dreams, follow *it,* I conjure thee. Arise, save thyself, be one of those that save thy country.

Bucaniers, Chactaw Indians, whose supreme aim in fighting is that they may get the scalps, the money, that they may amass scalps and money: out of such came no Chivalry, and never will! Out of such came only gore and wreck, infernal rage and misery; desperation quenched in annihilation. Behold it, I bid thee, behold there, and consider! What is it that thou have a hundred thousand-pound bills laid up in thy strong-room, a hundred scalps hung up in thy wigwam? I value not them or thee. Thy scalps and thy thousand-pound bills are as yet nothing, if no nobleness from within irradiate them; if no Chivalry, in action, or in embryo ever struggling towards birth and action, be there.

Love of men cannot be bought by cash-payment; and without love, men cannot endure to be together. You cannot lead a Fighting World without having it regimented, chivalried: the thing, in a day, becomes impossible; all men in it, the highest at first, the very lowest at last, discern consciously, or by a noble instinct, this necessity. And can you any more continue to lead a Working World unregimented, anarchic? I answer, and the Heavens and Earth are now answering, No! The thing becomes not "in a day" impossible; but in some two generations it does. Yes, when fathers and mothers, in Stockport hunger-cellars, begin to eat their children, and Irish widows have to prove their relationship by dying of typhus-fever; and amid Governing "Corporations of the Best and Bravest," busy to preserve their game by "bushing," dark millions of God's human creatures start up in mad Chartisms, impracticable *Sacred-Months*,[2] and Manchester Insurrections;—and there is a virtual Industrial Aristocracy as yet only half-alive, spellbound amid money-bags and ledgers; and an actual Idle Aristocracy seemingly near dead in somnolent delusions, in trespasses and double-barrels; "sliding," as on inclined-planes, which every new year they *soap* with new Hansard's-jargon under God's sky, and so are "sliding" ever faster, towards a "scale" and balance-scale whereon is written *Thou art found Wanting:*—in such days, after a generation or two, I say, it does become, even to the low and simple, very palpably impossible! No Working World, any more than a Fighting World, can be led on without a noble Chivalry of Work, and laws and fixed rules which follow out of that,— far nobler than any Chivalry of Fighting was. As an anarchic multitude on mere Supply-and-demand, it is becoming inevitable that we dwindle in horrid suicidal convulsion, and self-abrasion, frightful to the imagination, into *Chactaw* Workers. With wigwam and scalps,—with palaces and thousand-pound bills; with savagery, depopulation, chaotic desolation! Good Heavens, will not one French Revolution and Reign of Terror suffice us, but must there be two? There will be two if needed; there will be twenty if needed; there will be precisely as many as are needed. The Laws of Nature will have themselves fulfilled. That is a thing certain to me.

---

2. "Sacred month" was a Chartist designation for a month-long strike. [Ed.]

Your gallant battle-hosts and work-hosts, as the others did, will need to be made loyally yours; they must and will be regulated, methodically secured in their just share of conquest under you;—joined with you in veritable brotherhood, sonhood, by quite other and deeper ties than those of temporary day's wages! How would mere redcoated regiments, to say nothing of chivalries, fight for you, if you could discharge them on the evening of the battle, on payment of the stipulated shillings,—and they discharge you on the morning of it! Chelsea Hospitals, pensions, promotions, rigorous lasting covenant on the one side and on the other, are indispensable even for a hired fighter. The Feudal Baron, much more,—how could he subsist with mere temporary mercenaries round him, at sixpence a day; ready to go over to the other side, if sevenpence were offered? He could not have subsisted;—and his noble instinct saved him from the necessity of even trying! The Feudal Baron had a Man's Soul in him; to which anarchy, mutiny, and the other fruits of temporary mercenaries, were intolerable: he had never been a Baron otherwise, but had continued a Chactaw and Bucanier. He felt it precious, and at last it became habitual, and his fruitful enlarged existence included it as a necessity, to have men round him who in heart loved him; whose life he watched over with rigour yet with love; who were prepared to give their life for him, if need came. It was beautiful; it was human! Man lives not otherwise, nor can live contented, anywhere or anywhen. Isolation is the sum-total of wretchedness to man. To be cut off, to be left solitary: to have a world alien, not your world; all a hostile camp for you; not a home at all, of hearts and faces who are yours, whose you are! It is the frightfulest enchantment; too truly a work of the Evil One. To have neither superior, nor inferior, nor equal, united manlike to you. Without father, without child, without brother. Man knows no sadder destiny. "How is each of us," exclaims Jean Paul, "so lonely, in the wide bosom of the All!" Encased each as in his transparent "ice-palace;" our brother visible in his, making signals and gesticulations to us;—visible, but forever unattainable: on his bosom we shall never rest, nor he on ours. It was not a God that did this; no!

Awake, ye noble Workers, warriors in the one true war: all this must be remedied. It is you who are already half-alive, whom I will welcome into life; whom I will conjure in God's name to shake off your enchanted sleep, and live wholly! Cease to count scalps, gold-purses; not in these lies your or our salvation. Even these, if you count only these, will not long be left. Let bucaniering be put far from you; alter, speedily abrogate all laws of the bucaniers, if you would gain any victory that shall endure. Let God's justice, let pity, nobleness and manly valour, with more gold-purses or with fewer, testify themselves in this your brief Life-transit to all the Eternities, the Gods and Silences. It is to you I call; for ye are not dead, ye are already half-alive: there is in you a sleepless dauntless energy, the prime-matter of all nobleness in man. Honour to you in your kind. It is to you I call: ye know at least this, That the mandate of God to His creature man is: Work! The future Epic of the World rests not with those that are near dead, but with those that are alive, and those that are coming into life.

Look around you. Your world-hosts are all in mutiny, in confusion, destitution; on the eve of fiery wreck and madness! They will not march farther for you, on the sixpence a day and supply-and-demand principle: they will not; nor ought they, nor can they. Ye shall reduce them to order, begin reducing them. To order, to just subordination; noble loyalty in return for noble guidance. Their souls are driven nigh mad; let yours be sane and ever saner. Not as a bewildered bewildering mob; but as a firm regimented mass, with real captains over them, will these men march any more. All human interests, combined human endeavours, and social growths in this world, have, at a certain stage of their development, required organising: and Work, the grandest of human interests, does now require it.

God knows, the task will be hard: but no noble task was ever easy. This task will wear away your lives, and the lives of your sons and grandsons: but for what purpose, if not for tasks like this, were lives given to men? Ye shall cease to count your thousand-pound scalps, the noble of you shall cease! Nay the very scalps, as I say, will not long be left if you count only these. Ye shall cease wholly to be barbarous vulturous *Chactaws,*[3] and become noble European Nineteenth-Century Men. Ye shall know that Mammon, in never such gigs and flunky "respectabilities," is not the alone God; that of himself he is but a Devil, and even a Brute-god.

Difficult? Yes, it will be difficult. The short-fibre cotton; that too was difficult. The waste cotton-shrub, long useless, disobedient, as the thistle by the wayside,—have ye not conquered it; made it into beautiful bandana webs; white woven shirts for men; bright-tinted air-garments wherein flit goddesses? Ye have shivered mountains asunder, made the hard iron pliant to you as soft putty: the Forest-giants, Marsh-jötuns bear sheaves of golden grain; Ægir the Sea-demon himself stretches his back for a sleek highway to you, and on Fire-horses and Windhorses ye career. Ye are most strong. Thor red-bearded, with his blue sun-eyes, with his cheery heart and strong thunder-hammer, he and you have prevailed. Ye are most strong, ye Sons of the icy North, of the far East,—far marching from your rugged Eastern Wildernesses, hitherward from the grey Dawn of Time! Ye are Sons of the *Jötun*-land; the land of Difficulties Conquered. Difficult? You must try this thing. Once try it with the under-

---

3. "Chactaws" or Choctaws, were a nation of Native Americans who farmed in the Southeast United States until they were forced, in 1832, to "remove" to the Indian Territory in Oklahoma. They may have been featured in the British press for this reason and become familiar to Carlyle. [Ed.]

standing that it will and shall have to be done. Try it as ye try the paltrier thing, making of money! I will bet on you once more, against all Jötuns, Tailor-gods, Double-barrelled Law-wards, and Denizens of Chaos whatsoever!

KARL MARX

THE FACTORY

At the commencement of this chapter we considered that which we may call the body of the factory, i.e., machinery organised into a system. We there saw how machinery, by annexing the labour of women and children, augments the number of human beings who form the material for capitalistic exploitation, how it confiscates the whole of the workman's disposable time, by immoderate extension of the hours of labour, and how finally its progress, which allows of enormous increase of production in shorter and shorter periods, serves as a means of systematically getting more work done in a shorter time, or of exploiting labour-power more intensely. We now turn to the factory as a whole, and that in its most perfect form.

Dr. Ure, the *Pindar*[1] of the automatic factory, describes it, on the one hand as "Combined co-operation of many orders of work-people, adult and young, in tending with assiduous skill, a system of productive machines, continuously impelled by a central power" the prime mover; on the other hand, as "a vast automaton, composed of various mechanical and intellectual organs, acting in uninterrupted concert for the production of a common object, all of them being subordinate to a self-regulated moving force." These two descriptions are far from being identical. In one, the collective labourer, or social body of labour, appears as the dominant subject, and the mechanical automaton as the object; in the other, the automaton itself is the subject, and the workmen are merely conscious organs, co-ordinate with the unconscious organs of the automaton, and together with them, subordinated to the central moving-power. The first description is applicable to every possible employment of machinery on a large scale, the second is characteristic of its use by capital,

---

From *Capital: A Critique of Political Economy.* Vol. I. Samuel Moore and Edward Aveling, trans. New York: International Publishers, 1967.

1. Pindar is often regarded as the greatest of Greek lyric poets. This is a typically sarcastic comparison by Marx. [Ed.]

	Quantity Exported, 1848.	Quantity Exported, 1851.	Quantity Exported, 1860.	Quantity Exported, 1865.
COTTON				
Cotton yarn	lbs.	lbs.	lbs.	lbs.
	135,831,162	143,966,106	197,343,655	103,751,455
Sewing thread	lbs.	lbs.	lbs.	lbs.
		4,392,176	6,297,554	4,648,611
Cotton cloth	yds.	yds.	yds.	yds.
	1,091,373,930	1,543,161,789	2,776,218,427	2,015,237,851
FLAX & HEMP				
Yarn	lbs.	lbs.	lbs.	lbs.
	11,722,182	18,841,326	31,210,612	36,777,334
Cloth	yds.	yds.	yds.	yds.
	88,901,519	129,106,753	143,996,773	247,012,529
SILK				
Yarn	lbs.	lbs.	lbs.	lbs.
	466,825	462,513	897,402	812,589
Cloth	yds.	yds.	yds.	yds.
		1,181,455	1,307,293	2,869,837
WOOL				
Woollen and	lbs.	lbs.	lbs.	lbs.
Worsted yarns		14,670,880	27,533,968	1,669,267
Cloth	yds.	yds.	yds.	yds.
		241,120,973	190,381,537	278,837,438

and therefore of the modern factory system. Ure prefers therefore, to describe the central machine, from which the motion comes, not only as an automaton, but as an autocrat. "In these spacious halls the benignant power of steam summons around him his myriads of willing menials."[2]

Along with the tool, the skill of the workman in handling it passes over to the machine. The capabilities of the tool are emancipated from the restraints that are inseparable from human labour-power. Thereby the technical foundation on which is based the division of labour in Manufacture, is swept away. Hence, in the place of the hierarchy of specialised workmen that characterises manufacture, there steps, in the automatic factory, a tendency to equalise and reduce to one and the same level every kind of work that has to be done by the

2. Andrew Ure, *The Philosophy of Manufactures.* 2nd ed. London: 1835, p. 18 [Ed.]

	Value Exported, 1848.	Value Exported, 1851.	Value Exported, 1860.	Value Exported, 1865.
COTTON	£	£	£	£
Yarn	5,927,831	6,634,026	9,870,875	10,351,04
Cloth	16,753,369	23,454,810	42,141,505	46,903,796
FLAX & HEMP				
Yarn	493,449	951,426	1,801,272	2,505,497
Cloth	2,802,789	4,107,396	4,804,803	9,155,318
SILK				
Yarn		195,380	918,342	768,067
Cloth	77,789	1,130,398	1,587,303	1,409,221
WOOL				
Yarn	776,975	1,484,544	3,843,450	5,424,017
Cloth	5,733,828	8,377,183	12,156,998	20,102,259

See the Blue books "Statistical Abstract of the United Kingdom," Nos. 8 and 13. Lond., 1861 and 1866. In Lancashire the number of mills increased only 4 per cent. between 1839 and 1850; 19 per cent. between 1850 and 1856; and 33 per cent. between 1856 and 1862; while the persons employed in them during each of the above periods of 11 years increased absolutely, but diminished relatively. (See "Rep. of Insp. of Fact., for 31st Oct., 1862," p. 63.) The cotton trade preponderates in Lancashire. We may form an idea of the stupendous nature of the cotton trade in that district when we consider that, of the gross number of textile factories in the United Kingdom, it absorbs 45.2 per cent., of the spindles 83.3 per cent., of the powerlooms 81.4 per cent., of the mechanical horse-power 72.6 per cent., and of the total number of persons employed 58.2 per cent. (l. c., pp. 62–63.)

minders of the machines;[3] in the place of the artificially produced differentiations of the detail workmen, step the natural differences of age and sex.

So far as division of labour re-appears in the factory, it is primarily a distribution of the workmen among the specialised machines; and of masses of workmen, not however organised into groups, among the various departments of the factory, in each of which they work at a number of similar machines placed together; their co-operation, therefore, is only simple. The organised group, peculiar to manufacture, is replaced by the connexion between the head workman and his few assistants. The essential division is, into workmen who are actually employed on the machines (among whom are included a few who look after the engine), and into mere attendants (almost exclusively children) of these workmen. Among the attendants are reckoned more or less all "Feeders" who supply the machines with the material to be worked. In addi-

---

3. Ure, ibid., p. 31.

tion to these two principal classes, there is a numerically unimportant class of persons, whose occupation it is to look after the whole of the machinery and repair it from time to time; such as engineers, mechanics, joiners, &c. This is a superior class of workmen, some of them scientifically educated, others brought up to a trade; it is distinct from the factory operative class, and merely aggregated to it.[4] This division of labour is purely technical.

To work at a machine, the workman should be taught from childhood, in order that he may learn to adapt his own movements to the uniform and unceasing motion of an automation. When the machinery, as a whole, forms a system of manifold machines, working simultaneously and in concert, the co-operation based upon it, requires the distribution of various groups of workmen among the different kinds of machines. But the employment of machinery does away with the necessity of crystallising this distribution after the manner of Manufacture, by the constant annexation of a particular man to a particular function.[5] Since the motion of the whole system does not proceed from the workman, but from the machinery, a change of persons can take place at any time without an interruption of the work. The most striking proof of this is afforded by the *relays system,* put into operation by the manufacturers during their revolt from 1848–1850. Lastly, the quickness with which machine work is learnt by young people, does away with the necessity of bringing up for exclusive employment by machinery, a special class of operatives.[6] With regard to the work of the mere attendants, it can, to some extent, be re-

---

4. It looks very like intentional misleading by statistics (which misleading it would be possible to prove in detail in other cases too), when the English factory legislation excludes from its operation the class of labourers last mentioned in the text, while the parliamentary returns expressly include in the category of factory operatives, not only engineers, mechanics, &c., but also managers, salesmen, messengers, warehousemen, packers, &c., in short everybody, except the owner of the factory himself.

5. Ure grants this. He says, "in case of need," the workmen can be moved at the will of the manager from one machine to another, and he triumphantly exclaims: "Such a change is in flat contradiction with the old routine, that divides the labour, and to one workman assigns the task of fashioning the head of a needle, to another the sharpening of the point." He had much better have asked himself, why this "old routine" is departed from in the automatic factory, only "in case of need."

6. When distress is very great, as, for instance, during the American Civil War, the factory operative is now and then set by the Bourgeois to do the roughest of work, such as road-making, &c. The English "ateliers nationaux" of 1862 and the following years, established for the benefit of the destitute cotton operatives, differ from the French of 1848 in this, that in the latter the workmen had to do unproductive work at the expense of the state, in the former they had to do productive municipal work to the advantage of the bourgeois, and that, too, cheaper than the regular workmen, with whom they were thus thrown into competition. "The physical appearance of the cotton operatives is unquestionably improved. This I attribute . . . as to the men, to outdoor labour on public works." ("Rep. of Insp. of Fact., 31st Oct., 1863," p. 59.) The writer here alludes to the Preston factory operatives, who were employed on Preston Moor.

placed in the mill by machines, and owing to its extreme simplicity, it allows of a rapid and constant change of the individuals burdened with this drudgery.

Although then, technically speaking, the old system of division of labour is thrown overboard by machinery, it hangs on in the factory, as a traditional habit handed down from Manufacture, and is afterwards systematically re-moulded and established in a more hideous form by capital, as a means of exploiting labour-power. The life-long speciality of handling one and the same tool, now becomes the life-long speciality of serving one and the same machine. Machinery is put to a wrong use, with the object of transforming the workman, from his very childhood, into a part of a detail-machine.[7] In this way, not only are the expenses of his reproduction considerably lessened, but at the same time his helpless dependence upon the factory as a whole, and therefore upon the capitalist, is rendered complete. Here as everywhere else, we must distinguish between the increased productiveness due to the development of the social process of production, and that due to the capitalist exploitation of that process. In handicrafts and manufacture, the workman makes use of a tool, in the factory, the machine makes use of him. There the movements of the instrument of labour proceed from him, here it is the movements of the machine that he must follow. In manufacture the workmen are parts of a living mechanism. In the factory we have a lifeless mechanism independent of the workman, who becomes its mere living appendage. "The miserable routine of endless drudgery and toil in which the same mechanical process is gone through over and over again, is like the labour of Sisyphus. The burden of labour, like the rock, keeps ever falling back on the worn-out labourer."[8] At the same time that factory work exhausts the nervous system to the uttermost, it does away with the many-sided play of the muscles, and confiscates every atom of freedom, both in bodily and intellectual activity.[9] The lightening of the labour, even, becomes a sort of torture, since the machine does not free the labourer from work, but deprives the work of all interest. Every kind of capitalist production, in so far as it is not only a labour-process, but also a process of creating surplus-value, has this in common, that it is not the workman that employs the instruments of labour, but the instruments of labour that employ the work-

---

7. So much then for Proudhon's wonderful idea: he "construes" machinery not as a synthesis of instruments of labour, but as a synthesis of detail operations for the benefit of the labourer himself.

8. F. Engels, *Die Lage der arbeitenden Klasse in England*, Liepzig (1845), p. 217. Even an ordinary and optimist Free-trader, like Mr. Molinari, goes so far as to say, "Un homme s'use plus vite en surveillant, quinze heures par jour, l'évolution uniforme d'un mécanisme, qu'en exerçant, dans le même espace de temps, sa force physique. Ce travail de surveillance qui servirait peut-être d'utile gymnastique à l'intelligence, s'il n'était pas trop prolongé, détruit à la longue, par son excès, et l'intelligence, et le corps même." (G. de Molinari: "Études Économiques." Paris, 1846.)

9. F. Engels, ibid., p. 216.

man. But it is only in the factory system that this inversion for the first time acquires technical and palpable reality. By means of its conversion into an automaton, the instrument of labour confronts the labourer, during the labour-process, in the shape of capital, of dead labour, that dominates, and pumps dry, living labour-power. The separation of the intellectual powers of production from the manual labour, and the conversion of those powers into the might of capital over labour, is, as we have already shown, finally completed by modern industry erected on the foundation of machinery. The special skill of each individual insignificant factory operative vanishes as an infinitesimal quantity before the science, the gigantic physical forces, and the mass of labour that are embodied in the factory mechanism and, together with that mechanism, constitute the power of the "master." This "master," therefore, in whose brain the machinery and his monopoly of it are inseparably united, whenever he falls out with his "hands," contemptuously tells them: "The factory operatives should keep in wholesome remembrance the fact that theirs is really a low species of skilled labour; and that there is none which is more easily acquired, or of its quality more amply remunerated, or which by a short training of the least expert can be more quickly, as well as abundantly, acquired. . . . The master's machinery really plays a far more important part in the business of production than the labour and the skill of the operative, which six months' education can teach, and a common labourer can learn."[10] The technical subordination of the workman to the uniform motion of the instruments of labour, and the peculiar composition of the body of workpeople, consisting as it does of individuals of both sexes and of all ages, give rise to a barrack discipline, which is elaborated into a complete system in the factory, and which fully develops the before mentioned labour of overlooking, thereby dividing the workpeople into operatives and overlookers, into private soldiers and sergeants of an industrial army. "The main difficulty [in the automatic factory] . . . lay . . . above all in training human beings to renounce their desultory habits of work, and to identify themselves with the unvarying regularity of the complex automaton. To devise and administer a successful code of factory discipline, suited to the necessities of factory diligence, was the Herculean enterprise, the noble achievement of Arkwright! Even at the present day, when the system is perfectly organised and its labour lightened to the utmost, it is found nearly impossible to convert persons past the age of puberty, into useful factory hands."[11] The factory code in which capital formulates, like a private legislator, and at his own good will, his au-

---

10. "The Master Spinners' and Manufacturers' Defence Fund. Report of the Committee." Manchester, 1854, p. 17. We shall see hereafter, that the "master" can sing quite another song, when he is threatened with the loss of his "living" automaton.

11. Ure, op. cit. p. 15. Whoever knows the life history of Arkwright, will never dub this barber-genius "noble." Of all the great inventors of the 18th century, he was incontestably the greatest thiever of other people's inventions and the meanest fellow.

tocracy over his workpeople, unaccompanied by that division of responsibility, in other matters so much approved of by the bourgeoisie, and unaccompanied by the still more approved representative system, this code is but the capitalistic caricature of that social regulation of the labour-process which becomes requisite in co-operation on a great scale, and in the employment in common, of instruments of labour and especially of machinery. The place of the slave-driver's lash is taken by the overlooker's book of penalties. All punishments naturally resolve themselves into fines and deductions from wages, and the law-giving talent of the factory Lycurgus so arranges matters, that a violation of his laws is, if possible, more profitable to him than the keeping of them.[12]

---

12. "The slavery in which the bourgeoisie has bound the proletariat, comes nowhere more plainly into daylight than in the factory system. In it all freedom comes to an end both at law and in fact. The workman must be in the factory at half past five. If he come a few minutes late, he is punished; if he come 10 minutes late, he is not allowed to enter until after breakfast, and thus loses a quarter of a day's wage. He must eat, drink and sleep at word of command . . . The despotic bell calls him from his bed, calls him from breakfast and dinner. And how does he fare in the mill? There the master is the absolute law-giver. He makes what regulations he pleases; he alters and makes additions to his code at pleasure; and if he insert the veriest nonsense, the courts say to the workman: Since you have entered into this contract voluntarily, you must now carry it out . . . These workmen are condemned to live, from their ninth year till their death, under this mental and bodily torture." (F. Engels, op. cit., p. 217, sq.) What, "the courts say," I will illustrate by two examples. One occurs at Sheffield at the end of 1866. In that town a workman had engaged himself for 2 years in a steelworks. In consequence of a quarrel with his employer he left the works, and declared that under no circumstances would he work for that master any more. He was prosecuted for breach of contract, and condemned to two months' imprisonment. (If the master break the contract, he can be proceeded against only in a civil action, and risks nothing but money damages.) After the workman has served his two months, the master invites him to return to the works, pursuant to the contract. Workman says: No, he has already been punished for the breach. The master prosecutes again, the court condemns again, although one of the judges, Mr. Shee, publicly denounces this as a legal monstrosity, by which a man can periodically, as long as he lives, be punished over and over again for the same offence or crime. This judgment was given not by the "Great Unpaid," the provincial Dogberries, but by one of the highest courts of justice in London.—[*Added in the 4th German edition.*—This has now been done away with. With few exceptions, *e.g.,* when public gas-works are involved, the worker in England is now put on an equal footing with the employer in case of breach of contract and can be sued only civilly.—*F.E.*] The second case occurs in Wiltshire at the end of November 1863. About 30 power-loom weavers, in the employment of one Harrup, a cloth manufacturer at Leower's Mill, Westbury Leigh, struck work because master Harrup indulged in the agreeable habit of making deductions from their wages for being late in the morning; 6d. for 2 minutes; 1s. for 3 minutes, and 1s. 6d. for ten minutes. This is at the rate of 9s. per hour, and £4 10s. 0d. per diem; while the wages of the weavers on the average of a year, never exceeded 10s. to 12s. weekly. Harrup also appointed a boy to announce the starting time by a whistle, which he often did before six o'clock in the morning: and if the hands were not all there at the moment the whistle ceased, the doors were closed, and those hands who were outside were fined: and as there was no clock on the premises, the unfortunate hands were at the mercy of the young Harrup-inspired time-keeper. The hands on strike, mothers of families as well as girls, offered to resume work if the time-keeper were replaced by a clock, and a more reasonable scale of fines were intro-

We shall here merely allude to the material conditions under which factory labour is carried on. Every organ of sense is injured in an equal degree by artificial elevation of the temperature, by the dust-laden atmosphere, by the deafening noise, not to mention danger to life and limb among the thickly crowded machinery, which, with the regularity of the seasons, issues its list of the killed and wounded in the industrial battle.[13] Economy of the social means

duced. Harrup summoned 19 women and girls before the magistrates for breach of contract. To the utter indignation of all present, they were each mulcted in a fine of 6d. and 2s. 6d. for costs. Harrup was followed from the court by a crowd of people who hissed him.— A favourite operation with manufacturers is to punish the workpeople by deductions made from their wages on account of faults in the material worked on. This method gave rise in 1866 to a general strike in the English pottery districts. The reports of the Ch. Empl. Com. (1863–1866), give cases where the worker not only receives no wages, but becomes, by means of his labour, and of the penal regulations, the debtor to boot, of his worthy master. The late cotton crisis also furnished edifying examples of the sagacity shown by the factory autocrats in making deductions from wages. Mr. R. Baker, the Inspector of Factories, says, "I have myself had lately to direct prosecutions against one cotton mill occupier for having in these pinching and painful times deducted 10d. a piece from some of the young workers employed by him, for the surgeon's certificate (for which he himself had only paid 6d.), when only allowed by the law to deduct 3d., and by custom nothing at all . . . And I have been informed of another, who, in order to keep without the law, but to attain the same object, charges the poor children who work for him a shilling each, as a fee for learning them the art and mystery of cotton spinning, so soon as they are declared by the surgeon fit and proper persons for that occupation. There may therefore be undercurrent causes for such extraordinary exhibitions as strikes, not only wherever they arise, but particularly at such times as the present, which without explanation, render them inexplicable to the public understanding." He alludes here to a strike of power-loom weavers at Darwen, June, 1863. ("Reports of Insp. of Fact. for 30 April, 1863," pp. 50–51.) The reports always go beyond their official dates.

13. The protection afforded by the Factory Acts against dangerous machinery has had a beneficial effect. "But . . . there are other sources of accident which did not exist twenty years since; one especially, viz., the increased speed of the machinery. Wheels, rollers, spindles and shuttles are now propelled at increased and increasing rates; fingers must be quicker and defter in their movements to take up the broken thread, for, if placed with hesitation or carelessness, they are sacrificed. . . . A large number of accidents are caused by the eagerness of the workpeople to get through their work expeditiously. It must be remembered that it is of the highest importance to manufacturers that their machinery should be in motion, *i.e.,* producing yarns and goods. Every minute's stoppage is not only a loss of power, but of production, and the workpeople are urged by the overlookers, who are interested in the quantity of work turned off, to keep the machinery in motion; and it is no less important to those of the operatives who are paid by the weight or piece, that the machines should be kept in motion. Consequently, although it is strictly forbidden in many, nay in most factories, that machinery should be cleaned while in motion, it is nevertheless the constant practice in most, if not in all, that the workpeople do, unreproved, pick out waste, wipe rollers and wheels, &c., while their frames are in motion. Thus from this cause only, 906 accidents have occurred during the six months. . . . Although a great deal of cleaning is constantly going on day by day, yet Saturday is generally the day set apart for the thorough cleaning of the machinery, and a great deal of this is done while the machinery is in motion." Since cleaning is not paid for, the workpeople seek to get done with it as speedily as possible. Hence "the number of accidents which occur on Fridays, and especially on Saturdays, is much larger than on any other day. On the former day the excess is nearly 12 per cent. over the average number of the four first days of the week, and on the latter day the

of production, matured and forced as in a hothouse by the factory system, is turned, in the hands of capital, into systematic robbery of what is necessary for the life of the workman while he is at work, robbery of space, light, air, and of protection to his person against the dangerous and unwholesome accompaniments of the productive process, not to mention the robbery of appliances for the comfort of the workman.[14] Is Fourier wrong when he calls factories "tempered bagnos"?[15]

---

excess is 25 per cent. over the average of the preceding five days; or, if the number of working-hours on Saturday being taken into account—$7\frac{1}{2}$ hours on Saturday as compared with $10\frac{1}{2}$ on other days—there is an excess of 65 per cent. on Saturdays over the average of the other five days." ("Rep. of Insp. of Fact., 31st Oct., 1866," pp. 9, 15, 16, 17.)

14. Charles Fourier (1772–1837) was a French philosopher who formulated a theory of socialist utopia. [Ed.]

15. "Tempered bagno" probably means in this context a somewhat improved prison or brothel. The idea is that factories have been improved to accommodate advances in machinery and that workers have benefited from this but remain imprisoned or, like prostitutes, physically oppressed by their work. [Ed.]

CHAPTER FIVE

PRACTICE

GEORGE BEAUMONT
❈

from THE BEGGAR'S COMPLAINT

It will, no doubt, be gratifying to some Readers, to be made acquainted with the origin of *Luddism*. From the enquiries I made in Nottinghamshire, where Luddism originated, I learnt the following particulars, namely, That a good many years ago, there lived a poor man at Loughborough, in Leicestershire, about fifteen miles from Nottingham, whose name was *Edward Ludd:* This man was not one of the brightest cast, in regard to his intellects; and, as is commonly the case with such characters, was of an irritable temper. This *Edward Ludd,* called by his neighbours *Ned Ludd,* was by trade a *Frame Work Knitter:* or in plainer language, and which is all the same, a *Stocking Weaver.* This man, being irritated, either by his Employer, or his work, or both, took the desperate resolution of avenging himself, by breaking his *Stocking Frame.* As the value of a common Stocking Frame is considerable, being not much less than Forty Pounds, Ned's exploit was much more admired for its temerity than its utility.

However, the consequence of this affair was, a *Bon Mot:* for, whenever any Stocking Weaver was out of patience with his Employer or his Employment, he would say, speaking of his Frame, "I have good mind to *Ned Ludd* it": meaning, *I have a good mind to break it, &c.*

About the latter end of the year 1811, the Stocking and Lace Weavers of Nottingham, having been for a long time harrassed by abridged wages, and

---

From *The Luddites: Three Pamphlets, 1812–1839.* New York: Arno Press, 1972.

want of employment, in whole or in part, and consequently with want of bread, entered into a combination, (as report says, upon oath) to break certain proscribed Frames. But it should here be observed, that the interdicted Frames were not all of a new-invented kind, there being many destined to destruction for the sake of their *owner;* the owner having rendered himself notorious by abridging the workmen's wages, and underselling other manufacturers: therefore many Frames of an ordinary construction were broken.

These Frame-Breakers assumed the name of their proto-type *Ned Ludd.* Hence when they entered a house in order to break Frames, they would say *Ned Ludd* or *General Ludd,* commands us to break these Frames, &c. These men, collectively, were therefore called *Luddites,* and their system was, and is, called *Luddism.*

This system has been communicated to thousands; and as rumour says, to hundreds of thousands, and is still in existence. But it does not always exist where report places it; for every thief and highwayman now takes the name of *Ned Ludd* in his mouth when he is about to commit his depredations; and News Printers seem very willing to have it so; most of them caring very little about the difference betwixt truth and falsehood; their drift too commonly is, to enhance the value of their Papers, by saying something that will surprise and astonish their readers. The old and stale names of *thief, high-wayman,* and *robber,* will not now adorn the *great news* columns of those Papers which are ever seeking to treat their Readers with a mess of Wonderment! Therefore *Ned Ludd* being a new character, is made to bear the heat and burden of the day; for whatever enormities are committed in the counties where *Ned* lives, they are, for the most part, very carefully ascribed to him.

Of the fourteen unfortunate men who were executed at York, on the 15th Jan. 1813, not one-half of them, as I am informed, were in reality Luddites. Either five or six of them were Luddites, who were convicted of entering houses and demanding fire-arms, or breaking, or attempting to break machinery; part of them upon one charge, and part of them upon the other. As to the rest of the fourteen, they were, as I am informed, utter strangers to the system of Luddism: but knowing something of Luddism by popular rumour, they had designated themselves Luddites. Wherefore on entering a house they would preface their demand of money, by telling the people General Ludd was come: or that Ned Ludd had sent them to make such and such a demand. Information of the transaction soon reached the ears of a News Printer: who, glad enough of something fresh to tell his Readers, soon laid it before the public: his fellow Newsmen would copy his statement, and thus this wonderful news which was half true and half false, ran, in the compass of a week, all over the three kingdoms.

With regard to the conduct of the Luddites in breaking Machinery, I wholly disapprove of it: it is altogether condemnable: for in my opinion, Machinery ought to be encouraged to any extent whatever. It is also my opinion, that every man that invents any thing that will lessen human labour, is a benefactor to mankind, and ought to be rewarded, not by a patent, as is commonly the case, but out of the national purse, in order that he and others may be encouraged to new exertions, and the public benefitted by the free use of such inventions!

I pity the poor, and should hardly think myself innocent if any man felt more for them than I do; but the remedy for their grievances, lies not in the destruction of Machinery. They are oppressed exceedingly, but not by Machinery. Those who accuse Machinery of causing any part of the distresses of the poor, have very contracted views and narrow minds, and see but a little way. They do not seem to consider that almost every thing was new Machinery once. There was a time when corn was ground by the hand; and when Corn Mills and Wind Mills were first invented they were *New Machinery;* and therefore why not break and burn these as soon as any other kind of Machinery; for if they were all stopped, and corn again ground by the hand, there would be plenty of employment for many hands! Much the same observations might be made respecting every other kind of Machinery, and I have asked this question in order to shew the silliness of the practice.

The grievous distresses of the poor are occasioned by the Monopolization of Landed Property Rack Rents—Large Farms—War, and its Concomitants, Bad Trade and Excessive Taxation. The remedy for all which is, PEACE and REFORM; without these, bad will become worse, and worse will be utter *ruin!*

Nor can I forego the present opportunity of noticing the practice that has long obtained among Journeymen of various callings, respecting Apprentices. Ever since I can remember, feuds and quarrels have subsisted betwixt the Employers and the Employed respecting workmen called *illegal men;* and also an *allowed* number of *Apprentices:* and the proper, or *lawful time* of servitude in Apprenticeships, &c. &c. To me these altercations have always appeared highly reprehensible, because at the best they originate in ignorance, and not unfrequently in something less excuseable. But, be their origin what it may, they commonly generate litigations and enmity; and sometimes they separate chief friends, and greatly exasperate and injure individuals.

Now, is it not folly, or something worse, for one man to vex and harrass another, either respecting his servants as a Master, or his servitude as an Apprentice? What right, either in law or reason, has one man to teaze and distress another on these considerations? There is nothing, there can be nothing but what is both unjust and unreasonable in such conduct. With regard to Apprentices, there ought in reason to be no constraints or restrictions laid upon them or their Masters, respecting the length or shortness of their servitude: let the parties concerned arbitrate the conditions according to their own discretion.

And is it not notorious also, that there are some branches of trade, some arts and callings, that are not half so mysterious and difficult of attainment as others? and some young men there are who by dint of superior gifts and mental endowments from nature, will learn a trade in three, or even two years, as perfectly as others will learn the same trade in seven years. Is it not unjust then, is it not highly unreasonable that the narrow minded policy of selfish ignorance, should institute schemes of restriction to superscede the bounties of nature. Would it be equitable to compel a man of two yards high, to take as many strides in walking a mile, as a man of five feet? And is it any more equitable to compel young men of all geniuses and capacities, to run over the same precise round of seven years in the acquisition of a trade. It is in vain to declaim against aristocracies and privileged orders, until this selfish and vexatious conduct be abandoned: for what are all these petty monopolies and sinister exclusious, but the exhibitions of aristocracy in low life!

Hatters, Calico-Printers, Curriers, and indeed men of some other branches, have been extremely active in this kind of folly: for what is it but folly; seeing that when men are debarred from the readiest access to one calling, they will, they must betake themselves to another calling! Therefore all those laws of restriction and exclusion have no other effect than that of harrassing and shoving men from one place to another: for these harassed men are still in the world, and must be supported: the result of the whole therefore is, much trouble to individuals, and no gain to society.

Nor ought I to pass over the vexatious privileges and conduct of *Corporations*. The immunities and privileges of these bodies of men, have ever been, in my humble opinion, inimical to general happiness: for who does not see, or at least who may not see, that *Civil Privileges* granted to some, are *Civil Privations* to others. These privileges were, for the most part, granted by Kings in days of yore, and in times of ignorance; and whenever the time shall arrive that reason shall over-rule precedent, and general happiness be preferred to private interest, these laws of immunity shall be abrogated, and Corporations annihilated.

I have known a *Corporation,* not quite two hundred miles from *York,* extort from a poor Tailor, who wished to set up in business in that part of the world, either thirty or fifty pounds, I have forgot which, as the price of his *Freedom!* The poor Tailor toiled hard and long to pay this cruel extortion: however, he did pay it by instalments, and length of time; and thus obtained permission to labour quietly for his bread!

Here it will be a reasonable question to ask, to what purposes Corporations apply the monies they obtain by these extortions. I pretend not to know all the art and mystery of these Privileged Bodies of men, but of one thing I am certain, namely, that they make themselves very costly *Dinners* and *Suppers:* and that at these festivals they drink a good deal of what some people are pleased to call *good stuff:* and I must in conscience say, that it is neither decent nor honest for men, many of whom are worth hundreds, and some of whom are worth thousands, to sit and gormandize and guzzle the hard earnings of poor Tailors!

With regard to labourers and mechanics, and poor men in general, their case is evidently very deplorable; but I think it is much worse in reality than in appearance. *Law, Wealth,* and *War,* are all against the poor man. Hence, says a French Writer, ROUSSEAU,[1] *"The universal spirit of all laws in all countries, is to favor the strong in opposition to the weak; and to assist those who have possessions against those who have none."*—This Frenchman's allegation is sufficiently verified in the case of Masters and Workmen. Against combinations of Workmen, formed for the purpose of raising wages, there are *acts* and statutes plenty; but, says Dr. Adam Smith,[2] in his *Wealth of Nations,* "against Combinations of Masters for the purpose of lowering wages, there is no existing law!" And should any one say that Masters never combine for the purpose of lowering wages, I will answer him in the words of the Author just mentioned:——"We rarely hear, it has been said, of the combinations of Masters, though frequently of those of Workmen. But whoever imagines on this account, that Masters rarely combine, is as ignorant of the world as of the subject. Masters are always and every where in a sort of tacit, but constant and uniform combination, not to raise their wages above their actual rate. To violate this combination is every where a most unpopular action, and a sort of reproach to a Master among his neighbours and equals. We seldom, indeed, hear of this combination, because it is the usual, and one may say, the natural state of things which nobody ever hears of. Masters too sometimes enter into particular combinations to sink the wages of labour even below this rate. These are always conducted with the utmost silence and secrecy, till the moment of execution, and when the workmen yield, as they sometimes do, without resistance, though severely felt by them, they are never heard of by other people."

About two years ago, the Cotton Weavers of Manchester, and its vicinity, having long had their wages abridged in an extreme degree, were reduced by excessive labour, and half maintainance, nearly to skeletons. They were also become ragged and forlorn: and those who had wives and children, as many of them had, had the mortification to see these natural dependents as ghastly and wretched as themselves. Even single men, in general, found it impossible

---

1. Jean-Jacques Rousseau (1712–1778) was a Swiss-French philosopher who valued "nature" over what he saw as the depredations of social and cultural forms. He famously believed that humans are by nature good, but then corrupted by society. His doctrine of popular sovereignty had a great impact on French Revolutionary thought. He is the author of the novels *Julie, or the Nouvelle Heloïse* and *Emile,* of the theoretical *The Social Contract,* and the autobiographical *Confessions* among other works. [Ed.]
2. See the Biographies section at the end of this volume. [Ed.]

by all their exertions, to procure for themselves a sufficiency of the necessaries of life. The patience of the Weavers under these severe privations, was worthy of admiration. Disinclination to turbulence, and expectation of better times, induced many to hold their patience until they lost their lives, and when they had done, but few rich people cared a straw for them.

The Weavers moreover shewed their unwillingness to disturb the public tranquility, by peace ably sending two Delegates to Government, in order to represent their distressed situations. These Delegates found their way to *Mr. Secretary Ryder,* and to him they stated the purport of their mission, hoping that he would become the medium of their complaints so the supreme authorities. But, Mr. Secretary Ryder, who, no doubt, eats, well, drinks well, dresses well, and sleeps well, had learned the readiest way of dispatching *some sorts* of business, for he told the poor, meagre, ragged Weavers, through the medium of their Delegates, that, "*they must have patience!*"

Being defeated in this peaceable and prudent measure, the Weavers had recourse to another, which was, to convene a public meeting of all the Masters, and some chosen Weavers, who should conjointly arbitrate the rate of Wages for the various kinds of work: Some few of the Magistrates were also friendly to this plan of procedure. A few of the Masters seemed willing to subject themselves to this mode of decision; but the greater part of them, assumed an aristocratic air of superiority, and therefore affected to scorn the very idea of debating points and compromising differences with mere workmen! The consequence was, that at one of the meetings which had been convened by mutual consent, only three Masters made their appearance, and it was not without reason suspected, that even those three came with no better design than that of seeing who did come to the meeting and who did not, and also of carrying away all the information they could to their colleagues, respecting the transactions of the Meeting.

Here it will be proper to state the pleas of the respective parties, that is, of the *Masters* on the one side, and the *Workmen* on the other. The Masters pleaded in justification of their conduct in abridging of wages, "*the extreme badness of trade.*" The Weavers replied to this, by saying, that "*the Trade could not, at least be extremely bad, seeing they had found by long and painful experience, that in the midst of all the complaints of bad trade, there was still work enough for those who would do it for almost nothing!*" As this reply of the work people was founded in plain, broad fact, it was impossible it could be controverted with success. Indeed it is not without reason suspected that many men of capital greatly augmented their fortunes at that period, and chiefly by getting much work done for little money!

The Weavers finding the Masters unwilling to bind themselves to any terms, or to make any compromise with them, began to hold public Meetings in the open air. These Meetings were called, I apprehend, for the purpose of devising means of redress, independent of the Masters, unless the Masters would willingly accede. The Weavers also unanimously struck work, or at least, those who would not, had their work spoiled in their looms.

Now it was that Masters and Magistrates began to bestir themselves. Dragoons were called out: Special Constables were sworn: Power and alacrity were every where to be seen. Two men, I think, were killed on the occasion, at Manchester; one of the two who had no more to do in the business than the Emperor of Morocco, was shot by a Dragoon, when coming down a passage from his own house. Many Weavers were seized on this, and other occasions, and, as is usual on such occurrences, were called *Ringleaders.* They were sent to jails, and, after some time, tried, for breaking the peace, assembling tumultuously, rioting, &c. &c. and were accordingly variously dealt with as their *crimes* merited! In the affair at Manchester just mentioned, originated the prosecution and imprisonment of that respectable Gentleman, of independent fortune, *Colonel Hanson,* who was, in consequence, imprisoned six months, and amerced, I think, fifty pounds.

Here then, reader, a brief recapitulation will give thee a distinct view of this grievous business:—In the first place, the Weavers were long impoverished by abridged Wages, even until their existence became a burthen——they then took the prudent measure of sending Delegates to represent their condition to Government, and to implore redress; and this they did more than once: but this mode was ineffectual, as the Masters failed not to counteract their efforts, either openly or secretly. They then called upon the Masters to meet them and enter into fair discussion on the subject; they also called upon the Magistrates to join both parties, and act as Mediators in the business: but the Masters would never enter honestly and unanimously into conditions with those whom habit and commercial policy had taught them to keep at a distance; and the Magistrates, being more nearly allied to the Masters by rank and fortune, and also more familiar with them by convivial interviews, dealt in the business with but a slack hand. It may be added, likewise, that some of the Magistrates had been Masters themselves: and to all the rest it must be superadded, that there is no existing law against the practice of abridging Wages!

The Weavers seeing no prospect of any help from *others,* began now to think of helping *themselves.* They accordingly began to assemble in large bodies in the open air, and in the day time. They adopted strong measures: one of which was to work no more at all until their Wages should be augmented. They also spoiled the Work of those Weavers who entered not into their combination. They were then seized by Dragoons and Constables, and sent in groups to prison; besides being loaded with soul epithets, and disgraceful names, such as *litigious fellows, movers of sedition, mischief makers, disturbers of the public peace, &c.* for it is not the way of wealth and power in modern times, to redress grievances and remove oppressions; but rather to stifle complaints, and suppress remonstrances by Dragoons, Prisons, Gibbets, and and Foul Names! And to complete the miseries of the miserable, the News Printers generally echo the language of authority, seldom or never having the manly fortitude to slate to the public what they really believe respecting the actual condition of the poor. Thus are these words of Solomon verified, *The poor is hated,* (that is, despised and abandoned) *even of his own neighbour, but the Rich hath many friends* Prov. xiv, 20. And the observation of the Famous, or, as some would have it, the Infamous Machiavel[3] are not inapposite here, *Every man,* says he, *has liberty to speak what he pleases against the people, but against a Prince no man can task without a thousand apprehensions and dangers.*

Hear also, what Dr. Goldsmith[4] says, in his Citizen of the World:—"The slightest misfortune of the Great, the most imaginary uneasiness of the Rich, are aggravated with all the power of eloquence, and held up to engage our attention and sympathetic sorrow. The miseries of the Poor are entirely disregarded, though some undergo more real hardships in one day than the Great in their whole lives. These (the Great) may eat, drink, and sleep; have slaves to attend them, and are sure of subsistence for life; while many of their fellow-creatures are obliged to wander, without a friend to comfort or assist them, find enmity in every law, and are too poor to obtain even justice!"

The poor Mechanics of Nottinghamshire, Lancashire, Cheshire. Derbyshire, Yorkshire, and else where, finding themselves hemmed in by multiplied oppressions of long duration, such as, War with all its attendant evils; Provisions high; Taxes high; Wages low; frequently work scarce; *Law* and *Power* nearly all on the side of the oppressors; no Public Writers to state the case of the Poor, in a just and impartial manner; News Printers, for the most part, either Knaves or Cowards, who had courage enough to libel and defame the Oppressed, but not virtue sufficient to defend them.

What then, reader, was the consequence of all this? Why, LUDDISM! Here then, is as plain a statement of the origin of Luddism, as I am capable, with my present information, of drawing: I am not able to say from certain information that I have a personal acquaintance with any Luddite in the world. My knowledge of the business has been picked up in an indirect way, and partly from the Newspapers.

When the Luddites began first to break Machinery, the News Printers, and

---

3. Niccoló Machiavelli (1469–1527), a Florentine statesman and author most famous for his work *The Prince* (1532), in which he describes the amorality and cunning necessary to maintain political power, thus the adjective "Machiavellian," which suggests scheming for dominance without regard to ethical principle. [Ed.]
4. Oliver Goldsmith (1730?–1774) was a physician who became a journalist, essayist, poet, playwright, and novelist. *The Citizen of the World* (1762) is a collection of satirical essays. [Ed.]

especially those of London, abused them in the most unqualified language, calling them *infatuated men; deluded men; wicked men;* and *ill-designing men.* But I did not observe that any of these "infatuated" Printers had the candour to call the Poor Luddites *empty-bellied men—ragged men—or worn-out, emaciated, half-starved, dying men:* A few words of this kind might have been slipped in without any injury to the *truth:* though indeed it might have been greatly detrimental to the *interest* of those who derive a considerable revenue from the sale of truth and conscience, and who make their fortunes by deceiving and poisoning the public mind, and who are principals in bringing on national ruin; and who, strange to tell, are paid for their villainy out of the hard earnings of those whom they ruin!!!

I wholly disapprove of the conduct of the Luddites, as I have already stated, in their breaking Machinery: they ought in no wise to injure either persons or property, but then their real grievances are not to be denied and disregarded, because they are poor and imprudent. For if they be mad it is oppression that has made them mad; and Solomon says, *surely oppression maketh a wise man mad* Eccles vii, 7. how much more then will it make a *weak* man mad! Besides it is not only in the very nature of things, but farther evident from Scripture facts, that multifarious and long continued oppressions will ultimately make men deaf to the dictates of reason, and prompt them to seek redress in acts of violence and desperation. It is written, *And Moses speak so unto the Children of Israel; but they bearkened not unto Moses for anguish of spirit, and for cruel bondage.* Exodus vi. 9.

Now, say, ye Philanthrophists, ye men of reason, candour, and humanity, is it just, is it equitable; first to drive men mad by oppression, and then hang them by group in a day for being mad? Is it equitable and christian-like in *Judges* and *Juries,* and *Counsellors* to make a mighty stir about the *effects* of oppression, and yet never utter a word about the cause of it? Is it right to give a man a *halter* who only wants a *loaf?* Pray, Sirs, where shall we learn that *Hemp* would make a good substitute for *Bread?*

It is the opinion of both the wisest and best among men, that most of the outrages of the people in any nation whatever, are chiefly ascribable to men of wealth and power; because it is with wealth and power commonly, that ill example and oppression originate. It follows, therefore, that to the discerning few, many and horrid executions are strong indications of a bad government. And it is not without reason suspected that Foreigners appreciate the merits of British liberty and happiness, chiefly by the number of transportations and executions that take place in her dominions. Hear what Dr. Franklin[5] says in his Essays.

---

5. Benjamin Franklin (1706–1790) was an American statesman and writer whose aphoristic wit made his *Poor Richard's Almanack* a compendium of classic American proverbs. He helped to bring the American Constitution, and with it the United States, into being. [Ed.]

"It is said by those who know Europe generally, that there are more thefts committed and punished annually in England, than in all the other nations put together. If this be so, there must be a cause or causes for such depravity, in our common people. May not one be the deficiency of justice, and morality in our national government, manifested in our oppressive conduct to subjects, and unjust Wars on our neighbours?" Voltaire,[6] also, evidently entertained the same opinion; for he asks, "How comes it that so many are infected with the pestilence of wickedness? It is that they who bear rule over them, having caught the distemper, communicate it to others!" *Philosoph. Dict.*

If things be so, may we not farther ask, How is it that Judges can reconcile their consciences to the practice of hanging men who have committed no murder, by groups in a day? Whence did these Judges derive their authority for such conduct? Not from the Bible, I am certain; for the law of Moses warrants not the taking any man's life for any other crime but murder; neither can the practice be justified by advertance to what the learned call Primordial Laws. It will be said, that Judges have nothing to do with the Laws but to put them in execution: that they are not sent forth to legislate but only to execute. To this I answer, that if such a plea will satisfy the Divine Being, it may well enough satisfy me, or indeed any one else. But I have a suspicion that it will not satisfy the Divine Being: for though the Judges may have Coke's Institutes, Blackstone's Commentaries, and Burn's Justice[7] in their hands, yet they have a Bible also in their hands, or in their reach; and the Bible contains God's Code of Laws; and moreover, if I mistake not, in all points that affect men's lives and morals, the Laws of the Bible are paramount to all the laws in the world!

I am not very well skilled in human laws, having taken most pain to know plain right and wrong in a moral sense: but I think that most of the existing criminal laws of Europe were made in the days of ferocity and ignorance, and are now maintained and strengthened in these our days by cruelty, and avarice. And, to an ingenuous mind it must be extremely galling, to see, on the one hand, with what tyger-like fierceness, Judges, Juries, Counsellors, and Constables, set upon a poor depredator, who has neither killed nor lamed any man: and on the other hand, to observe what fawning, cringing, and honour-

---

6. François Marie Arouet de Voltaire (1694–1778) was a writer and philosopher who became an emblematic figure of the Enlightenment. Voltaire's *Candide* (1764) expressed a practical philosophy based on common sense. [Ed.]

7. These are three famous works of British jurisprudence. Sir Edward Coke (1552–1634) was a proponent of common law against royal prerogatives. *The Institutes* are among his most important legal writings. Sir William Blackstone (1723–1780) organized and explained English law in his four-volume work, *Commentaries on the Laws of England* (1765–69). Richard Burn (1709–1785) was a justice of the peace who wrote a significant guide to that office, *The Justice of the Peace and Parish Officer* (1755), which went through twenty-nine editions by the early eighteenth century. [Ed.]

ing are heaped upon men of wealth and power, who have distinguished themselves by nothing but by racking their tenants, debauching their neighbours' wives and daughters, fighting duels, and blasting the morals of the whole neighbourhood where they reside! Good God! What an unjust, unfeeling, and unreasonable world is this in which we live! Is it not time that it should either soon mend or soon end?

With regard to the Judges in every country where Grand Larceny, that is stealing the value of a shilling and upwards, can be made a Capital Crime, or in other words, can be punished with Death, their situation is awful in the extreme, because they have power to do what no good man would do for a thousand worlds! When I contemplate the conduct and character of Judge Jeffreys,[8] who lived and dispensed *halters* with unsparing hand, in the reign of James the Second, and likewise the conduct of similar Judges, I cannot help thinking that it will be an awful scene at the last day, if the greatest Judges should be found amongst the greatest Murderers!

It is not long since I saw a Judge sit in solemn pomp, and put his cap on and then pass sentence of death upon eleven poor wretches, telling them severally, that they should be hung by the neck until they were dead, and their bodies given to the Surgeons: not one of these poor wretches had committed, or even attempted to commit, Murder.—One of them had stolen a pair of old shoes from a Shoemaker, and put them on his own feet, because he needed them: the shoes were come a *second* time to be mended; but that they might subject the poor thief to capital punishment, that is Death, they were valued at *One Shilling,* which constituted the offence, Grand Larceny. I saw the shoes, and thought they were worth about *four-pence:* but the inhabitants of the town who were present, said *three-pence* was the full value of them. When therefore I saw the poor fellow condemned, with others, to be hung by the neck until he was dead, and his body given to the surgeons, I felt an indignation against men, and a contempt for Law and Lawyers, which it would not be prudent to describe and divulge. I thought within myself, how few there are amongst these prating, impudent Lawyers and Attornies, here present, who have not a thousand and times more villainy upon their consciences than this poor wretch: and how few there are in the whole assembly who do not frequently violate the obligations of morality as hemously as this poor unfortunate fellow has done. However, none of these poor creatures were hung: they were all respited, and then *only* transported for life! O cursed world, where lit-

---

8. Judge George Jeffreys was a notoriously severe judge under Charles II and James II. He presided over the "Bloody Assizes" of 1685, convened to punish those who participated in the rebellion of the Duke of Monmouth. He ordered two hundred persons to be hanged. James II made him Lord Chancellor that same year. [Ed.]

tle knaves are hanged or transported, and great ones swim in wealth and pleasure, and are also flattered with titles and dignities!

The conduct of Judges in reference to their addresses to criminals, is also worthy of notice.—When criminals are convicted, it is usual for the Judge to give them some verbal reproofs and exhortations suitable to their situation: and it must be allowed that all this is very proper when appropriately performed: but I do not think that this is always the case. I lately both heard and saw a Judge, before whom a criminal stood convicted of Petty Theft, austerely say to the poor culprit, "You are big enough, and able enough, to work, why don't you work instead of stealing?" This admonitory rebuke had the appearance of great wisdom and propriety, tho' I believe it was in fact founded in ignorance: for the Judge ought first to have been well assured that the poor man could have gotten work if he would have sought it. I believe the fact was, that the poor man could not get employment, and therefore he stole!

And though not all, yet I am seriously of opinion that most of the depredations committed on property in these days, might be traced to the same cause, namely, the want of employment! O wicked oppressive world: a comparatively few among men have engrossed to themselves all the Land in the world, which is the source of subsistence; the bulk of mankind are in consequence left to shift as they can; but if in this precarious state of shifting and contriving for a livelihood they should have the imprudence to transgress on the bounds prescribed by laws which wealth has made for its own security, then they are most severely dealt with; sometimes, to use Mr. Pitt's own language, even with *a vigour beyond the Law!* at least, beyond the Law of Moses! But, strange to tell, these *vigorous* measures are often repeated without one step being taken, or one word being uttered about removing the cause of these depredations, namely, *grievous Oppression!* It is not the way of the world now a-days to listen to reason, give way to humane sentiments, remove heavy burthens, and put it in the power of all honest men to get bread for themselves and dependents! No: it is the practice of modern Europe to oppress poor men, and almost force them to steal, and then hang them for stealing: and what then? Mend their condition? No: Oppress them again, and then hang some again!

I have sometimes fancied to myself the act of an angel leaning over the edge of a bright cloud and viewing the conduct of a Judge when putting on his cap and proceeding to pass sentence of Death upon a few poor wretches, some of whom may be quite callous and abandoned, but others of them not deeply depraved, not desperate knaves, but only poor and imprudent, and hurried into *one* desperate action through the pressure of pinching poverty. I have then imagined to myself that the angel knew that a Judge's salary is (as I think) three thousand pounds a-year, independent of private fortune, and that three thousand a-year amounts to more than *fifty-seven* pounds a week, and that some of the poor wretches whom the Judge so solemnly condemns and consigns to the gibbet, would never have transgressed against the laws had they been capable of procuring by hard labour, not *fifty seven pounds a week,* but *fifteen shillings a week!* Then I inferred, that the angel, disgusted with the numerous executions, and the oppressions which had caused them, would go up to heaven with holy indignation and join the company, and cry of those who say, *How long, O Lord, holy and true, dost thou not Judge and avenge our blood on them that dwell on the earth!* Rev. vi. 10.

Nor can I pass by the conduct of News Printers in reference to Judges. It is the common practice of fawning, and cowardly News Printers to speak in high terms of commendation on whatever may issue from the lips of a Judge. The Judge's speech, whatever it be, is always *opposite, appropriate,* and *learned!* I am not among those who would wantonly speak evil of dignities, or even encourage the practice of so doing, well knowing that respectability is essential to the character and office of a Judge; but, neither am I willing that *truth* should be violated in support of *character:* Not is it too much to say, that truth is infinitely greater than character! This is a secret which, judging from facts, most men have yet to learn, and among the rest of men, many News Printers. It is chiefly by supporting character at the expence of truth, that the world has been brought into its present awful situation. It is the duty of News Printers to commend the speeches of Judges whenever they are worthy of commendation; but if those speeches be unworthy, then the News Printer ought to act the part of a man of spirit and independence, and shew, by reason and argument, that he dares to differ in sentiment even from a Judge. This kind of conduct would produce incalculable benefit to the liberties of mankind!

Finally, Oppression is a consummate evil, inasmuch as it induces ferocity, misanthropy, disaffection between man and man, ignorance and cruelty; by it both the Oppressors and Oppressed are spoiled in their sentiment and and moral feeling. Hence on the part of the Oppressors, it is their frequent practice to make out a justification of their conduct by libelling human nature, and indeed the MAKER of human nature, and saying that mankind are so ill-disposed by their very nature, that nothing but Whips, Gibbets, and Dragoons, can keep them in order!

Now, this mode of argument might be retorted upon the Rulers of Mankind very much to their disadvantage: for unless those high-minded Rulers can prove themselves of a nature and kind quite different from those whom they govern, and too commonly oppress which I suspect they would be somewhat puzzled to do, they will have to come in for a share of the stigma and opprobrium with which they load their common nature. And moreover, if their allegations respecting the depravity of the human heart and character be true, then this would be the best imaginable reason for greatly abridging the power of all the Rulers in the world: for what can be more horrible, only to contemplate, than ill-disposed mefn, invested with great power! But if they will still abide by their opinion respecting the great depravity of human nature, then I must and will insist upon it, that their *own* conduct is the best illustration of their own theory!

Even Buonaparte,[9] in his oration which he made to his Senate, after his return from Moscow, could find it in his heart to libel both God and Man, by saying in substance what follows, namely, "That the fine theories of Philosophers respecting Governments, are impracticable; that history shews that men are bad; and that therefore governments must be adapted to the bad hearts of men, and not to the pleasing theories of Philosophers!"

To this I answer, *first,* that such language comes with a very bad grace from Buonaparte, seeing he has stood in such a variety of situations, and some of them so very dissimilar, that impartial posterity, whilst it allows his *greatness,* will think his *goodness* at least equivocal; every one knows that he has changed both his politics and his religion; that he wounded the Pope, and then healed the deadly wound: by which conduct he has put it in the power of men to say that he has adapted both his heart and his religion to his circumstances and his interest! *Secondly,* When Buonaparte assumes the language and character of a Philosopher, he is, like the fabled Bear in the Boat, utterly out of his element. His province is among Military Tactics; of these he understands both the Science and the Practice; and by these he has got an ample share of what a foolish world has agreed to call *glory* and *renown! Thirdly,* the practice of declaiming against fine theories, and of asserting their impracticability, is founded in ignorance; it being silly to say that any *theory* can be *good* and *fine* when it is *practically* the reverse. Wherefore a fine theory, can only be such when it is fine, practically. From all which I infer that the fine theories of government devised by the first revolutionary Philosophers of France, *Brissot, Barrere,*[10] and others, would have been highly conducive to the happiness of mankind, had they been put in practice. But, alas! alas! Pitt, Brunswick, Frederic, Francis,[11] and another sabled old *Gentleman* from Pandemonium, through their damnable malignity against the very theory of liberty, quickly turned the cheerful dawnings of human freedom into political darkness, animosity, hatred, persecution, prosecution, and bloody War: a war, which for

---

9. Napoleon Bonaparte, or Napoleon I (1769–1821) the French emperor. [Ed.]

10. Jacques-Pierre Brissot de Warville was a Girondin leader during the French Revolution. The Girondins were a moderate republican faction that opposed the radical Jacobins. Bertrand Barére was a leading Jacobin and a major propagandist against the aristocracy. Beaumont seems to be confused in this passage, conflating two competing ideologies of the period. [Ed.]

11. Beaumont is probably referring here several political scandals involving William Pitt the Younger, British prime minister from 1783–1801 and 1804–6, and his allies Charles Duke of Brunswick, Sir Philip Francis, and Frederick the Great of Prussia. [Ed.]

blood and ruin has no precedent in the whole compass of historical record! And, grievous to relate, when all this infernal mischief had been kindled up in the world, mankind were impudently told that all the whole scene was the legitimate offspring of republican principles! Whereas it is known to heaven and earth, that all these evils originated in the opposition which Aristocracy and Despotism threw in the way of Liberty and Equality! By this rancourous and malevolent opposition, all Europe which might now have been as the Garden of God, for liberty and happiness, is a howling wilderness, an Aceldama,[12] and a land of the valley and shadow of death!

Respecting the great characteristic of human nature so much controverted by Divines and Philosophers, some holding the opinion, that man is radically bad, and others, that he is radically good: My opinion is, that through the introduction of sin into the human heart, by the disobedience of Adam, man is radically depraved. On the other hand, I believe, that in every heart of man, there is also implanted, by the goodness of God, a principle of light and life, and that it is the predominance of either of these opposite principles that characterises the man, good or bad. I am farther of opinion, that with the Divine assistance which may always be had by those who will ask for it, it is in the power of man to make the good principle predominate in every heart! I believe therefore, that it is Education that makes the principal difference betwixt man and man. In short, man is the creature of *Education! Solomon* was also of this opinion, when he said, *Train up a Child in the way he should go, and when he is old he will not depart from it.* Prov. xxii. 6.

So much am I pre-possessed with the opinion that Education makes the difference between man and man, that I am firmly persuaded, and who can deny it, that had *Sir Isaac Newton* been born and educated among the Hottentots, at the Cape of Good Hope, he would have been just as wise, and just as mannerly as Hottentots commonly are ! Had the refined *Lord Chesterfield,*[13] who was said to be the politest man in Europe, in his day, been born in Lapland, I believe it very possible that he might have lived in unlettered rudeness, and died a Lapland Wizzard. And had *Mr. Howard,* the famous Philanthrophist, been born and educated in South America, he might have lived an ignorant Cannibal, and have left a character, when he died, remarkable for nothing but vindictive ferocity!

Now, Education may be divided into two parts, *Public and Private;* or *National* and *Domestic.* National Education centres in, and emanates from the

---

12. Aceldama was the name given to a field near Jerusalem, bought with blood-money received by Judas Iscariot. Figuratively, it suggests a scene of slaughter.
13. Philip Dormer Stanhope, fourth earl of Chesterfield (1694–1773), statesman and diplomat, is remembered for his wittiness, worldliness, and for some, his cynicism in regard to the ways of the world.

government. If then the government be Military, Corrupt, and Oppressive, it will be a centre of corruption and depravity, and will gradually, but surely, viciate the whole nation; and consequently, either prevent the practice, or destroy the effects, of private education. When therefore, a nation has become generally depraved and wicked, let not the rulers of such nation lay cruel and vindictive hands upon the people, and then think to justify their conduct by defaming both Man and his Maker. Seeing it is a truth legible on the face of history, and maintained by the wisest and best of men,—that every nation is good or bad, as it is well or ill governed! In a word, when a nation becomes so vicious, that it is necessary to hang great numbers of people, in order to keep the rest in subjection, it is a sure evidence that the Rulers of that nation have forfeited all claim to veneration and confidence!

My conclusion is, that the Ever Blessed God has made man fully capable of being good, and that his goodness depends upon his Education, and his Education depends, in great measure, upon the Government under which he lives. *Plato,* the great Philosopher, held the same opinion. So likewise did Lycurgus,[14] the famous Grecian Legislator. And among many other learned men, of modern times, the pious and learned Dr Jortin[15] held the same sentiment, as the following extract from his third dissertation will shew:

"The most judicious Philosophers, and the most acute observers of the human frame and constitution, (says he) have pronounced man to be a creature naturally tame and gentle, and sociable and tractable, who, by the help of *good laws,* and *good examples,* and *good teachers* and *Governors,* may be made good and useful to the world.

"Our adversaries will not admit thus much. They have commonly, no good opinion of God, so no favourable opinion of men; in short, some of them have no esteem of themselves, and finding little moral honesty at home, in their own breasts, they are willing to suppose the rest of the world to be no better. And this is probably one great motive which induces them to draw an hideous portrait of human nature, loaded with the ugly features of craft, baseness, malice, suspicion, selfishness, and dissimulation, by which they have transformed this earth into a hell, where, as many men, so many Devils surround us!"

---

14. Lycurgus was the founder of the Spartan constitution, which reformed the Spartan government to make it easier to quell social unrest. [Ed.]

15. John Jortin was the author of *Remarks on Ecclesiastical History* (1751). [Ed.]

CHARLES BABBAGE

from ON THE ECONOMY OF MACHINERY
AND MANUFACTURES

OF THE IDENTITY OF THE WORK WHEN IT IS
OF THE SAME KIND, AND ITS ACCURACY WHEN
OF DIFFERENT KINDS

. . . (79.) NOTHING is more remarkable, and yet less unexpected, than the perfect identity of things manufactured by the same tool. If the top of a circular box is to be made to fit over the lower part, it may be done in the lathe by gradually advancing the tool of the sliding-rest; the proper degree of tightness between the box and its lid being found by trial. After this adjustment, if a thousand boxes are made, no additional care is required; the tool is always carried up to the stop, and each box will be equally adapted to every lid. The same identity pervades all the arts of printing; the impressions from the same block, or the same copper-plate, have a similarity which no labour could produce by hand. The minutest traces are transferred to all the impressions, and no omission can arise from the inattention or unskilfulness of the operator. The steel punch, with which the card-wadding for a fowling-piece is cut, if it once perform its office with accuracy, constantly reproduces the same exact circle.

(80.) The accuracy with which machinery executes its work is, perhaps, one of its most important advantages: it may, however, be contended, that a considerable portion of this advantage may be resolved into saving of time; for it generally happens, that any improvement in tools increases the quantity of work done in a given time. Without tools, that is, by the mere efforts of the human hand, there are, undoubtedly, multitudes of things which it would be impossible to make. Add to the human hand the rudest cutting-instrument, and its powers are enlarged: the fabrication of many things then becomes easy, and that of others possible with great labour. Add the saw to the knife or the hatchet, and other works become possible, and a new course of difficult operations is brought into view, whilst many of the former are rendered easy. This observation is applicable even to the most perfect tools or machines. It would be *possible* for a very skilful workman, with files and polishing sub-

---

From *On the Economy of Machinery and Manufactures.* Philadelphia: Carey and Lea, 1832.

stances, to form a cylinder out of a piece of steel; but the time which this would require would be so considerable, and the number of failures would probably be so great, that for all practical purposes such a mode of producing a steel cylinder might be said to be impossible. The same process by the aid of the lathe and the sliding-rest is the every-day employment of hundreds of workmen.

(81.) Of all the operations of mechanical art, that of turning is the most perfect. If two surfaces are worked against each other, whatever may have been their figure at the commencement, there exists a tendency in them both to become portions of spheres. Either of them may become convex, and the other concave, with various degrees of curvature. A plane surface is the line of separation between convexity and concavity, and is most difficult to hit; it is more easy to make a good circle than to produce a straight line. A similar difficulty takes place in figuring specula for telescopes; the parabola is the surface which separates the hyperbolic from the elliptic figure, and is the most difficult to form. If a spindle, not cylindrical at its end, be pressed into a hole not circular, and kept constantly turning, there is a tendency in these two bodies so situated to become conical, or to have circular sections. If a triangular-pointed piece of iron be worked round in a circular hole the edges will gradually wear, and it will become conical. These facts, if they do not explain, at least illustrate the principles on which the excellence of work formed in the lathe depends.

OF COPYING

(82.) THE two last-mentioned sources of excellence in the work produced by machinery depend on a principle which pervades a very large portion of all manufactures, and is one upon which the cheapness of the articles produced seems greatly to depend. The principle alluded to is that of COPYING, taken in its most extensive sense. Almost unlimited pains are, in some instances, bestowed on the original, from which a series of copies is to be produced; and the larger the number of these copies, the more care and pains can the manufacturer afford to lavish upon the original. It may thus happen, that the instrument or tool actually producing the work, shall cost five or even ten thousand times the price of each individual specimen of its power.

As the system of copying is of so much importance, and of such extensive use in the arts, it will be convenient to classify a considerable number of those processes in which it is employed. The following enumeration however is not offered as a complete list; and the explanations are restricted to the shortest possible detail which is consistent with a due regard to making the subject intelligible.

Operations of copying are effected under the following circumstances:—

By printing from cavities.	By stamping.
By printing from surface.	By punching.
By casting.	With elongation.
By moulding.	With altered dimensions.

Of Printing from Cavities

(83.) The art of printing, in all its numerous departments, is essentially an art of copying. Under its two great divisions, printing from hollow lines, as in copper-plate, and printing from surface, as in block-printing, are comprised numerous arts.

(84.) *Copper-plate Printing.*—In this instance, the copies are made by transferring to paper, by means of pressure, a thick ink, from the hollows and lines cut in the copper. An artist will sometimes exhaust the labour of one or two years upon engraving a plate, which will not, in some cases, furnish above five hundred copies in a state of perfection.

(85.) *Engravings on Steel.*—This art is like that of engraving on copper, except that the number of copies is far less limited. A bank-note engraved as a copper-plate, will not give above three thousand impressions without a sensible deterioration. Two impressions of a bank-note engraved on steel were examined by one of our most eminent artists, who found it difficult to pronounce with any confidence, which was the earliest impression. One of these was a proof from amongst the first thousand, the other was taken after between seventy and eighty thousand had been printed off.

(86.) *Music-Printing.*—Music is usually printed from pewter plates, on which the characters have been impressed by steel punches. The metal being much softer than copper, is liable to scratches, which detain a small portion of the ink. This is the reason of the dirty appearance of printed music. A new process has recently been invented by Mr. Cowper, by which this inconvenience will be avoided. The improved method, which gives sharpness to the characters, is still an art of copying; but it is effected by surface-printing, nearly in the same manner as calico-printing from blocks, to be described hereafter, (96.) The method of printing music from pewter-plates, although by far the most frequently made use of, is not the only one employed, for music is occasionally printed from stone. Sometimes also it is printed with moveable type; and occasionally the musical characters are printed on the paper, and the lines printed afterwards. Specimens of both these latter modes of music-printing may be seen in the splendid collection of impressions from the types of the press of Bodoni at Parma: but notwithstanding the great care bestowed on the execution of that work, the perpetual interruption of continuity in the lines, arising from the use of moveable types, when the characters and lines are printed at the same time, is apparent.

(87.) *Calico-Printing from Cylinders.*—Many of the patterns on printed calicos are copies by printing from copper cylinders about four or five inches in diameter, on which the desired pattern has been previously engraved. One portion of the cylinders is exposed to the ink, whilst an elastic scraper of very thin steel, by being pressed forcibly against another part, removes all superfluous ink from the surface previously to its reaching the cloth. A piece of calico twenty-eight yards in length rolls through this press, and is printed in four or five minutes.

(88.) *Printing from perforated Sheets of Metal, or Stencilling.*—Very thin brass is sometimes perforated in the form of letters, usually those of a name; this is placed on any substance which it is required to mark, and a brush dipped in some paint is passed over the brass. Those parts which are cut away admit the paint, and thus a copy of the name appears on the substance below. This method, which affords rather a coarse copy, is sometimes used for paper with which rooms are covered, and more especially for the borders. If a portion be required to match an old pattern, this is, perhaps the most economical way of producing it.

(89.) Coloured impressions of leaves upon paper may be made by a kind of surface printing. Such leaves are chosen as have considerable inequalities: the elevated parts of these are covered, by means of an inking ball, with a mixture of some pigment ground up in linseed oil; the leaf is then placed between two sheets of paper, and being gently pressed, the impression from the elevated parts on each side appear on the corresponding sheets of paper.

(90.) The beautiful red cotton handkerchiefs dyed at Glasgow have their pattern given to them by a process similar to stencilling, except that instead of *printing* from a pattern, the reverse operation,—that of *discharging* a part of the colour from a cloth already dyed,—is performed. A number of handkerchiefs are pressed with very great force between two plates of metal, which are similarly perforated with round or lozenge-shaped holes, according to the intended pattern. The upper plate of metal is surrounded by a rim, and a fluid which has the property of discharging the red dye is poured upon that plate. This liquid passes through the holes in the metal, and also through the calico; but, owing to the great pressure opposite all the parts of the plates not cut away, it does not spread itself beyond the pattern. After this, the handkerchiefs are washed, and the pattern of each is a copy of the perforations in the metal-plate used in the process.

(91.) Another mode by which a pattern is formed by discharging colour from a previously dyed cloth, is to print on it a pattern with paste; then, passing it into the dying-vat, it comes out dyed of one uniform colour. But the paste has protected the fibres of the cotton from the action of the dye or mordant; and when the cloth so dyed is well washed, the paste is dissolved, and leaves uncoloured all those parts of the cloth to which it was applied.

Printing from Surface

This second department of printing is of more frequent application in the arts than that which has just been considered.

(92.) *Printing from wooden Blocks.*—A block of box wood is, in this instance, the substance out of which the pattern is formed: the design being sketched upon it, the workman cuts away with sharp tools every part except the lines to be represented in the impression. This is exactly the reverse of the process of engraving on copper, in which every line to be represented is cut away. The ink, instead of filling the cavities cut in the wood, is spread upon the surface which remains, and is thence transferred to the paper.

(93.) *Printing from moveable Types.*—This is the most important in its influence of all the arts of copying. It possesses a singular peculiarity, in the immense subdivision of the parts that form the pattern. After that pattern has furnished thousands of copies, the same individual elements may be arranged again and again in other forms, and thus supply multitudes of originals, from each of which thousands of their copied impressions may flow. It also possesses this advantage, that wood-cuts may be used along with the letter-press, and impressions taken from both at the same operation.

(94.) *Printing from Stereotype.*—This mode of producing copies is very similar to the preceding. There are two modes by which stereotype plates are produced. In that most generally adopted a mould is taken in plaster from the moveable types, and in this the stereotype plate is cast. Another method has been employed in France: instead of composing the work in moveable type, it was set up in moveable copper matrices; each matrix being in fact a piece of copper of the same size as the type, and having the impression of the letter sunk into its surface, instead of projecting in relief. A stereotype plate may, it is evident, be obtained at once from this arrangement of matrices. The objection to the plan is the great expense of keeping so large a collection of matrices.

As the original composition does not readily admit of change, stereotype plates can only be applied with advantage to cases where an extraordinary number of copies are demanded, or where the work consists of figures, and it is of great importance to ensure accuracy. Trifling alterations may, however, be made in it from time to time; and thus mathematical tables may, by the gradual extirpation of error, at last become perfect. This mode of producing copies possesses, in common with that by moveable types, the advantage of admitting the use of wood-cuts; the copy of the wood-cut in the stereotype plate being equally perfect with that of the moveable type. This union is of considerable importance, and cannot be accomplished with engravings on copper.

(95.) *Lettering Books.* The gilt letters on the backs of books are formed by placing a piece of gold leaf upon the leather, and pressing upon it brass letters previously heated: these cause the gold immediately under them to adhere to the leather, whilst the rest of the metal is easily brushed away. When a great number of copies of the same volume are to be lettered, it is found to be cheaper to have a brass pattern cut with the whole of the proper title: this is placed in a press, and being kept hot, the covers, each having a small bit of leaf-gold placed in the proper position, are successively brought under the brass, and stamped. The lettering at the back of the volume in the reader's hand was executed in this manner.

(96.) *Calico-Printing from Blocks.*—This is a mode of copying, by surface-printing, from the ends of small pieces of copper wire, of various forms, fixed into a block of wood. They are all of one uniform height, about the eighth part of an inch above the surface of the wood, and are arranged by the maker into any required pattern. If the block be placed upon a piece of fine woollen cloth, on which ink of any colour has been uniformly spread, the projecting copper wires receive a portion, which they give up when applied to the calico to be printed. By the former method of printing on calico, only one colour could be used; but by this plan, after the flower of a rose, for example, has been printed with one set of blocks, the leaves may be printed of another colour by a different set.

(97.) *Printing Oil-Cloth.*—After the canvass, which forms the basis of oil-cloth, has been covered with paint of one uniform tint, the remainder of the processes which it passes through, are a series of copyings by surface-printing, from patterns formed upon wooden blocks very similar to those employed by the calico printer. Each colour requiring a distinct set of blocks, those oil-cloths with the greatest variety of colours are most expensive.

There are several other varieties of printing which we shall briefly notice as arts of copying; which, although not strictly surface-printing, yet are more allied to it than that from copper-plates.

(98.) *Letter Copying.*—In one of the modes of performing this process, a sheet of very thin paper is damped, and placed upon the writing to be copied. The two papers are then passed through a rolling press, and a portion of the ink from one paper is transferred to the other. The writing is, of course, reversed by this process; but the paper to which it is transferred being thin, the characters are seen through it on the other side, in their proper position. Another common mode of copying letters is by placing a sheet of paper covered on both sides with a substance prepared from lamp-black, between a sheet of thin paper and the paper on which the letter to be despatched is to be written. If the upper or thin sheet be written upon with any hard pointed substance, the words written with this style will be impressed from the black paper upon both those adjoining it. The translucency of the upper sheet, which is retained by the writer, is in this instance necessary to render legible the writing which is on the back of the paper. Both these arts are very limited in their extent, the former affording two or three, the latter from two to perhaps ten or fifteen copies at the same time.

(99.) *Printing on China.*—This is an art of copying which is carried to a very great extent. As the surfaces to which the impression is to be conveyed are often curved, and sometimes even fluted, the ink, or paint,is first transferred from the copper to some flexible substance, such as paper, or an elastic compound of glue and treacle. It is almost immediately conveyed from this to the unbaked biscuit, to which it more readily adheres.

(100.) *Lithographic Printing.*—This is another mode of producing copies in almost unlimited number. The original which supplies the copies is a drawing made on a stone of a slightly porous nature; the ink employed for tracing it is made of such greasy materials that when water is poured over the stone it shall not wet the lines of the drawing. When a roller covered with printing-ink, which is of an oily nature, is passed over the stone previously wetted, the water prevents this ink from adhering to the uncovered portions; whilst the ink used in the drawing is of such a nature that the printing-ink adheres to it. In this state, if a sheet of paper be placed upon the stone, and then passed under a press, the printing-ink will be transferred to the paper, leaving the ink used in the drawing still adhering to the stone.

(101.) There is one application of lithographic printing which does not appear to have received sufficient attention, and perhaps further experiments are necessary to bring it to perfection. It is the reprinting of works which have just arrived from other countries. A few years ago one of the Paris newspapers was reprinted at Brussels as soon as it arrived by means of lithography. Whilst the ink is yet fresh, this may easily be accomplished: it is only necessary to place one copy of the newspaper on a lithographic stone; and by means of great pressure applied to it in a rolling press, a sufficient quantity of the printing ink will be transferred to the stone. By similar means, the other side of the newspaper may be copied on another stone, and these stones will then furnish impressions in the usual way. If printing from stone could be reduced to the same price per thousand as that from moveable types, this process might be adopted with great advantage for the supply of works for the use of distant countries possessing the same language. For a single copy might be printed off with *transfer ink,* and thus an English work, for example, might be published in America from stone, whilst the original, printed from moveable types, made its appearance on the same day in England.

(102.) It is much to be wished that such a method were applicable to the reprinting of fac-similes of old and scarce books. This, however, would require the sacrifice of two copies, since a leaf must be destroyed for each page. Such a method of reproducing a small impression of an old work, is peculiarly applicable to mathematical tables, the setting up of which in type is always expensive and liable to error: but how long ink will continue to be transferable to stone, from paper on which it has been printed, must be determined by experiment. The destruction of the greasy or oily portion of the ink in the character of old books, seems to present the greatest impediment; if one constituent only of the ink were removed by time, it might perhaps be hoped, that chemical means would ultimately be discovered for restoring it: but if this be unsuccessful, an attempt might be made to discover some substance having a strong affinity for the carbon of the ink which remains on the paper, and very little for the paper itself.

(103.) Lithographic prints have occasionally been executed in colours. In such instances a separate stone seems to have been required for each colour, and considerable care, or very good mechanism, must have been employed to adjust the paper to each stone. If any two kinds of ink should be discovered mutually inadhesive, one stone might be employed for two inks; or if the inking-roller for the second and subsequent colours had portions cut away corresponding to those parts of the stone inked by the previous ones, then several colours might be printed from the same stone: but these principles do not appear to promise much, except for coarse subjects.

(104.) *Register-Printing.*—It is sometimes thought necessary to print from a wooden block, or stereotype plate, the same pattern reversed upon the opposite side of the paper. The effect of this, which is technically called *Register-Printing,* is to make it appear as if the ink had penetrated through the paper, and rendered the pattern visible on the other side. If the subject chosen contains many fine lines, it seems at first sight extremely difficult to effect so exact a super-position of the two patterns, on opposite sides of the same piece of paper, that it shall be impossible to detect the slightest deviation; yet the process is extremely simple. The block which gives the impression is always accurately brought down to the same place by means of a hinge; this spot is covered by a piece of thin leather stretched over it; the block is now inked, and being brought down to its place, gives an impression of the pattern to the leather: it is then turned back; and being inked a second time, the paper intended to be printed is placed upon the leather, when the block again descending, the upper surface of the paper is printed from the block, and its under surface takes up the impression from the leather. It is evident that the perfection of this mode of printing depends in a great measure on finding some soft substance like leather, which will take as much ink as it ought from the block, and which will give it up most completely to paper. Impressions thus obtained are usually fainter on the lower side; and in order in some measure to remedy this defect, rather more ink is put on the block at the first than at the second impression.

Of Copying by Casting

(105.) The art of casting, by pouring substances in a fluid state into a mould which retains them until they become solid, is essentially an art of copying;

the form of the thing produced depending entirely upon that of the pattern from which it was formed.

(106.) *Of Casting Iron and other Metals.*—Patterns of wood or metal made from drawings are the originals from which the moulds for casting are made: so that, in fact, the casting itself is a copy of the mould; and the mould is a copy of the pattern. In castings of iron and metals for the coarser purposes, and, if they are afterwards to be worked, even for the finer machines, the exact resemblance amongst the things produced, which takes place in many of the arts to which we have alluded, is not effected in the first instance, nor is this necessary. As the metals shrink in cooling, the pattern is made larger than the intended copy; and in extricating it from the sand in which it is moulded, some little difference will occur in the size of the cavity which it leaves. In smaller works, where accuracy is more requisite, and where few or no after-operations are to be performed, a mould of metal is employed which has been formed with considerable care. Thus, in casting bullets, which ought to be perfectly spherical and smooth, an iron instrument is used, in which a cavity has been cut and carefully ground; and, in order to obviate the contraction in cooling, a *jet* is left which may supply the deficiency of metal arising from that cause, and which is afterwards cut off. The leaden toys for children are cast in brass moulds which open, and in which have been graved or chiselled the figures intended to be produced.

(107.) A very beautiful mode of representing small branches of the most delicate vegetable productions in bronze has been employed by Mr. Chantrey. A small strip of a fir-tree, a branch of holly, a curled leaf of broccoli, or any other vegetable production, is suspended by one end in a small cylinder of paper which is placed for support within a similarly formed tin case. The finest river silt, carefully separated from all the coarser particles, and mixed with water, so as to have the consistency of cream, is poured into the paper cylinder by small portions at a time, carefully shaking the plant a little after each addition, in order that its leaves may be covered, and that no bubbles of air may be left. The plant and its mould are now allowed to dry, and the yielding nature of the paper allows the loamy coating to shrink from the outside. When this is dry it is surrounded by a coarser substance; and, finally, we have the twig with all its leaves imbedded in a perfect mould. This mould is carefully dried, and then gradually heated to a red heat. At the ends of some of the leaves or shoots, wires have been left to afford air-holes by their removal, and in this state of strong ignition a stream of air is directed into the hole formed by the end of the branch. The consequence is, that the wood and leaves which had been turned into charcoal by the fire, are now converted into carbonic acid by the current of air; and, after some time, the whole of the solid matter of which the plant consisted is completely removed, leaving a hollow mould, bearing on its interior all the minutest traces of its late vegetable occupant.

When this process is completed, the mould being still kept at nearly a red heat, receives the fluid metal, which, by its weight, either drives the very small quantity of air, which at that high temperature remains behind, out through the air-holes, or compresses it into the pores of the very porous substance of which the mould is formed.

(108.) When the form of the object intended to be cast is such that the pattern cannot be extricated from its mould of sand or plaster, it becomes necessary to make the pattern with wax, or some other easily fusible substance. The sand or plaster is moulded round this pattern, and, by the application of heat, the wax is extricated through an opening left purposely for its escape.

(109.) It is often desirable to ascertain the form of the internal cavities, inhabited by molluscous animals, such as those of spiral shells, and of the various corals. This may be accomplished by filling them with fusible metal, and dissolving the substance of the shell by muriatic acid; thus a metallic solid will remain which exactly filled all the cavities. If such forms are required in silver, or any other difficultly fusible metal, the shells may be filled with wax or resin, then dissolved away; and the remaining waxen form may serve as the pattern from which a plaster mould may be made for casting the metal. Some nicety will be required in these operations; and perhaps the minuter cavities can only be filled under an exhausted receiver.

(110.) *Casting in Plaster.*—This is a mode of copying applied to a variety of purposes:—to produce accurate representations of the human form,—of statues,—or of rare fossils,—to which latter purpose it has lately been applied with great advantage. In all casting, the first process is to make the mould; and plaster is the substance which is almost always employed for the purpose. The property which it possesses of remaining for a short time in a state of fluidity, renders it admirably adapted to this object, and adhesion, even to an original of plaster, is effectually prevented by oiling the surface on which it is poured. The mould formed round the subject which is copied, removed in separate pieces and then reunited, is that in which the copy is cast. This process gives additional utility and value to the finest works of art. The students of the Academy at Venice are thus enabled to admire the sculptured figures of Egina, preserved in the gallery at Munich; as well as the marbles of the Parthenon, the pride of our own Museum. Casts in plaster of the Elgin marbles adorn many of the academies of the Continent; and the liberal employment of such presents affords us an inexpensive and permanent source of popularity.

(111.) *Casting in Wax.*—This mode of copying, aided by proper colouring, offers the most successful imitations of many objects of natural history, and gives an air of reality to them which might deceive even the most instructed. Numerous figures of remarkable persons, having the face and hands formed in wax, have been exhibited at various times; and the resemblances have, in some instances been most striking. But whoever would see the art of copying in wax carried to the highest perfection, should examine the beautiful collection of fruit at the house of the Horticultural Society; the model of the magnificent flower of the new genus Rafflesia—the waxen models of the internal parts of the human body which adorn the anatomical gallery of the Jardin des Plantes at Paris, and the Museum at Florence—or the collection of morbid anatomy at the University of Bologna. The art of imitation by wax does not usually afford the multitude of copies which flow from many similar operations. This number is checked by the subsequent stages of the process, which, ceasing to have the character of copying by a tool or pattern, become consequently more expensive. In each individual production, form alone is given by casting; the colouring must be the work of the pencil, guided by the skill of the artist.

Of Copying by Moulding

(112.) This method of producing multitudes of individuals having an exact resemblance to each other in external shape, is adopted very widely in the arts. The substances employed are, either naturally or by artificial preparation, in a soft or plastic state; they are then compressed by mechanical force, sometimes assisted by heat, into a mould of the required form.

(113.) *Of Bricks and Tiles.*—An oblong box of wood fitting upon a bottom fixed to the brick-maker's bench, is the mould from which every brick is formed. A portion of the plastic mixture of which the bricks consist is made ready by less skilful hands: the workman first sprinkles a little sand into the mould, and then throws the clay into it with some force; at the same time rapidly working it with his fingers, so as to make it completely close up to the corners. He next scrapes off, with a wetted stick, the superfluous clay, and shakes the new-formed brick dexterously out of its mould upon a piece of board, on which it is removed by another workman to the place appointed for drying it. A very skilful moulder has occasionally, in a long summer's day, delivered from ten to eleven thousand bricks; but a fair average day's work is from five to six thousand. Tiles of various kinds and forms are made of finer materials, but by the same system of moulding. Amongst the ruins of the city of Gour, the ancient capital of Bengal, bricks are found having projecting ornaments in high relief: these appear to have been formed in a mould, and subsequently glazed with a coloured glaze. In Germany, also, brickwork has been executed with various ornaments. The cornice of the church of St. Stephano, at Berlin, is made of large blocks of brick moulded into the form required by the architect. At the establishment of Messrs. Cubitt, in Gray's-inn lane, vases, cornices, and highly ornamented capitals of columns are thus formed which rival stone itself in elasticity, hardness, and durability.

(114.) *Of Embossed China.*—Many of the forms given to those beautiful specimens of earthenware which constitute the equipage of our breakfast and our dinner tables, cannot be executed in the lathe of the potter. The embossed ornaments on the edges of the plates, their polygonal shape, the fluted surface of many of the vases, would all be difficult and costly of execution by the hand; but they become easy and comparatively cheap, when made by pressing the soft material out of which they are formed into a hard mould. The care and skill bestowed on the preparation of that mould are repaid by the multitude it produces. In many of the works of the china manufactory, one part only of the article is moulded; the upper surface of the plate, for example, whilst the under side is figured by the lathe. In some instances, the handle, or only a few ornaments, are moulded, and the body of the work is turned.

(115.) *Glass Seals.*—The process of engraving upon gems requires considerable time and skill. The seals thus produced can therefore never become common. Imitations, however, have been made of various degrees of resemblance. The colour which is given to glass is, perhaps, the most successful part of the imitation. A small cylindrical rod of coloured glass is heated in the flame of a blow pipe, until the extremity becomes soft. The operator then pinches it between the ends of a pair of nippers, which are formed of brass, and on one side of which the device intended for the seal has been carved in relief. When the mould has been well finished and care is taken in heating the glass properly, the seals thus produced are not bad imitations; and by this system of copying they are so multiplied, that the more ordinary kinds are sold at Birmingham for three pence a dozen.

(116.) *Square Glass Bottles.*—The round forms which are usually given to vessels of glass are readily produced by the expansion of the air with which they are blown. It is, however, necessary in many cases to make bottles of a square form, and each capable of holding exactly the same quantity of fluid. It is also frequently desirable to have imprinted on them the name of the maker of the medicine or other liquid they are destined to contain. A mould of iron, or of copper, is provided of the intended size, on the inside of which are engraved the names required. This mould, which is used in a hot state, opens into two parts, to allow the insertion of the round, unfinished bottle, which is placed in it in a very soft state before it is removed from the end of the iron tube with which it was blown. The mould is now closed, and the glass is forced against its sides, by blowing strongly into the bottle.

(117.) *Wooden Snuff-Boxes.*—Snuff-boxes ornamented with devices, in imitation of carved work or of rose engine-turning, are sold at a price which proves that they are only imitations. The wood, or horn, out of which they are formed, is softened by long boiling in water, and whilst in this state it is forced into moulds of iron, or steel, on which are cut the requisite patterns, where it remains exposed to great pressure until it is dry.

(118.) *Horn Knife-Handles and Umbrella-Handles.*—The property which horn possesses of becoming soft by the action of water and of heat, fits it for many useful purposes. It is pressed into moulds, and becomes embossed with figures in relief, adapted to the objects to which it is to be applied. If curved, it may be straightened; or if straight, it may be bent into any forms which ornament or utility may require; and by the use of the mould these forms may be multiplied in endless variety. The commoner sorts of knives, the crooked handles for umbrellas, and a multitude of other articles to which horn is applied, attest the cheapness which the art of copying gives to the things formed of this material.

(119.) *Moulding Tortoise-shell.*—The same principle is applied to things formed out of the shell of the turtle, or the land tortoise. From the greatly superior price of the raw material, this principle of copying is, however, more rarely employed upon it; and the few carvings which are demanded, are usually performed by hand.

(120.) *Tobacco Pipe-Making.*—This simple art is almost entirely one of copying. The moulds are formed of iron, in two parts, each embracing one half of the stem; the line of junction of these parts may generally be observed running lengthwise from one end of the pipe to the other. The hole passing to the bowl is formed by thrusting a long wire through the clay before it is enclosed in the mould. Some of the moulds have figures, or names, sunk in the inside, which give a corresponding figure in relief upon the finished pipe.

(121.) *Embossing upon Calico.*—Calicoes of one colour, but embossed all over with raised patterns, though not much worn in this country, are in great demand in several foreign markets. This appearance is produced by passing them between rollers, on one of which is figured in intaglio the pattern to be transferred to the calico. The substance of the cloth is pressed very forcibly into the cavities thus formed, and retains its pattern after considerable use. The *watered* appearance in the cover of the volume in the reader's hands is produced in a similar manner. A cylinder of gun-metal, on which the design of the *watering* is previously cut, is pressed by screws against another cylinder, formed out of pieces of brown paper which have been strongly compressed together and accurately turned. The two cylinders are made to revolve rapidly, the paper one being slightly damped, and, after a few minutes, it takes an impression from the upper or metal one. The glazed calico is now passed between the rollers, its glossy surface being in contact with the metal cylinder, which is kept hot by a heated iron inclosed within it. Calicoes are sometimes *watered* by placing two pieces on each other in such a position that the longitudinal threads of the one are at right angles to those of the other, and compressing them in this state between flat rollers. The threads of the one piece produce indentations in those of the other, but they are not so deep as when produced by the former method.

(122.) *Embossing upon Leather.*—This art of copying from patterns previously engraved on steel rollers is in most respects similar to the preceding. The leather is forced into the cavities, and the parts which are not opposite to any cavity are powerfully condensed between the rollers.

(123.) *Swaging.*—This is an art of copying practised by the smith. In order to fashion his iron and steel into the various forms demanded by his customers, he has small blocks of steel into which are sunk cavities of different shapes; these are called *swages,* and are generally in pairs. Thus if he wants a round bolt, terminating in a cylindrical head of larger diameter, and having one or more projecting rims, he uses a corresponding *swaging-tool;* and having heated the end of his iron rod, and thickened it by striking the end in the direction of the axis, (which is technically called *upsetting,*) he places its head upon one part of the *swage;* and whilst an assistant holds the other part on the top of the hot iron, he strikes it several times with his hammer, occasionally turning the head one quarter round. The heated iron is thus forced by the blows to assume the form of the mould into which it is impressed.

(124.) *Engraving by Pressure.*—This is one of the most beautiful examples of the art of copying carried to an almost unlimited extent; and the delicacy with which it can be executed, and the precision with which the finest traces of the graving tool can be transferred from steel to copper, or even from hard steel to soft steel, is most unexpected. We are indebted to Mr. Perkins for most of the contrivances which have brought this art at once almost to perfection. An engraving is first made upon soft steel, which is hardened by a peculiar process without in the least injuring its delicacy. A cylinder of soft steel, pressed with great force against the hardened steel engraving, is now made to roll very slowly backward and forward over it, thus receiving the design, but in relief. The cylinder is in its turn hardened without injury; and if it be slowly rolled to and fro with strong pressure on successive plates of copper, it will imprint on a thousand of them a perfect fac-simile of the original steel engraving from which it was made. Thus the number of copies producible from the same design may be multiplied a thousand-fold. But even this is very far short of the limits to which the process may be extended. The hardened steel roller, bearing the design upon it in relief, may be employed to make a few of its first impressions upon plates of *soft steel,* and these being hardened become the representatives of the original engraving, and may in their turn be made the parents of other rollers, each generating copper-plates like their prototype. The possible extent to which fac-similes of one original engraving may thus be multiplied, almost confounds the imagination, and appears to be for all practical purposes unlimited.

This beautiful art was first proposed by Mr. Perkins for the purpose of rendering the forgery of banknotes a matter of great difficulty; and there are two principles which peculiarly adapt it to that object: first, the perfect identity of all the impressions, so that any variation in the minutest line would at once cause detection; secondly, that the original plates may be formed by the united labours of several artists most eminent in their respective departments; for as only one original of each design is necessary, the expense, even of the most elaborate engraving, will be trifling, compared with the multitude of copies produced from it.

(125.) It must, however, be admitted that the principle of copying itself furnishes an expedient for imitating any engraving or printed pattern, however complicated; and thus presents a difficulty which none of the schemes devised for the prevention of forgery appear to have yet effectually obviated. In attempting to imitate the most perfect bank note, the first process would be to place it with the printed side downwards upon a stone or other substance, on which, by passing it through a rolling-press, it might be firmly fixed. The next object would be to discover some solvent which should dissolve the paper, but neither affect the printing-ink, nor injure the stone or substance to which it is attached. Water does not seem to do this effectually, and perhaps weak alkaline or acid solutions would be tried. If, however, this could be fully accomplished, and if the stone or other substance, used to retain the impression, had those properties which enable us to print from it, innumerable fac-similes of the note might obviously be made, and the imitation would be complete. Porcelain biscuit, which has recently been used with a black-lead pencil for memorandum-books, seems in some measure adapted for such trials, since its porosity may be diminished to any required extent by regulating the dilution of the glazing.

(126.) *Gold and Silver Moulding.*—Many of the mouldings used by jewellers consist of thin slips of metal, which have received their form by passing between steel rollers, on which the pattern is embossed or engraved; thus taking a succession of copies of the devices intended.

(127.) *Ornamental Papers.*—Sheets of paper coloured or covered with gold or silver leaf, and embossed with various patterns, are used for covering books, and for many ornamental purposes. The figures upon these are produced by the same process, that of passing the sheets of paper between engraved rollers.

ANDREW URE

GENERAL VIEW OF MANUFACTURING INDUSTRY

Manufacture is a word, which, in the vicissitude of language, has come to signify the reverse of its intrinsic meaning, for it now denotes every extensive product of art which is made by machinery, with little or no aid of the human

---

From *Philosophy of Manufactures.* London: Charles Knight, 1835.

hand; so that the most perfect manufacture is that which dispenses entirely with manual labour. The philosophy of manufactures is therefore an exposition of the general principles on which productive industry should be conducted by self-acting machines. The end of a manufacture is to modify the texture, form, or composition of natural objects by mechanical or chemical forces, acting either separately, combined, or in succession. Hence the automatic arts subservient to general commerce may be distinguished into Mechanical and Chemical, according as they modify the external form or the internal constitution of their subject matter. An indefinite variety of objects may be subjected to each system of action, but they may be all conveniently classified into animal, vegetable, and mineral.

A mechanical manufacture being commonly occupied with one substance, which it conducts through metamorphoses in regular succession, may be made nearly automatic; whereas a chemical manufacture depends on the play of delicate affinities between two or more substances, which it has to subject to heat and mixture under circumstances somewhat uncertain, and must therefore remain, to a corresponding extent, a manual operation. The best example of *pure* chemistry on self-acting principles which I have seen, was in a manufacture of sulphuric acid, where the sulphur being kindled and properly set in train with the nitre, atmospheric air, and water, carried on the process through a labyrinth of compartments, and supplied the requisite heat of concentration, till it brought forth a finished commercial product. The finest model of an automatic manufacture of *mixed* chemistry is the five-coloured calico machine, which continuously, and spontaneously, so to speak, prints beautiful webs of cloth with admirable precision and speed. It is in a cotton-mill, however, that the perfection of automatic industry is to be seen; it is there that the elemental powers have been made to animate millions of complex organs, infusing into forms of wood, iron, and brass an intelligent agency. And as the philosophy of the fine arts, poetry, painting, and music may be best studied in their individual master-pieces, so may the philosophy of manufactures in this its noblest creation.

There are four distinct classes of textile fibres, cotton, wool, flax, and silk, which constitute the subjects of four, or, more correctly speaking, five distinct classes of factories: first, the cotton factories; second, the woollen; third, the worsted; fourth, the flax, hempen, or linen; and fifth, the silk. These five factories have each peculiarities proceeding from the peculiarities of its raw material and of its fabrics; but they all possess certain family features, for they all employ torsion to convert the loose slender fibres of vegetable or animal origin into firm coherent threads, and, with the exception of silk, they all employ extension also to attenuate and equalize these threads, technically styled yarn. Even one kind of silk which occurs in entangled tufts, called floss, is spun like cotton, by the simultaneous action of stretching and twisting.

The above-named five orders of factories are, throughout this kingdom, set in motion by steam-engines or water-wheels; they all give employment to multitudes of children or adolescents; and they have therefore been subjected to certain legislative provisions, defined in the Factories Regulation Act,[1] passed by Parliament on the 29th August, 1833.

It is ascertained that 344,623 work-people are constantly engaged within the factories of the United Kingdom; of which number 278,876 belong to England and Wales; 56,176 to Scotland; and 9571 to Ireland. About nine-twentieths are under eighteen years of age; and of these nine, fully five are female, and nearly four are male. It must be remembered, however, that besides these 344,623 inmates of factories, a vast population derives a livelihood from the manufactures of cotton, wool, flax, and silk, such as the hand-weavers, the calico-printers, and dyers, the frame-work knitters, the lace-makers, lace-runners, muslin-sewers, &c.

It appears from the Parliamentary Returns of 1831, that in Great Britain, out of a total population of 16,539,318 persons, there are of adult male agricultural labourers and labouring occupiers 1,055,982, and of adult male manufacturing labourers 404,317. Whence it would seem that there are only 383 manufacturing labourers to 1000 of the agricultural class. But if we include among manufacturers the adults employed in retail trade and in handicraft, as masters or workmen, =1,159,867, we shall have as the total adult males engaged in arts and trades 1,564,184, being about fifty per cent, more than those engaged in agriculture. The capitalists, bankers, professional and other educated men, amount to 214,396; labourers, non-agricultural, to 618,712. Even if we include in the agricultural department the occupiers employing labourers (few of whom, however, work), we shall have to add only 187,075 to the above number 1,055,057, constituting for the whole of the agriculturists, a sum of 1,243,057, being after all only 80 adult males for 100 employed in manufactures, arts, and trades.

When we take into account the vastly greater proportion of young persons constantly occupied with factory labour (who are not noticed in the above statement) than of those occupied with agricultural labour, we shall be then led to conclude, that at least double the amount of personal industry is engaged in the arts, manufactures, and trade, to what is engaged in agriculture. Upwards of one-eighth of the population of this island would therefore appear

---

1. The Factories Regulation Act of 1833 covered textile factories, excluding those making lace. It stipulated that no children under nine were allowed to work in factories; children under thirteen were restricted to working nine hours a day and forty-eight hours a week. Four paid factory inspectors were appointed to enforce this law, although they had no official way to verify the ages of children going into the factories they observed; moreover, child labor committee reports show again and again that many children did not actually know their own ages. [Ed.]

to be actually employed in manufactures; and probably not more than one-sixteenth in agriculture. This conclusion ought to lead our legislative land-owners to treat the manufacturing interests with greater respect than they have usually been accustomed to do. If we consider, moreover, how much greater a mass of productive industry a labourer, whether young or old, is equivalent to, in power-driven manufactures, than in husbandry, the balance in favour of the former will be greatly enhanced.

France, which has for upwards of a century and a half tried every scheme of public premium to become a great manufacturing country, has a much less proportion than one employed in trade for two employed in agriculture. M. Charles Dupin, indeed, has been led by his researches into the comparative industry of France and of the United Kingdom, to conclude that the agricultural produce of our country amounted in value to 240 millions sterling, and that of his own to 180 millions sterling, being the ratio of three to two; and that our manufacturing power is inferior to that of France in the proportion of sixty-three to seventy-two, or as seven to eight. There can be no doubt that his agricultural estimate underrates France, as much as his manufacturing estimate underrates Great Britain.

This island is pre-eminent among civilized nations for the prodigious development of its factory wealth, and has been therefore long viewed with a jealous admiration by foreign powers. This very pre-eminence, however, has been contemplated in a very different light by many influential members of our own community, and has been even denounced by them as the certain origin of innumerable evils to the people, and of revolutionary convulsions to the state. If the affairs of the kingdom be wisely administered, I believe such allegations and fears will prove to be groundless, and to proceed more from the envy of one ancient and powerful order of the commonwealth, towards another suddenly grown into political importance, than from the nature of things.

In the recent discussions concerning our factories, no circumstance is so deserving of remark, as the gross ignorance evinced by our leading legislators and economists,—gentlemen well informed in other respects,—relative to the nature of those stupendous manufactures which have so long provided the rulers of the kingdom with the resources of war, and a great body of the people with comfortable subsistence; which have, in fact, made this island the arbiter of many nations, and the benefactor of the globe itself. Till this ignorance be dispelled, no sound legislation need be expected on manufacturing subjects. To effect this purpose is a principal, but not the sole, aim of the present volume, for it is intended also to convey specific information to the classes directly concerned in the manufactures, as well as general knowledge to the community at large, and particularly to young persons about to make the choice of a profession.

The blessings which physico-mechanical science has bestowed on society, and the means it has still in store for ameliorating the lot of mankind, have been too little dwelt upon; while, on the other hand, it has been accused of lending itself to the rich capitalists as an instrument for harassing the poor, and of exacting from the operative an accelerated rate of work. It has been said, for example, that the steam-engine now drives the power-looms with such velocity as to urge on their attendant weavers at the same rapid pace; but that the hand-weaver, not being subjected to this restless agent, can throw his shuttle and move his treddles at his convenience. There is, however, this difference in the two cases, that in the factory, every member of the loom is so adjusted, that the driving force leaves the attendant nearly nothing at all to do, certainly no muscular fatigue to sustain, while it procures for him good, unfailing wages, besides a healthy workshop gratis: whereas the non-factory weaver, having everything to execute by muscular exertion, finds the labour irksome, makes in consequence innumerable short pauses, separately of little account, but great when added together; earns therefore proportionally low wages, while he loses his health by poor diet and the dampness of his hovel. Dr. Carbutt of Manchester says, "With regard to Sir Robert Peel's assertion a few evenings ago, that the hand-loom weavers are mostly small farmers, nothing can be a greater mistake; they live, or rather they just keep life together, in the most miserable manner, in the cellars and garrets of the town, working sixteen or eighteen hours for the merest pittance."[2]

The constant aim and effect of scientific improvement in manufactures are philanthropic, as they tend to relieve the workmen either from niceties of adjustment which exhaust his mind and fatigue his eyes, or from painful repetition of efforts which distort or wear out his frame. At every step of each manufacturing process described in this volume the humanity of science will be manifest. New illustrations of this truth appear almost every day, of which a remarkable one has just come to my knowledge. In the woollen-cloth trade there is a process between carding and spinning the wool, called *slubbing,* which converts the spongy rolls turned off from the cards into a continuous length of fine porous cord. Now, though carding and spinning lie within the domain of automatic science, yet slubbing is a handicraft operation, depending on the skill of the slubber, and participating therefore in all his irregularities. If he be a steady, temperate man, he will conduct his business regularly, without needing to harass his juvenile assistants, who join together the series of card rolls, and thus feed his machine; but if he be addicted to liquor, and passionate, he has it in his power to exercise a fearful despotism over the young pieceners, in violation of the proprietor's benevolent regulations. This

---

2. Letter of 3rd of May, 1833, to Dr. Hawkins in his Medical Report, Factory Commission, p. 282.

class of operatives, who, though inmates of factories, are not, properly speaking, factory workers, being independent of the moving power, have been the principal source of the obloquy so unsparingly cast on the cotton and other factories, in which no such capricious practices or cruelties exist. The wool slubber, when behind-hand with his work, after a visit to the beer-shop, resumes his task with violence, and drives his machine at a speed beyond the power of the pieceners to accompany; and if he finds them deficient in the least point, he does not hesitate to lift up the long wooden rod from his slubbing-frame, called a billy-roller, and beat them unmercifully. I rejoice to find that science now promises to rescue this branch of the business from handicraft caprice, and to place it, like the rest, under the safeguard of automatic mechanism. The details of this recent invention will be given in describing the woollen manufacture.

The processes that may be employed to give to portions of inert matter precise movements resembling those of organized beings are innumerable, as they consist of an indefinite number and variety of cords, pulleys, toothed-wheels, nails, screws, levers, inclined-planes, as well as agencies of air, water, fire, light, &c., combined in endless modes to produce a desired effect. Ingenuity has been long exercised on such combinations, chiefly for public amusement or mystification, without any object of utility. In ancient times the statue of Memnon was celebrated for emitting harmonious sounds at sunrise, and acted probably by concealed organ-pipes. The flying pigeon of Archytas was more manifestly an automatic mechanism, as it performed all the motions of an animal; and likewise the Android of Albert the Great, which opened a door when any one knocked, and muttered certain sounds, as if speaking to the visiter. The brass heads, or conversable busts of Abbé Mical, were probably a simple acoustic experiment on the transmission of sounds through tubes, like the Invisible Girl. More recently the flute-player of Vaucanson has puzzled the world. It presented the appearance of a human figure of the ordinary size, seated on a piece of rock, supported on a pedestal four feet and a half high. By the movements of its lips, fingers, and tongue, it modified the tones of the flute, and executed twelve different airs on the instrument. Vaucanson constructed also a drummer, which played on a flute with a three-holed mouthpiece no less than twenty airs. Standing upright on a pedestal, dressed like a dancing shepherd, holding its flageolet in one hand, and a rod in the other, it beat the drum at one time in single taps, and at another in a long roll, as accompaniments to the flageolet tune. This automaton seemed to be truly the animated leader of the pleasures of a ball, skilful in augmenting or diminishing the breathing sounds of its instrument, with equal precision and taste.

The duck of the same celebrated mechanician not only imitated the different movements of that animal, drinking, gobbling, swallowing, &c., but also represented faithfully the structure of the internal viscera for the digestion of the food. The play of every part necessary to discharge these functions was imitated to the life; for the duck drank, dabbled in the water, stretched out its neck to take grain when offered to it in the hand, drew back its head again to swallow it, doubled the quickness of the masticating movements in passing the grain into the stomach, like the living duck, which always swallows its food very hastily. The grain was then ground in the gizzard, as preparatory to digestion; and finally subjected to excrementitious actions. Its wings, neck, head, and whole frame, were imitated bone by bone, and arranged in their natural form and order. When once wound up, the duck went through all its vital evolutions without needing to be touched. These machines were purchased by Professor Bayreuss, of Helmstadt.

The chess-player of M. Maelzel, now under exhibition at Paris, and formerly shown in this country, has been often described. It imitates very remarkably a living being, endowed with all the resources of intelligence, for executing the combinations of profound study.

Raisin's automaton harpsichord was found to contain an infant performer.

Self-acting inventions like the preceding, however admirable as exercises of mechanical science, do nothing towards the supply of the physical necessities of society. Man stands in daily want of food, fuel, clothing, and shelter; and is bound to devote the powers of body and mind, of nature and art, in the first place to provide for himself and his dependents a sufficiency of these necessaries, without which there can be no comfort, nor leisure for the cultivation of the taste and intellect. To the production of food and domestic accommodation not many automatic inventions have been applied, or seem to be extensively applicable; though for modifying them to the purposes of luxury many curious contrivances have been made. Machines, more or less automatic, are embodied in the coal-mines of Great Britain; but such combinations have been mainly directed, in this as well as other countries, to the materials of clothing. These chiefly consist of flexible fibres of vegetable or animal origin, twisted into smooth, tenacious threads, which are then woven into cloth by being decussated in a loom. Of the animal kingdom, silk, wool, and hair are the principal textile products. The vegetable tribes furnish cotton, flax, hemp, besides several other fibrous substances of inferior importance.

Wool, flax, hemp, and silk, have been very generally worked up among the nations of Europe, both in ancient and modern times; but cotton attire was, till sixty years ago, confined very much to Hindostan, and some other districts of Asia. No textile filaments however are, by their facility of production as well as their structure, so well adapted as those of cotton to furnish articles of clothing, combining comfort with beauty and convenience in an eminent degree. Hence we can understand how cotton fabrics, in their endless variety of textures and styles, plain, figured, and coloured, have within the short period of one human life grown into an enormous manufacture, have become an object of the first desire to mankind all over the globe, and of zealous industry to the most civilized states. This business has received its great automatic development in England, though it was cultivated to a considerable extent on handicraft principles in France a century ago, and warmly encouraged by the government of that country, both as to the growth of the material and its conversion into cloth. The failure of the French, however, to establish a factory system prior to the English is a very remarkable fact, and proves clearly that mechanical invention, for which the former nation have long been justly celebrated, is not of itself sufficient to found a successful manufacture.

We have adverted to the mechanisms of Vaucanson. This inventive artisan directed his attention also to productive machines. He constructed one for winding silk so long ago as 1749; one for doubling and twisting it in 1751; a tapestry loom in 1758; another for winding silk in 1770; a machine for laminating stuffs in 1757, and a plan of mounting silk-mills in 1776. There can be no doubt as to the value of these inventions, as they were described with merited eulogiums in the above-named years by the Academy of Paris. In 1776 he published an account of the Indian mode of weaving fine muslins in the wet state, showing that his attention had been turned likewise to the cotton trade.

The term *Factory System,* in technology, designates the combined operation of many orders of work-people, adult and young, in tending with assiduous skill a series of productive machines continuously impelled by a central power. This definition includes such organizations as cotton-mills, flax-mills, silk-mills, woollen-mills, and certain engineering works; but it excludes those in which the mechanisms do not form a connected series, nor are dependent on one prime mover. Of the latter class, examples occur in iron-works, dye-works, soap-works, brass-foundries, &c. Some authors, indeed, have comprehended under the title *factory,* all extensive establishments wherein a number of people co-operate towards a common purpose of art; and would therefore rank breweries, distilleries, as well as the workshops of carpenters, turners, coopers, &c., under the factory system. But I conceive that this title, in its strictest sense, involves the idea of a vast automaton, composed of various mechanical and intellectual organs, acting in uninterrupted concert for the production of a common object, all of them being subordinated to a self-regulated moving force. If the marshalling of human beings in systematic order for the execution of any technical enterprise were allowed to constitute a factory, this term might embrace every department of civil and military engineering,—a latitude of application quite inadmissible.

In its precise acceptation, the Factory system is of recent origin, and may claim England for its birthplace. The mills for throwing silk, or making organzine, which were mounted centuries ago in several of the Italian states, and furtively transferred to this country by Sir Thomas Lombe in 1718, contained indeed certain elements of a factory, and probably suggested some hints of those grander and more complex combinations of self-acting machines, which were first embodied half a century later in our cotton manufacture by Richard Arkwright,[3] assisted by gentlemen of Derby, well acquainted with its celebrated silk establishment. But the spinning of an entangled flock of fibres into a smooth thread, which constitutes the main operation with cotton, is in silk superfluous; being already performed by the unerring instinct of a worm, which leaves to human art the simple task of doubling and twisting its regular filaments. The apparatus requisite for this purpose is more elementary, and calls for few of those gradations of machinery which are needed in the carding, drawing, roving, and spinning processes of a cotton-mill.

When the first water-frames for spinning cotton were erected at Cromford, in the romantic valley of the Derwent, about sixty years ago, mankind were little aware of the mighty revolution which the new system of labour was destined by Providence to achieve, not only in the structure of British society, but in the fortunes of the world at large. Arkwright alone had the sagacity to discern, and the boldness to predict in glowing language, how vastly productive human industry would become, when no longer proportioned in its results to muscular effort, which is by its nature fitful and capricious, but when made to consist in the task of guiding the work of mechanical fingers and arms, regularly impelled with great velocity by some indefatigable physical power. What his judgment so clearly led him to perceive, his energy of will enabled him to realize with such rapidity and success, as would have done honour to the most influential individuals, but were truly wonderful in that obscure and indigent artisan.

The main difficulty did not, to my apprehension, lie so much in the invention of a proper self-acting mechanism for drawing out and twisting cotton into a continuous thread, as in the distribution of the different members of the apparatus into one co-operative body, in impelling each organ with its appropriate delicacy and speed, and above all, in training human beings to renounce their desultory habits of work, and to identify themselves with the unvarying regularity of the complex automation. To devise and administer a successful code of factory discipline, suited to the necessities of factory diligence, was the Herculean enterprise, the noble achievement of Arkwright. Even at the present day, when the system is perfectly organized, and its labour lightened to the utmost, it is found nearly impossible to convert persons past the age of puberty, whether drawn from rural or from handicraft occupations, into useful factory hands. After struggling for a while to conquer their listless or restive habits, they either renounce the employment spontaneously, or are dismissed by the overlookers on account of inattention.

---

3. For biographical information, see the selection from Edward Baines, Jr., *A History of the Cotton Manufacture in Great Britain,* collected in this volume. [Ed.]

If the factory Briareus could have been created by mechanical genius alone, it should have come into being thirty years sooner; for upwards of ninety years have now elapsed since John Wyatt, of Birmingham, not only invented the series of fluted rollers, (the spinning fingers usually ascribed to Arkwright,) but obtained a patent for the invention, and erected "a spinning engine without hands" in his native town. The details of this remarkable circumstance, recently snatched from oblivion, will be given in our Treatise on the Cotton Manufactures. Wyatt was a man of good education, in a respectable walk of life, much esteemed by his superiors, and therefore favourably placed, in a mechanical point of view, for maturing his admirable scheme. But he was of a gentle and passive spirit, little qualified to cope with the hardships of a new manufacturing enterprise. It required, in fact, a man of a Napoleon nerve and ambition to subdue the refractory tempers of workpeople accustomed to irregular paroxysms of diligence, and to urge on his multifarious and intricate constructions in the face of prejudice, passion, and envy. Such was Arkwright, who, suffering nothing to stay or turn aside his progress, arrived gloriously at the goal, and has for ever affixed his name to a great era in the annals of mankind,—an era which has laid open unbounded prospects of wealth and comfort to the industrious, however much they may have been occasionally clouded by ignorance and folly.

Prior to this period, manufactures were everywhere feeble and fluctuating in their development; shooting forth luxuriantly for a season, and again withering almost to the roots, like annual plants. Their perennial growth now began in England, and attracted capital in copious streams to irrigate the rich domains of industry. When this new career commenced, about the year 1770, the annual consumption of cotton in British manufactures was under four millions of pounds weight, and that of the whole of Christendom was probably not more than ten millions. Last year the consumption in Great Britain and Ireland was about two hundred and seventy millions of pounds, and that of Europe and the United States together four hundred and eighty millions. This prodigious increase is, without doubt, almost entirely due to the factory system founded and upreared by the intrepid native of Preston. If, then, this system be not merely an inevitable step in the social progression of the world, but the one which gives a commanding station and influence to the people who most resolutely take it, it does not become any man, far less a denizen of this favoured land, to vilify the author of a benefaction, which, wisely administered, may become the best temporal gift of Providence to the poor,—a blessing destined to mitigate, and in some measure to repeal, the primeval curse pronounced on the labour of man, "in the sweat of thy face shalt thou eat bread." Arkwright well deserves to live in honoured remembrance among those ancient master-spirits, who persuaded their roaming companions to exchange the precarious toils of the chase, for the settled comforts of agriculture.

In my recent tour, continued during several months, through the manufacturing districts, I have seen tens of thousands of old, young, and middle-aged of both sexes, many of them too feeble to get their daily bread by any of the former modes of industry, earning abundant food, raiment, and domestic accommodation, without perspiring at a single pore, screened meanwhile from the summer's sun and the winter's frost, in apartments more airy and salubrious than those of the metropolis in which our legislative and fashionable aristocracies assemble. In those spacious halls the benignant power of steam summons around him his myriads of willing menials, and assigns to each the regulated task, substituting for painful muscular effort on their part, the energies of his own gigantic arm, and demanding in return only attention and dexterity to correct such little aberrations as casually occur in his workmanship. The gentle docility of this moving force qualifies it for impelling the tiny bobbins of the lace-machine with a precision and speed inimitable by the most dexterous hands, directed by the sharpest eyes. Hence, under its auspices, and in obedience to Arkwright's polity, magnificent edifices, surpassing far in number, value, usefulness, and ingenuity of construction, the boasted monuments of Asiatic, Egyptian, and Roman despotism, have, within the short period of fifty years, risen up in this kingdom, to show to what extent capital, industry, and science may augment the resources of a state, while they meliorate the condition of its citizens. Such is the factory system, replete with prodigies in mechanics and political economy, which promises in its future growth to become the great minister of civilization to the terraqueous globe, enabling this country, as its heart, to diffuse along with its commerce the life-blood of science and religion to myriads of people still lying "in the region and shadow of death."

When Adam Smith[4] wrote his immortal elements of economics, automatic machinery being hardly known, he was properly led to regard the division of labour as the grand principle of manufacturing improvement; and he showed, in the example of pin-making, how each handicraftsman, being thereby enabled to perfect himself by practice in one point, became a quicker and cheaper workman. In each branch of manufacture he saw that some parts were, on that principle, of easy execution, like the cutting of pin wires into uniform lengths, and some were comparatively difficult, like the formation and fixation of their heads; and therefore he concluded that to each a workman of appropriate value and cost was naturally assigned. This appropriation forms the very essence of the division of labour, and has been constantly made since the origin of society. The ploughman, with powerful hand and skilful eye, has been always hired at high wages to form the furrow, and the plough-

4. See the Biographies section at the end of this volume. [Ed.]

boy at low wages, to lead the team. But what was in Dr. Smith's time a topic of useful illustration, cannot now be used without risk of misleading the public mind as to the right principle of manufacturing industry. In fact the division, or rather adaptation of labour to the different talents of men, is little thought of in factory employment. On the contrary, wherever a process requires peculiar dexterity and steadiness of hand, it is withdrawn as soon as possible from the *cunning* workman, who is prone to irregularities of many kinds, and it is placed in charge of a peculiar mechanism, so self-regulating, that a child may superintend it. Thus,—to take an example from the spinning of cotton—the first operation in delicacy and importance, is that of laying the fibres truly parallel in the spongy slivers, and the next is that of drawing these out into slender spongy cords, called rovings, with the least possible twist; both being perfectly uniform throughout their total length. To execute either of these processes tolerably by a hand-wheel would require a degree of skill not to be met with in one artisan out of a hundred. But fine yarn could not be made in factory-spinning except by taking these steps, nor was it ever made by machinery till Arkwright's sagacity contrived them. Moderately good yarn may be spun indeed on the *hand-wheel* without any drawings at all, and with even indifferent rovings, because the thread, under the twofold action of twisting and extension, has a tendency to equalize itself.

The principle of the factory system then is, to substitute mechanical science for hand skill, and the partition of a process into its essential constituents, for the division or graduation of labour among artisans. On the handicraft plan, labour more or less skilled was usually the most expensive element of production—Materiem superabat opus;[5] but on the automatic plan, skilled labour gets progressively superseded, and will, eventually, be replaced by mere overlookers of machines.

By the infirmity of human nature it happens, that the more skilful the workman, the more self-willed and intractable he is apt to become, and, of course, the less fit a component of a mechanical system, in which, by occasional irregularities, he may do great damage to the whole. The grand object therefore of the modern manufacturers is, through the union of capital and science, to reduce the task of his work-people to the exercise of vigilance and dexterity,—faculties, when concentred to one process, speedily brought to perfection in the young. In the infancy of mechanical engineering, a machine-factory displayed the division of labour in manifold gradations—the file, the drill, the lathe, having each its different workmen in the order of skill: but the dextrous hands of the filer and driller are now superseded by the planing, the key-groove cutting, and the drilling-machines; and those of the iron and

5. "The work will overcome the material," meaning that hand labor was expensive because it was more consequential than that on which it worked. [Ed.]

brass turners, by the self-acting slide-lathe. Mr. Anthony Strutt, who conducts the mechanical department of the great cotton factories of Belper and Milford, has so thoroughly departed from the old routine of the schools, that he will employ no man who has learned his craft by regular apprenticeship; but in contempt, as it were, of the division of labour principle, he sets a ploughboy to turn a shaft of perhaps several tons weight, and never has reason to repent his preference, because he infuses into the turning apparatus a precision of action, equal, if not superior, to the skill of the most experienced journeyman.

An eminent mechanician in Manchester told me, that he does not choose to make any steam-engines at present, because, with his existing means, he would need to resort to the old principle of the division of labour, so fruitful of jealousies and strikes among workmen; but he intends to prosecute that branch of business whenever he has prepared suitable arrangements on the equalization of labour, or automatic plan. On the graduation system, a man must serve an apprenticeship of many years before his hand and eye become skilled enough for certain mechanical feats; but on the system of decomposing a process into its constituents, and embodying each part in an automatic machine, a person of common care and capacity may be intrusted with any of the said elementary parts after a short probation, and may be transferred from one to another, on any emergency, at the discretion of the master. Such translations are utterly at variance with the old practice of the division of labour, which fixed one man to shaping the head of a pin, and another to sharpening its point, with most irksome and spirit-wasting uniformity, for a whole life.

It was indeed a subject of regret to observe how frequently the workman's eminence, in any craft, had to be purchased by the sacrifice of his health and comfort. To one unvaried operation, which required unremitting dexterity and diligence, his hand and eye were constantly on the strain, or if they were suffered to swerve from their task for a time, considerable loss ensued, either to the employer, or the operative, according as the work was done by the day or by the piece. But on the equalization plan of self-acting machines, the operative needs to call his faculties only into agreeable exercise; he is seldom harassed with anxiety or fatigue, and may find many leisure moments for either amusement or mediation, without detriment to his master's interests or his own. As his business consists in tending the work of a well-regulated mechanism, he can learn it in a short period; and when he transfers his services from one machine to another, he varies his task, and enlarges his views, by thinking on those general combinations which result from his and his companions' labours. Thus, that cramping of the faculties, that narrowing of the mind, that stunting of the frame, which were ascribed, and not unjustly, by moral writers, to the division of labour, cannot, in common circumstances, occur under the equable distribution of industry. How superior in vigour and intelligence are the factory mechanics in Lancashire, where the latter system of labour prevails, to the handicraft artisans of London, who, to a great extent, continue slaves to the former! The one set is familiar with almost every physico-mechanical combination, while the other seldom knows anything beyond the pin-head sphere of his daily task.

It is, in fact, the constant aim and tendency of every improvement in machinery to supersede human labour altogether, or to diminish its cost, by substituting the industry of women and children for that of men; or that of ordinary labourers for trained artisans. In most of the water-twist, or throttle cotton-mills, the spinning is entirely managed by females of sixteen years and upwards. The effect of substituting the self acting mule for the common mule, is to discharge the greater part of the men spinners, and to retain adolescents and children. The proprietor of a factory near Stockport states, in evidence to the commissioners, that, by such substitution, he would save 50*l.* a week in wages, in consequence of dispensing with nearly forty male spinners, at about 25*s.* of wages each. This tendency to employ merely children with watchful eyes and nimble fingers, instead of journeymen of long experience, shows how the scholastic dogma of the division of labour into degrees of skill has been exploded by our enlightened manufacturers.

FRANCIS PLACE
✂✂✂

HAND LOOM WEAVERS AND FACTORY WORKERS
A Letter to James Turner, Cotton Spinner

Brompton, London, 29th September, 1835.

My Good Friend,

I thank you for your letter, and for the printed placard containing the "Address of the Cotton Spinners and Factory Workers."

That the style which you and your coadjutors think it wise to adopt, and the purpose you hope to accomplish, may be more extensively known, I have

------

"Hand Loom Weavers and Factory Workers: Letter to James Turner, Cotton Spinner, from Francis Place." J. A. Roebuck, M.P., ed. London: C. Ely, 1835.

caused your address to be reprinted, and have made such remarks upon it as time and space will permit.

These remarks may hereafter be extended, and others may be made, until the whole matter relating to the Working People has been developed, and the principles which govern profits and wages be so demonstrated, as to be made easily intelligible to every one. Until this has been done, and the Working People understand their relative condition to other classes, they will never attain to that state of comfort and independence they ought to attain, and in which every good man must heartily desire they should *place themselves.*

My doing this will, however, depend upon the disposition of the Working People themselves. If they in any considerable number shall appear to be disposed to desire the information so necessary to their welfare, and without which they cannot go on in the right way, I shall be ready to do my best for their service. If they shall not be so disposed, I shall be, as I have long been, compelled to wait in hope that the time will arrive when they may be willing to come to a right understanding of these matters to them of the very greatest importance.

Copy of the Placard

Let Labour Live!—Let Industry be Rewarded!—Let Children be Protected!

Fellow Workmen, Fellow Countrymen, and Fellow Sufferers,

We, the Operative: Cotton Spinners and Factory Workers, in Delegate Meeting assembled, at Preston, in the country of Lancaster, beg most respectfully to call your attention to this our humble

Address

To the honest Labourers and industrious Producers of the United Kingdom, of every class, Agriculturalists, Artisans, and Manufacturers.

If patience and perseverance can ensure victory in a good cause, *our* efforts must at last be crowned with success. Faint we sometimes are, but still we pursue our course.

From the hard earnings of our ill-required toil we have sacrificed for several years, what is to us a large portion, *not* to buy the bloody weapons of "civil discord or of a servile war," (which may God avert!) but to attempt, as we now do, to arouse the attention of our neighbours and countrymen to that most accursed system under which we and *our children* continue to groan.

What speculator of ages past ever dared or ventured to predict the monstrous evils of the British Factory System? Whoever imagined that human depravity could so far vitiate the best blessings of Heaven as to transfer, by means of our boasted "ingenuity," the labour of the parent to the infant, and of the man to the *woman?* and having thus rendered the lords of God's creation artificially "superfluous," would hand them over to the tender mercies of an Emigration Committee, and *force* them from their native home and their beloved country, to make room for the inanimate, untaxed, and monopolizing *Machines* of their covetousness, "that *they* may be placed alone in the earth!" And these, forsooth, are "Christians!"

In bare justice to Christianity, we do denounce every abettor of such a heartless system as a very apostle of Atheism. Christianity! Does *it* contain one precept to sanction such a system as that of the British Factories?—a system which immures in a foul and blighting atmosphere the thousands who now toil in these modern temples of Mammon. Does Christianity deprive the young of the balmy air of Heaven, and of the gay pastimes of childhood, and leave them, when Mammon's bond is paid when his cruel claim (15 hours a-day) for' labour and occupation together, is satisfied, neither TIME nor PHYSICAL CAPACITY for the schoolmaster's lessons, nor for the counsels of the ministers of *Christ's* religion? Is this "Christianity?" Is it not heathenism? Is not barbarism itself refinement to this, and is not Paganism divine when compared with such "Christianity" as this?

Those who, in "the dark ages," caused their children to pass through the fire to Moloch, and filled the Valley of Hinnom with infants' wailings—those who even now encourage the blind Hindoo to prostrate himself beneath the gory ear of Juggernaut—those who consign the hoary head of age, and even smiling infancy to Ganges' gloomy stream—*all* infinitely fall short of the depravity which, in a "Christian country," fattens systematically upon the hardships of innocent childhood and the groans of oppressed manhood!

This, Fellow Countrymen, is no over-drawn case, no poetic description of unreal woe. Towards all *productive* occupation, without exception, the *principle* of degradation and of spoliation is in exercise; and is contemplated, in still keener force, by the heartless money-mongers of this "enlightened" generation. "The monied interest" in this country, as they are called, have usurped the seat of government, have wielded "the lash of the law," and have jostled Justice from her throne. This lofty-eyed generation boldly *demand* our labour at a rate even lower than the due sustenance of nature admits. Coolly they doom us to "coarser food," to workhouses, gaols, or to the cruel alternative of compulsory emigration, which they most fiendishly call "voluntary," when they have first pinched us down to object submission! Meanwhile, they claim to enjoy all but entire immunity from toil, from taxation, and from restraint; and if among the crowd a murmuring word is uttered, they—"liberal" souls—are ready to introduce to us a park of artillery, or a forest of bayonets!

This, fellow-sufferers, to speak truly, is the real character of a very large portion of the mighty ones of this land. We gladly admit that there are exceptions.— But how have they obtained the power thus to crush us, and to make us bend down to the ground for them to tread over?

The first cause is our ignorance; and under the factory hours of labour, that ignorance is hopeless. The second is our *divisions* and *jealousies,* which spring in a great measure from our ignorance. The third cause is the worst of all, and the least excusable—our *intemperance!* We debase ourselves, and invite tyranny to trample upon us! Our enemies see in the vices of a large portion of our body the opportunity and pretext for oppression.

Fellow Workmen! let us, at all events, strive to deliver ourselves from the last of these evils. Unless this be done, our case is hopeless; we are and must be the victims of imposition; we can neither by pecuniary nor by moral means do anything for our emancipation from the yoke which others impose, till we have broken the iron fetters of intemperance, which our own hands have rivetted.

The producers of this land could soon, by moral unity, overturn every unjust and oppressive system, by God's help. But we are divided: we, like Sampson, are shorn of our strength, and these Philistines are upon us.

The money-mongers and the party politicians find us an easy prey. They perceive that we are easily amused and divided by party ribbons, and banners, and clap-traps, and thus we become, by turns, the playthings and tools of Whigs, Tories, and even Radicals. Each of these parties are striving for place, power, and pension—these are the gods of their idolatry. Each in turn is, or else would be, patriots when out of office, and tyrants when in, sucking voraciously the nation's life blood, and only stopping to take breath, and to utter the insulting cry of "Prosperity, prosperity," and to tell us that *for them* "the machine works well." Oh, the trickery of this game between the *Outs* and the *Ins!* Ambition inspires it, cupidity urges it, and hypocrisy disguises it:—we have, however, to pay the smart! Let us not be misunderstood. In each of these three parties there are some good men, real philanthropists; but they are led away by party spirit. This is our national ruin—scrambling for power and place under colour of patriotism.

Would to God that men of real benevolence would cease from this worse than child play, and learn, before it is too late, that the wealth of the producers is the wealth of all.

We are not for *confusion* and *bloodshed,* and therefore we speak thus plainly. Let not the trumpet of seasonable warning be disregarded, because it is sounded by a few plain Lancashire workers. We would spoil no man of his rightful property—we dream not of any absolute equality of condition—we entertain no visions of a Paradise below. We expect that the "brow" of man must "sweat" for his maintenance, but we expect also, according to the promise of the Most High, to "live" by it—to "eat our bread" by it; nor do we yet learn, that in his severest indignation, God has ever doomed the majority of the human family to toil, that a minority of idlers may eat all the "bread," and leave the producers to pine upon the *chaff* and the *husks.* We read no where that he has condemned *our children* to toil *for us, or to toil at all.* But if it must be so, if our children must toil, if ingenious avarice, the master idol of the land, has so contrived and ordained, at least let those who profess to reverence the God of love stand up for us, and claim some real protection for the factory child.

We know that great bodies of our fellow-countrymen are deluded by the idea that Lord Althorp's Act affords sufficient protection. Many suppose, especially those who live remote from manufacturing districts, that the system has been reformed to the model of our lamented friend, Mr Sadler. We tell them *it is a delusion.* That some amelioration may have taken place in many instances, we are willing to allow; but let it not be forgotten, that the great majority of the young factory workers are still working twelve hours a day, and are occupied nearly fifteen, when meals, &c. are included.

It is boasted, that children up to thirteen years are protected from more than eight hours' work, and allowed education.

Be it known to all who value the health or education of the young, that this Act is, as we always said it would prove, a complete failure. We therefore call for help. Charles Hindley, Esq. M.P. for Ashton, himself a large cotton manufacturer, is so convinced of this, that he has benevolently introduced, this session, a Bill to amend the failure of Lord Althorp and his factory commissioners. We ask that Mr. Hindley may have the support of the nation, *upon the express condition that the ten hours' clause be retained and never relinquished,* and also, that *the* restriction as to time be laid on the *moving power.* There are also some other improvements, which we trust he will admit. We regard this measure as a first instalment. We openly declare, that this is not all we require. We do not look upon a Ten Hour Bill, however effective, as a "cure all." There are many other measures required by strict justice for the labouring and productive classes, but this stands first on humanity's list.

We have indeed but little reason to hope for any good for our class from the House of Commons; but as Mr. Hindley is willing to try them *once more,* let him have the nation's support. And is it not a national measure? Certainly, as much so as the deliverance of the blacks from their bondage. And if those who made such ado about Black slavery do not heartily join to put down this *White* slavery, they brand hypocrisy on their own foreheads, and deserve the scorn of every real lover of his country and kind. Will not the farmers help us? Let there be no strife between us and them. Our interests are one—what is bad for us, is not good for them. The interests of all producers are common—what hurts one class of them hurts all. The money-mongers of every political party rush together in one phalanx, wherever our common cause is to be opposed. If labour cries for protection, for cessation from toil—if industry require that property should bear its due quota of taxation, you will soon find *Peel, Rice,* and *Hume* all "check by jowl."

Let, then, all petty jealousies and distinctions fall, and let us all join first to set our children free. Ours is a well-tried cause. No question has been more variously and amply discussed by the press and by public meetings; no question has undergone more thorough sifting no; position is more firmly established, especially by the highest medical authorities. Mr. Hindley is now at his post. In another session he will have to fight for us. Now, then, let us prepare to help him. From Preston, in the extreme north-west of the Factory Districts, we humbly venture to sound once more the tocsin of agitation; yes, we repeat it, of agitation, and in good earnest too—of such an agitation as has not yet been—peaceful in its character, but firm and resolute too. Our Manchester brethren are not less ready than we. They will forgive us if we say, we are now prepared to meet them; to confer with them; to act upon any well devised and uniform plan. Yorkshire will not be wanting—Scotland, we hope, will vie with us. Let us gather the material of the conflict; it shall not be one of blood, but it shall be one, if we can avail anything, which shall shake the Temple of Tyranny to its base, and teach the worshippers of gold that there is a power above them, and that there is a spirit in Britons that will not suffer them to see their children thus enslaved.

We claim the Bill of Mr. Hindley for *ourselves* as well. We are parents, we have families who look up to us for instruction, and we have no time either to acquire information for ourselves or to communicate it to them.

Once more, then, we ask the help of all who love their country. We invoke the arm of Omnipotence, humbly imploring his power and approbation! To our countrymen we say, cease from your ribbons and banners, support party strugglers no more, leave them to die—to exhaust themselves; support those men of all parties and shades who will espouse and maintain the good old rule of Christianity. "Do unto others as ye would they should do unto you." Here is our rallying point.

Farmers, help us, and we will help you. We call upon all to help us. We appeal to Christians and to Christian Ministers. By a firm union of moral energy we may, by God's help, save our country yet. *But if we now hang back and continue disunited, the sequel of its history will be written in blood.*

And now, fellow-countrymen, (in conclusion) we call upon you to arouse. Demand, or at least cry most urgently for a restriction to "ten hours," according to the plan of Mr. Hindley's Bill. *We shall never be able to stand our ground until we shorten time.*

From committees as they have done in Manchester, Preston, Bradford, Wigan, Warrington, &c. &c. Bradford, Yorkshire, is at present the centre of communication, and letters (post paid) addressed to J. B. Smeles, Bridge street, will receive attention.

(*Signed on behalf of the Meeting*),

H. E., Chairman.

B. J., Secretary.

August 23rd, 1835.

You appeal to your fellow workmen, to your employers and others, as to christians—you dwell on this topic as one likely to be useful to you: you depend upon a broken reed. You appeal to humanity and religion: you are suppliants in a way which cannot serve you. You deceive yourselves. There are to be sure, as you admit, some who from religion and humanity are desirous to see your condition improved, but they are few and far apart. Yours is a matter of business. You have the power to regulate your own concerns; and until you are sufficiently acquainted with that power, honest enough to one another to hold together as you ought to do, and wise enough to use your power discreetly, your condition cannot be improved. All appeals to religion and humanity will be useless, so long as you are unwise and unfaithful to one another.

Have you never read the fable of Hercules and the Waggoner. "As the Waggoner was driving his team, one of the wheels stuck fast in the mire; down fell the waggoner on his knees, and bawled, and prayed to Hercules to come and help him. Hercules looking down from a cloud, told him not to lie there like

a stupid idle rascal as he was, but to get up, flog his horses, put his shoulder to the wheel, and then if he called upon him, he would help him."
From this fable came the proverb

"God helps those who help themselves."

Drop all nonsensical appeals, get up from your knees, put your shoulders to the wheel, push the waggon out of the mire, and you will find that you want no Hercules to help you: you will find the power, whenever you find the resolution, to help yourselves.

Neither canting nor threatening, nor violence of any kind can serve you: drop all notions of such things. Take pains to understand all that relates to your condition; work together honestly, patiently, resolutely, and you will accomplish your purpose. You will never accomplish it by any other mode of proceeding.

You ask: "Whoever imagined that human *depravity* could transfer the labour of the parent to the infant, and the man to the woman, thus rendering *hands* artificially *superfluous.*"

There indeed is the evil; yes, there is the *depravity* which more than everything else put together ruins you.

You, as well as many others, know well that I have always deprecated the employment of women in every regularly conducted trade. Women have enough to do to attend to their homes, their husbands, their children, their relatives, and such light labour as can be done at home; their place is home; there they must be, or there can be no order, no satisfaction, no comfort. All is turned upside down, where the woman is turned out of her home,—turned into a mill or a workshop. Women who follow a regular trade like men, never can be either good wives, good mothers, or good companions; and yet, unless these are all the society must degenerate, until at length it can go no lower, until *depravity* has reached its lowest depth, until crime and misery can be pushed no further.

Let us then calmly inquire about this *depravity.* In the reports of Committees of the House of Commons, are statements made by both masters and men of the former earnings of spinners and weavers. The wages of weavers were it seems at one time higher than those in any other common trade. How then has it happened that they are now lower than in any other common trade? You have answered, "*pinching*" and "*grinding*" have lowered them, "the *avarice* of the rich has lowered them." Here is fallacy, here is self-deception. Ask yourselves another question: how is it that while the weavers' wages were gradually sinking, those in other trades were generally rising? Why has not "*pinching*" and "*grinding*" and "*avarice*" kept them down also, and made all workmen equally ill paid with the cotton weaver? Why have not these things compelled the wives and children in other trades (where they might be employed) to be employed as they are in mills and factories and hand looms? Why have not tailors and shoemakers and compositors, with their wives and sons and daughters, been compelled to work for fourteen, fifteen, and sixteen hours a day, for a pittance, which when put together, does not amount to so much as the man alone earns? Why, indeed? Hear me—hear your friend, who would not, if he could avoid it, say one word to you which you would not like to hear—whose greatest pleasure would be to praise you, as it is his greatest pain to blame you.

When the weavers in Lancashire were earning 36s. a week, the tailors in London were earning 18s. 6d.; when the weavers were earning 28s. a week, the tailors were earning 21s. 9d.; when the best of the weavers were earning 7s. 6d. for six days' labour of fourteen hours each, the tailors were earning 36s. for six days' labour of twelve hours each. In other trades a proportionate rise had taken place.

How has this happened? I will tell you: These trades had each of them a judicious combination, they knew that separately each man had no power at all, and that, unless they combined, their wages would be reduced to the lowest sum on which they could exist and perform their labour. Take an example. In 1810 the master-tailors combined, and went to Parliament for a bill. The bill was carefully and artfully drawn; its purpose was to give the masters power over the men, to enable them to employ women, and consequently children. The Bill was sent to a Committee, and was thrown out,—thrown out by the well-directed exertions of the men, aided by some of the wisest of the masters.

Had not the men been in a well-digested combination, they must have submitted; and if they had, the number of hands would have increased so rapidly that, in a few years, women and girls would have done so much of the trade, that the whole body would have been reduced to a very low state of degradation,—to horrid poverty, vice, crime, and misery.

The same course would have been pursued in many other trades, and instead of the increase of knowledge, and sobriety, and decency of behaviour,— and, above all, the growing desire to have their children better and better instructed, they would have been in the sad condition in which the cotton "*weavers and factory-workers*" are but too generally placed. One trade has, however, followed a different plan, and bitterly do they suffer for their want of sense. I mean the Spitalfields silk weavers. In that trade women and children work, have always worked, and have always, with few exceptions, been in poverty; and there they will remain so long as the practice is continued.

I now come back to the "*cotton-weavers and factory-workers*," and I ask you, how did it happen that when "*a cotton-weaver*" could earn better wages than men could earn in other common trades, they did not maintain those high wages? How did it happen that while, in other trades, wages rose, theirs fell?

Hear me, while I tell you the unpleasant—the appalling truth! At that time the men were much more ignorant—much more dissolute than they are now; for information has even reached them, spite of their poverty.

The men were then as idle as they were were ignorant and dissolute; nothing was saved—all was squandered. A few exceptions will not invalidate the rule.

They worked, at times, in their own looms; they contrived to put up other looms; they taught men and women to weave, that they might hire their looms. The pittance they got from this hiring enabled them to increase their idleness, and to indulge their debauchery. They were too besotted to think of the consequences—too selfish to think of anything beyond their own immediate indulgence. Thus were the cotton-workers increased with amazing rapidity, and this practice has continued to the present time. "Thus has the labour been transferred from the man to the woman; from the woman to the infant. Thus have hands been rendered superfluous." Thus have wages been reduced to nearly the starvation point.

It will be said again, as you have said now:—all this is a consequence of the factory system, and the masters are the cause of it. Ask yourself, then—Why have not the masters in other trades done the same? See if you can find any other answer than this—*The men would not let them.* See if you can find any other honest and true reason than this. The cotton-masters needed do no more than countenance the absurd conduct of the workmen, until they had accomplished the mischief, and then they had the power to do nearly as they pleased.

No trade, no manufacture, has gone on increasing like the cotton manufacture—no trade, no manufacture, has required so rapid an increase of hands. It ought, therefore, to have been one of the best paid. And so it would have been, but for the increase of hands still faster than the demand for them. The increase of hands seems almost incredible; it was, however, soon made *artificially superfluous,* and the sad consequences are before us.

"Oh," say you and your confederates, catching like drowning men at straws—"we have to contend with the *untaxed and monopolising machinery.*" Now, these machines have been the cause of the great increase of the manufacture, and of the immensity of trade connected with it; and had not the number of hands increased faster than the demand for them, wages must have been high. No efforts, however made, or by whom made, could have made wages low. Almost, if indeed not quite within the memory of persons yet living, there were not so many as 40,000 persons employed in the whole manufacture; yet sometime since, when Robert Owen,[1] after taking much pains to acquire accurate information, stated the number at *one million two hundred thousand.* Now then, ask yourself—let any one ask himself—if without the continued increase of machinery, one fourth part of this number could ever have been employed? Whether, if there had been no machinery, even a one-tenth part of

---

1. See the Biographies section at the end of this volume. [Ed.]

the number could have been employed at all? Let all, then, everyone, ask this question, and without prejudice answer it. If we had increased our number to 1,000,000, instead of 1,200,000, should we not have good wages still? One only answer can be given.

But the power-loom—ay, the power-loom. If I were to pass over this piece of machinery, it would be said I had omitted to notice it, because it would have confuted my assertions; and they who love to delude themselves with a fallacy, to cheat themselves with an idle excuse, would have triumphed in their mischievous self-delusion. The power-loom is not an universal loom; it cannot weave fancy articles, it cannot weave ginghams, it cannot weave fine fabrics, it cannot weave either muslin or cambric. Now then there are more of these fabrics to be woven than there were of all kinds of fabrics taken together when the power-loom was first introduced, and there are many more persons employed in hand-loom weaving now than there were at the time when the power-loom was first used. Here then is the answer. Had there been no increase, or only a proportionate increase of hand-loom weavers, wages could not have fallen; the power-loom might be left to do its coarse work, giving good wages to those who managed them, while good wages would also be given to every one of the hand-loom weavers.

You describe the oppressions of the monied interest, and say, "they have pinched us down to abject submission." This is railing to no purpose. You know—you all know—that no sooner does a workman find the means to employ other men, then he becomes a "pincher" as much as he can. You all know that the little master and the new master are the first to take advantage of the poverty of the workman, of his want of employment; that this leads upwards until wages are lowered all round. "Pinching," then, is the vice of all, whether monied or unmonied. I heartily dislike the rich man who, by manufacturing or trading, seeks to increase his too great riches. He who does this seldom cares at all for the condition of others—their happiness or unhappiness is no concern of his. But this, even this, should have no influence on the working man. What is it to him that some men care nothing about him? His business should be to care for himself, for his family, for his relatives, for his class, and to give himself no trouble about what the rich may think of him. Whenever the working people shall care as they ought to do for their own class, all will soon be well with them.

You come at length to something like the real matter-of-fact. Speaking of your degradation, you say:—

"The first cause is our ignorance; and, under the factory hours of labour, that ignorance (the removal of it) is hopeless.

"The second cause is our jealousies and divisions, which spring in a great measure from our ignorance.

"The third cause is the worst of all—and the least excusable—our intemperance! We debase ourselves, and invite tyranny to trample upon us!"

With one exception these are plain truths. You have it in your power, notwithstanding "the factory hours of labour," to do much. Yes, here are the truths all should attend—to which all must attend—or your case will become hopeless.

The only wise course for you is, to leave off railing at others, and go seriously to work for yourselves. "God helps those who help themselves," says the proverb; and you may depend upon it that you never will be helped by any but yourselves. If you reason on the matter closely, you will be *convinced* that you never will be helped by any but yourselves, even if all were disposed to help you, as but few ever will be.

Why then, if you are properly disposed to help yourselves, should not the factory hours of working be reduced? In other trades, the workmen refuse to work more than a certain number of hours: and the masters have never been able to make them work more hours than they themselves have decided shall be a day's work. Why do not you do as they have done? A mill cannot go on without spinners; spinners are the best paid, and would, if they were as well organised as other trades are, be just as able as they are to settle the hours of working. Depend upon it you will never have the number of working hours reduced until you yourselves have reduced them. You only waste your time in complaining of your grievances, and in praying for help to Hercules; actions, not prayers, must serve you, or nothing will.

Your proposed remedy of a short time-bill, is even more than absurd. It never will be granted. It ought not to be granted. No Parliament will ever pass a bill to prevent any class of manufacturers from carrying on their business in any manner they may think most advantageous, save only so far as relates to the employment of children; and a short time-bill[2] is not necessary for their protection. A short time-bill would make the condition of the "factory workers," beyond all that they have hitherto endured, miserable indeed.

You talk wildly of a "power above the worshippers of gold, which shall shake the temple of tyranny to its base, and shew that there is a spirit in Britons, which will not suffer them to see their children thus enslaved." This is calling upon Hercules with a vengeance. You have heard his reply—"get up, you lazy rascals;"—yes, get up: the power is in your own integrity, vigilance, and perseverance; "put your shoulders to the wheel;" help yourselves, and Hercules will help you—that is, when you help yourselves—when you want none of his help.

I wish I could see your own power in full exercise. It will not be a power from above to "shake the temple of tyranny to its foundations," but the power, the moral power of men, of men here below, who understand their duty to one another, and have wisdom and courage to use it discretely, yet effectually.

---

2. "A short time bill" was one restricting the number of hours a laborer could work in a day. [Ed.]

With respect to the employment of children, I agree with you that it is altogether improper; it is all but atrocious in many cases;—actually atrocious in many of their parents to let them go, and nearly, if not quite, as bad in the legislature to permit the practice. Children are especially under the control of the legislature. The law has declared that they are not free agents, that is, they are not free to choose for themselves. It has forbidden them to make contracts to dispose of themselves; it ought, therefore, to prevent others from disposing of them improperly, and to some extent it has done this. It has left them generally to the care of their parents and guardians, and it is itself the guardian of those who have no "natural guardian." It punishes parents who use them cruelly, and it takes them away from cruel parents; yet it permits them to be sent to factories, where the employment, the discipline, and all the consequences taken together, amount to cruelty much greater than the law will permit the parents to exercise in their own persons. This should be rectified. It might be rectified by a well directed simultaneous effort, and the time would soon arrive when no child under thirteen years of age should be suffered to enter any mill or factory as a labourer; and when admitted, even at that age, the hours of their work should be carefully limited. This step taken, the next as regards minors should be, that no girl should be employed as a labourer or worker in any mill or factory whatever. If the legislature should think it was pushing power too far, to prohibit girls being bound apprentices to those employed in mills or factories, after they were fourteen years of age, you, the men, should exclude them, by refusing to work with them. Keep them out, keep them up. Your future happiness depends too greatly on the education of girls from fourteen to twenty-one years of age, for you to allow their education destroyed, and themselves debased in mill and factory work.

If, then, the men refused to work in mills and factories with girls, as they ought to do, as other trades have done, in workshops, and for those masters who employ women and girls, the young women who will otherwise be degraded by factory labour will become all that can be desired as companionable wives, and the whole condition of factory-workers would soon be improved, the men will obtain competent wages for their maintenance. This the one will never be, nor the other ever obtain, under the present system.

I have never seen the inside of a cotton-factory. It is almost certain that I never shall see the inside of one. I have read all the evidence taken by Committees of Parliament; I have read books and pamphlets; I have conversed with numbers of cottoners, masters as well as men; I understand much of the machinery used in all sorts of mills, and should like to see it in use. But I cannot voluntarily submit to see the misery of working it before my eyes. I abhor such scenes of degradation as even the best of the cotton-mills cannot be free from.

This will be treated as a ridiculous feeling—as an absurd prejudice; but to me, to whom human beings are valuable as they are intellectual and free, a cotton-mill is more abhorrent than I can find words with which to describe it.

Here my good friends is a test of the wisdom and virtue of the factory-workers and the hand-loom weavers! Here is a reply to some parts of their address, of which they will not probably purchase five hundred copies! If they had the proper feeling, they would re-print it. It contains their own address, as well as the comment thereon. They would make a small subscription, continue it weekly, and circulate a penny pamphlet, say once a fortnight. Here is the opening of a controversy, which, if it were carried on with temper, might lead to almost inexpressible advantage.

Yours, my good friend,

FRANCIS PLACE.

THE EFFECTS OF MACHINERY ON MANUAL LABOUR, AND ON THE DISTRIBUTION OF THE PRODUCE OF INDUSTRY

The Justice or Injustice with which the New Productive Power of this age is exercised, and how far the existing application of this power to the benefit of the few, and the misery of the many, can be vindicated upon the principles of moral, natural, and civil justice, is a question of grand and paramount import at the present moment, when liberty under a new aspect is opened upon us, and all men are looking forward to vast changes in the relative condition of the different classes which constitute the social body; to a substantial equality of natural privileges, instead of that shadowy semblance of it, which has hitherto mocked our hopes and defeated our happiness.

There is no question so deeply interesting as that of the relative condition of labour and industry, in a community abounding, even to excess, in wealth, and in the means of multiplying and increasing it by a new and unprecedented productive power, which has enabled us to sink 1,000 millions in the coffer of National indolence—to pay 30 millions worth of industry annually into this coffer—and yet to remain rich; to exhibit the grossest extremes of splendour and beggary.

From *The English Chartist Circular.* Vol. 2 No. 82 (1842)

In a former paper, of *"The Respective Rights of Property and Industry,"* we observed, that "Human industry has received a new modification, while it has attained a new and unmeasurable power; and the poor man must now depend for subsistence upon the distribution and diffusion, *after another manner than heretofore,* of the advantages which a new and mighty agency is creating." It will be the object of the following remarks to illustrate this position.

In the actual state of human society, the market value of labour depends upon its *scarcity,* in the general view of the case; and, specifically, the value of labour in each particular line of industry must depend upon the scarcity or fewness of the hands in that line, by which they can be enabled to *command* a reasonable recompense; this circumstance being the only safeguard that labour can avail itself of against the cupidity of employers, which stimulates them to get their work done well at the lowest rate, *whatever may be their own profit!* But machinery *diminishes the scarcity of labour* in every line to which it is applied, and this in proportion to the perfection of the machinery employed in such line; and, in so doing, it robs labour of its only protection. Capital, wielding exclusively the almost unlimited productive power of the age, is altogether, in the sense we are now considering, and at the present moment, independent of the remonstrances of labour, to whom it can triumphantly say, "This, or nothing, is your reward!" The requirement for manual labour, in each branch, decreases in proportion to the perfection of the machinery in such branch, and is not necessarily increased by the increased demand for the article which the application of machinery, in making it, gives rise to; that is, by the increased quantity of the article required to be made by the aid of the machinery, since this quantity, after all, is *limited* by the *actual,* not the *presumed,* consumption of the article, and cannot go beyond this; a fact wholly lost sight of by reasoners on the effects of machinery. Whatever this limited quantity or demand may be, however great it may be, it *may* require comparatively but little assistance from manual labour to produce it with the aid of machinery. Thus, if 100,000 yards of lace we produced by 1,000 individuals, *without* the aid of machinery, there is no reason why a million of yards may not be produced *with* machinery, by half this number of individuals: thus throwing out of all employment 500 persons, and that *permanently,* in this particular branch of manufacture. Capital wielding the Productive Power, upon the principle of competition and individual gain, does not say to the 500 thus thrown out of employment, "You shall still work on, but you shall only work *half the former number of hours,* and be paid the same wages *for this half* that you formerly received; since Providence has designed this invention to mitigate your labour to improve your condition." No.—Only one half of the former number of hands are kept working, *at the old wages,* and the rest are turned off to starve, the difference gained being pocketed by the capitalist, deducting only the interest of the cost of his machinery and its wear and tear—a comparative trifle.

But it will be said, that machinery by increasing the general activity and the demand for fast supplies of raw materials, will occasion employment to present itself in other channels. We have, however, seen that this is *limited*—limited by demand, as demand is limited by actual consumption, which again is limited by the system of pauperism which is overtaking us, and which will be noticed as we proceed. Besides, machinery may be made successively applicable to many of these new branches of manufacture, and it is incumbent on those who use this argument to prove that the opening for the application of manual labour, thus assumed to have taken place, *has really taken place without being counteracted by machinery,* which would be, we conceive, no easy task. Where has machinery not been applied? Will any man in the face of facts assert, that with a demand limited by a limited consumption, an equivalent opening has been presented for the quantity of labour displaced by the operation of machinery? If he do assert this, then, as there is manifestly no branch in which labour is not a drug, he must set up the argument of over population, as the cause of the depreciation of labour; in which case he is bound to shew that the power of production is actually applied *to its full extent;* and thus applied is still *insufficient* to maintain this redundancy in the population. While the Productive Power remains bound and fettered by the self-interest of the few—and can no longer continue in motion than this interest is served—when the wheel stops at its bidding, though riches abound in the land, and thousands are in want and *idle,* who might set it going by their industry—the argument of over population is worthless, and if not urged in ignorance, is as wicked as it is worthless.

Does any individual in the United Kingdom feel the horrors of starvation, because there is not subsistence for all? It is not the lack of wealth and produce, or of the means of creating wealth and produce; but it is the partial and selfish distribution of wealth and produce which is the cause of our suffering. We can cure an Irish famine by the *distribution* of a little gold—there is no want of means or of power! We can *make* wealth, if we will but distribute wealth; but if we fail to promote distribution, the productive power will be rendered proportionally abortive. But let population, for the argument's sake, be so egregiously thinned down as to enhance the price of labour; what, in this case, becomes of the system of *Competition,* which depends for its prosperity upon the facility of paying labour at a starvation price;—of paying it as it wills! Were it possible thus to thin down the population, by emigration or otherwise, we should moreover in this case, be presented with the anomaly of increased and increasing productive powers, and the simultaneous necessity of a decreased and decreasing population.

But taking fact and experience for our guides, we here affirm, that this reduction of the number of hands will never take place. Let us therefore view the condition of manual labour, and of mere industry without capital, in the actual circumstances in which we find them placed, relatively with capital, and its minister—the productive power—machinery.

It is the direct effect of *Machinery* to produce an immediate supply of any given article, equal to the demand for such article; and it is the direct effect of *Competition* to render this supply at *the lowest possible price!*

Under the system of *Competition* generated by the new power of production, and stimulated by it, in proportion to the ability to produce will be the tendency to produce cheap. Labour will thus become depreciated in an exact ratio with the perfection of machinery; and in the degree in which consumption becomes limited by the depreciation of the value of labour, production will become *artificially superabundant!* For if a *foreign market* is open, to mitigate the evil, in order to command this market a starvation price will *still* be the only one labour will obtain, and however great our *exports,* the same unmitigated toil will be demanded from manual industry for the same iniquitous pittance! The *factories will still groan with the slavery of the employed* even to the immolation, at the altar of avarice, of the helpless innocency of infancy and childhood!

In this state of things, with the increased and increasing perfection of Machinery and a limited home consumption, there will obviously always remain a redundant proportion of manual labour, which capital and competition may work with as it wills, to the wringing of the last sigh of despair from the bosom of Industry. In such a state of things, to *scarcity* of labour, which may enhance its value, can possibly happen; the market price of the article, which includes the wages of labour, will be reduced, by the facility afforded by machinery to competition, to its *minimum*—its nearest approximation to the price of the raw material; and that this may be got cheap, the wages of those who are instrumental in procuring it will, in common with all other wages, be reduced to the lowest ebb—namely the starvation point! For with this competition and rivalry, *rendered practicable by machinery, and by machinery only,* it is needless to say, that human cupidity goes hand in hand. And who will trust the cupidity of any set of men with the rights of the rest? Justice must be the thing appealed to.

From these Premises, it follows, as a result of the increased and increasing perfection of machinery, and of the extreme competition on the part of capital arising from this perfection. *That the value of labour must necessarily recede to the starvation point; and not only so recede, but must* REMAIN PERMANENTLY DEPRESSED TO THIS POINT! In other words, the *Starvometer,* (if the inventive faculty be indulged for a term) will be applied to human industry, so long as competition, aided by machinery in its career, shall continue to be the prime principle of human activity.

Now, this is exactly our situation at the present moment. Competition wielding the Productive Power has run its career until great Capitalists alone can thrive, upon the principle of small profits on large quantities of production; while the wages of labour are ground down to the starvation point, or a too close approximation to it, for the vindication of humanity; and thus, while the productive power, Machinery, has gone on increasing wealth to an enormous extent, in a limited and partial sphere, this increase has been attended with the excessive impoverishment of the many! Is not the crisis arrived, or nearly so, in which the wages of labour are approaching a minimum pittance, taken in many cases out of a minimum profit, arising from the competition which brings the market price of an article to its lowest scale—or nearest approximation to the price of the raw material of which it is made? It is true that a great number of these small profits put together may make a splendid fortune for the capitalist. But what in this case becomes of the operative? who is, besides, thrown out of employment, when the machinery stands still, and his services are not wanted. Again, are we not arrived or arriving at that crisis, in which the great body, by becoming poor, must become non-consumers, and then what follows?—What, but that while consumers can be found abroad, the evil is remedied for the capitalist, and for him only; the condition of the operative remaining the same!

And it is melancholy to have to add, that however low the price of provisions may be brought, labour will still, under a system of competition, which cannot be restrained while it has the Productive Power at its command, continue to be oppressed, and chained down to the level of more than slavery—to an inhuman point of destitution.

THREE

CALCULATING LOSSES

In this section, reformers and radicals assess the damage inflicted on individuals and society as a result of factory production. None of the writers in this section seek to end factory production. Rather, they suggest the ways in which its effects might be mitigated so that the laboring population might live better lives, and, not incidentally, pose less of a threat—in political and public health terms—to the middle and upper classes.

Richard Oastler's letter to the *Leeds Mercury* describes factory work as a worse evil than colonial slavery; indeed, working in a factory is a form of slavery in Oastler's description. This analogy will become a familiar one over the course of the nineteenth century. Reformers like James Phillips Kay-Shuttleworth and Peter Gaskell are less concerned with working conditions and more focused on the home lives of workers. Indeed, it seems that the living conditions of the working class are more important than their working conditions: "the first step to recklessness," Kay writes, "may often be traced in a neglect of that self-respect, and of the love of domestic enjoyments, which are indicated by personal slovenliness, and discomfort of the habitation" (29). Poverty breeds not only disease, but also dissent—which may be expressed recklessly.

Gaskell specifically suggests that women who work in factories cannot provide a comfortable domestic life. Engels also bewails the loss of domesticity that working women represent: the health of women is sacrificed and in turn, the whole family suffers: it is turned "upside down" by women at work and men (because they demand higher wages) at home. Engels includes devastating examples of illness and deformity caused by factory work. Indeed, his list of accidents anticipates an unsigned article in *Household Words* of

1854 by Henry Morley in which he enumerates the dangers of the factory in a list so vivid that the reader can almost see the hands of children severed at the wrist, arms torn away from shoulders by machinery, and finally the agonizing deaths of these accident victims. Lord Macaulay's speech to Parliament on the Ten Hours Bill unites morality and health as issues in which the government must interfere. He appeals to the self-interest of the middle and upper classes in his description of a permanently weakened laboring class, full of stunted and chronically ill persons who will eventually be unable to work, to reproduce, or to fight in wars.

Charles Wing's *Evils of the Factory System*—like many books of this genre—includes long excerpts from Parliamentary hearings on child labor. Workers, mill owners, and physicians were interviewed at such hearings, and although the evidence fills many damning volumes, child labor persisted to the end of the century (and indeed persists now in many "developing" countries). The texture of nineteenth-century factory life comes through, though, in the testimony of workers—in their descriptions of many missed meals and much missed sleep, of unventilated rooms filled with cotton dust in which some workers stopped breathing altogether, of workers urinating on themselves because they were not permitted to leave the factory except at designated times, of "strappings" of children, of deformities of the legs caused by standing. In the excerpt from the autobiography of John Ward O'Neil, written in part during the British "cotton famine" of the 1860s, news from America about the progress of the Civil War precedes that of his daughter's wedding in one entry and suggests how critical that distant struggle became for British cotton workers.

None of the losses inflicted by industrialization were significant enough to stunt its growth: The dangers of the factory system and the ways of life it engendered were extensively and repeatedly described, but they changed very slowly. We might say that they produced a habit of horrified reaction, but that the major material reforms were realized in piecemeal and reluctant attempts to improve a system that seemed like it could not be altered it in any significant way.

CHAPTER SIX

CHILDHOOD AND DOMESTICITY

JAMES PHILLIPS KAY-SHUTTLEWORTH
※※※

from THE MORAL AND PHYSICAL CONDITION OF THE WORKING CLASSES

The population employed in the cotton factories rises at five o'clock in the morning, works in the mills from six till eight o'clock, and returns home for half an hour or forty minutes to breakfast. This meal generally consists of tea or coffee, with a little bread. Oatmeal porridge is sometimes, but of late rarely used, and chiefly by the men; but the stimulus of tea is preferred, and especially by the women. The tea is almost always of a bad, and sometimes of a deleterious quality; the infusion is weak, and little or no milk is added. The operatives return to the mills and workshops until twelve o'clock, when an hour is allowed for dinner. Amongst those who obtain the lower rates of wages this meal generally consists of boiled potatoes. The mess of potatoes is put into one large dish; melted lard and butter are poured upon them, and a few pieces of fried fat bacon are sometimes mingled with them, and but seldom a little meat. Those who obtain better wages, or families whose aggregate income is larger, add a greater proportion of animal food to this meal, at least three times in the week; but the quantity consumed by the labouring population is not great. The family sits round the table, and each rapidly appropriates his portion on a plate, or they all plunge their spoons into the dish, and with an animal eagerness satisfy the cravings of their appetite. At the expiration of the hour, they are all again employed in the workshops or mills, where

From *The Moral and Physical Condition of the Working Classes.* London: J. Ridgway, 1832.

185

they continue until seven o'clock or a later hour, when they generally again indulge in the use of tea, often mingled with spirits accompanied by a little bread. Oatmeal or potatoes are however taken by some a second time in the evening.

The comparatively innutritious qualities of these articles of diet are most evident. We are, however, by no means prepared to say that an individual living in a healthy atmosphere, and engaged in active employment in the open air, would not be able to continue protracted and severe labour, without any suffering, whilst nourished by this food. We should rather be disposed on the contrary to affirm, that any ill effects must necessarily be so much diminished, that, from the influence of habit, and the benefits derived from the constant inhalation of an uncontaminated atmosphere, during healthy exercise in agricultural pursuits, few if any evil results would ensue. But the population nourished on this aliment is crowded into one dense mass, in cottages separated by narrow, unpaved, and almost pestilential streets, in an atmosphere loaded with the smoke and exhalations of a large manufacturing city. The operatives are congregated in rooms and workshops during twelve hours in the day, in an enervating, heated atmosphere, which is frequently loaded with dust or filaments of cotton, or impure from constant respiration, or from other causes. They are engaged in an employment which absorbs their attention, and unremittingly employs their physical energies. They are drudges who watch the movements, and assist the operations, of a mighty material force, which toils with an energy ever unconscious of fatigue. The persevering labour of the operative must rival the mathematical precision, the incessant motion, and the exhaustless power of the machine.

Hence, besides the negative results—the abstraction of moral and intellectual stimuli—the absence of variety—banishment from the grateful air and the cheering influences of light, the physical energies are impaired by toil, and imperfect nutrition. The artisan too seldom possesses sufficient moral dignity or intellectual or organic strength to resist the seductions of appetite. His wife and children, subjected to the same process, have little power to cheer his remaining moments of leisure. Domestic economy is neglected, domestic comforts are too frequently unknown. A meal of coarse food is hastily prepared, and devoured with precipitation. Home has little other relation to him than that of shelter—few pleasures are there—it chiefly presents to him a scene of physical exhaustion, from which he is glad to escape. His house is ill furnished, uncleanly, often ill ventilated—perhaps damp; his food, from want of forethought and domestic economy, is meagre and innutritious; he generally becomes debilitated and hypochondriacal, and unless supported by principle, falls the victim of dissipation. In all these respects, it is grateful to add, that those among the operatives of the mills, who are employed *in the process of spinning,* and especially of fine spinning, (who receive a high rate of wages and who are elevated on account of their skill) are more attentive to their domestic arrangements, have better furnished houses, are consequently more regular in their habits, and more observant of their duties than those engaged in other branches of the manufacture.

The other classes of artisans of whom we have spoken, are frequently subject to a disease, in which the sensibility of the stomach and bowels is morbidly excited; the alvine secretions are deranged, and the appetite impaired. Whilst this state continues, the patient loses flesh, his features are sharpened, the skin becomes sallow, or of the yellow hue which is observed in those who have suffered from the influence of tropical climates. The strength fails, the capacities of physical enjoyment are destroyed, and the paroxysms of corporeal suffering are aggravated by deep mental depression. We cannot wonder that the wretched victim of this disease, invited by those haunts of misery and crime the gin shop and the tavern, as he passes to his daily labour, should endeavour to cheat his suffering of a few moments, by the false excitement procured by ardent spirits; or that the exhausted artisan, driven by ennui and discomfort from his squalid home, should strive, in the delirious dreams of a continued debauch, to forget the remembrance of his reckless improvidence, of the destitution, hunger, and uninterrupted toil, which threaten to destroy the remaining energies of his enfeebled constitution.

The contagious example which the Irish have exhibited of barbarous habits and savage want of economy, united with the necessarily debasing consequences of uninterrupted toil, have demoralized the people.

The inspection conducted by the District Boards of Health, chiefly referred to the state of the streets and houses, inhabited by the labouring population—to local nuisances, and more general evils. The greatest portion of these districts, especially of those situated beyond Great Ancoats-street, are of very recent origin; and from the want of proper police regulations are untraversed by common sewers. The houses are ill soughed, often ill ventilated, unprovided with privies, and, in consequence, the streets which are narrow, unpaved, and worn into deep ruts, become the common receptacles of mud, refuse, and disgusting ordure.

The Inspectors' reports do not comprise all the houses and streets of the respective districts, and are in some other respects imperfect. The returns concerning the various defects which they enumerate must be received, as the reports of evils, too positive to be overlooked. Frequently, when they existed in a slighter degree, the questions received no reply.

Predisposition to contagious disease is encouraged by every thing which depresses the physical energies, amongst the principal of which agencies may be enumerated imperfect nutrition; exposure to cold and moisture, whether from inadequate shelter, or from want of clothing and fuel, or from dampness of the habitation; uncleanliness of the person, the street, and the abode; an atmosphere contaminated, whether from the want of ventilation, or from impure effluvia; extreme labour, and consequent physical exhaustion; intemperance; fear; anxiety; diarrhœa, and other diseases. The whole of these subjects could not be included in the investigation, though it originated in a desire to remove, as far as possible, those ills which depressed the health of the population. The list of inquiries to which the inspectors were requested to make tabular replies is placed in the appendix, for the purpose of enabling the reader to form his own opinion of the investigation from which the classified results are deduced.

The state of the streets powerfully affects the health of their inhabitants. Sporadic cases of typhus chiefly appear in those which are narrow, ill ventilated, unpaved, or which contain heaps of refuse, or stagnant pools. The confined air and noxious exhalations, which abound in such places, depress the health of the people, and on this account contagious diseases are also most rapidly propagated there. The operation of these causes is exceedingly promoted by their reflex influence on the manners. The houses, in such situations, are uncleanly, ill provided with furniture; an air of discomfort if not of squalid and loathsome wretchedness pervades them, they are often dilapidated, badly drained, damp: and the habits of their tenants are gross—they are ill-fed, ill-clothed, and uneconomical—at once spendthrifts and destitute—denying themselves the comforts of life, in order that they may wallow in the unrestrained licence of animal appetite. An intimate connexion subsists, among the poor, between the cleanliness of the street and that of the house and person. Uneconomical habits, and dissipation are almost inseparably allied; and they are so frequently connected with uncleanliness, that we cannot consider their concomitance as altogether accidental. The first step to recklessness may often be traced in a neglect of that self-respect, and of the love of domestic enjoyments, which are indicated by personal slovenliness, and discomfort of the habitation. Hence, the importance of providing by police regulations or general enactment, against those fertile sources alike of disease and demoralization, presented by the gross neglect of the streets and habitations of the poor. When the health is depressed by the concurrence of these causes, contagious diseases spread with a fatal malignancy among the population subjected to their influence. The records of the Fever Hospital of Manchester, prove that typhus *prevails almost exclusively* in such situations.

The following table, arranged by the Committee of classification appointed by the Special Board of Health, from the reports of Inspectors of the various District Boards of Manchester, shows the extent to which the imperfect state of the streets of Manchester may tend to promote demoralization and disease among the poor.

A minute inspection of this table will render the extent of the evil affecting the poor more apparent. Those districts which are almost exclusively inhabited

No. of District	No. of streets inspected.	No. of streets unpaved.	No. of streets partially pvd.	No. of streets ill ventilated.	No. of streets containing heaps of refuse, stagnant pools, ordure, &c.
1	114	63	13	7	64
2	180	93	7	23	92
3	49	2	2	12	28
4	66	37	10	12	52
5	30	2	5	5	12
6	2	1	0	1	2
7	53	13	5	12	17
8	16	2	1	2	7
9	48	0	0	9	20
10	29	19	0	10	23
11	0	0	0	0	0
12	12	0	1	1	4
13	55	3	9	10	23
14	33	13	0	8	8
Total:	687	248	53	112	352

by the labouring population are Nos. 1, 2, 3, 4, and 10. Nos. 13 and 14, and 7, also contain, besides the dwellings of the operatives, those of shopkeepers and tradesmen, and are traversed by many of the principal thoroughfares. No. 11 was not inspected, and Nos. 5, 6, 8, and 9, are the central districts containing the chief streets, the most respectable shops, the dwellings of the more wealthy inhabitants, and the warehouses of merchants and manufacturers. Subtracting, therefore, from the various totals, those items in the reports which concern these divisions only, we discover in those districts which contain a large portion of poor, namely, in Nos. 1, 2, 3, 4, 7, 10, 13, and 14, that among 579 streets inspected, 243 were altogether unpaved—46 partially paved—93 ill ventilated—and 307 contained heaps of refuse, deep ruts, stagnant pools, ordure, &c.; and in the districts which are almost exclusively inhabited by the poor, namely, Nos. 1, 2, 3, 4, and 10, among 438 streets inspected, 214 were altogether unpaved—32 partially paved—63 ill ventilated—and 259 contained heaps of refuse, deep ruts, stagnant pools, ordure, &c.

The replies to the questions proposed in the second table relating to houses, contain equally remarkable results, which have been carefully arranged by the Classification Committee of the Special Board of Health, as follows.

District	No. of houses inspected.	No. of houses reported as requiring whitewashing	No. of houses reported as requiring repair	No. of houses in which the soughs wanted repair	No. of houses damp.	No. of houses reported as ill ventilated.	No. of houses wanting privies.
1	850	399	128	112	177	70	326
2	2489	898	282	145	497	109	755
3	213	145	104	41	61	52	96
4	650	279	106	105	134	69	250
5	413	176	82	70	101	11	66
6	12	3	5	5			5
7	343	76	59	57	86	21	79
8	132	35	30	39	48	22	20
9	128	34	32	24	39	19	25
10	370	195	53	123	54	2	232
11							
12	113	33	23	27	24	16	52
13	757	218	44	108	146	54	177
14	481	74	13	83	68	7	138
Total:	6951	2565	960	939	1435	452	2221

It is however to be lamented, that even these numerical results fail to exhibit a perfect picture of the ills which are suffered by the poor. The replies to the questions contained in the inspectors' table refer only to cases of the most positive kind, and the numerical results would therefore have been exceedingly increased, had they embraced those in which the evils existed in a scarcely inferior degree. Some idea of the want of cleanliness prevalent in their habitations, may be obtained from the report of the number of houses requiring whitewashing; but this column fails to indicate their gross neglect of order, and absolute filth. Much less can we obtain satisfactory statistical results concerning the want of furniture, especially of bedding, and of food, clothing, and fuel. In these respects the habitations of the Irish are most destitute. They can scarcely be said to be furnished. They contain one or two chairs, a mean table, the most scanty culinary apparatus, and one or two beds, loathsome with filth. A whole family is often accommodated on a single bed, and sometimes a heap of filthy straw and a covering of old sacking hide them in one undistinguished heap, debased alike by penury, want of economy, and dissolute habits. Frequently, the inspectors found two or more families crowded into one small house, containing only two apartments, one in which

Pauper Lodging Houses.

	No. of houses.		No. of houses.
District No. 1 , ...	0	District No. 9 , ...	0
2 , ...	108	10 , ...	12
3 , ...	51	11 , ...	26
4 , ...	0	12 , ...	—
5 , ...	6	13 , ...	60
6 , ...	0	14 , ...	1
7 , ...	3		—
8 , ...	0		267

they slept, and another in which they eat; and often more than one family lived in a damp cellar, containing only one room, in whose pestilential atmosphere from twelve to sixteen persons were crowded. To these fertile sources of disease were sometimes added the keeping of pigs and other animals in the house, with other nuisances of the most revolting character.

As the visits of the inspectors were made in the day, when the population is engaged in the mills, and the vagrants and paupers are wandering through the town, they could not form any just idea of the state of the pauper lodging houses. The establishments thus designated are fertile sources of disease and demoralization. They are frequently able to accommodate from twenty to thirty or more lodgers, among whom are the most abandoned characters, who, reckless of the morrow, resort thither for the shelter of the night—men who find safety in a constant change of abode, or are too uncertain in their pursuits to remain beneath the same roof for a longer period. Here, without distinction of age or sex, careless of all decency, they are crowded in small and wretched apartments; the same bed receiving a succession of tenants until too offensive even for their unfastidious senses. The Special Board being desirous that these lodging houses should be inspected by the Overseers, the Churchwardens obtained a report of the number in each district, which cannot fail to be a source of surprise and apprehension.

The temporary tenants of these disgusting abodes, too frequently debased by vice, haunted by want, and every other consequence of crime, are peculiarly disposed to the reception of contagion. Their asylums are frequently recesses where it lurks, and they are active agents in its diffusion. They ought to be as much the objects of a careful vigilance from those who are the guardians of the health, as from those who protect the property of the public.

PETER GASKELL
❧❧❧

SEPARATION OF FAMILIES

Domestic Manufacturer—Union of his Family—Its Consequences and Advantages—No Child-labour—Effects of this upon the Male and Female Portion of his Household described—Factory Labour—Destruction of Home—Separation of Families—Effects of these upon social Character—Payment of Wages to Children, its Evils described—Conversion of Homes into Lodging-houses—Loss of domestic Virtues, description of—Early Period at which Factory Labour begins—The Mind, &c. of Childhood—Division of Families—Cultivation of Home Affections—Infancy of the Factory Child described—Comparison of the Condition of the Agricultural Labourer—Its Advantages—Domestic Economy—Non-existence of, in the Factory Woman—Separation of Man and Wife.

It has been truly remarked by Bacon,[1] that "the culture and manurance of mind in youth, hath such a forcible though unseen operation, as hardly any length of time or contention of labour, can countervail its influence."

The domestic manufacturer possessed one great advantage over the factory labourer, which was—that his occupation was carried on beneath the roof of his own cottage, and in the midst of his family: also, that his children, growing up under his own eye, and around his fire-side, retained for him the respect and awe due to parental authority, by remaining members of one home and under the direction of one head. By keeping up this natural and proper order of things, he secured one means of making his offspring domestic in their habits, and it was his own fault if their social character was not what it ought to be.

So long as families were thus bound together by the strong link of interest and affection, each member in its turn, as it attained an age fitted for the loom, joined its labour to the general stock, its earnings-forming part of a fund, the whole of which was placed at the disposal of the father or mother, as the case

---

From *The Manufacturing Population of England.* London: Baldwin and Cradock, 1833.
1. An early proponent of the inductive method in scientific study, Francis Bacon (1561–1626) was a philosopher and the author of *The Advancement of Learning* (1605) and the *Novum Organum* (1620). [Ed.]

might be; and each individual looked to him or to her for the adequate supply of its wants. No separate or distinct interests was ever acknowledged or dreamt of. If any one, by superior industry or skill, earned more in proportion than another, no separate claim was made for such excess on the part of that individual; on the contrary, it was looked upon equally as a part of the wages of the family,—perhaps gratefully and affectionately acknowledged, but leading to no other result.

This family compact, of course, existed no longer than the usual period when parental control yields before the maturity of offspring. This was rarely before twenty-two or twenty-three years of age, and often much later. Grown up, as each member had, as part and parcel of a little community, these divisions seldom took place before marriage opened a series of new cares and new prospects to son or daughter, which, in consequence seceded, or, as was frequently the case, brought a wife or husband to be joined to the family union. Generally, however, at this period an offset or branching took place, which was best for all parties.

This preserved in all their vigour the moral obligations of father and mother, brother and sister, son and daughter, and that till a time of life was gained, which had given abundant opportunity for the formation of character—a character most assuredly the best calculated to render the labouring man happy and virtuous, viz., a domestic one; without which, no adventitious aid can ever secure him their possession.

The greatest misfortune—the most unfavourable change which has resulted from factory labour, is the breaking up of these family ties; the consequent abolition of the domestic circle, and the perversion of all the social obligations which should exist between parent and child on the one hand, and between children themselves on the other.

The age at which a child became useful to its parents, so long as the great mass of manufacturing was manual and confined to private dwelling-houses, was from fourteen to sixteen. At an earlier age it was useful in a minor degree as winder, &c.; but that was the period at which it became an auxiliary to the incomings of the family by working at the loom.

Before this it was a mere child, entirely dependent upon the exertions of its parents or older brothers and sisters for support. During this time it was taught, by daily experience, habits of subordination to its seniors. The period at which it ranked itself by the side of the efficient portions of the household, was a happy medium between too early an application and too late a procrastination of its physical energies; for the child was sufficiently matured, in its material organization, to bear without injury moderate and continued exertion; and no time had, as yet, been allowed for the acquirement of slothful habits: it came, too, at a time when the first impulses of puberty were beginning to stir new associations in his mind. These it checked by keeping him occupied, while he was removed from the influence of bad example, and laboured in an open workshop, free from the stimulus of warmth, and in the presence of his sisters, brothers, and parents,—the very best anodyne for allaying and keeping in due restraint his nascent passions,—whilst his moral and social instincts were under a process of incessant cultivation.

The same observations apply with still greater force to the females of the family. With them labour commenced at a somewhat earlier period, or they supplied the place of their mother in the household offices, leaving her at liberty to work for their sustenance, if such a course of proceeding was deemed necessary, or forced upon them by the pressure of circumstances. Whichever it was, she was kept from promiscuous intercourse with the other sex, at an age when it was to her of the utmost importance—her young sensibilities rendering her peculiarly liable to powerful and irresistible impressions. It is true that the sports of her own sex were to some extent libidinous; but to these she was not admitted till a much later period; and these, though coarse and highly objectionable, rarely ended in mischief, being considered as a sort of prelude to marriage, universally existing amongst them—a custom most certainly "more honoured in the breach than in the observance."

Her occupations and feelings were therefore exclusively home-bred, and no idea existed that distinct or detached interests could intervene betwixt her parents and herself.

It is in these respects that the family of the factory labourers offers such strong contrasts and unhappy differences.

In the first place, there is no home labour. It becomes therefore a mere shelter, in which their meals are hastily swallowed, and which offers them repose for the night. It has no endearing recollections which bind it on their memories—no hold upon their imaginations.

In the next place, the various members not only do not labour under their own roof, but they do not labour in common, neither in one mill; or if in one mill, so separated, that they have no opportunity of exchanging a single glance or a word throughout the long hours they are engaged there. Children are thus entirely removed from parental guardianship;—and not only so, but they are brought into immediate contact with parties, generally of their own age, equally removed with themselves from inspection, and equally unchecked by a consciousness that the eye of a brother, sister, or parent may be fixed upon them. They are placed, too, under the control of an overlooker, who from a sense of duty to his employer, if aggravated by no baser feeling, treats them frequently with harshness, often with brutal coarseness, making no allowance for childish simplicity, bashfulness, delicacy, or female failings; and this is most fatal to self-esteem,—for nothing so soon injures or destroys this, as unworthy treatment, suffered in themselves or witnessed in others, without the power of redress or even of appeal.

Again, they are subjected on all sides to the influence of vicious examples—in an heated atmosphere, and have no occupation, save watching the passage of a thread or the revolution of a spindle. The mind is but little engaged, there is no variety for it to feed upon,—it has none of the pure excitements which home affords,—it becomes crowded with images of the very opposite quality, and has its delicacy utterly and irretrievably ruined, and no opportunity is given for the growth of modesty on the one hand, or of the social obligations of brother, sister, or child on the other.

The next evil which removes factory labour another step still more widely apart from the condition of domestic manufacture is, that the wages of children have become, either by universal consent, or by the growth of disobedience, payable to the person earning them. This has led to another crying and grievous misfortune; namely, that each child ceases to view itself as a subordinate agent in the household; so far indeed loses the character and bearing of a child, that it pays over to its natural protector a stated sum for food and lodging; thus detaching itself from parental subjection and control. The members, therefore, of a spinner's or weaver's family become a body of distinct individuals, occupying occasionally, but by no means universally, the same home, each paying its quota to the joint expenses, and considering themselves as lodgers merely, and appropriating any surplus which may remain of their wages to their own private purposes, accountable to no one for the mode in which it happens to be used or wasted.

It is to be feared, that the mischiefs resulting from such an unnatural arrangement, must, in the first instance, be saddled upon the errors of parents—such a dereliction from filial duty being hardly likely to happen spontaneously on the side of the children; and that a plan originally adopted in a few cases, by the family of idle and depraved parents[2]—and many such are to be found, who would willingly batten upon the toil of their children—has become general, in consequence of the lowering in the reciprocal confidence and affection which ought to exist between parent and child.

In numerous examples then, at the present day, parents are thus become the keepers of lodging-houses for their offspring, between whom little intercourse beyond that relating to pecuniary profit and loss is carried on. In a vast number of others, children have been entirely driven away from their homes, either by unnatural treatment, or have voluntarily deserted them, and taken up their abode in other asylums, for the sake of saving a small sum in the amount of payment required for food and house-room.

---

2. Too frequently the father, enjoying perfect health, and ample opportunities of employment, is supported in idleness on the earnings of his oppressed children.—Dr. Kay's pamphlet, p. 64. (*The Moral and Physical Condition of the Working Classes* (1832); see selection in this volume. [Ed.])

This disruption of all the ties of home, is one of the most fatal consequences of the factory system. The social relations which should distinguish the members of the same family, are destroyed. The domestic virtues—man's natural instincts, and the affections of the heart, are deadened and lost. Those feelings and actions which should be the charm of the fire-side—which should prepare young men and young women for fulfilling the duties of parents, are displaced by a selfishness utterly repugnant to all such sacred obligations. Tenderness of manner—solicitude during sickness—the foregoing of personal gratification for the sake of others—submission to home restraint—all these are lost, and their place occupied by individual independence—private avarice—the withholding assistance,[3] however slight, from those around them, who have a natural claim upon their generosity—calculations and arrangements, based solely upon pecuniary matters,—with a gradual extinction of those sympathies and feelings, which are alone fitted to afford happiness—a wearing away of the more delicate shades of character, which render home a world of pleasures, leaving nothing but attention to the simple wants of nature, in addition to the depraved appetites which are the result of other circumstances connected with their condition;—and in the end reducing them, as a mass, to a heartless assemblage of separate and conflicting individuals, each striving for their "own hand," uninfluenced, unmodified by the more gentle, the more noble, and the more humanized cares, aspirations and feelings, which could alone render them estimable as fathers, mothers, brothers and sisters.

When it is borne in mind, at what an early period of life this separation of family takes place, its effects will be better and more correctly appreciated, and the permanence of the injurious impression produced by it, will be more clearly comprehended.

Factory labour, in many of its processes, requires little else but manual dexterity, and no physical strength; neither is there any thing for the mind to do in it; so that children, whose fingers are taught to move with great facility and rapidity, have all the requisites for it. Hence one reason for introducing mere infants into mills, though this is by no means the only one; and were the hours of labour sufficiently limited, and under proper regulation, when the present habits of their parents are considered, the evil—great in some respects as it is—would almost cease to be one. Children from nine to twelve years of age, are now become part of the staple hands, and are consequently subjected at this tender period to all the mischiefs incident to the condition of the older work-people.

It may be urged, that the mind of a child at this age, cannot, from its very

---

3. "When age and decrepitude cripple the energies of the parents, their adult children abandon them to the scanty maintenance derived from parochial relief."—Dr. Kay's pamphlet, p. 64.

structure and previous impressions, be susceptible of the more vicious and immoral parts of the system; and that its previous education, which it is presumed must have been home, will, to some extent, guard it against evil communications.

It has been truly observed, and not the less beautifully than truly, that "heaven is around us in our infancy." This might have been extended, and said, that "heaven is around and within us in our infancy;" for the happiness of childhood springs full as much from an internal consciousness of delight, as from the novelty of its impressions from without. Its mind, providing the passions are properly guided, is indeed a swelling fountain of all that is beautiful—all that is amiable;—overflowing with joy and tenderness; and its young heart is a living laboratory of love, formed to be profusely scattered on all around it.

The very copiousness of its sensations, however, prevents stability in their direction, if not carefully tended—and if its heart and mind have capabilities for exhibiting and lavishing the treasures of their awakening energies, they are, from their very immaturity, more easily warped and misdirected. The hacknied quotation, "just as the twig is bent," &c., is not the less true for being hacknied. Most unhappily, every thing which goes on before the eyes of the unfortunate factory children, is but too well calculated to nip in the bud—to wither in the spring-time of its growth—the flower which was springing up within them, to adorn and beautify their future existence—and in its stead to bring forth an unsightly mass of ill-assorted and rugged excrescences, equally hateful to sight and injurious to the parent stem.

The independence assumed by older brothers and sisters, the total inattention to parental remonstrance or wishes, soon produce their influence upon a child—which is quite as ready to learn evil as good. Then, driven at the early age it is, into the mill, and at once placed amongst crowds of children similarly circumstanced with itself, the impressions made upon it at home soon become permanent. The subsequent possession of money, with the bickerings that arise therefrom, alienate any spark of affection which might still be lingering in its breast for its parents, and when a mere infant, it establishes itself either as an independent inmate of its paternal dwelling, or seeks out a lodging with other parties, as the case may happen to be.

The existence of a divided interest in a household, whether the division is between man and wife, or between parent and child, is alike fatal to its best interests. No home can ever be what it ought without proper government, or where all the inmates are on such terms of equality as to give to each an equal right to the direction of the whole—and even a household so constituted will not hang long together. In the homes of the manufacturing population, the divisions between parents and children, arising from the assumption of managing their own earnings, so generally acknowledged amongst them, deprives them of the most valuable portion of their influence.

Thus, whether at home or abroad, unfettered by wholesome restraints, the factory child grows up, acquiring vices of all shades, and utterly losing that which might render its condition one of respectability and comfort—the social and domestic virtues. Year after year rolls on, unfitting it more and more for the best purposes of life, and if it should become a parent, it transmits to its offspring the evils of a system of which it has been the victim.

The entire breaking up of households, which is an inevitable consequence of mill-labour, as it now exists, is one which may be regarded as the most powerfully demoralizing agent attendant upon it. This is, however, aided by many other causes, some of which have been already described, and others will be noticed in the course of the work. The domestic affections, if they are to assume strength, must be steadily cultivated, and cultivated, too, in the only way of which they are capable. This is by parental kindness in the first place, which, by rendering home pleasant, and weaving its delightful associations in the young imagination, forms one of the most sacred, most delightful, and most permanent feelings of the human heart. In the next place, the example of proper household subordination, for without this the first will be destroyed, or so weakened as to be inefficient and inoperative. Neither of these agents are brought to bear actively and properly upon the factory child. From its birth it sees nothing around it but dissension; its infant cries are hushed, not by maternal tenderness, but by doses of gin or opiates, or it is left to wail itself asleep from exhaustion. In thousands of cases it is abandoned throughout the day by its parents, both of whom are egaged in the mill, and left to the care of a stranger or a mere child—badly used—badly fed—its little heart hardened by harshness even in the cradle; then badly clothed—unattended during its growth by regular and systematic kindness—constantly hearing execrations, curses, blasphemy, and every thing coarse and obscene in expression—seeing on all sides strife, drunkenness, beastiality, and abominations, and finally sent shivering into the mill, to swell the hordes of children which have been similarly educated, and similarly abandoned to their own resources.

It may be said, that the agricultural labourer is subjected to a separation from his family, and that the members of his family are also, after a time, separated from home. This is granted, and that, thus, primâ facie, he appears circumstanced in these respects like the factory labourer. Nothing can, however, be more dissimilar than the two cases, when looked at in their true bearings.

The agricultural labourer, it is true, pursues his occupation from home—but he pursues it in nine cases out of ten solitarily, or if he works in company, it is in small gangs; he works too in an atmosphere natural in its temperature, and favourable to bodily health, saying nothing of the moral influences of the sights and sounds which are his familiar companions; his labour is physically severe, and is just sufficient to require what intellectual capacity he generally possesses; his diet is plain and wholesome; he is freed from the example of many vices, by his situation, to which the factory labourer is exposed, and his habits and modes of life are simpler and purer. His family, separated from each other, and from home after a time, remain long enough under the paternal roof to have acquired some notion of domestic discipline, and that too under the best of all possible teachers—a mother, whose avocations are exclusively household. The labour of the sons, when old enough to pursue it, which is not till sixteen years of age, is that of the father, under similar circumstances. The daughters become household servants, either to persons of their own class, or, what is more general, in the houses of respectable families in the neighbourhood, or seek service in the surrounding towns and villages; their family interest thus, of course, merging in that of their employers. In all these cases a strict watch is kept over their morals.[4] No point of similarity exists then between them, except in the single one of separation of families, and that too at a period and in a way to be as little injurious as possible to the moral character of the parties.

The agricultural labourer has other moral advantages over those possessed by the manufacturing one. He is frequently under the direct inspection of his employer, in the middle class of land proprietors, or respectable land-holders; and in the inferior order of both these, he is the personal assistant, and works in conjunction with it. In the highest order, he has the reflected benefit of hereditary rank and wealth, circumstances of more importance than the superficial observer is aware of, but which are rendered sufficiently apparent by examining into the condition of the cottagers and labourers upon those estates which are benefited by the residence of their proprietors.

These are a few of the moral advantages which he possesses still, to some extent, over the factory labourer. Of late years, indeed, the breaking-up of small farms—and other causes, have brought into operation upon him, the demoralizing agency of poverty and want of employ, and its influence has done much to deprive him of many of the benefits he once enjoyed.

In addition to the enumeration already given of the evils which result from the division of families, and the early age at which children are impressed into earning their own support, with the moral degradation which is their universal effect, another misfortune, of a very prominent character, attends upon the female division of the manufacturing population. This is, the entire want of instruction or example in learning the plainest elements of domestic economy; and this single circumstance goes far to explain many of the improvident habits

---

4. "It may be safely affirmed, that the virtue of female chastity does not exist amongst the lower orders of England, except to a certain extent among domestic female servants, who know that they hold their situations by that tenure, and are more prudent in consequence." [—*Report of Poor Laws' Commission.*] Great Britain. Report of the Poor Law Commissioners to the Marquis of Normanby. London: s.n., 1840

which form a chief part of the curse upon their social condition. No earnings, however liberal, can compensate for this. It at once robs the home of the labouring man of every chance of being rightly or even decently conducted. If minute economy, which is the only true economy, is to be of service, it must be carefully taught, and with the best means of furnishing the supplies of a family, and making these supplies go to their utmost length. Of all these essentials to the head of a household, she is utterly ignorant, and her arrangements, if arrangements they can be called, where every thing is left to chance, are characterised by sluttish waste, negligence, carelessness as to the quality of food, and indifference as to the mode of cooking, and an absence of all that tidiness, cleanliness, and forethought which are requisite to a good housewife.

So complete is the separation of families, and so entirely are all their members absorbed by mill labour, that it very frequently happens that man and wife do not meet during the day at all. Working at different mills, perhaps at opposite sides of the town, their various meals are procured at some lodging-house in the immediate neighbourhood—thus adding another evil—another cause of the dissolution of the domestic links,—to the long list already brought under review.

THOMAS MACAULAY

SPEECH ON THE TEN HOURS ACT

Delivered in the House of Commons on the 22d of May, 1846

On the 29th of April, 1846, Mr. Fielden, Member for Oldham, moved the second reading of a bill for limiting the labor of young persons in factories to ten hours a day. The debate was adjourned, and was repeatedly resumed at long intervals. At length, on the 22d of May, the bill was rejected by 203 votes to 193. On that day the following Speech was made:

It is impossible, sir, that I can remain silent after the appeal which has been made to me in so pointed a manner by my honorable friend, the Member for

From *The Miscellaneous Works of Lord Macaulay.* Lady Trevelyan, ed. New York: G.P. Putnam's Sons, 1900.

Sheffield. And even if that appeal had not been made to me, I should have been very desirous to have an opportunity of explaining the grounds on which I shall vote for the second reading of this bill.

It is, I hope, unnecessary for me to assure my honorable friend that I utterly disapprove of those aspersions which have, both in this house and out of it, been thrown on the owners of factories. For that valuable class of men I have no feeling but respect and good-will. I am convinced that with their interests the interests of the whole community, and especially of the laboring classes, are inseparably bound up. I can also with perfect sincerity declare that the vote which I shall give to-night will not be a factious vote. In no circumstances, indeed, should I think that the laws of political hostility warranted me in treating this question as a party question. But at the present moment I would much rather strengthen than weaken the hands of Her Majesty's Ministers. It is by no means pleasant to me to be under the necessity of opposing them. I assure them, I assure my friends on this side of the House with whom I am so unfortunate as to differ, and especially my honorable friend, the Member for Sheffield, who spoke, I must say, in rather too plaintive a tone, that I have no desire to obtain credit for humanity at their expense. I fully believe that their feeling towards the laboring people is quite as kind as mine. There is no difference between us as to ends; there is an honest difference of opinion as to means; and we surely ought to be able to discuss the points on which we differ without one angry emotion or one acrimonious word.

The details of the bill, sir, will be more conveniently and more regularly discussed when we consider it in committee. Our business at present is with the principle; and the principle, we are told by many gentlemen of great authority, is unsound. In their opinion, neither this bill, nor any other bill regulating the hours of labor, can be defended. This, they say, is one of those matters about which we ought not to legislate at all: one of those matters which settle themselves far better than any government can settle them. Now, it is most important that this point should be fully cleared up. We certainly ought not to usurp functions which do not properly belong to us. But, on the other hand, we ought not to abdicate functions which do properly belong to us. I hardly know which is the greater pest to society; a paternal government, that is to say, a prying, meddlesome government, which intrudes itself into every part of human life, and which thinks that it can do everything for everybody better than anybody can do anything for himself; or a careless, lounging government, which suffers grievances, such as it could at once remove, to grow and multiply, and which to all complaint and remonstrance has only one answer: "We must let things alone: we must let things take their course: we must let things find their level." There is no more important problem in politics than to ascertain the just mean between these two most pernicious extremes; to draw correctly the line which divides those cases in which it is the duty of the

State to interfere from those cases in which it is the duty of the State to abstain from interference. In old times the besetting sin of rulers was undoubtedly an inordinate disposition to meddle. The lawgiver was always telling people how to keep their shops, how to till their fields, how to educate their children, how many dishes to have on their tables, how much a yard to give for the cloth which made their coats. He was always trying to remedy some evil which did not properly fall within his province; and the consequence was that he increased the evils which he attempted to remedy. He was so much shocked by the distress inseparable from scarcity that he made statutes against forestalling and regrating, and so turned the scarcity into a famine. He was so much shocked by the cunning and hard-heartedness of money-lenders that he made laws against usury; and the consequence was that the borrower, who, if he had been left unprotected, would have got money at ten per cent., could hardly, when protected, get it at fifteen per cent. Some eminent political philosopher of the last century exposed with great ability the folly of such legislation, and, by doing so, rendered a great service to mankind. There has been a reaction, a reaction which has doubtless produced much good, but which, like most reactions, has not been without evils and dangers. Our statesmen cannot now be accused of being busybodies. But I am afraid that there is, even in some of the ablest and most upright among them, a tendency to the opposite fault. I will give an instance of what I mean. Fifteen years ago it became evident that railroads would soon, in every part of the kingdom, supersede to a great extent the old highways. The tracing of the new routes, which were to join all the chief cities, ports, and naval arsenals of the island was a matter of the highest national importance. But, unfortunately, those who should have acted for the nation refused to interfere. Consequently, numerous questions which were really public questions, which concerned the public convenience, the public security, were treated as private questions. That the whole society was interested in having a good system of internal communication seemed to be forgotten. The speculator who wanted a large dividend on his shares, the land-owner who wanted a large price for his acres, obtained a full hearing. But nobody applied to be heard on behalf of the community. The effects of that great error we feel, and we shall not soon cease to feel. Unless I am greatly mistaken we are in danger of committing tonight an error of the same kind. The honorable Member for Montrose and my honorable friend the Member for Sheffield think that the question before us is merely a question between the old and the new theories of commerce. They cannot understand how any friend of free-trade can wish the Legislature to interfere between the capitalist and the laborer. They say

You do not make a law to settle the price of gloves, or the texture of gloves, or the length of credit which the glover shall give. You leave it to him to determine whether he will charge high or low prices, whether he will use strong or flimsy materials, whether he will trust or insist on ready money. You acknowledge that these are matters which he ought to be left to settle with his customers, and that we ought not to interfere. It is possible that he may manage his shop ill. But it is certain that we shall manage it ill. On the same grounds on which you leave the seller of gloves and the buyer of gloves to make their own contract, you ought to leave the seller of labor and the buyer of labor to make their own contract.

I have a great respect, sir, for those who reason thus: but I cannot see this matter in the light in which it appears to them; and, though I may distrust my own judgment, I must be guided by it. I am, I believe, as strongly attached as any Member of this House to the principle of free-trade, rightly understood. Trade, considered merely as trade, considered merely with reference to the pecuniary interest of the contracting parties, can hardly be too free. But there is a great deal of trade which cannot be considered merely as trade, and which affects higher than pecuniary interests. And to say that government never ought to regulate such trade is a monstrous proposition, a proposition at which Adam Smith would have stood aghast. We impose some restrictions on trade for purposes of police. Thus, we do not suffer everybody who has a cab and a horse to ply for passengers in the streets of London. We do not leave the fare to be determined by the supply and the demand. We do not permit a driver to extort a guinea for going half a mile on a rainy day when there is no other vehicle on the stand. We impose some restrictions on trade for the sake of revenue. Thus, we forbid a farmer to cultivate tobacco on his own ground. We impose some restrictions on trade for the sake of national defence. Thus, we compel a man who would rather be ploughing or weaving to go into the militia; and we fix the amount of pay which he shall receive without asking his consent. Nor is there in all this anything inconsistent with the soundest political economy. For the science of political economy teaches us only that we ought not on commercial grounds to interfere with the liberty of commerce; and we, in the cases which I have put, interfere with the liberty of commerce on higher than commercial grounds.

And now, sir, to come closer to the case with which we have to deal, I say, first, that where the health of the community is concerned, it may be the duty of the State to interfere with the contracts of individuals; and to this proposition I am quite sure that Her Majesty's government will cordially assent. I have just read a very interesting report signed by two members of that government, the Duke of Buccleuch, and the noble earl who was lately Chief Commissioner of the Woods and Forests, and who is now Secretary for Ireland; and, since that report was laid before the House, the noble earl himself has, with the sanction of the Cabinet, brought in a bill for the protection of the public health. By this bill it is provided that no man shall be permitted to build a house on his own land in any great town without giving notice to certain

Commissioners. No man is to sink a cellar without the consent of these Commissioners. The house must not be of less than a prescribed width. No new house must be built without a drain. If an old house has no drain, the Commissioners may order the owner to make a drain. If he refuses, they make a drain for him, and send him in the bill. They may order him to whitewash his house. If he refuses, they may send people with pails and brushes to whitewash it for him, at his charge. Now, suppose that some proprietor of houses at Leeds or Manchester were to expostulate with the government in the language in which the government has expostulated with the supporters of this bill for the regulation of factories. Suppose that he were to say to the noble earl,

> Your lordship professes to be a friend to free-trade. Your lordship's doctrine is that everybody ought to be at liberty to buy cheap and to sell dear. Why then may not I run up a house as cheap as I can, and let my rooms as dear as I can? Your lordship does not like houses without drains. Do not take one of mine, then. You think my bedrooms filthy. Nobody forces you to sleep in them. Use your own liberty; but do not restrain that of your neighbors. I can find many a family willing to pay a shilling a week for leave to live in what you call a hovel. And why am not I to take the shilling which they are willing to give me? And why are not they to have such shelter as, for that shilling, I can afford them? Why did you send a man without my consent to clean my house, and then force me to pay for what I never ordered? My tenants thought the house clean enough for them, or they would not have been my tenants; and, if they and I were satisfied, why did you, in direct defiance of all the principles of free-trade, interfere between us?

This reasoning, sir, is exactly of a piece with the reasoning of the honorable Member for Montrose, and of my honorable friend, the Member for Sheffield. If the noble earl will allow me to make a defence for him, I believe that he would answer the objection thus: "I hold," he would say,

> the sound doctrine of free-trade. But your doctrine of free-trade is an exaggeration, a caricature of the sound doctrine; and by exhibiting such a caricature you bring discredit on the sound doctrine. We should have nothing to do with the contracts between you and your tenants, if those contracts affected only pecuniary interests. But higher than pecuniary interests are at stake. It concerns the commonwealth that the great body of the people should not live in a way which makes life wretched and short, which enfeebles the body and pollutes the mind. If, by living in houses which resemble hogsties, great numbers of our countrymen have contracted the tastes of hogs, if they have become so familiar with filth and stench and contagion, that they burrow without reluctance in holes which would turn the stomach of any man of cleanly habits, that is only an additional proof that we have too long neglected our duties, and an additional reason for our now performing them.

Secondly, I say that where the public morality is concerned, it may be the duty of the State to interfere with the contracts of individuals. Take the traffic in licentious books and pictures. Will anybody deny that the State may with propriety interdict that traffic? Or take the case of lotteries. I have, we will suppose, an estate for which I wish to get twenty thousand pounds. I announce my intention to issue a thousand tickets at twenty pounds each. The holder of the number which is first drawn is to have the estate. But the magistrate interferes; the contract between me and the purchasers of my tickets is annulled; and I am forced to pay a heavy penalty for having made such a contract. I appeal to the principle of free-trade, as expounded by the honorable gentlemen, the Members for Montrose and Sheffield. I say to you, the legislators who have restricted my liberty, "What business have you to interfere between a buyer and a seller? If you think the speculation a bad one, do not take tickets; but do not interdict other people from judging for themselves." Surely you would answer, "You would be right if this were a mere question of trade; but it is a question of morality. We prohibit you from disposing of your property in this particular mode, because it is a mode which tends to encourage a most pernicious habit of mind, a habit of mind incompatible with all the qualities on which the well-being of individuals and of nations depends."

It must then, I think, be admitted that where health is concerned, and where morality is concerned, the State is justified in interfering with the contracts of individuals. And, if this be admitted, it follows that the case with which we now have to do is a case for interference.

Will it be denied that the health of a large part of the rising generation may be seriously affected by the contracts which this bill is intended to regulate? Can any man who has read the evidence which is before us; can any man who has ever observed young people; can any man who remembers his own sensations when he was young, doubt that twelve hours a day of labor in a factory is too much for a lad of thirteen?

Or will it be denied that this is a question in which public morality is concerned? Can any one doubt—none, I am sure, of my friends around me doubts—that education is a matter of the highest importance to the virtue and happiness of a people? Now we know that there can be no education without leisure. It is evident that, after deducting from the day twelve hours for labor in a factory, and the additional hours necessary for exercise, refreshment, and repose, there will not remain time enough for education.

I have now, I think, shown that this bill is not in principle objectionable; and yet I have not touched the strongest part of our case. I hold that, where public health is concerned, and where public morality is concerned, the State may be justified in regulating even the contracts of adults. But we propose to regulate only the contracts of infants. Now, was there ever a civilized society in which the contracts of infants were not under some regulation? Is there a single member of this House who will say that a wealthy minor of thirteen ought to be at perfect liberty to execute a conveyance of his estate, or to give a bond for fifty thousand pounds? If anybody were so absurd as to say, "What has the Legislature to do with the matter? Why cannot you leave trade free? Why do you pretend to understand the boy's interest better than he understands it?"—you would answer, "When he grows up, he may squander his fortune away if he likes: but at present the State is his guardian; and he shall not ruin himself till he is old enough to know what he is about." The minors whom we wish to protect have not indeed large property to throw away, but they are not the less our wards. Their only inheritance, the only fund to which they must look for their subsistence through life, is the sound mind in the sound body. And is it not our duty to prevent them from wasting that most precious wealth before they know its value?

But, it is said, this bill, though it directly limits only the labor of infants, will, by an indirect operation, limit also the labor of adults. Now, sir, though I am not prepared to vote for a bill directly limiting the labor of adults, I will plainly say that I do not think that the limitation of the labor of adults would necessarily produce all those frightful consequences which we have heard predicted. You cheer me in very triumphant tones, as if I had uttered some monstrous paradox. Pray, does it not occur to any of you that the labor of adults is now limited in this country? Are you not aware that you are living in a society in which the labor of adults is limited to six days in seven? It is you, not I, who maintain a paradox opposed to the opinions and the practices of all nations and ages. Did you ever hear of a single civilized State since the beginning of the world in which a certain portion of time was not set apart for the rest and recreation of adults by public authority? In general, this arrangement has been sanctioned by religion. The Egyptians, the Jews, the Greeks, the Romans, had their holidays: the Hindoo has his holidays: the Mussulman[1] has his holidays: there are holidays in the Greek Church, holidays in the Church of Rome, holidays in the Church of England. Is is not amusing to hear a gentleman pronounce with confidence that any legislation which limits the labor of adults must produce consequences fatal to society, without once reflecting that in the society in which he lives, and in every other society that exists, or ever has existed, there has been such legislation without any evil consequence? It is true that a Puritan government in England, and an Atheistical government in France, abolished the old holidays as superstitious. But those governments felt it to be absolutely necessary to institute new holidays. Civil festivals were instituted for religious festivals. You will find among the

---

1. A Muslim. [Ed.]

ordinances of the Long Parliament a law providing that, in exchange for the days of rest and amusement which the people had been used to enjoy at Easter, Whitsuntide, and Christmas, the second Tuesday of every month should be given to the working-man, and that any apprentice who was forced to work on the second Tuesday of any month might have his master up before a magistrate. The French Jacobins[2] decreed that the Sunday should no longer be a day of rest; but they instituted another day of rest—the Decade. They swept away the holidays of the Roman Catholic Church; but they instituted another set of holidays—the Sans-culottides—one sacred to Genius, one to Industry, one to Opinion, and so on. I say, therefore, that the practice of limiting by law the time of the labor of adults, is so far from being, as some gentlemen seem to think, an unheard of and monstrous practice, that it is a practice as universal as cookery, as the wearing of clothes, as the use of domestic animals.

And has this practice been proved by experience to be pernicious? Let us take the instance with which we are most familiar. Let us inquire what has been the effect of those laws which, in our own country, limit the labor of adults to six days in every seven. It is quite unnecessary to discuss the question whether Christians be or be not bound by a divine command to observe the Sunday. For it is evident that, whether our weekly holiday be of divine or of human institution, the effect on the temporal interests of society will be exactly the same. Now, is there a single argument in the whole speech of my honorable friend, the Member for Sheffield, which does not tell just as strongly against the laws which enjoin the observance of the Sunday as against the bill on our table? Surely, if his reasoning is good for hours, it must be equally good for days.

He says, "If this limitation be good for the working-people, rely on it that they will find it out, and that they will themselves establish it without any law." Why not reason in the same way about the Sunday? Why not say, "If it be a good thing for the people of London to shut their shops one day in seven, they will find it out, and will shut their shops without a law?" Sir, the answer is obvious. I have no doubt that, if you were to poll the shopkeepers of London, you would find an immense majority, probably a hundred to one, in favor of closing shops on the Sunday; and yet it is absolutely necessary to give to the wish of the majority the sanction of a law; for, if there were no such law, the minority, by opening their shops, would soon force the majority to do the same.

---

2. Jacobins were a faction within the French Revolution who were initially radical republicans, but who were then responsible for the Reign of Terror. Macaulay suggests here that the Jacobins ordered, among other things, rest. [Ed.]

But, says my honorable friend, you cannot limit the labor of adults unless you fix wages. This proposition he lays down repeatedly, assures us that it is incontrovertible, and, indeed, seems to think it self-evident; for he has not taken the trouble to prove it. Sir, my answer shall be very short. We have, during many centuries, limited the labor of an adult to six days in seven; and yet we have not fixed the rate of wages.

But, it is said, you cannot legislate for all trades; and therefore you had better not legislate for any. Look at the poor seamstress. She works far longer and harder than the factory child. She sometimes plies her needle fifteen, sixteen hours in the twenty-four. See how the house-maid works; up at six every morning, and toiling up-stairs and down-stairs till near midnight. You own that you cannot do anything for the seamstress and the house-maid. Why then trouble yourself about the factory child? Take care that by protecting one class you do not aggravate the hardships endured by the classes which you cannot protect. Why, sir, might not all this be said, word for word, against the laws which enjoin the observance of the Sunday? There are classes of people whom, you cannot prevent from working on the Sunday. There are classes of people whom, if you could, you ought not to prevent from working on the Sunday. Take the seamstress of whom so much has been said. You cannot keep her from sewing and hemming all Sunday in her garret. But you do not think that a reason for suffering Covent Garden Market, and Leadenhall Market, and Smithfield Market, and all the shops from Mile End to Hyde Park to be open all Sunday. Nay, these factories about which we are debating, does anybody propose that they shall be allowed to work all Sunday? See, then, how inconsistent you are. You think it unjust to limit the labor of the factory child to ten hours a day, because you cannot limit the labor of the seamstress; and yet you see no injustice in limiting the labor of the factory child, ay, and of the factory man, to six days in the week, though you cannot limit the labor of the seamstress.

But, you say, by protecting one class we shall aggravate the sufferings of all the classes which we cannot protect. You say this, but you do not prove it; and all experience proves the contrary. We interfere on the Sunday to close the shops. We do not interfere with the labor of the house-maid. But are the house-maids of London more severely worked on the Sunday than on other days? The fact notoriously is the reverse. For your legislation keeps the public feeling in a right state, and thus protects indirectly those whom it cannot protect directly.

Will my honorable friend, the Member for Sheffield, maintain that the law which limits the number of working-days has been injurious to the working population? I am certain that he will not. How then can he expect me to believe that a law which limits the number of working-hours must necessarily be injurious to the working population? Yet he and those who agree with him seem to wonder at our dulness because we do not at once admit the truth of the doctrine which they propound on this subject. They reason thus: We cannot reduce the number of hours of labor in factories without reducing the amount of production. We cannot reduce the amount of production without reducing the remuneration of the laborer. Meanwhile, foreigners, who are at liberty to work till they drop down dead at their looms, will soon beat us out of all the markets of the world. Wages will go down fast. The condition of our working-people will be far worse than it is; and our unwise interference will, like the unwise interference of our ancestors with the dealings of the corn-factor and the money-lender, increase the distress of the very class which we wish to relieve.

Now, sir, I fully admit that there might be such a limitation of the hours of labor as would produce the evil consequences with which we are threatened; and this, no doubt, is a very good reason for legislating with great caution, for feeling our way, for looking well to all the details of this bill. But it is certainly not true that every limitation of the hours of labor must produce these consequences. And I am, I must say, surprised when I hear men of eminent ability and knowledge lay down the proposition that a diminution of the time of labor must be followed by a diminution of the wages of labor, as a proposition capable of being strictly demonstrated, as a proposition about which there can be no more doubt than about any theorem in Euclid. Sir, I deny the truth of the proposition; and for this plain reason: We have already, by law, greatly reduced the time of labor in factories. Thirty years ago, the late Sir Robert Peel told the House that it was a common practice to make children of eight years of age toil in mills fifteen hours a day. A law has since been made which prohibits persons under eighteen years of age from working in mills more than twelve hours a day. The law was opposed on exactly the same grounds on which the bill before us is opposed. Parliament was told then, as it is told now, that with the time of labor the quantity of production would decrease, that with the quantity of production the wages would decrease, that our manufacturers would be unable to contend with foreign manufacturers, and that the condition of the laboring population, instead of being made better by the interference of the Legislature, would be made worse. Read over those debates, and you may imagine that you are reading the debate of this evening. Parliament disregarded these prophecies. The time of labor was limited. Have wages fallen? Has the cotton trade left Manchester for France or Germany? Has the condition of the working-people become more miserable? Is it not universally acknowledged that the evils which were so confidently predicted have not come to pass? Let me be understood. I am not arguing that, because a law which reduced the hours of daily labor from fifteen to twelve did not reduce wages, a law reducing those hours from twelve to ten or eleven cannot possibly reduce wages. That would be very inconclusive reasoning. What I

say is this, that, since a law which reduced the hours of daily labor from fifteen to twelve has not reduced wages, the proposition that every reduction of
the hours of labor must necessarily reduce wages is a false proposition. There
is evidently some flaw in that demonstration which my honorable friend
thinks so complete; and what the flaw is we may perhaps discover if we look
at the analogous case to which I have so often referred.

Sir, exactly three hundred years ago, great religious changes were taking
place in England. Much was said and written, in that inquiring and innovat-
ing age, about the question whether Christians were under a religious obligation to rest from labor on one day in the week; and it is well known that the
chief Reformers, both here and on the Continent, denied the existence of any
such obligation. Suppose then that, in 1546, Parliament had made a law that
there should thenceforth be no distinction between the Sunday and any other
day. Now, sir, our opponents, if they are consistent with themselves, must hold
that such a law would have immensely increased the wealth of the country and
the remuneration of the working-man. What an effect, if their principles be
sound, must have been produced by the addition of one sixth to the time of
labor! What an increase of production! What a rise of wages! How utterly unable must the foreign artisan, who still had his days of festivity and of repose,
have found himself to maintain a competition with a people whose shops were
open, whose markets were crowded, whose spades, and axes, and planes, and
hods, and anvils, and looms were at work from morning till night on three
hundred and sixty-five days a year! The Sundays of three hundred years make
up fifty years of our working-days. We know what the industry of fifty years
can do. We know what marvels the industry of the last fifty years has wrought.
The arguments of my honorable friend irresistibly lead us to this conclusion,
that if, during the last three centuries, the Sunday had not been observed as a
day of rest, we should have been a far richer, a far more highly civilized people than we now are, and that the laboring class especially would have been
far better off than at present. But does he, does any Member of the House, seriously believe that this would have been the case? For my own part, I have
not the smallest doubt that if we and our ancestors had, during the last three
centuries, worked just as hard on the Sundays as on the week-days, we should
have been at this moment a poorer people and a less civilized people than we
are; that there would have been less production than there has been, that the
wages of the laborer would have been lower than they are, and that some other
nation would have been now making cotton stuffs and woollen stuffs and cut-
lery for the whole world.

Of course, sir, I do not mean to say that a man will not produce more in a
week by working seven days than by working six days. But I very much doubt
whether, at the end of a year, he will generally have produced more by work-

ing seven days a week than by working six days a week; and I firmly believe that, at the end of twenty years, he will have produced much less by working seven days a week than by working six days a week. In the same manner I do not deny that a factory child will produce more, in a single day, by working twelve hours than by working ten hours, and by working fifteen hours than by working twelve hours. But I do deny that a great society in which children work fifteen, or even twelve hours a day, will, in the lifetime of a generation, produce as much as if those children had worked less. If we consider man merely in a commercial point of view, if we consider him merely as a machine for the production of worsted or calico, let us not forget what a piece of mechanism he is, how fearfully and wonderfully made. We do not treat a fine horse or a sagacious dog exactly as we treat a spinning-jenny. Nor will any slaveholder, who has sense enough to know his own interest, treat his human chattels exactly as he treats his horses and his dogs. And would you treat the free laborer of England like a mere wheel or pulley? Rely on it that intense labor, beginning too early in life, continued too long every day, stunting the growth of the body, stunting the growth of the mind, leaving no time for healthful exercise, leaving no time for intellectual culture, must impair all those high qualities which have made our country great. Your overworked boys will become a feeble and ignoble race of men, the parents of a more feeble and more ignoble progeny; nor will it be long before the deterioration of the laborer will injuriously affect those very interests to which his physical and moral energies have been sacrificed. On the other hand, a day of rest recurring in every week, two or three hours of leisure, exercise, innocent amusement or useful study, recurring every day, must improve the whole man, physically, morally, intellectually; and the improvement of the man will improve all that the man produces. Why is it, sir, that the Hindoo cotton manufacturer, close to whose door the cotton grows, cannot, in the bazaar of his own town, maintain a competition with the English cotton manufacturer, who has to send thousands of miles for the raw material, and who has then to send the wrought material thousands of miles to market? You will say that it is owing to the excellence of our machinery. And to what is the excellence of our machinery owing? How many of the improvements which have been made in our machinery do we owe to the ingenuity and patient thought of working-men? Adam Smith[3] tells us, in the first chapter of his great work, that you can hardly go to a factory without seeing some very pretty machine—that is his expression—devised by some laboring-man. Hargraves,[4] the inventor of the spinning-jenny,

---

3. See Biographies section at the end of this volume. [Ed.]
4. See the selection from Edward Baines, Jr., *A History of the Cotton Manufacture in Great Britain,* in this volume. [Ed.]

was a common artisan. Crompton,[5] the inventor of the mule-jenny, was a working-man. How many hours of the labor of children would do so much for our manufacturers as one of these improvements has done? And in what sort of society are such improvements most likely to be made? Surely in a society in which the faculties of the working-people are developed by education. How long will you wait before any negro, working under the lash in Louisiana, will contrive better machinery for squeezing the sugar canes? My honorable friend seems to me, in all his reasonings about the commercial prosperity of nations, to overlook entirely the chief cause on which that prosperity depends. What is it, sir, that makes the great difference between country and country? Not the exuberance of soil; not the mildness of climate; not mines, nor havens, nor rivers. These things are indeed valuable when put to their proper use by human intelligence: but human intelligence can do much without them; and they without human intelligence can do nothing. They exist in the highest degree in regions of which the inhabitants are few, and squalid, and barbarous, and naked, and starving; while on sterile rocks, amidst unwholesome marshes, and under inclement skies, may be found immense populations, well fed, well lodged, well clad, well governed. Nature meant Egypt and Sicily to be the gardens of the world. They once were so. Is it anything in the earth or in the air that makes Scotland more prosperous than Egypt, that makes Holland more prosperous than Sicily? No; it was the Scotchman that made Scotland: it was the Dutchman that made Holland. Look at North America. Two centuries ago the sites on which now arise mills, and hotels, and banks, and colleges, and churches, and the Senate-houses of flourishing commonwealths, were deserts, abandoned to the panther and the bear. What has made the change? Was it the rich mould, or the redundant rivers? No: the prairies were as fertile, the Ohio and the Hudson were as broad and as full then as now. Was the improvement the effect of some great transfer of capital from the Old World to the New? No: the emigrants generally carried out with them no more than a pittance; but they carried out the English heart, and head, and arm; and the English heart, and head, and arm turned the wilderness into cornfield and orchard, and the huge trees of the primeval forest into cities and fleets. Man, man is the great instrument that produces wealth. The natural difference between Campania and Spitzbergen is trifling when compared with the difference between a country inhabited by men full of bodily and mental vigor, and a country inhabited by men sunk in bodily and mental decrepitude. Therefore it is that we are not poorer but richer, because we have, through many ages rested from our labor one day in seven. That day is not lost. While industry is

---

5. Samuel Crompton (1753–1827) invented the mule spinner (see Glossary), an improvement on the Hargreaves jenny. He developed his invention after working on the spinning jenny himself in a mill. [Ed.]

suspended, while the plough lies in the furrow, while the Exchange is silent, while no smoke ascends from the factory, a process is going on quite as important to the wealth of nations as any process which is performed on more busy days. Man, the machine of machines, the machine compared with which all the contrivances of the Watts and the Arkwrights are worthless, is repairing and winding up, so that he returns to his labors on the Monday with clearer intellect, with livelier spirits, with renewed corporal vigor. Never will I believe that what makes a population stronger, and healthier, and wiser, and better, can ultimately make it poorer. You try to frighten us by telling us that, in some German factories, the young work seventeen hours in the twenty-four, that they work so hard that among thousands there is not one who grows to such a stature that he can be admitted into the army; and you ask whether, if we pass this bill, we can possibly hold our own against such competition as this? Sir, I laugh at the thought of such competition. If ever we are forced to yield the foremost place among commercial nations, we shall yield it, not to a race of degenerate dwarfs, but to some people pre-eminently vigorous in body and mind.

For these reasons, sir, I approve of the principle of this bill, and shall, without hesitation, vote for the second reading. To what extent we ought to reduce the hours of labor is a question of more difficulty. I think that we are in the situation of a physician who has satisfied himself that there is a disease, and that there is a specific medicine for the disease, but who is not certain what quantity of that medicine the patient's constitution will bear. Such a physician would probably administer his remedy by small doses, and carefully watch its operation. I cannot help thinking that, by at once reducing the hours of labor from twelve to ten, we should hazard too much. The change is great, and ought to be cautiously and gradually made. Suppose that there should be an immediate fall of wages, which is not impossible. Might there not be a violent reaction? Might not the public take up a notion that our legislation had been erroneous in principle, though, in truth, our error would have been an error, not of principle, but merely of degree? Might not Parliament be induced to retrace its steps? Might we not find it difficult to maintain even the present limitation? The wisest course would, in my opinion, be to reduce the hours of labor from twelve to eleven, to observe the effect of that experiment, and if, as I hope and believe, the result should be satisfactory, then to make a further reduction from eleven to ten. This is a question, however, which will be with more advantage considered when we are in Committee.

One word, sir, before I sit down, in answer to my noble friend near me. He seems to think that this bill is ill-timed. I own that I cannot agree with him. We carried up on Monday last to the bar of the Lords a bill which will remove the most hateful and pernicious restriction that ever was laid on trade. Nothing can be more proper than to apply, in the same week, a remedy to a great evil of a directly opposite kind. As law-givers, we have two great faults to confess and to repair. We have done that which we ought not to have done. We have left undone that which we ought to have done. We have regulated that which we should have left to regulate itself. We have left unregulated that which we were bound to regulate. We have given to some branches of industry a protection which has proved their bane. We have withheld from public health and public morals the protection which was their due. We have prevented the laborer from buying his loaf where he could get it cheapest; but we have not prevented him from ruining his body and mind by premature and immoderate toil. I hope we have seen the last both of a vicious system of interference and of a vicious system of non-interference, and that our poorer countrymen will not longer have reason to attribute their sufferings either to our meddling or to our neglect.

CHAPTER SEVEN

LIMBS AND LIVES

RICHARD OASTLER

YORKSHIRE SLAVERY

TO THE EDITORS OF THE LEEDS MERCURY

It is the pride of Britain that a slave cannot exist on her soil; and if I read the genius of her constitution aright, I find that slavery is most abhorrent to it—that the air which Britons breathe is free—the ground on which they tread is sacred to liberty.'

—*Rev. R. W. Hamilton's Speech at the Meeting held in the Cloth-hall Yard, Sept. 22nd, 1830.*

Gentlemen,—No heart responded with truer accents to the sounds of liberty which were heard in the Leeds Cloth-hall yard, on the 22nd instant, than did mine, and from none could more sincere and earnest prayers arise to the throne of Heaven, that hereafter slavery might only be known to Britain in the pages of her history. One shade alone obscured my pleasure, arising not from any difference in principle, but from the want of application of the general principle *to the whole empire.* The pious and able champions of *negro* liberty and *colonial* rights should, if I mistake not, have gone farther than they did; or perhaps, to speak more correctly, before they had travelled so far as the West Indies, should, at least for a few moments, have sojourned in our own

Originally printed in *Leeds Mercury* (September 29, 1830). Reprinted in *The History of the Factory Movement.* Vol. I. London: Simpkin, Marshall, and Co., 1857.

immediate neighbourhood, and have directed the attention of the meeting to scenes of misery, acts of oppression, and victims of slavery, even on the threshold of our homes. Let truth speak out, appalling as the statement may appear. The fact is true. Thousands of our fellow-creatures and fellow-subjects, both male and female, the miserable inhabitants of a *Yorkshire town,* (Yorkshire now represented in parliament by the giant of anti-slavery principles,) are this very moment existing in a state of slavery, *more horrid* than are the victims of that hellish system—"*colonial slavery.*" These innocent creatures drawl out, unpitied, their short but miserable existence, in a place famed for its profession of religious zeal, whose inhabitants are ever foremost in *professing* "temperance" and "reformation," and are striving to outrun their neighbours in missionary exertions, and would fain send the Bible to the farthest corner of the globe—ay, in the very place where the anti-slavery fever rages most furiously, her *apparent charity,* is not more admired on earth, than her *real cruelty* is abhorred in heaven. The very streets which receive the droppings of an "Anti-slavery Society" are every morning wet by the tears of innocent victims at the accursed shrine of avarice, who are *compelled* (not by the cart-whip of the negro slave-driver) but by the dread of the equally-appalling thong or strap of the overlooker, to hasten, half-dressed, *but not half-fed,* to those magazines of British infantile slavery—*the worsted mills in the town and neighbourhood of Bradford!!!*

Would that I had Brougham's[1] eloquence, that I might rouse the hearts of the nation, and make every Briton swear, "These innocents shall be free!"

Thousands of little children, both male and female, *but principally female,* from seven to fourteen years of age, are daily *compelled* to *labour* from six o'clock in the morning to seven in the evening, with only—Britons, blush while you read it!—*with only thirty minutes allowed for eating and recreation.* Poor infants! ye are indeed sacrificed at the shrine of avarice, *without even the solace of the negro slave;* ye are no more than he is, *free agents;* ye are compelled to work as long as the *necessity* of your needy parents may require, or the cold-blooded avarice of your worse than barbarian masters *may demand!* Ye live in the boasted land of freedom, and *feel* and mourn that *ye are slaves,* and slaves without the only comfort which the negro has. He knows it is his sordid, mercenary master's interest that he should *live,* be *strong* and *healthy. Not so with you.* Ye are doomed to labour from morning to night for one who cares not how soon your weak and tender frames are stretched to breaking! You are not mercifully valued at so much per head; this would assure you at least (even with the worst and most cruel masters) of the

---

1. Henry Brougham (1778–1868) was a prominent abolitionist. [Ed.]

mercy shown to their own labouring beasts. No, no! your soft and delicate limbs are tired and fagged, and jaded, at only *so much per week,* and when your joints can act no longer, your emaciated frames are cast aside, the boards on which you lately toiled and wasted life away, are instantly supplied with other victims, who in this boasted land of liberty are HIRED—not sold—as slaves, and daily forced to *hear* that they are free. Oh! Duncombe![2] Thou hatest slavery—I know thou dost resolve that "Yorkshire children shall no more be slaves." And Morpeth![3] who justly gloriest in the Christian faith—Oh, Morpeth! listen to the cries and count the tears of these poor babes, and let St Stephen's hear thee swear "they shall no longer groan in slavery!" And Bethell,[4] too! who swears eternal hatred to the name of slave, whene'er thy manly voice is heard in Britain's senate, assert the rights and liberty of Yorkshire youths. And Brougham! thou who art the chosen champion of liberty in every clime! oh bend thy giant's mind, and listen to the sorrowing accents of these poor Yorkshire little ones, and note their tears; then let thy voice rehearse their woes, and touch the chord thou only holdest—the chord that sounds above the silvery notes in praise of heavenly liberty, and down descending at thy will, groans in the horrid caverns of the deep in muttering sounds of misery accursed to hellish bondage; and as thou sound'st these notes, let Yorkshire hear thee swear, "Her *children* shall be free!" Yes, all ye four protectors of our rights, chosen by freemen to destroy oppression's rod,

> *Vow one by one, vow altogether, vow*
> *With heart and voice, eternal enmity*
> *Against oppression by your brethren's hands;*
> *Till man nor woman under Britain's laws,*
> *Nor son nor daughter born within her empire,*
> *Shall buy, or sell, or* HIRE, *or* BE A SLAVE!

The nation is now most resolutely determined that negroes shall be free. Let them, however, not forget that Britons have common rights with Afric's sons.

The blacks may be fairly compared to beasts of burden, *kept for their master's use;* the whites, to those *which others keep and let for hire.* If I have succeeded in calling the attention of your readers to the horrid and abominable system on which the worsted mills in and near Bradford is conducted, I have

---

2. Thomas Slingsby Duncombe (1776–1861) was a member of parliament for Finsbury. [Ed.]
3. Viscount Morpeth was the title taken by George Howard (1802–1864) who, as a Whig, represented the borough of Morpeth. [Ed.]
4. Christopher Bethell (1773–1859) was the bishop of Bangor. [Ed.]

done some good. Why should not children working in them be protected by legislative enactments, as well as those who work in cotton mills? Christians should feel and act for those whom Christ so eminently loved, and declared that "of such is the kingdom of Heaven."—I remain, yours, &c.,

—RICHARD OASTLER.

Fixby Hall, near Huddersfield, Sept. 29, 1830.

CHARLES WING

PARLIAMENTARY TESTIMONY ON CHILD LABOUR

ABRIDGMENT OF EVIDENCE

Aberdeen, Charles, age about 53,—examined 7th July, 1832,—a card-grinder in a cotton factory at Salford, in Manchester; apprenticed, when about 12, by the parish of St. James, Westminster, to Douglas and Co., of Hollywell, Flintshire; employed in different factories ever since; discharged by Messrs. Lambert, Hoole, and Jackson, on the 20th of April, for announcing his determination to support Mr. Sadler's Bill, and for refusing to sign a petition against it.

1. What was the nature of your employment?—I worked in a cardroom, when first I commenced working in a factory, spreading cotton.
2. Is it a very dusty apartment of the mill?—Very dusty; but it is superseded by machines; there is no spreading now by boys.
3. But still are there not various apartments of the cotton-mill now where there are many flues, and much dust?—Yes, men that are more lusty than myself, I have seen die daily for want of breath; because they were not allowed to let the fresh air in, and the foul air out.
4. Why so?—They consider that it damages the work; and that by not admitting so much air in the room, it makes a smaller surface on the flies of cotton; and that if they let too much air in, it becomes ouzy.
5. You are aware that it has been frequently asserted that the work-people in the mill have an objection to work in a tolerably cool and ventilated air?—I never heard an objection stated to let the foul air out and the fresh in; but a cry and craving for it.

From *Evils of the Factory System.* London: Saunders and Otley, 1837.

6. What were the hours of labour in the first mill you were in?—From six in the morning, to seven in the evening: carding went on during the day; it was only spinning that went on in the night, while I was an apprentice.

7. What time had you for refreshment?—A whole hour for dinner, none for breakfast, or anything else.

8. During the hour that the moving power was suspended, had you to clean the machinery?—In the dinner hour, I, for one, used to have to clean and oil the machinery, and I could do that in half an hour, and eat my morsel afterwards.

9. Was it the common practice to employ the children in that interval to clean the machinery?—Not the children generally; but the scavengers for the mills were obliged to stop; they were the smallest of the children.

10. Does the business of the scavengers demand constant attention, and to be in perpetual motion, and to assume a variety of attitudes, so as to accommodate their business in cleaning the machinery to its motions?—Yes, to go under the machine, while it is going, in all attitudes, and in a most deplorable dress; perhaps a mantle made of the coarse stuff in which the cotton is brought, called the bagging.

11. Is it a dangerous employment in point of exposing persons to accidents?—Very dangerous when first they come, but by constant application they become used to it.

12. Do you think that the people who worked at night were less healthy than those who worked in the day?—I do.

13. Would the people have preferred to work by day, if they had had their choice?—They would have preferred to work in the day.

14. Do you think that the children who worked through the night took the rest in the day-time that they ought to have done?—I do not think they did.

15. That they were tempted, in point of fact, to play and move about in the day-time, instead of going to bed?—Yes; and in such weather as this, to go a blackberrying, and so on.

16. So that night-work left them without a proper degree of rest, and consequently deprived them of health?—Yes.

17. Could a hand choose whether he would be a day-worker or a night-worker?—If the hand, a male or female, would not come in the night, they would not give them a place in the day; and it has been rather compulsory to make them go to night-work.

18. So as to keep up their stock of night-labourers from those who have been employed by day?—Yes; it has been known that they have discharged persons who have refused to go to night-work often.

19. Are the hours longer or shorter at present, than when you were apprentice to a cotton-mill?—Much the same; especially at the place where I

was last discharged. The master that I was last discharged from, had observed the Act of Parliament more than any master that I ever knew; indeed, it was framed, and hung up at the bottom of the factory stairs.

20. You say that the time of labour which is required from the children in those mills is much the same as when you first entered upon that employment; will you now inform the committee, whether the labour itself has increased, or otherwise?—The labour has increased more than twofold.

21. Explain in what way; do you merely mean that a double quantity is thrown off by some superiority in the machinery, or that a greater degree of exertion is demanded from the hands, and to the extent you mention?—The one is consequent upon the other; if the machine is speeded, it will turn off a double quantity; and it requires a double exertion and labour from the child, or from any person that is attending it.

22. Do you think there is double the quantity of labour required from the children that there used to be?—I am confident of it; since I have been working at the firm of Lambert, Hoole, and Jackson, I have done twice the quantity of work that I used to do, for less wages. The exertion of the body is required to follow up the speed of the machine.

23. Has this increased labour any visible effect upon the appearance of the children?—It has, indeed, a remarkable effect; it causes a paleness and a wanness; a factory-child may be known easily from another child that does not work in a factory.

24. Do you think it interferes with their growth, as well as with their health?—I do.

25. Has it had the effect of shortening their lives, do you suppose?—I am beyond supposing it.

26. Are you, then, confident as to that important and distressing fact?—Yes, I am confident of it from what experience I have had; and I think I have had a good deal.

27. What grounds have you for thinking so?—I have seen many instances, but cannot state particularly: I have seen men and women that have worked in a factory all their lives, like myself, and that get married; and I have seen the race become diminutive and small; I have myself had seven children, not one of which survived six weeks; my wife is an emaciated person, like myself, a little woman, and she worked during her childhood, younger than myself, in a factory.

28. What is the common age to which those that have been accustomed from early youth to work in factories survive, according to the best of your observation?—I have known very few that have exceeded me in age. I think that most of them die under forty.

29. Of course, if the period of their death is so much anticipated, a great deal of sickness must prevail before that event takes place?—I suppose there is not a week but what there are persons that are sick, who work in a factory; sometimes there may be ten; sometimes a dozen; sometimes half a dozen.

30. In consequence of their labour?—Not altogether in consequence of their labour, but for want of fresh air.

31. So that you consider that the hardship of the children and young persons confined to labour in factories does not altogether rest upon the circumstance of their being kept too long hours at their labour, but also has reference to the heated and unwholesome atmosphere which they have to breathe while at their work?—Yes; the friction of the brass, and the iron, and the oil, and the necessaries being in the same room; this all has a tendency to make them look ill.

32. Adverting to the trade, generally speaking, have you heard it as a usual remark and serious complaint, among the hands employed in factories, that their hours of labour were too long for them to endure with any comfort or safety?—I have heard it repeatedly said so by many.

33. What else have you to say with reference to the system?—I have something else to relate respecting the overlookers. They are men that are well paid, and are a great check to an advance of wages; I have known overlookers get 30*s.* a week, and 20£ a quarter bounty-money; according to the quantity of work that is thrown off, they get the bounty-money; but it is not half so much as they used to have.

34. Have the children any additional wages in proportion to the quantity of work done by their overlookers?—No; this all goes to the overlookers.

35. So that it only operates as an infliction of cruelty upon them?—Yes; those that do the most labour are the worst paid.

36. You have already stated your impressions as to the effect of the factory system, as now pursued, in reference to the health of those who are employed in it; will you state to this committee, whether it has not also a very pernicious consequence in regard to their education; and, first, have they a sufficient opportunity of attending night-schools?—I think they have not.

37. If after those hours of confinement and of labour they were to attend night-schools generally, do you think they are in a proper state, either of body or mind, adequately to avail themselves of the opportunity that might be afforded them under such circumstances?—I do not think they are.

38. Do you think that Sunday-schools are, in themselves, sufficient to obviate the great and manifest evils that must result from a total want of edu-

cation?—By no means; the young persons, after they have been laboured during the whole of the week, are disinclined to attend Sunday-schools.

39. Will you state what, in the mill in which you were employed, according to your observation for the considerable number of years during which you have been engaged in it, is the actual state of morals, as resulting from excessive labour and want of education?—The morals of the children are in a bad state there; if their parents, and the Sunday-schools combined, were to use all their power to teach them morality, the superabundant hours and extreme debaucheries that are practised in factories would entirely choke it.

40. Do you say that from your own knowledge and belief?—From my own knowledge and belief; both debaucheries in words and in actions.

Adamson, James, age 48,—examined 30th June, 1832,—overseer and manager at Arbroath, about eighteen miles from Dundee, upon the coast.

1. Have you any experience in mills and factories?—Yes, I have occasionally been engaged as an overseer, but rather more as a manager.

2. What were the hours of labour at the first mill in which you were employed?—Twelve were the stated hours, but then we made up all lost time.

3. Twelve hours independently of the time of refreshment?—Yes; we had one half hour for breakfast and another half hour for dinner, and the actual going hours were twelve; and if we lost time by holydays, or by any thing going wrong about the machinery, which stopped the mill in ordinary working hours, then we had to make it up.

4. Do you find that the children and young persons more particularly are fatigued with that length of labour?—I have seen its effects upon the young, and upon the old; I have found them upon myself.

5. The fatigue is more than the constitution can well bear?—Yes.

6. What were the hours at the next mill in which you were employed?—Twelve hours, the stated hours.

7. Still with the addition of the hours for meals, and having to make up lost time?—Yes.

8. At how early an age have you known children to labour in the mills?—I have known my own family labour before they were eight years of age, between seven and eight.

9. You have, as a parent, found that the hours of labour were too long for your children to endure, consistently with their health?—I have seen them, when they returned at night, so very tired, that if their meal was not ready when they came into the house, they were so sound asleep that we found it difficult to awake them to take their meal, and go to bed.

10. Have you observed in the mills in which you have been, that any considerable number of the hands have been absent from actual sickness, in

consequence of the length of their labour?—We always found that we had occasionally a want of hands on account of sickness; and some part of the day it has been difficult to keep the work going for want of hands, on account of sickness.

11. Is it usual for you to beat the children up to that length of labour, so as to keep them attentive and vigilant at their work?—Yes; I must confess that I have beaten them a little myself.

12. It becomes necessary, when you have to exact that length of labour from children and young persons, to keep them up to it by downright chastisement?—Yes, I have found that to be the case.

13. And that not from any fault of the children, but from their inability to attend to the business with sufficient activity and success?—Yes.

14. Are you well acquainted with the operatives of Arbroath?—Yes, I am pretty well acquainted with them.

15. Are they favourable to the proposed limitation of the hours of labour of their children?—They seem very anxious for a reduction of the hours of labour.

16. How many mills are there in Arbroath of the nature to which you have alluded,—that is, flax or tow mills?—I think there are thirteen or fourteen different mills.

17. Have all those mills schools attached to them?—No, there are none that have schools, with the exception of one. There is a Mr. Gordon, that pays a teacher for attending at the mill two hours after labour: he has a school-room in one of his mills for that purpose.

18. Then supposing that the hours of labour, including the hour for meals, extend to thirteen hours and a half a day, and that there are two hours more for children to attend the night-school, making fifteen hours and a half a day, besides the time that must be taken in going to and from their homes, is there not a very little time for either rest or recreation, so as to preserve health, in the case of those children?—I think the time is too short for even the necessary rest, without any relaxation.

19. Can you state the general impression that prevails as to the health of the children so employed in the town of Arbroath; state your own impression, whether it is favourable, in the first instance?—I certainly consider that it is against the health of the children; and I have a certificate from the medical gentlemen of Arbroath to the same effect.

[*The witness delivered in the same, which was read, as follows:*]

Arbroath, May 21st, 1832.

We, the undersigned, medical practitioners in Arbroath, have no hesitation in stating it as our decided opinion, that the employment of children and young persons in the confined and impure atmosphere of spinning-mills, during the present long hours, must be, and from our observation and experience actually is, highly prejudical to health, soundness of constitution, and longevity. We need scarcely add further, that it is very unfavourable to morality, and leaves scarcely any time for mental culture.

Wm. Traill, Surgeon.
John Traill, Surgeon.
Alexr. Mitchell, Surgeon.
Wm. J. Thomson, Surgeon.
Chas. Ginslay, Surgeon.
Robert W. Bruce, M.D.

20. Will you state your impression as to the effect that it has upon the character and the morals of the rising generation, those long hours of labour, interfering as they must do with instruction, both domestic and public?—My opinion is, that the length of the hours of labour puts out of their power their moral improvement, on account of their want of education, and I have a certificate from the ministers of religion to that effect.

[*The witness delivered in the same, which was read, as follows:*]

Arbroath, 2d May, 1832.

The undersigned have no hesitation in offering it as their decided opinion, that the present extended hours of labour in the flax-mills of this place have a most pernicious effect, both in a physical and in a moral point of view, upon the young persons employed in them. They have uniformly observed, that such young persons want the healthful aspect of children not similarly confined; that, in respect of education, they are far behind what used to be the average advancement of the same class of children in this part of the country, and that their moral and religious condition is such as was to be expected in the case of persons who are removed from school to the unwhole-some air and dangerous companionship of a manufactory, at the age which is most available for the formation either of virtuous or of vicious habits. Although the practice of employing a great number of children at the mills is, in this place, only of recent date, yet enough has already appeared to prove that the tendency of such an unnatural system is to effect a rapid and certain deterioration of the race. And there is nothing of which the undersigned are more firmly persuaded than this, that if something be not speedily done to enable parents to resist the temptation, or dispense with the necessity of sending their children to work in mills for a longer period than is consistent with the preservation of their health and the improvement of their minds, Parliament will have, at no distant day, to legislate for a population tenfold more ignorant, improvident, pauperized, and immoral, than the present.

Thomas Doig, Assistant Minister of Arbroath.
J. M'Culloch, Minister of St. Vigean's Chapel of Ease.
J. J. M'Farland, Minister of the Abbey Chapel.
William Henderson, Minister of the Episcopal Chapel.
P. Davidson, Minister of the Second Secession Congregation.
John Ramsay, Minister of the Independent Chapel.
William Allan, Minister of the Relief Congregation.
Robert Nicholson, Minister of the Methodist Chapel.
Joseph Hay, Minister of the First Secession Congregation.
George M'Ash, Teacher, Arbroath Academy.
David Grant, ditto——ditto.
John Straton, ditto——ditto.
Alex. Webster, ditto——ditto.
Walter Low, Private Teacher, Arbroath.
John Grant, Infant-school Teacher, Arbroath.
John Adam, Teacher, Arbroath.
John Lundie, ditto.
Dd. Littlejohns, ditto.
R. Naughton, ditto.
John Hastings, ditto.
John Hackney, ditto.
George Sheriffs, Preacher of the Gospel, Arbroath.

Allett, John, age 53,—examined 21st May, 1832,—a blanket manufacturer, began to work in manufactories when 14; eight children living.

1. Will you state, upon your own knowledge, whether the hours of labour have not been considerably increased (that is, in brisk times) since you were acquainted with factories?—When I went at first to factories I was at work about eleven hours a day, but time has increased to fifteen, to sixteen, and sometimes to eighteen, and sometimes to higher, even to twenty-four hours.

2. The labour of children and young persons has been increased as you have now stated?—Yes.

3. Is the work done harder than formerly?—It is much harder, and if we worked only ten hours now it is harder, because our machines are faster speeded than they were when they first began.

4. How long have you known children labour in brisk times?—Fourteen or fifteen hours a day, just as the work was.

5. How did you perceive them to bear it, especially at the latter part of the day?—I have seen my own children, when I have been in that department of business, spinning for Monday, Tuesday, and Wednesday, and they seemed to be quite lively; but towards the other end of the week, when they began to be fatigued, whilst at every interval we have been

getting refreshment, they have been sitting down, and could not abide playing, as they could at the fore-end of the week.

6. Are they not almost continually upon their feet?—Always upon their feet; there can be no rest at all.

7. Were they excessively sleepy?—Very sleepy; I have seen them sleeping while we were at our drinking, and when in the evening my youngest boy has said, "Father, what o'clock is it?" I have said perhaps, "It is seven o'clock;" "Oh! is it two hours to nine o'clock?" I cannot bear it; I have thought I had rather almost have seen them starve to death, than to be used in that manner. I have heard that child crying out, when getting within a few yards of the door, "Oh! mother, is my supper ready?" and I have seen him, when he has been taken from my back, fall asleep before he could get it.

8. When did that child first go to the mill?—Between six and seven years old.

9. How are they kept up when they begin to be fatigued by this intense and long-continued labour?—If it be not a tender parent that is over them, they are kept up to their work by something like the lash of a slave-driver; this I have frequently seen.

10. Is the chastisement generally at the latter end of the day?—Yes, gener-ally so; I have seen it also in the morning, because they have had so lit-tle sleep that they were hardly awakened; and I have known more acci-dents happen at the fore-end of the day than at the latter part; I mean before breakfast time. I was an eye-witness of one in the same place that I worked at many years: a child was working wool, that is, to prepare the wool for the machine; but the strap caught him, as he was hardly awake, and it carried him into the machinery; and we found one limb in one place and one in another, and he was cut to bits almost; his whole body went in, and was mangled.

11. Did you ever see any accidents happen at the latter end of the day from fatigue?—No, I cannot say; I have seen a spinner strike a child with a roller; I took up the child, and thought he was killed, but he got better afterwards. That man could not get any one to work for him in the whole town, and he went to another place, and he had spun there but very little time, not more than a week or a fortnight, before he took the roller, which is not less than three yards long, and four inches round about, and struck another child, and in six days he died. There was a coroner's inquest on the body, and it was brought in "accidental death."

12. You say that your children worked fourteen or fifteen hours a day; did you ever ask the overlooker to keep them only to the short hours?—Yes; I have myself asked the master, and said that we could not bear it; and

my master told me that if we could not bear it, there were others that could, and we might go about our business.

13. Do not those long hours of labour not only render it impossible for the children to attend a night-school, or the Sunday-school, as they ought to do, but also prevent parents from having the opportunity of being with, and properly instructing their children themselves, and training them up in habits of domestic industry and virtue?—Yes, I am sure they do.

Bennett, Thomas, age 48,—examined, 18th May, 1832,—a slubber, at Dewsbury, eight children.

1. What were the regular hours of work at Mr. Halliley's mill?—Our regular hours, when we were not so throng, were from six to seven.

2. And when you were the throngest, what were your hours?—From five to nine, and from five to ten, and from four to nine.

3. What intervals for meals had the children at that period?—Two hours: an hour for breakfast, and an hour for dinner.

4. Did they always allow two hours for meals at Mr. Halliley's?—Yes, it was allowed; but the children did not get it; for they had business to do at that time, such as fettling and cleaning the machinery.

5. How long a time together have you known those excessive hours to continue?—I have wrought so myself very nearly two years together.

6. Were your children working under you then?—Yes, two of them.

7. State the effect upon your children?—Of a morning, when they had to get up, they have been so fast asleep, that I have had to go up stairs, and lift them out of bed, and have heard their crying with the feelings of a parent; I have been much affected by it.

8. Were not they much fatigued at the termination of such a day's labour as that?—Yes: many a time I have seen their hands moving while they have been nodding almost asleep; they have been doing their business almost mechanically.

9. While they have been almost asleep, they have attempted to work?—Yes; and they have missed the carding, and spoiled the thread, and we have had to beat them for it.

10. Will you state what effect it had upon your children at the end of their day's work?—At the end of their day's work, when they have come home, instead of taking their victuals, they have dropped asleep with the victuals in their hand; and sometimes, when we have sent them to bed with a little bread or something to eat in their hand, I have found it in their bed the next morning.

11. Were your own children obliged to employ most of their time, at breakfast and at the drinking, in cleansing the machine, and in fettling the spindles?—I have seen at that mill, and I have experienced and men-

tioned it with grief, that the English children were enslaved worse than the Africans. Once, when Mr. Wood was saying to the carrier who brought his work in and out, "How long has that horse of mine been at work?" and the carrier told him the time, and he said, "Loose him directly, he has been in too long," I made this reply to him—"You have more mercy and pity for your horse than for your men."

12. Do the accidents principally occur at the latter end of those long days of labour?—Yes, I believe mostly so.

13. Do you know of any that have happened?—I know of one; it was at Mr. Wood's mill. Part of the machine caught a lass who had been drowsy and asleep, and the strap, which ran close by her, caught her at about the middle, and bore her to the ceiling, and down she came, and her neck appeared broken, and the slubber ran up to her, and pulled her neck, and I carried her to the doctor myself.

14. Did she get well?—Yes, she came about again.

15. What time was that?—In the evening.

16. Could you not have got other children to supply the place of your children occasionally?—No, it was forbidden; and if one neighbour wished to take another neighbour's children, unless they were out of work they would not come.

17. When you were working in the mill, were you bound, when required, to work the long hours?—Yes, if I had not done it, my master would have got somebody else that would.

18. And the parish officers would not have relieved you if you had left?—No; they would have said, "You refused to work."

19. You would then have been left to starve?—Yes.

20. Did you ever know a case in which that question has been tried in a court of justice?—No, but I have tried it myself in practice. I came to some distress, and I went to the parish, and the parish then relieved me, but I obtained relief with great trouble; I was told to go back to my work; I was nearly a fortnight away; my master sent me a letter to come to my work, and we agreed again.

Bentley, Elizabeth, age 23,—examined, 4th June, 1832,—as doffer, began to work, when six years old, in a flax mill, at Leeds.

1. What were your hours of labour?—From five in the morning, till nine at night, when they were thronged.

2. For how long a time together have you worked that excessive length of time?—For about half a year.

3. What were your usual hours of labour, when you were not so thronged?—From six in the morning, till seven at night.

4. What time was allowed for your meals?—Forty minutes at noon.

5. Had you any time to get your breakfast, or drinking?—No, we got it as we could.

6. And when your work was bad, you had hardly any time to eat it at all?—No; we were obliged to leave it or to take it home, and when we did not take it, the overlooker took it, and gave it to his pigs.

7. Do you consider doffing a laborious employment?—Yes; when the frames are full, they have to stop the frames, and take the flyers off, and take the full bobbins off, and carry them to the roller, and then put empty ones on, and set the frames going again.

8. Does that keep you constantly on your feet?—Yes; there are so many frames, and they run so quick.

9. Suppose you flagged a little, or were too late, what would they do?—Strap us.

10. Girls as well as boys?—Yes.

11. Have you ever been strapped?—Yes, severely.

12. Were you strapped if you were too much fatigued to keep up with the machinery?—Yes; the overlooker I was under was a very severe man, and when we have been fatigued, and worn out, and had not baskets to put the bobbins in, we used to put them in the window bottoms, and that broke the panes sometimes, and I broke one one time, and the overlooker strapped me on the arm, and it rose a blister, and I ran home to my mother.

13. How long were you in your first situation?—Three or four years.

14. Where did you go to then?—To Benyon's factory.

15. What were you there?—A weigher in the card-room.

16. How long did you work there?—From half-past five, till eight at night.

17. The carding-room is more oppressive than the spinning department?—Yes, it is so dusty; they cannot see each other for dust.

18. Did working in the card-room affect your health?—Yes; it was so dusty, the dust got up my lungs, and the work was so hard; I was middling strong when I went there, but the work was so bad; I got so bad in health, that when I pulled the baskets down, I pulled my bones out of their places.

19. You are considerably deformed in your person in consequence of this labour?—Yes, I am.

20. At what time did it come on?—I was about thirteen years old when it began coming, and it has got worse since; it is five years since my mother died, and my mother was never able to get me a pair of good stays to hold me up; and when my mother died, I had to do for myself, and got me a pair.

21. Were you straight till you were thirteen?—Yes, I was.

22. Have you been attended to by any medical gentleman at Leeds, or the neighbourhood?—Yes, I have been under Mr. Hares.

23. To what did he attribute it?—He said it was owing to hard labour, and working in the factories.
24. Where are you now?—In the poor-house.
25. Do any of your former employers come to see you?—No.
26. Did you ever receive anything from them when you became afflicted?—When I was at home, Mr. Walker made me a present of 1*s.* or 2*s.;* but since I have left my work and gone to the poor-house, they have not come nigh me.
27. You are supported by the parish?—Yes.
28. You are utterly incapable now of any exertion in the factories?—Yes.
29. You were very willing to have worked as long as you were able, from your earliest age?—Yes.
30. And to have supported your widowed mother as long as you could?—Yes.

Best, Mark, age 56,—examined, 2nd June, 1832,?—an overlooker in flax-mills.

1. What were your hours of labour in Mr. Marshall's mill?—The regular hours were from six to seven.
2. How many hours a day have you worked there, when they were throng?—From five to eight, or nine sometimes.
3. Was it the same in the other mills in which you were employed?—Yes.
4. What time was allowed in getting their meals?—Forty minutes.
5. Was any time allowed to take your breakfast, or your drinking?—No.
6. Speaking of the long hours of labour, how were the children treated when they were kept at their work for such a time?—In those rooms I have been in, spinning-rooms, they have small boys and girls to doff the bobbins off, and those that are the last they beat with a strap to make them look sharp.
7. Have you reason to think that, in any of the mills, the masters or the managers were aware that the children were thus beaten and strapped?—Yes, they knew it very well; they encouraged them to do it. Mr. Stirk's was the last place I was at; and the young Mr. Stirk made a strap for me himself, and told me to use it freely, and make them look sharp.
8. Do you think that you could have got the quantity of work out of the children, for so great a number of hours, without that cruel treatment?—No, I dare say I should not; the speed of the machinery is calculated, and they know how much work it will do, and unless they are driven and flogged up, they cannot get the quantity of work they want from them.
9. Does the better machinery increase the fatigue and labour of those engaged in watching it, or does it lessen their fatigue?—It gives more fatigue than it used to do; there are frames invented within the last few years, that they call water-frames. They spin all wet; they are heated by steam, and the place where the girls are minding them is all full of steam.

10. Is not that much more fatiguing employment for children than any spinning previously known?—Yes; this fresh system, which is called fine spinning, is spun all wet and in steam; and the frames stand so close in some places, and the water flies from one frame to another, so that they are wet through to the skin.
11. Are they not liable to be exceedingly injured in consequence of this new process of spinning?—In winter-time the clothes of those that have a long distance to go from their work will be frozen to their back, and quite stiff, before they get home.
12. Had you ever any visitors come to examine your mills?—Yes; many a time.
13. Were you in the habit of making any preparation previous to strangers coming to look at your work?—Yes, they used generally to come round half an hour before those gentlemen came, to tell us to clean and get our machines tidy against that time.
14. Did any of this strapping and cruelty go on when the visitors came to look at the mills?—No.
15. Supposing a stranger comes to see a mill, would it be possible to make a room appear less dusty at that moment than it usually is?—In those dusty places, when any person is coming round to look at them, they generally send some one to acquaint them, and get all cleaned up; and during the time of their cleaning, the machinery is standing; so that if any gentleman comes up the room is clear of dust at that time.

Binns, Stephen, age 39,—examined 2nd June, 1832,—began when about seven years old, to work as a piecener in a cotton factory; afterwards employed as an overlooker in several factories.

1. What is the temperature of the rooms in which hot-water spinning is carried on?—It varies; at the factory where I was employed, it was about 80°.
2. Is there any reason why the windows should not be kept open?—Yes; because as soon as the windows are opened the yarn becomes injured, because the temperature of the room is lessened; it cools the water, and the hot water dissolves the gum, and assists the rollers in breaking the flax.
3. Is not the water kept continually hot by a fresh supply?—No, by steam.
4. What is the temperature of the water?—About 110°, sometimes about 120°.
5. Have the children to plunge their hands and arms into the water?—Yes; continually, almost.
6. Has not the heat of the rooms, and the water, and the steam, the effect of almost macerating their bodies?—Yes; and their clothes are, as it were, all steamed, partially wet.

7. Are not the children so wet as to be very much endangered in going out into the street after a few hours' labour, especially in winter time?—Yes, I should think they would be frozen; I never saw any frozen, on account of having stopped last to lock up, and I never made any inquiry.

8. Do you consider this new system of spinning much more detrimental to the health than the old system?—Yes, on account of the steam and the hot water.

9. As long as this system is continued, must not they suffer in the mill, both from the steam and by being wet?—Yes; but shortening the time will lessen the evil in a certain proportion.

10. What were the hours of labour at Mr. Stirk's factory?—Thirteen hours a day, actual labour.

11. Could you keep the children to their work for that length of time without chastisement?—No; it is impossible to get the quantity of work from them without.

Burns, Charles; age 13; examined 1st June, 1832.

1. What were your hours of working at Mr. Hives's, of Leeds?—From half past five in the morning till eight at night.

2. Had you any time allowed you for your breakfast there?—No.

3. Nor for your drinking?—No.

4. How much time had you allowed you for your dinner?—Forty minutes.

5. Had you sometimes to clean the machinery at your dinner hour?—Yes; and had to wipe all the machines.

6. How long did that take you generally?—About a quarter of an hour, and sometimes twenty minutes.

7. Pray how often were you allowed to make water?—Three times a day.

8. And were you allowed to make water at any time that you wanted?—No; only when a boy came to tell you it was your turn, and whether we wanted or not, that was the only time allowed us; if we did not go when he came round, we could not go at all.

9. Could you hold your water all that time?—No; we were forced to let it go.

10. Did you then spoil or wet your clothes constantly?—Every noon and every night.

11. Did you ever hear of that hurting any body?—Yes; there was a boy died.

12. Did he go home ill with attempting to suppress his urine?—Yes; and after he had been at home a bit, he died.

13. Were you beaten at your work?—If we looked off our work, or spoke to one another, we were beaten.

14. If you had not gone so fast as the machine, should you have been beaten?—If we let the machine stop half a minute we should have been beaten.

15. When you retired for the purposes of nature, how long would they allow you to stop?—If we were longer than five minutes we got beaten; and if we stopped longer they would not let us go out another time, when it was our turn.

16. Was the mill very dusty?—Yes.

17. What effect had it upon your health?—The dust got down our throats, and when we went home at night and went to bed, we spit up blood.

18. Is it not likewise, in what is called hot-water spinning, extremely hot in these mills?—Yes, very hot.

19. Is not the place full of steam?—Yes, and the machinery throws off water perpetually; so that we are wet to the skin by the hot water. And in winter time as soon as we get home our clothes are quite stiff with the frost.

20. What did you get for your breakfast and drinking?—I had tea, sometimes coffee, and butter, and bread; and my tea, for fear of wanting to make water, I used to throw out of the window.

21. In either of the mills you were in, Mr. Marshall's or Mr. Hives's, were you allowed to sit down?—No.

22. Were you not allowed to sit down during the whole of the day?—If we did we should get beaten; we had nothing to sit on unless we sat upon the frame by getting upon it.

23. Is it a common thing for you children to be beaten in this sort of way?—Yes; there used to be screaming among the boys and the girls every time of the day, and they made black and blue marks on the shoulders.

24. Where was this?—At Mr. Hives's.

25. Are accidents often occurring at these mills?—Yes.

26. State any that occurred within your own knowledge?—I had a sister who worked at Marshall's, and she got killed there by accident.

27. Were you able to attend the night-school?—No.

28. Were you able to attend the Sunday-school?—I was not able to go; I should have been too late; I had to rest on the Sunday morning.

Bywater, David; age 17; examined 13th April, 1832.

1. What age were you when you began to work?—I believe I was twelve, not turned.

2. Where did you work at first?—At Mr. Hobblethwaite's, at Leeds.

3. Where did you work next?—At Mr. Brown's.

4. How old were you then?—I believe I was near thirteen then.

5. At what age were you when you entered upon night work in the steaming department?—I was nearly fourteen.

6. Will you state to this committee the labour which you endured when you were put upon long hours, and the night work was added?—We started at one o'clock on Monday morning, and then we went on till five, and stopped for half an hour for refreshment; then we went on again till eight o'clock, at breakfast time; then we had half an hour; and then we went on till twelve o'clock, and had an hour for dinner; and then we went on again till five o'clock, and had half an hour for drinking; and then we started at half past five; and if we had a mind, we could stop at nine and have half an hour then; but we thought it would be best to have an hour and a half together, which we might have at half past eleven; so we went on from half past five, and stopped at half past eleven for refreshment for an hour and a half at midnight; then we went on from one till five again, and then we stopped for half an hour; then we went on again till breakfast time, when we had half an hour; and then we went on again till twelve o'clock, at dinner time, and then we had an hour: and then we stopped at five o'clock again on Tuesday afternoon for half an hour for drinking; then we went on till half past eleven, and then we gave over till five o'clock on Wednesday morning.

7. Did you go home then?—No; we slept in the mill.

8. How did you sleep in the mill?—We slept among the white pieces, baulks, as they call them.

9. Did you undress yourself when you slept?—Yes; we took all our clothes off, except our shirts, and got into the warmest part of the mill, and amongst the driest cloth we could.

10. When did you commence on Wednesday morning?—At five o'clock, and then we worked till eight o'clock, and then we had half an hour again; then we went on to dinner time, and had an hour at twelve o'clock; and then at one o'clock we went on again till five, and then we had half an hour; and then we went on till half past eleven again; and then we started again at one o'clock on Thursday morning, and went on till five o'clock; than we had half an hour, and then we went on till eight o'clock; we had half an hour for breakfast, and then we went on till twelve, and got our dinner; then at one o'clock we went on till five o'clock, and then we had half an hour; then we went on till half-past eleven, and then we gave over till five o'clock on Friday morning; then we started again at five o'clock, and went on till eight; then we went on till dinner-time, at twelve o'clock; then at one o'clock we went on till five; then we had half an hour, and then we went on till half-past eleven; then we started again at one o'clock on Saturday morning, and went on till five; then we had half an hour, and went on till eight; then we had half

an hour for breakfast, and went on till twelve; then we had an hour for dinner, and then went on from one o'clock till seven, or eight, or nine o'clock; we had no drinking-time on Saturday afternoon; we could seldom get to give over on the Saturday afternoon as the other people did.

11. Do you mean that you, as a steamer, could not give over as the rest of the people of the mill did?—Yes.

12. Did you take your meals standing, or was there a table set out for you?—We put our baskets on the boxes.

13. Did you attend a Sunday-school under these circumstances?—No.

14. How did you spend your Sundays?—I used to sleep till seven o'clock on Sunday morning, and then we got up and went a walking.

15. Did you go to any place of worship?—Yes; I always used to go to a place of worship.

16. Did you keep awake?—Yes; when I was working those long times I used to go twice or three times to the church on Sundays.

17. Were you perfect in your limbs when you undertook that long and excessive labour?—Yes, I was.

18. Shew what effect it had upon your limbs?—It made me very crooked.

[*Here the witness shewed his knees and legs.*]

19. Are your thighs also bent?—Yes; the bone is quite bent.

20. How long was it after you had to endure this long labour before your limbs were in that way?—I was very soon told of it, before I found it out myself.

21. What did they tell you?—They told me I was getting very crooked in my knees; my mother found it out first. She said I should kill myself with working this long time.

22. If you had refused to work those long hours, and have wished to have worked a moderate length of time only, should you have been retained in your situation?—I should have had to go home; I should have been turned off directly.

23. Have you received an intimation as to what will be the consequences of your having given evidence?—I was sent for to the White Swan, in Leeds, and when I got there they questioned me about what time I worked, and I told them, and they told me that I was to stop there all night; and the next morning the overlooker sent my brother down; and when he came, he said that I was to go back, or else both he and I were to be turned away; and when he went back the overlooker told him, that if I came up to London here I should never have any employment any more, nor my brother neither; but when he came again at night the overlooker cooled over it, and he told him to be at work in good time in the

morning, and he has told him since that I should not be employed any more. My brother said he could not help it; that it was not wrong in him; but I expect the first time he does a job which does not please that he will turn him away directly; because, if they work in a family, and one does wrong, they must all go.

Carpenter, James, age 41; examined 4th June, 1832.

1. Where do you live?—At Leeds, at Benk.
2. Have you worked in mills most of your life?—Yes; I began working when I was about seven years of age.
3. What were the hours of your labour when you were busy?—In the commencement of my working in factories we worked from six to seven; that was at the commencement, but afterwards we increased.
4. To what length of time was your labour increased when you became busy?—We worked from sometimes five, and sometimes half-past five, to eight at night, or half-past eight.
5. Did you ever work later than half-past eight?—Sometimes till nine.
6. In what branch of the business?—In the card-room, as a rover.
7. What time had the children allowed for refreshment?—Forty minutes at dinner.
8. Was that all?—Yes; that was all.
9. Had you to stand the remainder of the time during those long hours?—I had to stand altogether; I had no sitting; it would have been a great easement to me had I been allowed to sit.
10. State the effect which the nature of the employment had upon you?—It caused great weakness and loss of appetite; I felt gradually decreased strength of body.
11. What effect had it upon your limbs?—By becoming weak, and having to stand such a length of time, my legs were not able to bear the weight of my body, and they became crooked, as they are at present.
12. At what time was it your legs began to get deformed, as they are at present?—I was just turned twelve years of age.
13. Did this deformity come upon you accompanied with great pain?—Yes; it was great pain indeed, and had been attended with pain ever since. It was in my ankles and my knees that I felt the most pain; I did not feel much elsewhere.
14. Was your work frequently interrupted by your becoming so poorly and so deformed?—Yes; I was frequently off my work for a week, or sometimes two weeks; and I have been off a month together, and sometimes a longer time than that.

15. Do the masters, when the children become ill and diseased by labouring at the mills, continue to pay them their wages?—No; when they leave off work they leave off wages.

16. Do they usually employ a medical man to recover them?—No; they have to find their own doctor, and their own medicine, when out of work.

17. So that the master then completely loses sight of his hands?—Yes; when they are off work, they are, he considers, entirely out of his care.

18. Therefore the master, however much disposed he may be to make a fair return of the deaths of the hands, would not be able to do so?—No; their calculation would be a very imperfect one.

19. Were not the children excessively sleepy towards the termination of the day?—Yes; very much so.

20. What means were taken to keep the children to their work?—They had various means; sometimes they would tap them over the head, or nip the nose, or give them a pinch of snuff, or throw water in their faces, or pull them off where they were, and jog them about, to keep them waking.

Kenworthy, Daniel; age 38; examined 15th May, 1832.

1. What is your present employment?—Woollen-weaving.

2. Are you the father of William Kenworthy?—Yes.

3. Was he a strong and healthy boy in his early youth?—He never had any sickness in his life till that weakness.

4. How long is it since he began to be deformed in his limbs and knees?—It is not past eighteen months, but I cannot speak exactly to the time; it is not more than that since he began to be so crooked.

5. Originally he was quite a straight and strong boy?—Yes; he was straight enough for any boy.

6. What do you consider was the cause of his deformity?—I think being over-worked, but what it is I cannot say.

7. What has been your employment?—When I began to work I was in a cotton factory.

8. What age were you?—I was turned six years of age.

9. What were the hours of labour at that period?—We began to work at six and worked till eight.

10. With what intervals?—We had one hour in the afternoon.

11. What was the general treatment at that period?—I never got any bad treatment from my employers.

12. Do you conceive that the usage of persons in mills has improved or got worse since you have had experience in them?—By all accounts it has

got worse; but I have never seen any cruel treatment for my own part; I have heard tell of it.

13. What is your opinion of the effect of the long hours of labour early in life, commencing as you did as a cotton-spinner, and continuing in the different branches of business for so many years; what has been the effect on your own health?—I think it has done me a great deal of harm; I am very ill to do for many years.

14. What is the nature of your complaint?—I am troubled with an asthma.

15. You consider that a complaint people are frequently troubled with in cotton mills?—It is a very smothering, unhealthy job altogether.

16. Do you not conceive that your memory and your mental faculties have suffered by this constant confinement and labour?—I have a very poor memory to what I used to have; I am very much troubled with a pain in my head and in my back-bone.

17. You find yourself totally out of sorts?—I am scarcely able to do anything in the winter-time in consequence of the asthma.

Kenworthy, William; age 14; examined 15th May, 1832.

1. What is your business?—A scribbler-feeder.

2. When did you first begin to work in a factory?—When I was under seven and a half years old.

3. In whose factory did you then work?—Mr. Starkie's.

4. What were your hours of work?—I cannot say exactly what the hours of work were then; we began at six in the morning; I cannot tell at what time we left at night; I was too young then to recollect.

5. Where did you work next?—My father and mother then went to Leeds; I got jobs at different places, till I worked at Messrs. Riples and Ogle's.

6. State their business?—Woollen manufacturers.

7. How many hours did you work there?—We began at six and worked till seven; two hours for meals.

8. At what sort of work?—I was [a] piecener.

9. How long did you work when you were busy?—When we were right busy, making seven days a week, we began at five and worked till eight; two hours out of it.

10. What were your wages at that time?—Three shillings and sixpence a week.

11. With over hours?—No; 4s. 1d. with over hours; we were paid for our over hours.

12. Where did you work when you left Messrs. Riples and Ogle's?—I went to Messrs. Starkie's, at Huddersfield.

13. Were you still a piecener?—Yes, till lately.
14. What were your hours at Mr. Starkie's mill?—We began at six and worked till half past eight.
15. What time had you for meals?—One hour and a half.
16. What effect had that long labour on your health and limbs?—It had no effect on me then.
17. How, then, did you become ill?—It was from the hard work I had.
18. Did you apply to any doctor?—The overlooker said I was to tell my father and mother that I had something the matter with me, I grew very crooked, and had better go to some doctor; so my father and mother took me to Dr. Day, but he did not seem to do me any good; and then they said I had better go to the Dispensary at Huddersfield, under Dr. Walker, and he did me a vast deal of good; he right cured me.
19. What did the doctor say was the matter with you?—He said I had an affection of the spine.
20. Will you just shew your legs?

[*Here the witness shewed his legs and knees, which appeared excessively deformed.*]

21. How long have your legs and knees been in that state?—I was as straight as ever I could be two years since.
22. What did the doctor state to be the cause of your becoming deformed?—He said it was hard work; it was being overworked.

CLASS III

Sir Charles Bell, K.G.H., F.R.S., called in, and examined, 7th August, 1832.

1. What is your profession?—A surgeon.
2. Are you an officer in any of the great medical establishments?—I am surgeon of Middlesex Hospital.
3. You have been in the habit of teaching your profession to medical students in the metropolis for a series of years?—I am a retired teacher of anatomy, and professor to the Royal College of Surgeons.
4. It is a universally received maxim in your profession, that exercise, confined within moderate limits, and with due intervals rest, is ordinarily necessary for the preservation of health?—Undoubtedly; that is an acknowledged principle in our profession.
5. Is it not also held by the profession as an undoubted principle, that undue labour, so as to produce great fatigue and weariness from its character or

long continuance, and without due intervals for rest and refreshment, ordinarily considered, is prejudicial to life?—That corresponds with the suggestions of common sense.

6. Do you think that the customary day's labour in this and other countries, alluding mainly to the usual avocations of industrious life in agricultural and the mechanical arts, extending about twelve hours, including the usual intervals for meals, is, ordinarily speaking, as much as the human constitution can bear, with due attention to health?—Indeed I think so, sustained for any considerable time.

7. Assuming that the labour in the mills and factories of this country greatly exceeds that term, and extends sometimes to fourteen hours and upwards, and is endured in a confined situation, and often in an impure atmosphere, heated to a high temperature, can there be any doubt whatever that, generally speaking, labour of that description must be prejudicial to the human health?—I have no doubt of that; you present a very painful picture; and such a system must be attended with unhappy consequences.

8. Do you not conceive that undue labour, so long continued as to afford but short intervals of rest, whether for recreation or sleep, is yet more prejudicial to children and young persons than it would be to adults in the prime and vigour of life?—Certainly; all circumstances unfavourable to health will have a great influence on the constitution before it is settled, and before the strength is matured.

9. The labour in question to be endured for the length of time described often stretches into the night, more especially in the winter time; can you give any opinion whether labour is more insalubrious when undergone in the night-time than in the day?—That answer requires some detail; it implies want of comfort; it implies want of exercise, since they must sleep during the day; it more effectually, therefore, implies deficient exercise in the open air; in short, close apartments and confinement.

10. Perhaps the working by artificial lights also might have a pernicious effect, is as much as the vital principle of the air would be, in some measure consumed?—Additional light in an apartment has nearly the same effect as if so many more people were admitted into the apartment, exhausting the vital air.

11. Have you had any personal experience regarding the work and labor of children in mills and factories?—No.

12. Appealing, then, to the general principles of your profession, to the analogies which your extensive practice has afforded, and the studies you have pursued, have you any hesitation in tracing many injurious consequence to that system of labour, consequences which have been described to the committee at great length, as affecting the health and the limits, and shortening the life, of those exposed to it?—I should answer in the affirmative, upon the acknowledged principles that such a state as

that described would be very injurious to the constitution, and engender a variety of diseases; the great disease, emphatically using that word, is scrofula: wherever there is a want of exercise, deficient ventilation, depression of mind, and want of interest in the occupation, I should say, especially in young persons, scrofula, in its hundred forms, would be the consequence.

13. Does not that latent disorder affect the osseous part of the system as well as the glandular?—That is one of its effects, undoubtedly.

14. It has been alleged before this committee, that distressing cases of deformity are produced in the mills and factories, and that they take their rise in young persons sometimes as late as perhaps the 13th, 14th, 15th, or 16th year of their age; is not that an unusual occurrence, when unconnected with over exertion in improper attitudes?—I shall divide the distortions into two kinds; distortion coming indirectly from constitutional defect or disease, and distortion arising from continued exertion of one kind, to which some artisans are liable; so that I should imagine the common distortion, the rickets, would make its appearance early in life; and that at a later period, deformities arise from the mechanical effort being continued in one mode, and without that variety which nature dictates.

15. Do you think that the female is as competent to long and continued exertions, and particularly in a standing position, as the male sex—I rather think, where the work is light, that she is.

16. Do you think that there is any particular risk, at the age of puberty from that description of labour long continued?—The period of puberty is a period of delicacy, and requires more particular attention.

17. Do you think that a child under nine years of age ought to be kept to the constant labour of a mill or factory?—It may be an alternative; on the general question, certainly not; but it may be a question of degree of suffering; the condition of the parents must be considered; the child may be starving.

18. But as a general question, you would think that long-continued labour under that age would be unfavorable to the health and future welfare of the child—Very unfavourable.

19. From that period to the time of life at which it is generally supposed the osseous system may be about completed, is not ten hours' labour a day, to which must be added the time necessary for the taking of meals and refreshment, making therefore twelve hours a day, as much as can be endured, generally speaking, with impunity by those so occupied?—I should say yes; and more than that is a painful idea.

20. Are you of opinion, with the late Dr. Baillie, and many other eminent medical men who have appeared before preceding select communities of both Houses on this particular subject, that, under ordinary circum-

stances, and in a great plurality of cases, ten hours' labour a day is as much as can be safely imposed on human beings of either sex, and at any age?—I consider that if a person is interested in his subject, and the mind is carried on, he may labour as many hours, and often many more, with impunity; but where he is mechanically employed, without interest in his work, I think that is fully enough.

21. It is almost superfluous to ask whether the mind is capable of imbibing instruction when it is suffering under considerable degree of fatigue?—Certainly, it is not; but to the contrary. Thus, a soldier cannot be kept too long on the parade without losing what he has gained in the exercise.

22. Allowing to one object which the framers of this bill have in view, namely, affording education to the lower orders of society by means of evening schools, it would be necessary to limit the hours of labour so as to render such instruction available to the lower classes of the poor?—If the child were to be instructed by its parent that would be well; but as the question supposes a public school and a crowded room, the proposal would tend to aggravate its hard condition: that child is to be carried from a crowded manufactory into a hot and crowded school-room: it is adding to the hours of confinement.

23. You would judge, then, that to devote the only remaining day of the week, when the rest have been employed in factories, to the purposes of tuition, the question alluding to Sunday-schools, while the body continues to suffer under a considerable degree of fatigue, would add to the physical sufferings of those exposed to that system?—All the circumstances which we have considered disadvantageous to the constitution being incurred during the week-days, and repeated in this new form on the Sunday, of course they become more subject to the disorders proceeding from their mode of life.

24. Without alluding at all to the view of the question which a political economist might take, can there be a doubt on the mind of any medical man of knowledge and experience, that a remission of the hours of labour would be highly beneficial, in point of health and welfare, to the lower classes of society?—Certainly it would be highly advantageous to the health, and I should say, consequently, to the powers of the mind, to the improvement both of the mind and the body.

25. You have considered the subject of factory employment?—Only in one point of view; that in passing through England, and seeing the different hospitals in the manufacturing towns, I was very much struck with the nature and number of the accidents received.

26. You mean from machinery?—Yes.

27. It is stated, that those accidents mainly occur at the termination of the day's labour, and that they accumulate towards the conclusion of every

week; would not that of itself be a strong indication that those engaged in this employment were generally over-worked?—It is the most pointed proof that can be given, I think.

28. Have you not been of opinion that some legislative means ought to be taken to decrease the number of those accidents, by inducing or obliging those masters who are careless in the fencing of those machines to adopt proper methods for protecting the persons of those so employed?—I did entertain such a notion some years ago: I mentioned it to the late Mr. Francis Horner, and he applied to some of his parliamentary friends; the answer that I then got was, it was not a practicable thing; but it is strongly in my mind that something ought to be done.

Sir William Blizard, F.R.S., called in, and examined, 2nd Aug. 1832.

1. What is your profession?—I am a surgeon; surgery is my profession.
2. Are you an officer in any of the great medical charities of this metropolis?—I am; and have been for upwards of fifty years surgeon to the London Hospital.
3. Have you been a medical or surgical lecturer?—Yes; for upwards of twenty years a lecturer on surgery, anatomy and physiology, in the London Hospital and the Royal College of Surgeons.
4. Your mind has consequently been directed, generally, to the causes and cure of those diseases to which the labouring classes of society are liable?—Undoubtedly.
5. May not the committee ask you, therefore, whether with moderate labour or employment proper intermissions for meals, refreshment and sleep are not ordinarily necessary to the preservation of health?—Undoubtedly they are.
6. Are not those advantages still less to be dispensed with as regards children and young persons of either sex?—Unquestionably.
7. Do you not also hold it to be a maxim of the profession, that excessive labour, or labour so long protracted as to inflict great and continued fatigue of either body or mind, and endured without such due intermissions for meals, for sleep; and for refreshment, is inconsistent, generally speaking, with the preservation of health?—Certainly.
8. Would not such an excessive degree of labour, continued as described, without due intermissions, and inducing so much fatigue, be still more injurious to children and growing persons?—Undoubtedly.
9. In reference to adults, do you not think that the ordinary day's labour, whether in agricultural or handicraft pursuits, namely, twelve hours, with proper intervals of rest, is, generally speaking, as much as can be endured with impunity to the frame?—That is consonant with general observation.

10. Alluding to the labouring classes of society, are not such moderate intervals from their labour as are sufficient for taking their meals necessary to the preservation of their health, particularly with reference to the digestive organs?—Undoubtedly; with reference to those organs most important to health and life.

11. Supposing, then, that the labour of persons in mills and factories greatly exceeds the term in question, and extends to thirteen, fourteen, or fifteen hours one of the twenty-four, and sometimes to seventeen; or eighteen hours, or more, should you have any doubt in saying that such a degree of labour must, in a great plurality of cases, be injurious to the health and the constitution?—Horribly so.

12. You of course mean to apply that expression to the extremity of the labour described to you?—Yes; and there is a question before, the spirit of which is involved in this; that which respects the relaxation and time required for taking food and exercise, and having relation to the digestive organs, and so on: all that is included then when you go to the maximum. I meant to reply generally, so that the application of my answer might be general, as I express it, and be taken in degree and ratio, as it would apply to the minimum and maximum respectively.

13. But you would think the average of such hours of labour would be an extravagant imposition upon the human frame?—Dreadful.

14. Then, when still further extended, so as to be continued for thirty or more successive hours, with inadequate intermissions, you would conceive it must lead to the most pernicious, and often fatal consequences?—I do.

15. You would perhaps scarcely believe, as your practice has been in this metropolis principally in the upper ranks of society, that children and young persons could be brought to endure that labour without the effects being immediately perceptible?—I should think it hardly possible.

16. Is it your opinion that labour pursued during the night is generally less congenial to the constitution than that undergone in the day-time?—It is contrary to the general course of nature; contrary to what nature seems to warrant.

17. Is not the employment in question, though it may, if contemplated for a moment, seem light or easy, yet when continued for such a length of time as to induce much fatigue of both mind and body, as it is asserted it does, likely to be more prejudicial than even more strenuous labour pursued for a moderate length of time, and with due intervals for rest and refreshment?—I am clearly of that opinion; however light it may be, yet extended as it has been described, the consequence must be, in my opinion, as stated.

18. May the committee ask you, appealing now to the principles of your pro-

fession, whether it does not require some considerable degree of muscular exertion to maintain the erect position for a great length of time together?—No doubt of it; and it is a position which, if long maintained, is unfavourable in many respects, and leading to consequences very serious.

19. Then this labour having to be endured for that length of time in that position must, of course, render it more distressing to the feelings and exhausting to the animal frame?—I have no doubt of it at all.

20. If that description and degree of labour is to be undergone in a polluted atmosphere, rendered impure by the admixture of dust and flues constantly passing off from the material wrought, would that, in your opinion, constitute an additional hardship as it regards the hands so employed?—Oh, no doubt of it; I might enlarge upon this very much, but it is hardly necessary here or elsewhere: as to a polluted atmosphere, we know the deterioration that the health suffers from it. One should hardly imagine that what is separated from the material (though it will render the atmosphere unfit for respiratory purposes) could be called a thing that pollutes the air; but, when you come to the heated state of the atmosphere, the effect upon that atmosphere is very great from so much breathing; for, with regard to the office of the lungs, there is a certain quantity of pure air required; and if not supplied, there is something vitiated produced in the atmosphere that will pollute the whole frame. Now we know very well that heat does this; and that respiration does it by means of what is exhaled from the surface of the body and from the lungs: the surface of the body and the action of the lungs are continually affecting the atmosphere that is most suited to the existence of living persons, by exhalation and by absorption; and if there be a state of air not admitting of that which is exhaled from the lungs and the skin passing off, it will not admit of that which is of a vital character being absorbed; and the circumstances named are such as are most unfavourable and most pernicious to human existence, and to the health of any human being. With regard to that which is separated from the raw material, it is a foreign body, and, by being inhaled into the system, has a very material effect upon the small vessels of the lungs; it mingles with the mucus from the lining membrane of the lungs; and the air-pipes, which become smaller and smaller, until they terminate in what we call vesicles, have their functions impaired; for here you have those particles obstructing those tubuli, and rendering difficult the admission of that portion which should be received from the circumambient air.

21. Rendering the necessity for abridging the hours of labour in such an atmosphere still more imperative?—Most undoubtedly.

22. In alluding to the temperature in which this work is usually performed, should you not think it more healthy to pursue labour in an atmosphere

at a given temperature, though high, but which was rendered so by natural causes, than one artificially heated and defiled by the adscititious matter alluded to?—No doubt; for though, on the one hand, there is what might be abstractedly considered an evil; on the other, there is that which counteracts it, which is not the case where the atmosphere is heated by artificial means.

23. Then you would conceive, that children and young persons in this country, not being free agents, who are doomed to labour in an atmosphere like that, are entitled, upon every principle of justice and humanity, to protection equally to slaves in a tropical climate?—I have no doubt of it, both physically and morally.

24. To allude more particularly to children: taking into view all that has been described to you, that the length of their labour corresponds with that of all the rest of the hands in the factory, that it has to be pursued, therefore, for the same number of hours, sometimes in a heated temperature, and subject to other circumstances, to which allusion has been made; do you not think that, in regard of such children and young persons, a regulation of labour, so as to bring its duration within something like moderate limits, is highly necessary, and is imperative upon the legislature?—No doubt of it; it is a corollary of what you have stated.

25. It has been said by eminent men of your profession, who have had constant practical experience of the effects of the system as described to you, that to reconcile it to health would be to reverse all the principles of the profession; you have already stated your views upon this subject, and, from philosophical and general principles, you coincide with their declaration, deduced from actual experience?—Without a doubt.

26. During the course of this inquiry, and many preceding ones, it has been found that various afflicting diseases are attributed to this system of factory labour, as it has been described to you: may the committee ask you whether, reasoning upon the principles of your profession and the causation of disease, you do not think that that system would not only be very liable to cause certain disease, but also to aggravate them, where there should be a constitutional tendency to them?—I have no doubt of it; long standing in one position has a very considerable influence on the circulating system; the veins become, as we denominate it, varicose or distended, and, of course, the return of the blood to the right side of the heart is not regular, nor in the right quantity or quality; and if it is either deficient in the one or the other, it is robbed of a certain degree of its stimulus, which is necessary, that all the other organs may be in a proper state. The heart is nothing more than a propelling organ, and the state of the circulation must become much affected by long standing.

27. That may be the cause which produces the languor of which these per-

sons complain?—There is no doubt of it, and a thousand other distressing signs and consequences of debility.

28. Would ulcerated legs in many instances ensue?—Yes, and edema, or a general swelling of the ankles.

29. Should you think that struma would be likely to be aggravated by this sort of labour?—Yes, and perhaps a strumous habit primarily induced by it. It is a disease of the lymphatic system, or lymphatic glands, and the various causes that have been expressed disturb the whole system and functions of the absorbents and their glands.

30. In alluding to the impure state of the atmosphere and to the irritating substances mixed up with it, should you conceive that pulmonary and bronchial affections might result from that sort of employment too long continued?—No doubt such a question involves in it the answer; when the structure of the lungs is attended to, how can it be otherwise? Pulmonary affections of every description may be induced by this disorganization of the pulmonary system.

31. In allusion to the tender age at which this labour is often, and, in fact, mainly to be undergone, should you conceive that pernicious effects also might be produced by it upon the osseous system?—No doubt; the progress of the perfecting of the bony parts is gradual. In some parts there is no bone. At the extremities you have, not a union of the bones, but epiphyses; these are a long while before they are united to the bones themselves, and in all those the parts are imperfect; whence it is that you have distortions of the spine. The ribs and the cartilages are not formed with that relative perfection they ought to have for respirable purposes; hence you have such a train of complaints, and even distortion and disease of the spine itself.

32. Many distortions in the lower extremities have been exhibited to this committee, where the frame has been perfectly straight and well formed, even to so late a period as twelve, fourteen, or sixteen years of age; you would not confound those cases with ordinary affections of the limbs, or what are called rickets?—No rickets have associated with them an imperfect formation of the bones, and an enlargement of the extremities of those bones; and, as the bones are not perfectly formed, they have ductility, so that they yield.

33. Is not rickets a disorder that is usually apparent in a much earlier period of life than those I have mentioned?—I can hardly say that; I am not quite certain upon that point; but what are called rickets are often ascribable to some or most of the causes you have stated.

34. So that the employment itself might induce that deformity of the skeleton that is sometimes called rickets, or at all events confounded with it?—Yes, unquestionably; I meant to convey that idea.

35. It has been stated, that the growth of children so circumstanced, compared with other children otherwise employed, is considerably stunted; should you be prepared for that effect also, as resulting from the system developed to you?—I have no doubt of it, both as to the extent of osseous growth and as to the condition of the bones, so far as they are formed.

36. Then it follows, that the muscular power and weight of the children so compared would exhibit similar variations, which also is found to be the case?—Undoubtedly there would not be an equal specific gravity in any of the parts; the bones would be lighter.

37. A paper has been ordered by this committee, and delivered to it, by which it appears that wherever this system prevails, it is accompanied by an extraordinary degree of mortality, especially in the earlier periods of life; taking the view you have done of the pernicious effects of labour so long pursued, and under the circumstances explained, you would be prepared for that result, namely, a greatly increased degree of mortality?— I do not know the fact; but, a priori, I should have no doubt of it, not the shadow of one.

35. It is a known fact, and often referred to as a sort of apology for this system, that it affords employment to females principally; would you conceive, arguing upon physiological principles, that the female is as well calculated to endure long and active labour as the male?—Certainly not; and universal observation would confirm that opinion.

36. Is it not necessary, with regard to any protection that the legislature may think it necessary to give to females so employed, that is should be extended at least to the period of puberty?—No doubt.

37. Is not the female constitution particularly liable to present and permanent injury, by undue exertion or improper treatment at that particular period—No doubt of it; it is admitted that at an early period the bones are not permanently formed, and cannot resist pressure to the same degree as at mature age, and that is the state of young females; they are liable, particularly from the pressure of the thigh bones upon the lateral parts, to have the pelvis pressed inwards, which creates what is called distortion; and although distortion does not prevent procreation, yet it most likely will produce deadly consequences, either to the mother or the child, when the period of parturition arrives; it is a mechanical effect, produced by lateral pressure.

38. Do not you think that the labour as described to you, pursued often in a heated temperature, under the circumstances of sexual excitement, would be likely to anticipate the period of puberty?—It might, and I believe would; whatever affects one particular important organ tends to disorganize the whole frame; there is a dependence of one organ upon

another, and particularly of certain organs, which have great influence with reference to all the other organs; these are the lungs and the liver. There is nothing in the world that is more readily affected than the circulation of the viscera by the causes mentioned, for its trunks go to form the *vena portae* of the liver; this has reference to every organ in the cavity of the abdomen: then the other organ is the lungs. Now with regard to the liver, it is very important; it separates the bile; and if that is not properly separated, the blood retains it, and returns to the right side of the heart in a very imperfect state; and from thence it goes to the lungs. The heart is to be regarded as being no more than a projecting organ. The lungs and the liver and the surface of the body are the great organs; and every thing that has been stated goes to alter and deteriorate the healthy functions of those parts; it is not that organ or this organ; but there is that harmonizing movement in all the parts of the body, that when one of those organs is affected every organ is affected.

39. Should not you conceive that the languor and debility that this kind of labour is known to produce has a direct tendency to produce that tippling which is said to prevail so lamentably in these manufacturing districts?—I have not a doubt of it, for there is nothing in the world more inviting from their influence than spirits; spirits produce that which is most delusive; they produce a delightful sensation in the stomach; they tend to sooth and comfort, and to produce a favourable effect to the sense upon the whole system, but, ah! deadly is the consequence.

40. You think that degree of languor that seems to require a stimulus is likely to lead to tippling and all its injurious consequences?—Yes, beyond anything in this world; and when that habit is established, break it if you can.

41. Should you not conceive that the body is in a very unfit state to renew its daily exertions when it is not habitually refreshed by a necessary degree of repose?—Yes, no doubt; whoever has dwelt upon the intellectual functions must admit that at once.

42. And must not that labour which can alone be stimulated by the lash and cruel inflictions at the latter part of the day be peculiarly pernicious?— I have not a doubt of it.

43. Do you think that a child under nine years of age ought, under any circumstances, to be sent to the labour of the mill?—Certainly not.

44. Do you think that the limitation of the hours of labour to ten, which, including the meal-times, will make the day's work twelve hours, is an unreasonable limitation, or more than ought to be demanded in behalf of young persons between the ages of nine and eighteen?—Not more than that ought to be demanded; and it is consonant with general experience, like that of large seminaries and schools, where reason is the guide of humanity.

45. You are perhaps of opinion, with the late Dr. Baillie and other eminent medical men, that the usual duration of a day's labour, namely, ten hours of actual work, which, with the time necessary for refreshment, extends to about twelve hours, is quite enough, and as much as can be ordinarily endured at any age with impunity?—I heartily concur in that opinion with my late honoured friend; it is mine also.

46. One pernicious consequence of this promiscuous and long-continued labour is stated to be gross immorality; in answer to that allegation, it is sometimes said that the number of illegitimate children is not greater among those employed under the system described; do you think that that would of itself be a proof of superior morality in that case than amongst an equal number of grown-up females in other pursuits?—No, certainly not; let any man reason upon that point, and he will decide otherwise.

47. You think that early and promiscuous profligacy is rarely accompanied by fertility?—Certainly.

48. Should you not consider it additionally injurious if, after those long days of labour, another hour or two were to be imposed upon the children by sending them to night-schools?—I should think it would have very little beneficial effect, but be demonstratively unfavourable.

49. Then supposing that the degree of labour leaves such fatigue and exhaustion as are now felt throughout the Sunday, often inducing the children to refrain from going to Sunday-schools, and rendering their attendance there very unprofitable, does not the institution of the Sunday-school increase the physical suffering of those children without those advantages being produced which would otherwise result?—Certainly; it increases their sufferings, and can produce very little benefit.

50. Can the youthful mind profit by instruction when the body is under a sense of great languor and fatigue?—No; every person's experience must have taught him that in some degree.

51. Then it is clear that it would be necessary to abate the extreme labour of those children and young persons if we mean to give them a decent and proper education?—Yes, no doubt. The mind, it is to be recollected, has reference to the brain and every nerve of the body, and every organ of the body has reference also to the brain; so that, morally speaking, and physically speaking, if you have reference to the brain and the functions of the brain, they cannot be properly performed under the influences named. The same thing may be said as to the nerves of the body, and the muscles, and every organ of sense; whence it is that every organ of sense and sight may become imperfect. There are two distinctive offices with relation to the brain; what has relation to the intellectual functions, and what has reference to the various organs of the body as to sensibility.

52. So that the employment that requires minute and incessant attention, and

which makes constant demands upon the brain, would be most fatiguing?—Yes, certainly.

53. Would not, upon the whole, such a remission in the hours of the labour and toil of young persons as should afford them better opportunities of becoming educated, whether at home, or in evening or other schools, at the same time securing their health more effectually, be a great public as well as individual advantage in your opinion?—Very great; it would be to the personal comfort of the individual, and to the benefit of society at large.

FRIEDRICH ENGELS

SINGLE BRANCHES OF INDUSTRY

They published last year elaborate tables to prove that machinery does not supersede adult male operatives. According to these tables, rather more than half of all the factory-workers employed, viz. 52 per cent, were females and 48 per cent males, and of these operatives more than half were over 18 years old. So far, so good. But the manufacturers are very careful not to tell us, how many of the adults were men and how many women. And this is just the point. Besides this, they have evidently counted the mechanics, engineers, carpenters, all the men employed in any way in the factories, perhaps even the clerks, and still they have not the courage to tell the whole truth. These publications teem generally with falsehoods, perversions, crooked statements, with calculations of averages, that prove a great deal for the uninitiated reader and nothing for the initiated, and with suppressions of facts bearing on the most important points; and they prove only the selfish blindness and want of uprightness of the manufacturers concerned. Let us take some of the statements of a speech with which Lord Ashley introduced the Ten Hours Bill,[1] on 15 March 1844, into the House of Commons. Here he gives some data as to the relations of sex and age of the operatives, not yet refuted by the manufacturers, whose statements, as

From *The Condition of the Working Class in England* (1845). David McLellan, ed. Oxford: Oxford Univ. Press, 1993.

1. The Ten Hours Bill of 1947 covered textile factories only and stipulated that women and "young persons" were to work no more than ten hours per day. No child under eight could be employed at all. [Ed.]

quoted above, cover moreover only a part of the manufacturing industry of England. Of 419,560 factory operatives of the British Empire in 1839, 192,887, or nearly half, were under 18 years of age, and 242,296 of the female sex, of whom 112,192 were less than 18 years old. There remain, therefore, 80,695 male operatives under 18 years, and 96,569 adult male operatives, *or not one full quarter* of the whole number. In the cotton factories, 56.5 per cent; in the woollen mills, 69.5 per cent; in the silk mills, 70.5 per cent; in the flax-spinning mills, 70.5 per cent of all operatives are of the female sex. These numbers suffice to prove the crowding out of adult males. But you have only to go into the nearest mill to see the fact confirmed. Hence follows of necessity that inversion of the existing social order which, being forced upon them, has the most ruinous consequences for the workers. The employment of women at once breaks up the family; for when the wife spends twelve or thirteen hours every day in the mill, and the husband works the same length of time there or elsewhere, what becomes of the children? They grow up like wild weeds; they are put out to nurse for a shilling or eighteenpence a week, and how they are treated may be imagined. Hence the accidents to which little children fall victims multiply in the factory districts to a terrible extent. The lists of the Coroner of Manchester[2] showed for nine months: 69 deaths from burning, 56 from drowning, 23 from falling, 77 from other causes, or a total of 225[3] deaths from accidents, while in non-manufacturing Liverpool during twelve months there were but 146 fatal accidents. The mining accidents are excluded in both cases; and since the Coroner of Manchester has no authority in Salford, the population of both places mentioned in the comparison is about the same. The *Manchester Guardian* reports one or more deaths by burning in almost every number. That the general mortality among young children must be increased by the employment of the mothers is self-evident, and is placed beyond all doubt by notorious facts. Women often return to the mill three or four days after confinement, leaving the baby, of course; in the dinner-hour they must hurry home to feed the child and eat something, and what sort of suckling that can be is also evident. Lord Ashley repeats the testimony of several workwomen:

> M. H., twenty years old, has two children, the youngest a baby, that is tended by the other, a little older. The mother goes to the mill shortly after five o'clock in the morning, and comes home at eight at night; all day the milk pours from her breasts, so that her clothing drips with it. H. W. has three children, goes away Monday morning at five o'clock, and comes back Saturday evening; has so much to do for the children then that she cannot get to bed before three o'clock in the morning; often wet through to the skin, and obliged to work in that state. She

---

2. Report of Factories' Inquiry Commission. Testimony of Dr Hawkins, p. 3.
3. In 1842, among the accidents brought to the Infirmary in Manchester, 189 were from burning.

said: "My breasts have given me the most frightful pain, and I have been dripping wet with milk."

The use of narcotics to keep the children still is fostered by this infamous system, and has reached a great extent in the factory districts. Dr Johns, Registrar-in-Chief for Manchester, is of opinion that this custom is the chief source of the many deaths from convulsions. The employment of the wife dissolves the family utterly and of necessity, and this dissolution, in our present society, which is based upon the family, brings the most demoralizing consequences for parents as well as children. A mother who has no time to trouble herself about her child, to perform the most ordinary loving services for it during its first year, who scarcely indeed sees it, can be no real mother to the child, must inevitably grow indifferent to it, treat it unlovingly like a stranger. The children who grow up under such conditions are utterly ruined for later family life, can never feel at home in the family which they themselves found, because they have always been accustomed to isolation, and they contribute therefore to the already general undermining of the family in the working class. A similar dissolution of the family is brought about by the employment of the children. When they get on far enough to earn more than they cost their parents from week to week, they begin to pay the parents a fixed sum for board and lodging, and keep the rest for themselves. This often happens from the fourteenth or fifteenth year.[4] In a word, the children emancipate themselves, and regard the paternal dwelling as a lodging-house, which they often exchange for another, as suits them.

In many cases the family is not wholly dissolved by the employment of the wife, but turned upside down. The wife supports the family, the husband sits at home, tends the children, sweeps the room and cooks. This case happens very frequently; in Manchester alone, many hundred such men could be cited, condemned to domestic occupations. It is easy to imagine the wrath aroused among the working men by this reversal of all relations within the family, while the other social conditions remain unchanged. There lies before me a letter from an English working man, Robert Pounder, Baron's Buildings, Woodhouse, Moorside, in Leeds (the bourgeoisie may hunt him up there; I give the exact address for the purpose), written by him to Oastler.[5]

He relates how another working man, being on tramp, came to St. Helens, in Lancashire, and there looked up an old friend.

> He found him in a miserable, damp cellar, scarcely furnished; and when my poor friend went in, there sat poor Jack near the fire, and what did he, think you? why

---

4. Factories' Inquiry Commission's Report, Power's Report on Leeds, *passim;* Tufnell Report on Manchester, p. 17, etc.
5. This letter is re-translated from the German, no attempt being made to reproduce either the spelling or the original Yorkshire dialect.

he sat and mended his wife's stockings with the bodkin; and as soon as he saw his old friend at the doorpost, he tried to hide them. But Joe, that is my friend's name, had seen it, and said: "Jack, what the devil art thou doing? Where is the missus? Why, is that thy work?" and poor Jack was ashamed, and said: "No, I know this is not my work, but my poor missus is i' th' factory; she has to leave at half-past five and works till eight at night, and then she is so knocked up that she cannot do aught when she gets home, so I have to do everything for her what I can, for I have no work, nor had any for more nor three years, and I shall never have any more work while I live"; and then he wept a big tear. Jack again said: "There is work enough for women folks and childer hereabouts, but none for men; thou mayest sooner find a hundred pound on the road than work for men—but I should never have believed that either thou or any one else would have seen me mending my wife's stockings, for it is bad work. But she can hardly stand on her feet; I am afraid she will be laid up, and then I don't know what is to become of us, for it's a good bit that she has been the man in the house and I the woman; it is bad work, Joe;" and he cried bitterly, and said, "It has not been always so." "No," said Joe; "but when thou hadn't no work, how hast thou not shifted?" "I'll tell thee, Joe, as well as I can, but it was bad enough; thou knowest when I got married I had work plenty, and thou knows I was not lazy." "No, that thou wert not." "And we had a good furnished house, and Mary need not go to work. I could work for the two of us; but now the world is upside down. Mary has to work and I have to stop at home, mind the childer, sweep and wash, bake and mend; and, when the poor woman comes home at night, she is knocked up. Thou knows, Joe, it's hard for one that was used different." "Yes, boy, it is hard." And then Jack began to cry again, and he wished he had never married, and that he had never been born; but he had never thought, when he wed Mary, that it would come to this. "I have often cried over it," said Jack. Now when Joe heard this, he told me that he had cursed and damned the factories, and the masters, and the Government, with all the curses that he had learned while he was in the factory from a child.

Can any one imagine a more insane state of things than that described in this letter? And yet this condition, which unsexes the man and takes from the woman all womanliness without being able to bestow upon the man true womanliness, or the woman true manliness—this condition which degrades, in the most shameful way, both sexes, and, through them, Humanity, is the last result of our much-praised civilization, the final achievement of all the efforts and struggles of hundreds of generations to improve their own situation and that of their posterity. We must either despair of mankind, and its aims and efforts, when we see all our labour and toil result in such a mockery, or we must admit that human society has hitherto sought salvation in a false direction; we must admit that so total a reversal of the position of the sexes can have come to pass only because the sexes have been placed in a false position from the beginning. If the reign of the wife over the husband, as inevitably brought about by the factory system, is inhuman, the pristine rule of the husband over the wife must have been inhuman too. If the wife can now base her supremacy upon the fact that she supplies the greater part, nay, the whole of the common possession, the necessary inference is that this community of possession is no true and rational one, since one member of the family boasts offensively of contributing the greater share. If the family of our present society is being thus dissolved, this dissolution merely shows that, at bottom, the binding tie of this family was not family affection, but private interest lurking under the cloak of a pretended community of possessions. The same relation exists on the part of those children who support unemployed parents[6] when they do not directly pay board as already referred to. Dr. Hawkins testified in the Factories' Inquiry Commission's Report that this relation is common enough, and in Manchester it is notorious. In this case the children are the masters in the house, as the wife was in the former case, and Lord Ashley gives an example of this in his speech:[7] A man berated his two daughters for going to the public house, and they answered that they were tired of being ordered about, saying, "Damn you, we have to keep you!" Determined to keep the proceeds of their work for themselves, they left the family dwelling, and abandoned their parents to their fate.

The unmarried women, who have grown up in mills, are no better off than the married ones. It is self-evident that a girl who has worked in a mill from her ninth year is in no position to understand domestic work, whence it follows that female operatives prove wholly inexperienced and unfit as housekeepers. They cannot knit or sew, cook or wash, are unacquainted with the most ordinary duties of a housekeeper, and when they have young children to take care of, have not the vaguest idea how to set about it. The Factories' Inquiry Commission's Report gives dozens of examples of this, and Dr. Hawkins, Commissioner for Lancashire, expresses his opinion as follows:[8]

The girls marry early and recklessly; they have neither means, time, nor opportunity to learn the ordinary duties of household life; but if they had them all, they would find no time in married life for the performance of these duties. The mother is more than twelve hours away from her child daily; the baby is cared for by a young girl or an old woman, to whom it is given to nurse. Besides this, the dwelling of the mill-hands is too often no home but a cellar, which contains no cooking or washing utensils, no sewing or mending materials, nothing which makes life agreeable and civilised, or the domestic hearth attractive. For these and

6. How numerous married women are in the factories is seen from information furnished by a manufacturer: In 412 factories in Lancashire, 10,721 of them were employed; of the husbands of these women, but 5,314 were also employed in the factories, 3,927 were otherwise employed, 821 were unemployed, and information was wanting as to 659; or two, if not three men for each factory, are supported by the work of their wives.

7. House of Commons, 15th Mar. 1844.

8. Factories' Inquiry Commission's Report, p. 4.

other reasons, and especially for the sake of the better chances of life for the little children, I can but wish and hope that a time may come in which married women will be shut out of the factories.[9]

But that is the least of the evil. The moral consequences of the employment of women in factories are even worse. The collecting of persons of both sexes and all ages in a single workroom, the inevitable contact, the crowding into a small space of people, to whom neither mental nor moral education has been given, is not calculated for the favourable development of the female character. The manufacturer, if he pays any attention to the matter, can interfere only when something scandalous actually happens; the permanent, less conspicuous influence of persons of dissolute character, upon the more moral, and especially upon the younger ones, he cannot ascertain, and consequently cannot prevent. But precisely this influence is the most injurious. The language used in the mills is characterized by many witnesses in the report of 1833, as "indecent", "bad", "filthy", etc.[10] It is the same process upon a small scale which we have already witnessed upon a large one in the great cities. The centralization of population has the same influence upon the same persons, whether it affects them in a great city or a small factory. The smaller the mill the closer the packing, and the more unavoidable the contact; and the consequences are not wanting. A witness in Leicester said that he would rather let his daughter beg than go into a factory; that they are perfect gates of hell; that most of the prostitutes of the town had their employment in the mills to thank for their present "situation.[11] Another, in Manchester, did not hesitate to assert that three-fourths of the young factory employees, from fourteen" to twenty years of age, were unchaste."[12] Commissioner Cowell expresses it as his opinion, that the morality of the factory operatives is somewhat below the average of that of the working class in general.[13] And Dr. Hawkins says:[14]

An estimate of sexual morality cannot readily be reduced to figures; but if I may trust my own observations and the general opinion of those with whom I have spoken, as well as the whole tenor of the testimony furnished me, the aspect of the influence of factory life upon the morality of the youthful female population is most depressing.

It is, besides, a matter of course that factory servitude, like any other, and to

---

9. For further examples and information compare Factories' Inquiry Commission's Report, Cowell Evidence, pp. 37, 38, 39, 72, 77, 82; Tufnell Evidence, pp. 9, 15, 45, 54, etc.
10. Cowell Evidence, pp. 35, 37, and elsewhere.
11. Power Evidence, p. 8.
12. Cowell Evidence, p. 57.
13. Ibid. 82.
14. Factories' Inquiry Commission's Report, p. 4, Hawkins.

an even higher degree, confers the *jus primae noctis*[16] upon the master. In this respect also the employer is sovereign over the persons and charms of his employees. The threat of discharge suffices to overcome all resistance in nine cases out of ten, if not in ninety-nine out of a hundred, in girls who, in any case, have no strong inducements to chastity. If the master is mean enough, and the official report mentions several such cases, his mill is also his harem; and the fact that not all manufacturers use their power, does not in the least change the position of the girls. In the beginning of manufacturing industry, when most of the employers were upstarts without education or consideration for the hypocrisy of society, they let nothing interfere with the exercise of their vested rights.

To form a correct judgement of the influence of factory-work upon the health of the female sex, it is necessary first to consider the work of children, and then the nature of the work itself. From the beginning of manufacturing industry, children have been employed in mills, at first almost exclusively by reason of the smallness of the machines, which were later enlarged. Even children from the workhouses were employed in multitudes, being rented out for a number of years to the manufacturers as apprentices. They were lodged, fed, and clothed in common, and were, of course, completely the slaves of their masters, by whom they were treated with the utmost recklessness and barbarity. As early as 1796, the public objection to this revolting system found such vigorous expression through Dr. Percival and Sir Robert Peel (father of the Cabinet Minister, and himself a cotton manufacturer), that in 1802 Parliament passed an Apprentices' Bill,[15] by which the most crying evils were removed. Gradually the increasing competition of free workpeople crowded out the whole apprentice system; factories were built in cities, machinery was constructed on a larger scale, and workrooms were made more airy and wholesome; gradually, too, more work was found for adults and young persons. The number of children in the mills diminished somewhat, and the age at which they began to work rose a little; few children under 8 or 9 years were now employed. Later, as we shall see, the power of the State intervened several times to protect them from the money-greed of the bourgeoisie.

The great mortality among children of the working class, and especially among those of the factory operatives, is proof enough of the unwholesome conditions under which they pass their first years. These influences are at work, of course, among the children who survive, but not quite so powerfully

---

15. The Apprentices Bill of 1802 was the first factory legislation. It covered textile mills and applied to "Poor Law" apprentices only, that is children sent to factories by parishes who were supporting them. It limited their work to twelve hours a day, and made night work illegal. Employers were enjoined to supply minimal education, clothing, and accommodation. For all mills employing more than twenty persons, proper ventilation was mandated and whitewashing of walls twice per year. [Ed.]

16. The right of the lord to be the first to have sexual relations with the women (or girls) of his realm. [Ed.]

as upon those who succumb. The result in the most favourable case is a tendency to disease, or some check in development, and consequent less than normal vigour of the constitution. A 9-year-old child of a factory operative that has grown up in want, privation, and changing conditions, in cold and damp, with insufficient clothing and unwholesome dwellings, is far from having the working force of a child brought up under healthier conditions. At 9 years of age it is sent into the mill to work $6\frac{1}{2}$ hours (formerly 8, earlier still, 12 to 14, even 16 hours) daily, until the thirteenth year; then twelve hours until the eighteenth year. The old enfeebling influences continue, while the work is added to them. It is not to be denied that a child of 9 years, even an operative's child, can hold out through $6\frac{1}{2}$ hours' daily work, without anyone being able to trace visible bad results in its development directly to this cause; but in no case can its presence in the damp, heavy air of the factory, often at once warm and wet, contribute to good health; and, in any case, it is unpardonable to sacrifice to the greed of an unfeeling bourgeoisie the time of children which should be devoted solely to their physical and mental development, withdraw them from school and the fresh air, in order to wear them out for the benefit of the manufacturers. The bourgeoisie says: "If we do not employ the children in the mills, they only remain under conditions unfavourable to their development"; and this is true on the whole. But what does this mean if it is not a confession that the bourgeoisie first places the children of the working class under unfavourable conditions, and then exploits these bad conditions for its own benefit, appeals to that which is as much its own fault as the factory system, excuses the sin of today with the sin of yesterday? And if the Factory Act did not in some measure fetter their hands, how this "humane," this "benevolent" bourgeoisie, which has built its factories solely for the good of the working class, would take care of the interests of these workers! Let us hear how they acted before the factory inspector was at their heels. Their own admitted testimony shall convict them in the report of the Factories' Inquiry Commission of 1833.

The report of the Central Commission relates that the manufacturers began to employ children rarely of 5 years, often of 6, very often of 7, usually of 8 to 9 years; that the working day often lasted fourteen to sixteen hours, exclusive of meals and intervals; that the manufacturers permitted overlookers to flog and maltreat children, and often took an active part in so doing themselves. One case is related of a Scots manufacturer, who rode after a 16-year-old runaway, forced him to return, running after the employer as fast as the master's horse trotted, and beat him the whole way with a long whip.[17] In the large towns where the operatives resisted more vigorously, such things natu-

17. Stuart Evidence, p. 35.

rally happened less often. But even this long working day failed to satisfy the greed of the capitalists. Their aim was to make the capital invested in the building and machinery produce the highest return, by every available means, to make it work as actively as possible. Hence the manufacturers introduced the shameful system of night-work. Some of them employed two sets of operatives, each numerous enough to fill the whole mill, and let one set work the twelve hours of the day, and the other the twelve hours of the night. It is needless to picture the effect upon the frames of young children, and even upon the health of young persons and adults, produced by permanent loss of sleep at night, which cannot be made good by any amount of sleep during the day. Irritation of the whole nervous system, with general lassitude and enfeeblement of the entire frame, were the inevitable results, with the fostering of temptation to drunkenness and unbridled sexual indulgence. One manufacturer testifies[18] that during the two years in which night-work was carried on in his factory, the number of illegitimate children born was doubled, and such general demoralization prevailed that he was obliged to give up night-work. Other manufacturers were yet more barbarous, requiring many hands to work thirty to forty hours at a stretch, several times a week, letting them get a couple of hours sleep only, because the night-shift was not complete, but calculated to replace a part of the operatives only.

The reports of the Commission touching this barbarism surpass everything that is known to me in this line. Such infamies, as are here related, are nowhere else to be found—yet we shall see that the bourgeoisie constantly appeals to the testimony of the Commission as being in its own favour. The consequences of these cruelties became evident quickly enough. The Commissioners mention a crowd of cripples who appeared before them, who clearly owed their distortion to the long working hours. This distortion usually consists of a curving of the spinal column and legs, and is described as follows by Francis Sharps, MRCS, of Leeds:[19]

I never saw the peculiar bending of the lower ends of the thigh bones before I came to Leeds. At first I thought it was rachitis, but I was soon led to change my opinion in consequence of the mass of patients who presented themselves at the hospital, and the appearances of the disease at an age (from eight to fourteen) in which children are usually not subject to rachitis, as well as by the circumstance that the malady had first appeated after children began to work in the mills. Thus far I have seen about a hundred such cases, and can, most decidedly, express the opinion that they are the consequences of overwork. So far as I know they were all mill children, and themselves attributed the evil to this cause. The number of

---

18. Tufnell Evidence, p. 91.
19. Dr Loudon Evidence, pp. 12, 13.

cases of curvature of the spine which have fallen under my observation, and which were evidently consequent upon too protracted standing, was not less than three hundred.

Precisely similar is the testimony of Dr. Hey, for eighteen years physician in the hospital in Leeds:[20]

Malformations of the spine are very frequent among mill-hands; some of them consequent upon mere overwork, others the effect of long work upon constitutions originally feeble, or weakened by bad food. Deformities seem even more frequent than these diseases; the knees were bent inward, the ligaments very often relaxed and enfeebled, and the long bones of the legs bent. The thick ends of these long bones were especially apt to be bent and disproportionately developed, and these patients came from the factories in which long work-hours were of frequent occurrence.

Surgeons Beaumont and Sharp, of Bradford, bear the same testimony. The reports of Drinkwater, Power, and Dr. Loudon contain a multitude of examples of such distortions, and those of Tufnell and Sir David Barry, which are less directed to this point, give single examples.[21] The Commissioners for Lancashire, Cowell, Tufnell, and Hawkins, have almost wholly neglected this aspect of the physiological results of the factory system, though this district rivals Yorkshire in the number of cripples. I have seldom traversed Manchester without meeting three or four of them, suffering from precisely the same distortions of the spinal columns and legs as that described, and I have often been able to observe them closely. I know one personally who corresponds exactly with the foregoing description of Dr. Hey, and who got into this condition in Mr. Douglas's factory in Pendleton, an establishment which enjoys an unenviable notoriety among the operatives by reason of the former long working periods continued night after night. It is evident, at a glance, whence the distortions of these cripples come, they all look exactly alike. The knees are bent inward and backwards, the ankles deformed and thick, and the spinal column often bent forwards or to one side. But the crown belongs to the philanthropic manufacturers of the Macclesfield silk district. They employed the youngest children of all, even from 5 to 6 years of age. In the supplementary testimony of Commissioner Tufnell, I find the statement of a certain factory manager Wright, both of whose sisters were most shamefully crippled, and who had once counted the cripples in several streets, some of them the cleanest and neatest streets of Macclesfield. He found in Townley Street ten,

---

20. Dr Loudon Evidence, p. 16.
21. Drinkwater Evidence, pp. 72, 80, 146, 148, 150 (two brothers); 69 (two brothers); 155, and many others. Power Evidence, pp. 63, 66, 67 (two cases); 68 (three cases); 69 (two cases); in Leeds, pp. 29, 31, 40, 43, 53 ff.

George Street five, Charlotte Street four, Watercots fifteen, Bank Top three, Lord Street seven, Mill Lane twelve, Great George Street two, in the work-house two, Park Green one, Peckford Street two, whose families all unanimously declared that the cripples had become such in consequence of overwork in the silk-twisting mills. One boy is mentioned so crippled as not to be able to go upstairs, and girls deformed in back and hips.

HENRY MORLEY

GROUND IN THE MILL

"It is good when it happens," say the children,—"that we die before our time." Poetry may be right or wrong in making little operatives who are ignorant of cowslips say anything like that. We mean here to speak prose. There are many ways of dying. Perhaps it is not good when a factory girl, who has not the whole spirit of play spun out of her for want of meadows, gambols upon bags of wool, a little too near the exposed machinery that is to work it up, and is immediately seized, and punished by the merciless machine that digs its shaft into her pinafore and hoists her up, tears out her left arm at the shoulder joint, breaks her right arm, and beats her on the head. No, that is not good; but it is not a case in point, the girl lives and may be one of those who think that it would have been good for her if she had died before her time.

She had her chance of dying, and she lost it. Possibly it was better for the boy whom his stern master, the machine, caught as he stood on a stool wickedly looking out of window at the sunlight and the flying clouds. These were no business of his, and he was fully punished when the machine he served caught him by one arm and whirled him round and round till he was thrown down dead. There is no lack of such warnings to idle boys and girls. What right has a gamesome youth to display levity before the supreme engine. "Watch me do a trick!" cried such a youth to his fellow, and put his arm familiarly within the arm of the great iron-hearted chief. "*I'll* show you a trick," gnashed the pitiless monster. A coil of strap fastened his arm to the shaft, and round he went. His leg was cut off, and fell into the room, his arm was broken in three or four places, his ankle was broken, his head was battered; he was not released alive.

From *Household Words*. No. 213. April 22, 1854.

Why do we talk about such horrible things? Because they exist, and their existence should be clearly known. Because there have occurred during the last three years, more than a hundred such deaths, and more than ten thousand (indeed, nearly twelve thousand) such accidents in our factories, and they are all, or nearly all, preventible.

These few thousands of catastrophes are the results of the administrative kindness so abundant in this country. They are all the fruits of mercy. A man was lime-washing the ceiling of an engine-room: he was seized by a horizontal shaft and killed immediately. A boy was brushing the dust from such a ceiling, before whitewashing: he had a cloth over his head to keep the dirt from falling on him; by that cloth the engine seized and held him to administer a chastisement with rods of iron. A youth while talking thoughtlessly took hold of a strap that hung over the shaft: his hand was wrenched off at the wrist. A man climbed to the top of his machine to put the strap on the drum: he wore a smock which the shaft caught; both of his arms were then torn out of the shoulder-joints, both legs were broken, and his head was severely bruised: in the end, of course, he died. What he suffered was all suffered in mercy. He was rent asunder, not perhaps for his own good; but, as a sacrifice to the commercial prosperity of Great Britain. There are few amongst us—even among the masters who share most largely in that prosperity—who are willing, we will hope and believe, to pay such a price as all this blood for any good or any gain that can accrue to them.

These accidents have arisen in the manner following. By the Factory Act, passed in the seventh year of Her Majesty's reign, it was enacted, among other things, that all parts of the mill-gearing in a factory should be securely fenced. There were no buts and ifs in the Act itself; these were allowed to step in and limit its powers of preventing accidents out of a merciful respect, not for the blood of the operatives, but for the gold of the mill-owners. It was strongly represented that to fence those parts of machinery that were higher than the heads of workmen—more than seven feet above the ground—would be to incur an expense wholly unnecessary. Kind-hearted interpreters of the law, therefore, agreed with mill-owners that seven feet of fencing should be held sufficient. The result of this accommodation—taking only the accounts of the last three years—has been to credit mercy with some pounds and shillings in the books of English manufacturers; we cannot say how many, but we hope they are enough to balance the account against mercy made out on behalf of the English factory workers thus:—Mercy debtor to justice, of poor men, women, and children, one hundred and six lives, one hundred and forty-two hands or arms, one thousand two hundred and eighty-seven (or, in bulk, how many bushels of) fingers, for the breaking of one thousand three hundred and forty bones, for five hundred and fifty-nine damaged heads, and for eight thousand two hundred and eighty-two miscellaneous injuries. It remains to be settled how much cash saved to the purses of the manufacturers is a satisfactory and proper off-set to this expenditure of life and limb and this crushing of bone in the persons of their work-people.

For, be it strictly observed, this expenditure of life is the direct result of that good-natured determination not to carry out the full provision of the Factory Act, but-to consider enough done if the boxing-off of machinery be made compulsory in each room to the height of seven feet from the floor. Neglect as to the rest, of which we have given the sum of a three-years' account, could lead, it was said, only to a few accidents that would not matter—that would really not be worth much cost of prevention. As kings do no wrong, so machines never stop; and what great harm is done, if A, putting a strap on a driving pulley, is caught by the legs and whirled round at the rate of ninety revolutions in a minute?—what if B, adjusting gear, gets one arm and two thighs broken, an elbow dislocated and a temple cracked?—what if C, picking some cotton from the lathe strips, should become entangled, have an arm torn off, and be dashed up and down, now against the floor, and now against the ceiling?—what if D, sowing a belt, should be dragged up by the neckerchief and bruised by steampower as if he were oats?—what if the boy E, holding a belt which the master had been sewing, be suddenly snapped up by it, whirled round a hundred and twenty times in a minute, and at each revolution knocked against the ceiling till his bones are almost reduced to powder?—what if F, oiling a shaft, be caught first by the neckerchief, then by the clothes, and have his lungs broken, his arm crushed, and his body torn?—what if G, packing yarn into a cart, and stretching out his hand for a corner of the cart-cover blown across a horizontal shaft, be caught up, partly dismembered, and thrown down a corpse?—what if H, caught by a strap, should die with a broken back-bone, and I die crushed against a beam in the ceiling, and little K, carrying waste tow from one part to another, be caught up by it and have his throat cut, and L die after one arm had been torn off and his two feet crushed, and M die of a fractured skull, and N die with his left leg and right arm wrenched from their sockets, and O, not killed, have the hair of his head torn away, and P be scalped and slain, and Q be beaten to death against a joist of the ceiling, and R, coming down a ladder, be caught by his wrapper, and bruised, broken, and torn till he is dead, and S have his bones all broken against a wall, and all the rest of the alphabet be killed by boiler explosions or destroyed in ways as horrible, and many more men be killed than there are letters in the alphabet to call them by? *Every case here instanced has happened, and so have many others, in the last three years.* Granted, but what can all this matter, in the face of the succeeding facts?—that to enclose all horizontal shafts in mills would put the mill-owners to great expense; that little danger is to be apprehended from such shafts to prudent persons, and that mill-owners have a most anxious desire to protect the lives and limbs of their work people. These are the facts urged by a deputation of manufacturers that has been deprecating any attempt to make this anxiety more lively than it has hitherto been.

They found such deprecation necessary. When it became very evident that, in addition to a large list of most serious accidents, there were but forty lives offered up annually to save mill-owners a little trouble and expense, a circular was issued by the factory-inspectors on the last day of January in the present year, expressing their determination to enforce the whole Factory Act to the utmost after the first of June next, and so to compel every shaft of machinery, at whatever cost and of whatever kind, to be fenced off. Thereupon London beheld a deputation, asking mercy from the Government for the aggrieved and threatened manufacturers. We have, more than once, in discussing other topics of this kind, dwelt upon the necessity of the most strict repression of all misplaced tenderness like that for which this committee seems to have petitioned. Preventible accidents must be sternly prevented.

Let Justice wake, and Rigour take her time,
For, lo! our mercy is become our crime.

The result of the deputation is not wholly satisfactory. There follows so much interference by the Home Office in favour of the mill-owners, as to absolve them from the necessity of absolutely boxing-up all their machines, and to require only that they use any precautions that occur to them for the prevention of the accidents now so deplorably frequent. Machinery might, for example, be adjusted when the shafts are not in motion; ceilings whitewashed only when all the machinery is standing still; men working near shafts should wear closely-fitting dresses, and so forth. Manufacturers are to do as they please, and cut down in their own way the matter furnished for their annual of horrors. Only of this they are warned, that they must reduce it; and that, hereafter, the friends of injured operatives will be encouraged to sue for compensation upon death or loss of limb, and Government will sometimes act as prosecutor. What do we find now in the reports? For severe injury to a young person caused by gross and cognisable neglect to fence or shaft, the punishment awarded to a wealthy firm is a fine of ten pounds twelve shillings costs. For killing a woman by the same act of indifference to life and limb, another large firm is fined ten pounds, and has to pay one guinea costs. A fine of a thousand pounds and twelve months at the treadmill would, in the last case, have been an award much nearer the mark of honesty, and have indicated something like a civilised sense of the sacredness of human life. If the same firm had, by an illegal act of negligence, caused the death of a neighbour's horse, they would have had forty, fifty, sixty pounds to pay for it. Ten pounds was the expense of picking a man's wife, a child's mother, limb from limb.

We have not spoken too strongly on this subject. We are indignant against no class, but discuss only one section of a topic that concerns, in some form, almost every division of society. Since, however, we now find ourselves speaking about factories, and turning over leaves of the reports of Factory Inspectors, we may as well have our grumble out, or, at any rate, so far prolong it as to make room for one more subject of dissatisfaction. It is important that Factory management should be watched by the public; in a friendly spirit indeed—for it is no small part of our whole English mind and body—but with the strictness which every man who means well should exercise in judgment on himself, in scrutiny of his own actions. We are told that in one Inspector's district—only in one district—mills and engines have so multiplied, during the last three years, in number and power, that additional work has, in that period, been created for the employment of another forty thousand hands. Every reporter has the same kind of tale to tell. During the last year, in our manufacturing districts, additions to the steam power found employment for an additional army of operatives, nearly thirty thousand strong. The Factory system, therefore, is developing itself most rapidly. It grows too fast, perhaps; at present the mills are, for a short time, in excess of the work required, and in many cases lie idle for two days in the week, or for one or two hours in the day. The succession of strikes, too, in Preston, Wigan, Hindley, Burnley, Padiham, and Bacup and the other places, have left a large number of men out of employ, and caused, for a long time, a total sacrifice of wages, to the extent of some twenty thousand pounds a week. These, however, are all temporary difficulties: the great extension of the Factory system is a permanent fact, and it must be made to bring good with it, not evil.

The law wisely requires that mill-owners, who employ children, shall also teach them, and a minimum, as to time, of schooling is assigned. Before this regulation was compulsory, there were some good schools kept as show-places by certain persons; but, when the maintenance of them became a necessity, and schools were no longer exceptional curiosities, these show-places often fell into complete neglect; they were no longer goods that would attract the public. In Scotland this part of the Factory Law seems to be well worked; and, for its own sake, as a beneficial requirement. That does not, however, seem to be the case in England. All the Inspectors tell us of the lamentable state of the factory schools in this country; allowance being, of course, made for a few worthy exceptions. It is doubtful whether much good will come out of them, unless they be themselves organised by men determined that they shall fulfil their purpose. English Factory children have yet to be really taught.

> *Let them prove their inward souls against the notion*
> *That they live in you, or under you, O wheels!*
> *Still, all day, the iron wheels go onward,*
> *Grinding life down from its mark;*

And the children's souls, which God is calling sunward,
   Spin on blindly in the dark.

Here they are left spinning in the dark. Let Mr. Redgrave's account of a factory school visited by him, near Leeds, suffice to show:—

> It was held in a large room, and the Inspector visiting it at twenty minutes before twelve, found the children at play in the yard, and the master at work in the school-room, sawing up the black board to make fittings of a house to which he proposed transferring his business. The children being summoned, came in carelessly, their disorderly habits evidently not repressed by their master, but checked slightly by the appearance of a strange gentleman. Two girls lolling in the porch were summoned in, and the teacher then triumphantly drew out of his pocket a whistle, whereupon to blow the order for attention. It was the only whole thing that he had to teach with. There were the twenty children ranged along the wall of a room able to contain seven times the number; there were the bits of black board, the master's arms, with a hand-saw, and a hammer for apparatus, and there were the books, namely, six dilapidated Bibles, some copy books, one slate, and half-a-dozen ragged and odd leaves of a "Reading made Easy." To such a school factory children were being sent to get the hours of education which the law makes necessary. Doubtless, that sample is very bad one, but too many resemble it.

They know the grief of man but not the wisdom, these poor childish hearts. They are now rescued from day-long ache and toil; we have given them some leisure for learning, though, as yet but little more than the old lesson to learn.

<hr>

JOHN WARD (O'NEIL)
※※※

FROM HIS DIARY

<hr>

APRIL 1861

1st All the mills in Clitheroe commenced work this morning. At Low Moor there is a great many off. There is above a hundred looms standing. It has been a fine day and I feel very tired after being out so long.

<hr>

From *Annals of Labor: Autobiographies of British Working-Class People 1820–1920,* John Burnett, ed. Bloomington, Ind.: Indiana Univ. Press, 1974.

2nd Another very fine day. Some odd weavers got to their work today.

3rd Another fine day. The weavers' committee have chosen their arbitrators and sent them in to the solicitor.

4th Another fine day. The arbitrators met at the Swan Hotel and elected the Rev. Mr Fielding umpire. They had some discussion and adjourned to this day week, when they hope to settle it.

6th Another fine day. I went up to Clitheroe to a committee meeting, when it was decided to have a public meeting after the decisions of the arbitrators was known.

7th This has been a very fine day. I cleaned myself and had a walk up to Clitheroe and saw the newspapers. There is a very good article in the Preston paper upon the arbitration case.

11th Another fine day. The arbitrators met today and after a long discussion they came to no decision, because the Masters' arbitrators would have 5 per cent for local disadvantages. They made their statement and would have nothing else, nor would they listen to anything else, although the weavers' arbitrators could prove to them that their statements were false and that there was no disadvantages whatever; but they would listen to nothing but what they stated themselves. But as the other side would not agree the umpire had to be called in, but he said before he gave his decision he would like a number of the operatives and Masters to be present so that they could all hear his decision. After some little delay a number of operatives and Masters was got together, when he delivered judgement. He said that he had been inquiring into the question, and from the best of his information there was a difference of $2\frac{1}{2}$ per cent between Clitheroe and Blackburn, but he did not think the weavers should pay it all, therefore he decided that the Masters should pay 1 per cent and the operatives $1\frac{1}{2}$. The Masters was greatly enraged at this decision because they were bent upon having 5 per cent. At night we had a public meeting. John Wood was in the chair, when Mr. Banks and Mr. Heaton, two of the arbitrators, gave an account of the whole proceedings, when a motion was made and carried that we accept the decision until we can mend ourselves. A vote of thanks to the arbitrators and to the umpire and the chairman was passed and the meeting broke up.

12th This has been another fine day. We got the list of prices this forenoon what we have to be paid for the future. There was a deal of grumbling among the narrow weavers because they have taken a farthing a cut too much off them. There was a turn-out among them at noon, and one of the committee men, John Wood, was discharged of the ground as being a ringleader, although he was innocent of the crime, but they seem determined to get rid of every committee man, both at Low Moor and Clitheroe, as all the blame is attached to them for resisting the reduction of 10 per cent; so we all look for nothing else when they can find an opportunity.

13th Another fine day. We had a committee meeting tonight to consider how those men should be dealt with that was made victims to the tyranny of the Masters. It was agreed that they should have 15s. per week until they get work again, and that each member be called upon to pay a penny per week towards a fund to be called the victim fund.

14th This was a fine day. I sat in the house all day reading the newspaper. I have not had much time since the lockout to see any papers, but the news is not of much interest, except that there is a probability of a civil war in the United States.

17th Another fine day. This was our quarterly meeting tonight and my term of office as President expired. It was strongly [pressed] upon me to take it again for another year but I would not, but they were determined not to do without me so they elected me a committee man for six months, and Robert Garner our secretary told the meeting that he had lost his work that afternoon for being a committee man, as he knew of nothing else. It was then put to the meeting that they should be supported, and all that might be made victims, and was carried unanimously.

19th Another fine day. They came round tonight collecting for the victim fund. They got 5d. in our house.

20th Another fine day. I went up to the committee room, and the collectors got more money than they expected for the victim fund, so it was agreed they should only go once a fortnight. . . .

27th It has been cold and stormy all day and a great deal of snow has fallen. I went up to Clitheroe and saw the newspaper. Civil war has broke out in the United States and Fort Sumter has been captured by the secessionists. . . .

NOVEMBER

16th Cold and frosty all day and a great deal of snow has fallen. I went up to Clitheroe. It was snowing very fast and there was very little to be seen. I read the newspaper but there is nothing fresh from America nor any word from the naval expedition that has gone to the south. There is great distress all through the manufacturing districts; they are all running short time through the scarcity of cotton.

21st It has rained all this day. Ribble is so high that we had to stop half an hour sooner for backwater.

22nd Another very wet day. We commenced working at half past eight this morning and stopped at four o'clock—an hour a day less time.

23rd This has been a fine clear frosty day. All the hills are again covered with snow. I went up to Clitheroe and read the newspaper. Things are much

about the same, but a rebel privateer captured and burned a steam-ship belonging to the Federals in the English Channel yesterday. . . .

26th It was very wet and stormy all night, and Ribble was so high with the
flood that we could not start to work until the afternoon.

30th Cold and wet again. I went up to Clitheroe and saw the newspaper.
There is a great deal of excitement owing to a Federal warship boarding a
British steamer and forcibly taking the two rebel commissioners and their sec-
retaries. England has sent a Queen's messenger to Washington to demand
restitution and reparation.

DECEMBER

2nd A clear frosty day but now tonight is raining. I have joined the Low Moor
Mechanics' Institute and Reading-room. It is a penny per week, so I will see
a daily paper regular. They have put me on the Committee.

3rd This has been a very wet dark day. We commenced to light gas tonight
and have gone on full time, but there is nothing but weavers to work full
time. . . .

7th Ribble was so high this morning that we had to give over for three
hours before we could make a start. The latest news from America this day
says that the people in the Northern states are filled with joy at the capture of
the rebel commissioners, but still there seems to be a doubt about the legality
of the proceeding. . . .

10th It has been a little better today, but cold. The news from America is
all about the taking of the rebel commissioners out of the British steamer
Trent. There seems to be great rejoicing through the States.

12th A cold dark day. The newspapers is filled with accounts of great
preparations making for war. Very large reinforcements are to be sent out to
Canada and a great number of ships of war to be sent to the American
coast. . . .

14th A clear cold day. The papers is all taken up with the preparations for
war with America unless the rebels' commissioners are not given up and every
reparation made. The Guards should have gone this week, but the Prince Consort, who is their Colonel, could not review them as he is confined to his
chamber with a severe cold.

15th A dark misty day. There is a rumour tonight that the Prince Consort
is dead.[1]

---

1. Prince Albert (1819–1861), consort of Queen Victoria. [Ed.]

16th It is true that Prince Albert is dead. The newspapers are all in mourning. There was no one expected such a sad calamity, he being a young man and had only a slight cold. Every one has got a shock by it being so sudden. . . .

21st Another clear frosty day. There is nothing fresh in the newspapers. I went up to Clitheroe to get some things for Christmas day, but it was very cold and I did not stop long.

23rd As this is the day that the Prince Consort is buried the mill was stopped all day, so I took the opportunity and whitewashed the house.

25th Christmas day, and the finest I ever seen. It was as warm as some summer days. I spent the day very pleasant. I had plenty of currant cake and whiskey but I kept myself sober and did not go to any public house.

26th Another very fine day, but now tonight is very frosty. The news from America is very scanty. The papers are all taken up discussing the *Trent* affair. . . .

31st The last day of the year and a cold damp day it is, and no news from America. Now as the year is finished I must say that I am not so well off as I have been for several years, owing to so much short time and a prospect of war with the United States.

JANUARY 1862

1st We are beginning the New Year under very poor prospects. Bad trade, short time, and a prospect of a war with America, which, if it should take place, will be worse than ever, as we will get no cotton from it. Every one is anxious for the arrival of the next mail, which is expected every day. We have been working all day—it has been cold and damp.

2nd Another dark soft day, and the news from America is better than we expected as it is of a peaceable kind; but we must wait for the answer to the despatches sent by our Government before we can rely upon anything.

4th A fine clear frosty day, and later news from America is of the same peaceful tone. My daughter was married today[2] at the old church in Clitheroe. It passed off very quietly and nobody got drunk. . . .

8th Another wet cold day, and owing to the scarcity of cotton we are working such rubbish as I never saw in my life. We cannot do the half work that we used to do.

10th A dark wet day, and the latest news from America states that the rebel agents are to be released. . . .

---

2. His daughter Jane, aged twenty-five, married Bernard Knowles, of Low Moor, widower, aged thirty-four, spinner.

17th Dark weather, bad yarn and short time answers very badly. A great number of weavers have given up their odd looms [i.e., third loom] as they cannot keep it on, the yarn is so bad.

20th We started full time this morning. It has been snowing all forenoon, but now tonight it is raining. . . .

22nd A clear day but cold. The newspaper is filled with an account of a coal-pit that has closed and buried 220 human beings near Newcastle.

23rd A dark dull day, and very bad for us poor weavers with rotten cotton.

24th There is no later news from America, and we stopped at half past four this afternoon again.

25th They have got the debris cleared away from the shaft of the Hartley coal-pit near Newcastle upon Tyne, but every one was dead, having been suffocated with gas. . . .

30th Wet again today. The Confederate commissioners, Slidell and Mason, who were taken out of a British ship by a Federal warship, has arrived in England.

FEBRUARY

2nd It has been very mild and calm all day, just like a spring day. I had a walk after dinner and home again. . . .

9th Another hard frosty day. I cleaned myself up and had a walk round by Clitheroe to look at the Co-operative mill which is getting on very fast. They are now at the cock loft. . . .

21st A fine day. I had a very narrow escape with my life this morning. The shaft above my head broke and fell just as I was coming from under it. As it is it broke a deal of yarn. . . .

MARCH

1st A very fine day. The news from America confirms the taking of Ronoake Island, but the loss of the Federals was not more than 350 men.

2nd This has been a very fine day. I had a walk round by Clitheroe to look at the Co-operative mill which has just got the timber on. . . .

18th Another fine day. We had a break down this morning which is likely to last all week.

19th Another fine day. We have stopped tonight for all week.

21st Another very bitter cold day. I had thought to have a walk out in the country but 'twas so cold. The news from America contains a message from President Lincoln recommending the emancipation of the slaves.

22nd There was a hard frost last night and it has been very fine all day. I had a walk in the country round by Waddington and Clitheroe and saw the newspapers, but there is nothing of importance in them.

26th Another very cold day and we have stopped today for all week.

27th It has not been so cold today. My daughter was confined this afternoon with a very fine son.

28th This has been a very fine day and I went and gathered some sticks for kindling fires. There is great news from America. The rebel army has retreated from the Potomac and the Federals have got possession of all their strongholds and another battle was fought in Missouri, when the rebels was routed with the loss of 1500 men, and there has been a great naval battle fought in James's River, when the rebel steamer *Merrimac* attacked the Federal fleet and destroyed two frigates and blew up three gun-boats. She is mail-clad, so that none of them could hurt, but next morning a Federal iron steamer *Monitor,* not half its size and only two guns, attacked the *Merrimac,* and after five hours fighting the rebel was glad to run back disabled, while the *Monitor* was not in the least injured.

30th This has been a fine day. I had a walk in the evening round by Waddington and Bashall Eaves [eight or nine miles].

31st We started at half past eight this morning and stopped at half past four, and things are likely to get worse if cotton gets no cheaper. . . .

APRIL

8th Another cold day and it seems our Government is taking alarm since the American fight with iron steamers, and have given orders that no more wooden ships of war are to be built, but that a fleet of iron ships be built as soon as possible.

13th Another hard frost last night and the hills all round Clitheroe are covered with snow. I went to Church this morning, it being Palm Sunday, and after dinner I had a walk with my son-in-law round by Hodder bridge and Hodder House and home by Mitton [about eight miles]. It was a fine day but cold. . . .

20th Easter Sunday. This has been a very fine day. I had a good deal of walking this afternoon. . . .

MAY

2nd A cold windy day. We stopped at noon and won't start until Monday morning. The news from America is much about the same as last mail. . . .

10th A fine day but rather cold. I feel very poorly myself. It is a bad cold I have got.

11th I have been very poorly all day and never been out of the house.

13th Another very fine day. The news from America tells of the capture of New Orleans by the Federals without a blow.

14th Another fine day. It seems that the siege of Yorktown is going on favourably.

15th Another mail from America confirms the capture of New Orleans and of Baton Rouge, the capital of Louisiana.

16th This was a fine day, and as I had nothing to do I went a gathering sticks and heard the Cuckoo several times. . . .

22nd Another fine day, and we stopped this forenoon for all week.

23rd Another fine day. I have been playing cards nearly all day.

24th Another fine day. I have been reading nearly all day. I went up to Clitheroe in the evening and saw new potatoes for the first time. They were 4d a pound. . . .

JUNE

4th Another wet day and the news from America says that the Federal army was within seven miles of Richmond, but that the rebels would make a stand there and fight to the last, and also that the blockade was raised in New Orleans, Port Royal and Beaufort.

7th This has been a very cold day. I went up to Clitheroe and stood awhile in the street and my feet and hands got as cold as if it had been midwinter.

8th This has been a very wet day and I have never been out of the house all day.

[The Diary breaks off here in the middle of a page, and resumes on the next page with:]

APRIL 1864

10th It is nearly two years since I wrote anything in the way of a diary. I now take up my pen to resume the task. It has been a very poor time for me all the time owing to the American war, which seems as far off being settled as ever. The mill I work in was stopped all last winter, during which time I had 3s. per week allowed by the relief committee, which barely kept me alive. When we started work again it was with Surat[3] cotton, and a great number of weavers

---

3. "Surat" was an inferior kind of cotton from southern India. [Ed.]

can only mind two looms. We can earn very little. I have not earned a shilling a day this last month, and there are many like me. My clothes and bedding is wearing out very fast and I have no means of getting any more, as what wages I get does hardly keep me, my daughter and son-in-law having gone to a house of their own during the time I was out of work. I went twice to Preston to see ― my brother Daniel, but him and his family were no better off than myself, having nothing better than Surat to work at, and it is the same all through Lancashire. There has been some terrible and bloody battles fought in America these last two years. . . . The principal reason why I did not take any notes these last two years is because I was sad and weary. One half of the time I was out of work and the other I had to work as hard as ever I wrought in my life, and can hardly keep myself living. If things do not mend this summer I will try somewhere else or something else, for I can't go much further with what I am at.

17th I have had another weary week of bad work. I have just earned 7s. $3\frac{1}{2}$. off three looms and there are plenty as bad off as me, and if any one complains to the Master of bad work he says, if you don't like [it] you can leave. He wants no one to stop that does not like it, and that is all the satisfaction we can get. . . .

MAY

1st There has been some little rain today, the first we have had for three weeks. It is much wanted. . . . I have given up my odd loom as I cannot keep two looms going, and last week I had only 5s. $1\frac{1}{2}$. after a very hard week's work, but they have promised us better work as soon as the cotton is done that they have on hand. They have promised so often that we can hardly believe them.

8th We have had a very fine week of sunshine and showers, and everything is growing very fast in fields and gardens, and markets are coming down very fast . . . The work at our place is beginning to mend. I have got two beams in, the best I have had for twelve months, but they are for shifting the looms out of our shop into a new shed that is ready for starting, so I hope to get better on than I have done this last winter. In Denmark the Danes are retreating and the Austrians and Prussians are advancing.[4] There is a conference sitting in London on the war, but how it will end there is no one knows.

15th Whitsunday. It has been very hot all day and I have been out walking nearly all afternoon. The news from America gives an account of the defeat

---

4. Frederick VII of Denmark became involved in a war with Prussia (1848–1850) over the status of Schleswig-Holstein. Denmark was defeated. [Ed.]

of the Federal army under General Banks on the Red River[5] with the loss of 4000 men and twenty pieces of cannon, and in the course of another week we may hear of one of the greatest battles that ever was fought. . . . At home things are much about the same. I have been shifted into the new shed and got two very bad looms and bad work in them, so I am no better off than I was. We are to have a holiday tomorrow, but I am too poor to go anywhere so I must stay at home.

22nd It has been very hot all this week, with some thunder showers. I have been walking all this afternoon, and everything looks well in fields and gardens, with every prospect of a good fruit year. . . . In Denmark all is quiet just now, and the Polish inserection is over and many hundreds of families are sent to Siberia; and at our mill things is likely to get worse. The spinners turned out, and a deputation waited upon the Masters, wanting them to mend the work as it was so bad they could scarce get a living. The Masters said they would not mend it and if they did not like it they could leave, so they had to go work again.

29th Another week of bad work. It is as bad now as ever it was, and no signs of it mending. . . .

JUNE

19th It has been fine growing weather this last week, and hay harvest has commenced. . . . In Europe the Danish armistice [is] prolonged another fortnight, and if nothing definite is come to, there will be war again; and at Low Moor things are as bad as ever. I went up to Clitheroe last night. There was a great temperance demonstration and procession which passed off very well. New potatoes were selling at two pound for $3\frac{1}{2}$.

26th There has been a great deal of rain this last week and today is very cold and boisterous. . . . There was a great battle fought last Sunday morning off the French coast near Cherbourg between the Federal war steamer *Kearsa[r]ge* and the Confederate cruiser the *Alabama,* which had burned and destroyed one hundred merchantmen belonging to the United States. The fight lasted an hour and ten minutes when the rebel ship was sent to the bottom. The captain and some of the officers escaped on board an English yacht that came out of Cherbourg with her. They had eleven killed and twenty wounded, and about ten or a dozen were drowned, along with the surgeon; while the *Kearsa[r]ge* was very little damaged and had only three men

5. Civil War Union General Nathaniel Prentiss Banks (1819–1894) was defeated on the Red River, a major southern tributary of the Mississippi, in 1863. [Ed.]

wounded. They picked up sixty-eight men from the sinking ship. . . . In Clitheroe last night new potatoes were selling five pounds for 6d., so I got some for my dinner and came home again.

JULY

10th It has been very fine warm weather since Wednesday, and a great deal of hay has been got in in good condition. . . . In Denmark the Prussians are taking every place they come to, the Danes offering very little resistance. In Parliament the Tories brought forward a motion for a vote of censure upon the Government for the way they have treated the Danish question. The debate lasted all week, and on a division the Ministers had a majority of eighteen. There is no other news of importance this week. . . .

AUGUST

14th This has been a fine warm week and we stopped yesterday as the engine wanted repairs, so I whitewashed and cleaned the house and today I am very stiff and tired. The latest news from America shews that Sherman has not captured Atlanta but that he has invested it with a view to make it surrender; and General Grant[6] has blown up a fort at Petersburg with a rebel regiment and had taken the outer line of defences. There is nothing else of importance. . . . At our mill we have had two turn-outs for bad work. It has been getting worse all summer until we could stand it no longer, and the last time we were out we stopped out all day, when the Master told the deputation that waited upon him that he would work his present stock of cotton up and then he would buy better sorts and have as good work as any in Clitheroe. It is shameful the work we have in at present. I had only 6s. this last week with very hard work, and there was some had less than me; and then our machinery is running very slow owing to the great drought as Ribble is very near dry. We have had frosty nights and warm days this last fortnight, and harvest has been commenced. There were thirty mills stopped in Blackburn this last week for want of water, and will not start again until wet weather sets in. I don't know that there is anything else of importance.

---

6. William Tecumseh Sherman (1820–1891) was a Union general; Ulysses S. Grant (1822–1885) was a Union general and then president of the United States. O'Neil's interest in the Civil War is related to the "cotton famine" it produced in the north of England. [Ed.]

SEPTEMBER

11th We have had a week of very wet weather which was much wanted. . . . Things are much about the same at Atlanta and Mobile, but the principle news from America just now is the coming election for President, because it depends upon which of the candidates is chosen whether there will be peace or a continuance of the war, and as the position of the parties are about evenly balanced there is no knowing yet how things may be, because if there should be peace, then the price of cotton must come down 2s. per pound, and that is the reason why the cotton trade is so bad just now. The merchants will not buy cloth, as they expect the price will come down one half, and the Manufacturers will not buy cotton for the same reason. There are several mills in Lancashire begun to run short time and some are stopping altogether. At our mills the cotton was done last Tuesday and no signs of any coming. There is none working now but weavers, and if no cotton comes, why then, we must stop next, so everything has a black look—and winter coming on!

18th Another wet week and bad prospects for trade. We got as much cotton last week as kept the mill running two days and a half, and as cotton has come down 4d. per pound it is thought we may get some more. . . . The Chicago convention have met and have put General M'Clellan in nomination as President in opposition to Abraham Lincoln, so now both sides are fairly at work, and as the election comes off on the fourth of November the cotton trade in the meanwhile will be greatly depressed until the result is known.

25th We have had some fine weather these days, and harvest is nearly over. . . . The cotton trade is getting worse every day. There is no market whatever, and mills are closing every day. The weft we have had this last week is worse than ever, but we are forced to put up with it, as we don't know how soon we will have to stop altogether.

OCTOBER

2nd It has been very fine all week and things are looking very bad. At our mill they are all working three days a week, except the weavers, who are yet on full time; but as the material is very bad they make very little wages. I have given up my odd loom and I find that two is as many as I can manage with such bad weft. There is a complete stagnation in trade, both in the cotton and cloth market, and nothing doing. . . .

9th Another fine week and very little doing. There has been nothing but the weavers working at our mill this week. All the rest are doing nothing, but they have got some cotton which will last three days, and all have to start tomorrow morning. . . . There is great distress all through Lancashire at present owing to so many mills stopping, and Clithero will soon be as bad as anywhere else.

16th We commenced short time last Monday, and on Thursday we stopped altogether and does not know when we will start again. The cotton that was bought last week—about forty bales—fell a penny a pound about two hours after he had bought it and he will buy no more until the market settles. I should have gone to Preston this morning but it was so wet, but I shall go tomorrow if all be well. . . .

23rd We have been stopped all week and likely for stopping a little longer as there is no cotton bought yet, although it has fallen 2 pence per pound last week, but in the cloth market there is nothing doing whatever. I went to Preston last Monday but only to find that my brother and family had left last Whitsuntide owing to the mill they were working in stopping. They have gone to Dolphinholme near Lancaster and never sent me word. I saw McMurray and family, who gave me all the information, so I found it was no use stopping there so I walked all the way to Blackburn [ten miles] and took the train to Clitheroe. It has been very stormy all week and we have had little pleasure. I applied with several others to the Relief Committee yesterday and got 3s., and our Masters gave every hand 2s., so we are not so badly off this week, whatever they may do next week. It was the great fair yesterday, and a very poor one it was owing to the stormy weather and so many people out of work. The news from America is much about the same as last week, very little doing on either side. The friends of Mr Lincoln say they are sure of winning the election by a large majority.[7]

30th We commenced work last Thursday and started full time, as our Masters have bought a large supply of cotton which will last a few weeks; and the cloth market is a trifle better this last week and it is thought that it has got a turn for the better. . . . The public mind is taken up with the Presidential contest, both sides say they are sure of winning, but in a week or two we shall know all about it. There is nothing else of any importance.

NOVEMBER

6th The weavers have been on full time all week, but the rest of the hands have only had four days and the markets are as gloomy as ever. . . .

---

7. Lincoln did win the election by about four hundred thousand votes. [Ed.]

DECEMBER

4th There is very little news of any kind lately that I have made no note of it. Lincoln has been re-elected President of America and there has been nothing but skirmishing since, and it is likely that there will not be much done until spring. At home we have nothing but stormy weather and bad work, and a poor prospect for Christmas.

[And on that dismal note the Diary ends, half-way down the last page of the book.]

BY HAND

This section could be much longer; it might include many major aesthetic theorists of the nineteenth century who were in various ways horrified by mass production and recommended a return, or a partial return, to earlier methods of manufacture. Or, a return to the original meaning of manufacture, which was "to make by hand." Ruskin's "The Nature of Gothic" influenced many later thinkers, including William Morris and Mahatma Gandhi, his fellow writers in this section. His is undoubtedly one of the great arguments against mass production. Acknowledging what he knows his audience experiences as the virtues of machine-made goods—regularity, perfection, quantity—Ruskin goes on to celebrate the apparent flaws of handmade items as the sign of their humanity, and as the sign of an elevated humanity in those who purchase such goods. William Morris took Ruskin's return to the Gothic architecture of the Middle Ages quite literally: His designs for furniture and wallpaper evoke that period, as did their manufacture in Morris's workshop. Morris, like Ruskin, invokes the humanity that inheres in handmade things and argues for the enjoyment of fewer well-made things over many badly made ones.

Gandhi's interest in the spinning wheel was political and economic: He cites Britain's destruction of the indigenous cotton industry in India as the root of British domination and argues that independence will only be fully realized if Indians end their dependence on foreign-made goods and start making and buying their own products. Gandhi also believed that home spinning would provide significant economic relief to the most impoverished Indians. To produce goods at home and by hand becomes the solution for the depredations of a distant factory system, one that changed production systems throughout the world, with often disastrous results.

CHAPTER EIGHT

THE HUMANITY OF THE HANDMADE

JOHN RUSKIN
⊗⊗⊗

THE NATURE OF GOTHIC

. . . But in the mediæval, or especially Christian, system of ornament, this slavery[1] is done away with altogether; Christianity having recognized, in small things as well as great, the individual value of every soul. But it not only recognizes its value; it confesses its imperfection, in only bestowing dignity upon the acknowledgment of unworthiness. That admission of lost power and fallen nature, which the Greek or Ninevite felt to be intensely painful, and, as far as might be, altogether refused, the Christian makes daily and hourly, contemplating the fact of it without fear, as tending, in the end, to God's greater glory. Therefore, to every spirit which Christianity summons to her service, her exhortation is: Do what you can, and confess frankly what you are unable to do; neither let your effort be shortened for fear of failure, nor your confession silenced for fear of shame. And it is, perhaps, the principal admirableness of the Gothic schools of architecture, that they thus receive the results of the labour of inferior minds; and out of fragments full of imperfection, and betraying that imperfection in every touch, indulgently raise up a stately and unaccusable whole.

But the modern English mind has this much in common with that of the Greek, that it intensely desires, in all things, the utmost completion or perfec-

From *The Complete Works of John Ruskin.* E.T. Cook and Alexander Wedderburn, eds. London: Longmans, Green and Company, 1907.
1. The "slavery" to which Ruskin refers here is explained in the previous paragraph of the text, not given in this excerpt: it is ornament of the Greek, Ninevite, and Egytian schools that required "absolute precision." [Ed.]

tion compatible with their nature. This is a noble character in the abstract, but becomes ignoble when it causes us to forget the relative dignities of that nature itself, and to prefer the perfectness of the lower nature to the imperfection of the higher; not considering that as, judged by such a rule, all the brute animals would be preferable to man, because more perfect in their functions and kind, and yet are always held inferior to him, so also in the works of man, those which are more perfect in their kind are always inferior to those which are, in their nature, liable to more faults and shortcomings. For the finer the nature, the more flaws it will show through the clearness of it; and it is a law of this universe, that the best things shall be seldomest seen in their best form. The wild grass grows well and strongly, one year with another; but the wheat is, according to the greater nobleness of its nature, liable to the bitterer blight. And therefore, while in all things that we see or do, we are to desire perfection, and strive for it, we are nevertheless not to set the meaner thing, in its narrow accomplishment, above the nobler thing, in its mighty progress; not to esteem smooth minuteness above shattered majesty; not to prefer mean victory to honourable defeat; not to lower the level of our aim, that we may the more surely enjoy the complacency of success. But, above all, in our dealings with the souls of other men, we are to take care how we check, by severe requirement or narrow caution, efforts which might otherwise lead to a noble issue; and, still more, how we withhold our admiration from great excellencies, because they are mingled with rough faults. Now, in the make and nature of every man, however rude or simple, whom we employ in manual labour, there are some powers for better things; some tardy imagination, torpid capacity of emotion, tottering steps of thought, there are, even at the worst; and in most cases it is all our own fault that they *are* tardy or torpid. But they cannot be strengthened, unless we are content to take them in their feebleness, and unless we prize and honour them in their imperfection above the best and most perfect manual skill. And this is what we have to do with all our labourers; to look for the *thoughtful* part of them, and get that out of them, whatever we lose for it, whatever faults and errors we are obliged to take with it. For the best that is in them cannot manifest itself, but in company with much error. Understand this clearly: You can teach a man to draw a straight line, and to cut one; to strike a curved line, and to carve it; and to copy and carve any number of given lines or forms, with admirable speed and perfect precision; and you find his work perfect of its kind: but if you ask him to think about any of those forms, to consider if he cannot find any better in his own head, he stops; his execution becomes hesitating; he thinks, and ten to one he thinks wrong; ten to one he makes a mistake in the first touch he gives to his work as a thinking being. But you have made a man of him for all that. He was only a machine before, an animated tool.

And observe, you are put to stern choice in this matter. You must either make a tool of the creature, or a man of him. You cannot make both. Men were not intended to work with the accuracy of tools, to be precise and perfect in all their actions. If you will have that precision out of them, and make their fingers measure degrees like cog-wheels, and their arms strike curves like compasses, you must unhumanize them. All the energy of their spirits must be given to make cogs and compasses of themselves. All their attention and strength must go to the accomplishment of the mean act. The eye of the soul must be bent upon the finger-point, and the soul's force must fill all the invisible nerves that guide it, ten hours a day, that it may not err from its steely precision, and so soul and sight be worn away, and the whole human being be lost at last—a heap of sawdust, so far as its intellectual work in this world is concerned: saved only by its Heart, which cannot go into the form of cogs and compasses, but expands, after the ten hours are over, into fireside humanity. On the other hand, if you will make a man of the working creature, you cannot make a tool. Let him but begin to imagine, to think, to try to do anything worth doing; and the engine-turned precision is lost at once. Out come all his roughness, all his dulness, all his incapability; shame upon shame, failure upon failure, pause after pause: but out comes the whole majesty of him also; and we know the height of it only when we see the clouds setting upon him. And, whether the clouds be bright or dark, there will be transfiguration behind and within them.

And now, reader, look round this English room of yours, about which you have been proud so often, because the work of it was so good and strong, and the ornaments of it so finished. Examine again all those accurate mouldings, and perfect polishings, and unerring adjustments of the seasoned wood and tempered steel. Many a time you have exulted over them, and thought how great England was, because her slightest work was done so thoroughly. Alas! if read rightly, these perfectnesses are signs of a slavery in our England a thousand times more bitter and more degrading than that of the scourged African, or helot Greek. Men may be beaten, chained, tormented, yoked like cattle, slaughtered like summer flies, and yet remain in one sense, and the best sense, free. But to smother their souls with them, to blight and hew into rotting pollards the suckling branches of their human intelligence, to make the flesh and skin which, after the worm's work on it, is to see God, into leathern thongs to yoke machinery with,—this is to be slave-masters indeed; and there might be more freedom in England, though her feudal lords' lightest words were worth men's lives, and though the blood of the vexed husbandman dropped in the furrows of her fields, than there is while the animation of her multitudes is sent like fuel to feed the factory smoke, and the strength of them is given daily to be wasted into the fineness of a web, or racked into the exactness of a line.

And, on the other hand, go forth again to gaze upon the old cathedral front, where you have smiled so often at the fantastic ignorance of the old sculptors: examine once more those ugly goblins, and formless monsters, and stern statues, anatomiless and rigid; but do not mock at them, for they are signs of the life and liberty of every workman who struck the stone; a freedom of thought, and rank in scale of being, such as no laws, no charters, no charities can secure; but which it must be the first aim of all Europe at this day to regain for her children.

Let me not be thought to speak wildly or extravagantly. It is verily this degradation of the operative into a machine, which, more than any other evil of the times, is leading the mass of the nations everywhere into vain, incoherent, destructive struggling for a freedom of which they cannot explain the nature to themselves. Their universal outcry against wealth, and against nobility, is not forced from them either by the pressure of famine, or the sting of mortified pride. These do much, and have done much in all ages; but the foundations of society were never yet shaken as they are at this day. It is not that men are ill fed, but that they have no pleasure in the work by which they make their bread, and therefore look to wealth as the only means of pleasure. It is not that men are pained by the scorn of the upper classes, but they cannot endure their own; for they feel that the kind of labour to which they are condemned is verily a degrading one, and makes them less than men. Never had the upper classes so much sympathy with the lower, or charity for them, as they have at this day, and yet never were they so much hated by them: for, of old, the separation between the noble and the poor was merely a wall built by law; now it is a veritable difference in level of standing, a precipice between upper and lower grounds in the field of humanity, and there is pestilential air at the bottom of it. I know not if a day is ever to come when the nature of right freedom will be understood, and when men will see that to obey another man, to labour for him, yield reverence to him or to his place, is not slavery. It is often the best kind of liberty,—liberty from care. The man who says to one, Go, and he goeth, and to another, Come, and he cometh, has, in most cases, more sense of restraint and difficulty than the man who obeys him. The movements of the one are hindered by the burden on his shoulder; of the other by the bridle on his lips: there is no way by which the burden may be lightened; but we need not suffer from the bridle if we do not champ at it. To yield reverence to another, to hold ourselves and our likes at his disposal, is not slavery; often it is the noblest state in which a man can live in this world. There is, indeed, a reverence which is servile, that is to say, irrational or selfish: but there is also noble reverence, that is to say, reasonable and loving; and a man is never so noble as when he is reverent in this kind; nay, even if the feeling pass the bounds of mere reason, so that it be loving, a man is raised by it. Which had, in reality, most of the serf nature in him,—the Irish peasant who was lying in wait yesterday for his landlord, with his musket muzzle thrust through the ragged hedge;[2] or that old mountain servant, who 200 years ago, at Inverkeithing, gave up his own life and the lives of his seven sons for his

---

2. Rural violence in Ireland was prevalent at this time as tenant farmers fought for their rights against largely absentee English landowners. [Ed.]

chief?—as each fell, calling forth his brother to the death, "Another for Hector!" And therefore, in all ages and all countries, reverence has been paid and sacrifice made by men to each other, not only without complaint, but rejoicingly; and famine, and peril, and sword, and all evil, and all shame, have been borne willingly in the causes of masters and kings; for all these gifts of the heart ennobled the men who gave, not less than the men who received them, and nature prompted, and God rewarded the sacrifice. But to feel their souls withering within them, unthanked, to find their whole being sunk into an unrecognized abyss, to be counted off into a heap of mechanism numbered with its wheels, and weighed with its hammer strokes—this, nature bade not,—this, God blesses not,—this, humanity for no long time is able to endure.

We have much studied and much perfected, of late, the great civilized invention of the division of labour; only we give it a false name. It is not, truly speaking, the labour that is divided; but the men:—Divided into mere segments of men—broken into small fragments and crumbs of life; so that all the little piece of intelligence that is left in a man is not enough to make a pin, or a nail, but exhausts itself in making the point of a pin or the head of a nail. Now it is a good and desirable thing, truly, to make many pins in a day; but if we could only see with what crystal sand their points were polished,—sand of human soul, much to be magnified before it can be discerned for what it is—we should think there might be some loss in it also. And the great cry that rises from all our manufacturing cities, louder than their furnace blast, is all in very deed for this,—that we manufacture everything there except men; we blanch cotton, and strengthen steel, and refine sugar, and shape pottery; but to brighten, to strengthen, to refine, or to form a single living spirit, never enters into our estimate of advantages. And all the evil to which that cry is urging our myriads can be met only in one way: not by teaching nor preaching, for to teach them is but to show them their misery, and to preach to them, if we do nothing more than preach, is to mock at it. It can be met only by a right understanding, on the part of all classes, of what kinds of labour are good for men, raising them, and making them happy; by a determined sacrifice of such convenience, or beauty, or cheapness as is to be got only by the degradation of the workman; and by equally determined demand for the products and results of healthy and ennobling labour.

And how, it will be asked, are these products to be recognized, and this demand to be regulated? Easily: by the observance of three broad and simple rules:

1. Never encourage the manufacture of any article not absolutely necessary, in the production of which *Invention* has no share.
2. Never demand an exact finish for its own sake, but only for some practical or noble end.

3. Never encourage imitation or copying of any kind, except for the sake of preserving records of great works.

The second of these principles is the only one which directly rises out of the consideration of our immediate subject; but I shall briefly explain the meaning and extent of the first also, reserving the enforcement of the third for another place.

Never encourage the manufacture of anything not necessary, in the production of which invention has no share.

For instance. Glass beads are utterly unnecessary, and there is no design or thought employed in their manufacture. They are formed by first drawing out the glass into rods; these rods are chopped up into fragments of the size of beads by the human hand, and the fragments are then rounded in the furnace. The men who chop up the rods sit at their work all day, their hands vibrating with a perpetual and exquisitely timed palsy, and the beads dropping beneath their vibration like hail. Neither they, nor the men who draw out the rods or fuse the fragments, have the smallest occasion for the use of any single human faculty; and every young lady, therefore, who buys glass beads is engaged in the slave-trade, and in a much more cruel one than that which we have so long been endeavouring to put down.

But glass cups and vessels may become the subjects of exquisite invention; and if in buying these we pay for the invention, that is to say, for the beautiful form, or colour, or engraving, and not for mere finish of execution, we are doing good to humanity.

WILLIAM MORRIS
☙☙☙

THE REVIVAL OF HANDICRAFT
An Article in the "Fortnightly Review," November 1888

For some time past there has been a good deal of interest shown in what is called in our modern slang Art Workmanship, and quite recently there has been a growing feeling that this art workmanship to be of any value must have some of the workman's individuality imparted to it beside whatever of art it may have

From *The Collected Works of William Morris,* volume XXII. London: Longmans, Green and Company, 1915.

got from the design of the artist who has planned, but not executed the work. This feeling has gone so far that there is growing up a fashion for demanding handmade goods even when they are not ornamented in any way, as, for instance, woollen and linen cloth spun by hand and woven without power, hand-knitted hosiery, and the like. Nay, it is not uncommon to hear regrets for the hand-labour in the fields, now fast disappearing from even backward districts of civilized countries. The scythe, the sickle, and even the flail are lamented over, and many are looking forward with drooping spirits to the time when the hand-plough will be as completely extinct as the quern, and the rattle of the steam-engine will take the place of the whistle of the curly-headed ploughboy through all the length and breadth of the land. People interested, or who suppose that they are interested, in the details of the arts of life feel a desire to revert to methods of handicraft for production in general; and it may therefore be worth considering how far this is a mere reactionary sentiment incapable of realization, and how far it may foreshadow a real coming change in our habits of life as irresistible as the former change which has produced the system of machine-production, the system against which revolt is now attempted.

In this paper I propose to confine the aforesaid consideration as much as I can to the effect of machinery *versus* handicraft upon the arts; using that latter word as widely as possible, so as to include all products of labour which have any claims to be considered beautiful. I say as far as possible: for as all roads lead to Rome, so the life, habits, and aspirations of all groups and classes of the community are founded on the economical conditions under which the mass of the people live, and it is impossible to exclude socio-political questions from the consideration of æsthetics. Also, although I must avow myself a sharer in the above-mentioned reactionary regrets, I must at the outset disclaim the mere æsthetic point of view which looks upon the ploughman and his bullocks and his plough, the reaper, his work, his wife, and his dinner, as so many elements which compose a pretty tapestry hanging, fit to adorn the study of a contemplative person of cultivation, but which it is not worth while differentiating from each other except in so far as they are related to the beauty and interest of the picture. On the contrary, what I wish for is that the reaper and his wife should have themselves a due share in all the fulness of life; and I can, without any great effort, perceive the justice of their forcing me to bear part of the burden of its deficiencies, so that we may together be forced to attempt to remedy them, and have no very heavy burden to carry between us.

To return to our æsthetics: though a certain part of the cultivated classes of to-day regret the disappearance of handicraft from production, they are quite vague as to how and why it is disappearing, and as to how and why it should or may reappear. For to begin with the general public is grossly ignorant of all the methods and processes of manufacture. This is of course one result of the machine-system we are considering. Almost all goods are made apart from the life of those who use them; we are not responsible for them, our will has had no part in their production, except so far as we form a part of the market on which they can be forced for the profit of the capitalist whose money is employed in producing them. The market assumes that certain wares are wanted; it produces such wares, indeed, but their kind and quality are only adapted to the needs of the public in a very rough fashion, because the public needs are subordinated to the interest of the capitalist masters of the market, and they can force the public to put up with the less desirable article if they choose, as they generally do. The result is that in this direction our boasted individuality is a sham; and persons who wish for anything that deviates ever so little from the beaten path have either to wear away their lives in a wearisome and mostly futile contest with a stupendous organization which disregards their wishes, or to allow those wishes to be crushed out for the sake of a quiet life.

Let us take a few trivial but undeniable examples. You want a hat, say, like that you wore last year; you go to the hatter's, and find you cannot get it there, and you have no resource but in submission. Money by itself won't buy you the hat you want; it will cost you three months' hard labour and twenty pounds to have an inch added to the brim of your wideawake; for you will have to get hold of a small capitalist (of whom but few are left), and by a series of intrigues and resolute actions which would make material for a three-volume novel, get him to allow you to turn one of his hands into a handicraftsman for the occasion; and a very poor handicraftsman he will be, when all is said. Again, I carry a walking-stick, and like all sensible persons like it to have a good heavy end that will swing out well before me. A year or two ago it became the fashion to pare away all walking-sticks to the shape of attenuated carrots, and I really believe I shortened my life in my attempts at getting a reasonable staff of the kind I was used to, so difficult it was. Again, you want a piece of furniture, which the trade (mark the word, Trade, not Craft!) turns out blotched over with idiotic sham ornament; you wish to dispense with this degradation, and propose it to your upholsterer, who grudgingly assents to it; and you find that you have to pay the price of two pieces of furniture for the privilege of indulging your whim of leaving out the trade finish (I decline to call it ornament) on the one you have got made for you. And this is because it has been made by handicraft instead of machinery. For most people, therefore, there is a prohibitive price put upon the acquirement of the knowledge of methods and processes. We do not know how a piece of goods is made, what the difficulties are that beset its manufacture, what it ought to look like, feel like, smell like, or what it ought to cost apart from the profit of the middleman. We have lost the art of marketing, and with it the due sympathy with the life of the workshop, which would, if it existed, be such a wholesome check on the humbug of party politics.

It is a natural consequence of this ignorance of the methods of making wares, that even those who are in revolt against the tyranny of the excess of division of labour in the occupations of life, and who wish to recur more or less to handicraft, should also be ignorant of what that life of handicraft was when all wares were made by handicraft. If their revolt is to carry any hope with it, it is necessary that they should know something of this. I must assume that many or perhaps most of my readers are not acquainted with Socialist literature, and that few of them have read the admirable account of the different epochs of production given in Karl Marx' great work entitled "Capital." I must ask to be excused, therefore, for stating very briefly what, chiefly owing to Marx, has become a common-place of Socialism, but is not generally known outside it. There have been three great epochs of production since the beginning of the Middle Ages. During the first or mediæval period all production was individualistic in method; for though the workmen were combined into great associations for protection and the organization of labour, they were so associated as citizens, not as mere workmen. There was little or no division of labour, and what machinery was used was simply of the nature of a multiplied tool, a help to the workman's hand-labour and not a supplanter of it. The workman worked for himself and not for any capitalistic employer, and he was accordingly master of his work and his time; this was the period of pure handicraft. When in the latter half of the sixteenth century the capitalist employer and the so-called free workman began to appear, the workmen were collected into workshops, the old tool-machines were improved, and at last a new invention, the division of labour, found its way into the workshops. The division of labour went on growing throughout the seventeenth century, and was perfected in the eighteenth, when the unit of labour became a group and not a single man; or in other words the workman became a mere part of a machine composed sometimes wholly of human beings and sometimes of human beings plus labour-saving machines, which towards the end of this period were being copiously invented; the fly-shuttle may be taken for an example of these. The latter half of the eighteenth century saw the beginning of the last epoch of production that the world has known, that of the automatic machine which supersedes hand-labour, and turns the workman who was once a handicraftsman helped by tools, and next a part of a machine, into a tender of machines. And as far as we can see, the revolution in this direction as to kind is complete, though as to degree, as pointed out by Mr. David A. Wells[1] last year (1887), the tendency is towards the displacement of ever more and more "muscular" labour, as Mr. Wells calls it.

This is very briefly the history of the evolution of industry during the last

---

1. David A. Wells was an American economist and author of "Our Burden and Our Strength" (1864), a pamphlet dealing with the financial consequences of the Civil War. [Ed.]

five hundred years; and the question now comes: Are we justified in wishing that handicraft may in its turn supplant machinery? Or it would perhaps be better to put the question in another way: Will the period of machinery evolve itself into a fresh period of machinery more independent of human labour than anything we can conceive of now, or will it develop its contradictory in the shape of a new and improved period of production by handicraft? The second form of the question is the preferable one, because it helps us to give a reasonable answer to what people who have any interest in external beauty will certainly ask: Is the change from handicraft to machinery good or bad? And the answer to that question is to my mind that, as my friend Belfort Bax[2] has put it, statically it is bad, dynamically it is good. As a condition of life, production by machinery is altogether an evil; as an instrument for forcing on us better conditions of life it has been, and for some time yet will be, indispensable.

Having thus tried to clear myself of mere reactionary pessimism, let me attempt to show why statically handicraft is to my mind desirable, and its destruction a degradation of life. Well, first I shall not shrink from saying bluntly that production by machinery necessarily results in utilitarian ugliness in everything which the labour of man deals with, and that this is a serious evil and a degradation of human life. So clearly is this the fact that though few people will venture to deny the latter part of the proposition, yet in their hearts the greater part of cultivated civilized persons do not regard it as an evil, because their degradation has already gone so far that they cannot, in what concerns the sense of seeing, discriminate between beauty and ugliness: their languid assent to the desirableness of beauty is with them only a convention, a superstitious survival from the times when beauty was a necessity to all men. The first part of the proposition (that machine-industry produces ugliness) I cannot argue with these persons, because they neither know, nor care for, the difference between beauty and ugliness; and with those who do understand what beauty means I need not argue it, as they are but too familiar with the fact that the produce of all modern industrialism is ugly, and that whenever anything which is old disappears, its place is taken by something inferior to it in beauty; and that even out in the very fields and open country. The art of making beautifully all kinds of ordinary things, carts, gates, fences, boats, bowls, and so forth, let alone houses and public buildings, unconsciously and without effort, has gone; when anything has to be renewed among these simple things the only question asked is how little it can be done for, so as to tide us over our responsibility and shift its mending on to the next generation.

---

2. Ernest Belfort Bax (1854–1926) was an English socialist who helped to found, with William Morris, the Socialist League. [Ed.]

It may be said, and indeed I have heard it said, that since there is some beauty still left in the world and some people who admire it, there is a certain gain in the acknowledged eclecticism of the present day, since the ugliness which is so common affords a contrast whereby the beauty, which is so rare, may be appreciated. This I suspect to be only another form of the maxim which is the sheet-anchor of the laziest and most cowardly group of our cultivated classes, that it is good for the many to suffer for the few; but if any one puts forward in good faith the fear that we may be too happy in the possession of pleasant surroundings, so that we shall not be able to enjoy them, I must answer that this seems to me a very remote terror. Even when the tide at last turns in the direction of sweeping away modern squalor and vulgarity, we shall have, I doubt, many generations of effort in perfecting the transformation, and when it is at last complete, there will be first the triumph of our success to exalt us, and next the history of the long wade through the putrid sea of ugliness which we shall have at last escaped from. But furthermore, the proper answer to this objection lies deeper than this. It is to my mind that very consciousness of the production of beauty for beauty's sake which we want to avoid; it is just what is apt to produce affectation and effeminacy amongst the artists and their following. In the great times of art conscious effort was used to produce great works for the glory of the City, the triumph of the Church, the exaltation of the citizens, the quickening of the devotion of the faithful; even in the higher art, the record of history, the instruction of men alive and to live hereafter, was the aim rather than beauty; and the lesser art was unconscious and spontaneous, and did not in any way interfere with the rougher business of life, while it enabled men in general to understand and sympathize with the nobler forms of art. But unconscious as these producers of ordinary beauty may be, they will not and cannot fail to receive pleasure from the exercise of their work under these conditions, and this above all things is that which influences me most in my hope for the recovery of handicraft. I have said it often enough, but I must say it once again, since it is so much a part of my case for handicraft, that so long as man allows his daily work to be mere unrelieved drudgery he will seek happiness in vain. I say further that the worst tyrants of the days of violence were but feeble tormentors compared with those Captains of Industry who have taken the pleasure of work away from the workmen. Furthermore I feel absolutely certain that handicraft joined to certain other conditions, of which more presently, would produce the beauty and the pleasure in work above mentioned; and if that be so, and this double pleasure of lovely surroundings and happy work could take the place of the double torment of squalid surroundings and wretched drudgery, have we not good reason for wishing, if it might be, that handicraft should once more step into the place of machine-production?

I am not blind to the tremendous change which this revolution would mean. The maxim of modern civilization to a well-to-do man is, Avoid taking trouble! Get as many of the functions of your life as you can performed by others for you! Vicarious life is the watchword of our civilization, and we well-to-do and cultivated people live smoothly enough while it lasts. But, in the first place, how about the vicars, who do more for us than the singing of mass for our behoof for a scanty stipend? Will they go on with it for ever? For indeed the shuffling off of responsibilities from one to the other has to stop at last, and somebody has to bear the burden in the end. But let that pass, since I am not writing politics, and let us consider another aspect of the matter. What wretched lop-sided creatures we are being made by the excess of the division of labour in the occupations of life! What on earth are we going to do with our time when we have brought the art of vicarious life to perfection, having first complicated the question by the ceaseless creation of artificial wants which we refuse to supply for ourselves? Are all of us (we of the great middle class I mean) going to turn philosophers, poets, essayists—men of genius, in a word, when we have come to look down on the ordinary functions of life with the same kind of contempt wherewith persons of good breeding look down upon a good dinner, eating it sedulously however? I shudder when I think of how we shall bore each other when we have reached that perfection. Nay, I think we have already got in all branches of culture rather more geniuses than we can comfortably bear, and that we lack, so to say, audiences rather than preachers. I must ask pardon of my readers; but our case is at once so grievous and so absurd that one can scarcely help laughing out of bitterness of soul. In the very midst of our pessimism we are boastful of our wisdom, yet we are helpless in the face of the necessities we have created, and which, in spite of our anxiety about art, are at present driving us into luxury unredeemed by beauty on the one hand, and squalor unrelieved by incident or romance on the other, and will one day drive us into mere ruin.

Yes, we do sorely need a system of production which will give us beautiful surroundings and pleasant occupation, and which will tend to make us good human animals, able to do something for ourselves, so that we may be generally intelligent instead of dividing ourselves into dull drudges or duller pleasure-seekers according to our class, on the one hand, or hapless pessimistic intellectual personages, and pretenders to that dignity, on the other. We do most certainly need happiness in our daily work, content in our daily rest; and all this cannot be if we hand over the whole responsibility of the details of our daily life to machines and their drivers. We are right to long for intelligent handicraft to come back to the world which it once made tolerable amidst war and turmoil and uncertainty of life, and which it should, one would think, make happy now we have grown so peaceful, so considerate of each other's temporal welfare.

Then comes the question, How can the change be made? And here at once we are met by the difficulty that the sickness and death of handicraft is, it seems, a natural expression of the tendency of the age. We willed the end, and therefore the means also. Since the last days of the Middle Ages the creation of an intellectual aristocracy has been, so to say, the spiritual purpose of civilization side by side with its material purpose of supplanting the aristocracy of status by the aristocracy of wealth. Part of the price it has had to pay for its success in that purpose (and some would say it is comparatively an insignificant part) is that this new aristocracy of intellect has been compelled to forgo the lively interest in the beauty and romance of life, which was once the portion of every artificer at least, if not of every workman, and to live surrounded by an ugly vulgarity which the world amidst all its changes has not known till modern times. It is not strange that until recently it has not been conscious of this degradation; but it may seem strange to many that it has now grown partially conscious of it. It is common now to hear people say of such and such a piece of country or suburb: "Ah! it was so beautiful a year or so ago, but it has been quite spoilt by the building." Forty years back the building would have been looked on as a vast improvement; now we have grown conscious of the hideousness we are creating, and we go on creating it. We see the price we have paid for our aristocracy of intellect, and even that aristocracy itself is more than half regretful of the bargain, and would be glad if it could keep the gain and not pay the full price for it. Hence not only the empty grumbling about the continuous march of machinery over dying handicraft, but also various elegant little schemes for trying to withdraw ourselves, some of us, from the consequences (in this direction) of our being superior persons; none of which can have more than a temporary and very limited success. The great wave of commercial necessity will sweep away all these well-meant attempts to stem it, and think little of what it has done, or whither it is going.

Yet after all even these feeble manifestations of discontent with the tyranny of commerce are tokens of a revolutionary epoch, and to me it is inconceivable that machine-production will develop into mere infinity of machinery, or life wholly lapse into a disregard of life as it passes. It is true indeed that powerful as the cultivated middle class is, it has not the power of re-creating the beauty and romance of life; but that will be the work of the new society which the blind progress of commercialism will create, nay, is creating. The cultivated middle class is a class of slave-holders, and its power of living according to its choice is limited by the necessity of finding constant livelihood and employment for the slaves who keep it alive. It is only a society of equals which can choose the life it will live, which can choose to forgo gross luxury and base utilitarianism in return for the unwearying pleasure of tasting the fulness of life. It is my firm belief that we shall in the end realize this society of equals, and also that when it is realized it will not endure a vicarious life by means of machinery; that it will in short be the master of its machinery and not the servant, as our age is.

Meantime, since we shall have to go through a long series of social and political events before we shall be free to choose how we shall live, we should welcome even the feeble protest which is now being made against the vulgarization of all life: first because it is one token amongst others of the sickness of modern civilization; and next, because it may help to keep alive memories of the past which are necessary elements of the life of the future, and methods of work which no society could afford to lose. In short, it may be said that though the movement towards the revival of handicraft is contemptible on the surface in face of the gigantic fabric of commercialism; yet, taken in conjunction with the general movement towards freedom of life for all, on which we are now surely embarked, as a protest against intellectual tyranny, and a token of the change which is transforming civilization into socialism, it is both noteworthy and encouraging.

CHAPTER NINE

"MANUAL" LABOR
AND NATIONAL INDEPENDENCE

MAHATMA GANDHI
❧

THE DUTY OF SPINNING

In "The Secret of Swaraj"[1] I have endeavoured to show what home-spinning means for our country. In any curriculum of the future, spinning must be a compulsory subject. Just as we cannot live without breathing and without eating, so is it impossible for us to attain economic independence and banish pauperism from this ancient land without reviving home-spinning. I hold the spinning wheel to be as much a necessity in every household as the hearth. No other scheme that can be devised will ever solve the problem of the deepening poverty of the people.

How then can spinning be introduced in every home? I have already suggested the introduction of spinning and systematic production of yarn in every national school. Once our boys and girls have learnt the art they can easily carry it to their homes.

But this requires organisation. A spinning wheel must be worked for twelve hours per day. A practised spinner can spin two tolas and a half per hour. The price that is being paid at present is on an average four annas per forty tolas or one pound of yarn, i. e., one pice per hour. Each wheel therefore should give three annas per day. A strong one costs seven rupees. Working,

---

From *Swaraj in One Year.* Madras: Ganesh & Co., 1921.
1. Self-rule. [Ed.]

therefore, at the rate of twelve hours per day it can pay for itself in less than 38 days. I have given enough figures to work upon. Anyone working at them will find the results to be startling.

If every school introduced spinning, it would revolutionize our ideas of financing education. We can work a school for six hours per day and give free education to the pupils. Supposing a boy works at the wheel for four hours daily, he will produce every day 10 tolas of yarn and thus earn for his school one anna per day. Suppose further that he manufactures very little during the first month, and that the school works only twenty-six days in the month, He can earn after the first month Rs. 1–10 per month, A class of thirty boys would yield, after the first month, an income of Rs. 48–12 per month.

I have said nothing about literary training. It can be given during the two hours out of the six. It is easy to see that every school can be made self-supporting without much effort and the nation can engage experienced teachers for its schools.

The chief difficulty in working out the scheme is the spinning wheel. We require thousands of wheels if the art becomes popular. Fortunately, every village carpenter can easily construct the machine. It is a serious mistake to order them from the Ashram or any other place. The beauty of spinning is that it is incredibly simple, easily learnt, and can be cheaply introduced in every village.

The course suggested by me is intended only for this year of purification and probation. When normal times are reached and Swaraj is established one hour only may be given to spinning and the rest to literary training.

Young India—Feb. 2nd, 1921.

HAND-SPINNING AGAIN

The Servant of India has a fling too at spinning and that is based as I shall presently show an ignorance of the facts. Spinning does protect a women's virtue, because it enables women who are to-day working on public roads and are often in danger of having their modesty outraged, to protect themselves, and I know no other occupation that *lacs* of women can follow save spinning. Let me inform the Jesting writer that several women have already returned to the sanctity of their homes and taken to spinning which they say is the one occupation which means so such *barkat* (blessing). I claim for it the properties of a musical instrument, for whilst a hungry and a naked woman will refuse to dance to the accompaniment of a piano, I have seen women beaming with joy to see the spinning wheel work, for they know that they can through that rustic instrument both feed and clothe themselves.

Yes, it does solve the problem of India's chronic poverty and is an insurance against famine. The writer of the jests may not know the scandals that I know about irrigation and relief works. These works are largely a fraud. But if my wise counsellors will devote themselves to introducing the wheel in every home, I promise that the wheel will be an almost complete protection against famine. It is idle to cite Austria. I admit the poverty and limitations of my humanity. I can only think of India's *Kamadhenu*,[1] and the spinning wheel is that for India. For India had the spinning wheel in every home before the advent of the East India Company. India being a cotton growing country, it must be considered a crime to import a single yard of yarn from outside. The figures quoted by the writer are irrelevant.

The fact is that inspite of the manufacture of 62-7 crores pounds of yarn in 1917–18 India imported several crore yards of foreign yarn which were woven by the mills as well as the weavers. The writer does not also seem to know that more cloth is to-day woven by our weavers than by mills, but the bulk of it is foreign yarn and therefore our weavers are supporting foreign spinners. I would not mind it much if we were doing something else instead. When spinning was almost compulsorily stopped nothing replaced it save slavery and idleness. Our mills cannot to-day spin enough for our wants, and if they did, they will not keep down prices unless they were compelled. They are frankly Money-makers and will not therefore regulate prices according to the needs of the nations. Hand-spinning is therefore designed to put millions of rupees in the hands of poor villagers. Every agricultural country requires a supplementary industry to enable the peasants to utilise the spare hours. Such industry for India has always been spinning. Is it such a visionary ideal—an attempt to revive an ancient occupation whose destruction has brought on slavery, pauperism and disappearance of the inimitable artistic talents which was once all expressed in the wonderful fabric of India and which was the envy of the world?

And now a few figures. One boy could, if he worked say four hours daily, spin $\frac{1}{4}$ lb. of yarn. 64,000 students would, therefore, spin 16,000 lbs per day and therefore feed 8,000 weavers if a weaver wove two lbs of hand-spun yarn. But the students and others are required to spin during this year of purification by way of penance in order to popularise spinning and to add to the manufacture of hand-spun yarn so as to overtake full manufacture during the current year. The nation may be too lazy to do it. But if all put their hands to this work, it is incredibly easy, it involves very little sacrifice and saves an annual drain of sixty crores even if it does nothing else. I have discussed the matter

---

1. The cow of prosperity in Hindu mythology. [Ed.]

with many mill-owners, several economists, men of business and no one has yet been able to challenge the position herein set forth. I do expect the "Servant of India" to treat a serious subject with seriousness and accuracy of information.

Young India—Feb. 16, 1921.

THE SECRET OF SWARAJ

The Congress resolution has rightly emphasised the importance of Swadeshi[1] and the amount of greater sacrifice by merchants.

India cannot be free so long as India voluntarily encourages or tolerates the economic drain which has been going on for the past century and a half. Boycott of foreign goods means no more and no less than boycott of foreign cloth. Foreign cloth constitutes the largest drain voluntarily permitted by us. It means sixty crores of rupees annually paid by us for piecegoods. If India could make a successful effort to stop that drain, she can gain Swaraj by that one act.

India was enslaved for satisfying the greed of the foreign cloth manufacturer. When the East India Company came in, we were able to manufacture all the cloth we needed, and more for export. By processes that need not be described here, India has become practically wholly dependent upon foreign manufacture for her clothing.

But we ought not to be dependent. India has the ability to manufacture all her cloth if her children will work for it. Fortunately India has yet enough weavers to supplement the out-turn of her mills. The mills do not and cannot immediately manufacture all the cloth we want. The reader may not know that, even at the present moment, the weavers weave more cloth than the mills. But the latter weave five crore yards of fine foreign counts, equal to forty crore yards of coarser counts. The way to carry out a successful boycott of foreign cloth is to increase the output of yarn. And this can only be done by hand-spinning.

To bring about such a boycott, it is necessary for our merchants to stop all foreign importation, and to sell out, even at a loss, all foreign cloth already stocked in India, preferably to foreign buyers. They must cease to speculate in cotton, and keep all the cotton required for home use. They must stop purchasing all foreign cotton.

---

1. An Indian nationalist policy of economic self-reliance based on buying indigenous goods and reviving industries in India, such as cotton spinning, that had been decimated by British imperialism. [Ed.]

The mill-owners should work their mills not for their profits but as a national trust and therefore cease to spin finer counts, and weave only for the home market.

The householder has to revise his or her ideas of fashion and, at least for the time being, suspend the use of fine garments which are not always worn to cover the body. He should train himself to see art and beauty in the spotlessly white *khaddar*[2] and to appreciate its soft unevenness. The householder must learn to use cloth as a miser uses his horde.

And even when the householders have revised their tastes about dress, somebody will have to spin yarn for the weavers. This can only be done by every one spinning during spare hours either for love or money.

We are engaged in a spiritual war. We are now living in abnormal times. Normal activities are always suspended in abnormal times. And if we are out to gain *Swaraj* in a year's time, it means that we must concentrate upon our goal to the exclusion of every thing else. I therefore venture to suggest to the students all over India to suspend their normal studies for one year and devote their time to the manufacture of yarn by hand-spinning. It will be their greatest act of service to the motherland, and their most natural contribution to the attainment of *Swaraj*. During the late war our rulers attempted to turn every factory into an arsenal for turning out bullets of lead. During this war of ours, I suggest every national school and college being turned into a factory for preparing cones of yarns for the nation. The students will lose nothing by the occupation: they will gain a kingdom here and hereafter. There is a famine of cloth in India. To assist in removing this dearth is surely an act of merit. If it is sinful to use foreign yarn, it is a virtue to manufacture more Swadeshi yarn in order to enable us to cope with the want that would be created by the disuse of foreign yarn.

The obvious question asked would be, if it is so necessary to manufacture yarn, why not pay every poor person to do so? The answer is that handspinning is not, and never was, a calling like weaving, carpentry, etc. Under the pre-British economy of India, spinning was an honourable and leisurely occupation for the women of India. It is difficult to revive the art among the women in the time at our disposal. But it is incredibly simple and easy for the school-goers to respond to the nation's call. Let not one decry the work as being derogatory to the dignity of men or students. It was an art confined to the women of India because the latter had more leisure. And being graceful, musical, and as it did not involve any great exertion, it had become the monopoly of women. But it is certainly as graceful for either sex as is music for instance. In hand-spinning is hidden the protection of women's virtue, the in-

---

2. Cotton cloth produced by the spinning wheel. [Ed.]

surance against famine and the cheapening of prices. In it is hidden the secret of *Swaraj*. The revival of hand-spinning is the least penance we must do for the sin of our forefathers in having succumbed to the satanic influences of the foreign manufacturer.

The school-goers will restore hand-spinning to its respectable status. They will hasten the process of making *khaddar* fashionable. For no mother or father worth the name will refuse to wear cloth made out of yarn spun by their children. And the scholars, practical recognition of art will compel the attention of the weavers of India. If we are to wean the Punjabi from the calling not of a soldier but of the murderer of innocent and free people of other lands, we must give back to him the occupation of weaving. The race of the peaceful Julahis of the Punjab is all but extinct. It is for the scholars of the Punjab to make it possible for the Punjabi weaver to return to his innocent calling.

I hope to show in a future issue how easy it is to introduce this change in the schools and how quickly, on these terms, we can nationalise our schools and colleges. Everywhere the students have asked me what new things I would introduce into our nationalised schools. I have invariably told them I would certainly introduce spinning. I feel, so much more clearly than ever before that during the transition period, we must devote exclusive attention to spinning and certain other things of immediate national use, so as to make up for past neglect. And the students will be better able and equipped to enter upon the new course of studies.

Do I want to put back the hand of the clock of progress? Do I want to replace the mills by hand-spinning and hand-weaving? Do I want to replace the railway by the country cart? Do I want to destroy machinery altogether? These questions have been asked by some journalists and public men. My answer is: I would not weep over the disappearance of machinery or consider it a calamity. But I have no design upon machinery as such. What I want to do at the present moment is to supplement the production of yarn and cloth through our mill, save the millions we send out of India, and distribute them in our cottages. This I cannot do unless and until the nation is prepared to devote its leisure hours to hand-spinning. To that end we must adopt the methods I have ventured to suggest for popularising spinning as a duty rather than as a means of livelihood.

Young India—January 19, 1921.

Glossary

Bobbin a cylinder around which thread or yarn is wound so that it can be easily unwound for weaving or other forms of textile production.

Boxing in surrounding machinery with protective fencing or boxing to prevent accidents.

Carding cotton or wool that has been combed; the action of combing cotton or wool.

Collier a coal miner.

Decussate having the shape of an "x."

Doffing, doffer the action of stripping cotton or wool from a carding machine's spools or bobbins. A doffer was a worker, usually a child, who stripped bits of cotton or wool or removed full bobbins from carding machines.

Drawing various operations of pulling threads through other threads or through spindles in the manufacture of textiles.

Effluvia particulate matter in the air, thought to be the primary cause of infectious disease in the mid-nineteenth century.

Fencing in see "boxing in" above.

Fettling the action of lining a furnace.

Flying shuttle shuttle operated by pulling a cord that sent the shuttle from side to side, freeing up one hand of the weaver to press the weft.

Fustian coarse cloth made of cotton and linen combined.

Mule spinner in 1779, Samuel Crompton combined the features of the spinning jenny with those of the water frame to produce a finer quality of yarn than had previously been possible.

Operative worker.

Piecer or piecener one who twists (by hand) broken strands of yarn back together. This job was usually done by children in the nineteenth-century mill.

Rove cotton or wool when it has been drawn out and slightly twisted. "Roving" is the process.

Scrofula in nineteenth-century medicine, a disease characterized by swelling and degeneration of lymph glands. Also called struma.

Scribbler a carding machine.

Sough   to drain, to build drains.

Spindle   a spool or bobbin.

Spinning jenny   a machine invented by James Hargreaves sometime between 1764–67. The machine allowed one wheel to turn many spindles and radically increased the speed of production of thread or yarn.

Stocking frame   a knitting machine.

Struma   see "scrofula."

Surat cotton   Indian cotton, of generally low quality, from the region near Bombay.

Swadeshi   in Indian Nationalism, the economic program that encouraged the support of indigenous industries, especially that of hand-spun cotton (an industry that had been virtually wiped out by the mechanized textile industry of Britain).

Sweat, sweating   sweated labor refers usually to work done at home, by the piece, usually distributed by a middleman who acts as a subcontractor.

Thronged   to be distressed, afflicted.

Turn-out   a strike.

Warp   threads that are at right angles to the weft or woof; usually stronger than the weft threads.

Water frame   a spinning machine invented by Richard Arkwright that was powered by water.

Weft or woof   threads that are at right angles to the warp.

Contributors' Biographies

Babbage, Charles (1792–1871)   A mathematician, Babbage started work in 1819 on the project that was to occupy much of his life: a machine to calculate numerical tables. His plans for a "difference engine" won the financial backing of the Royal Society and the chancellor of the exchequer. In 1823, Babbage received the first gold medal from the Astronomical Society (which he had helped found), its president saying the proposed machine was "in scope, as in execution, unlike anything before accomplished." Babbage's travels to study mechanical works abroad led to *On the Economy of Machinery and Manufactures* (1832) and to the idea for a new machine, an "analytic engine" using two sets of perforated cards that could solve multiple functions.

Baines, Sir Edward (1800–1890)   At age fifteen, Baines started reporting for the *Leeds Mercury,* one of the leading provincial newspapers, and he became the editor three years later. He also began to teach Sunday school at the Congregational chapel in 1815, a task he continued for over forty years His books include *History of the Cotton Manufacture of Great Britain* (1835), *Crosby Hall Lectures* (1848), and *Testimony and Appeal on the Effects of Total Abstinence* (1853). In 1859, Baines was elected to the House of Commons, where he was principally involved in widening the electorate and fostering a set of issues important to nonconformists.

Beaumont, George   Biographical information is unavailable.

Bell, Lady Florence (1851–1930)   Florence Eveleen Eleonore Olliffe Bell, a writer of plays, children's stories, novels, and essays, grew up in Paris during the Second Empire, but left during the Franco-Prussian war of 1870. In 1876, she married Hugh Bell, who had inherited his family's ironworks. Bell's book *At the Works* (1907, revised ed. 1911) grew out of her thirty years' experience as the wife of a leading industrialist.

Carlyle, Thomas (1795–1881)   Carlyle, born in Scotland, spent his early career teaching while he wrote articles for the *Edinburgh Encyclopaedia* and translated Legendre's *Geometry* (1824), Goethe's *Wilhelm Meister* (1824), and *German Ro-*

mances (1827). He also began in 1822 a series of "Portraits of Men of Genius and Character," which started with a life of Schiller that was published separately in 1825. He wrote for the *Edinburgh Review* and other periodicals, mostly on German literature and especially on Goethe with whom he corresponded. His satire and spiritual autobiography, *Sartor Resartus,* was serialized in *Fraser's Magazine* in 1833–1834, but was not well received. Besides numerous articles and essays, Carlyle wrote *Chartism* (1839), *On Heroes, Hero-worship, and the Heroic in History* (1841), *Past and Present* (1843), *Life and Letters of Oliver Cromwell* (1845), *Latter-day Pamphlets* (1850), *The Life of Sterling* (1851), *History of Friedrich II of Prussia* (1858–1865), *Inaugural Address at Edinburgh* (1866), *Reminiscences of my Irish Journey in 1849* (1882), and *Last Words of Thomas Carlyle* (1882).

Dilke, Lady Emilia Francis Strong (1840–1904) Dilke studied at the South Kensington Art School at the advice of Ruskin, but she eventually became an art critic and historian rather than an artist. She wrote for a number of periodicals, and after 1872 she specialized in the French renaissance, publishing five influential books on the subject. Dilke advocated the technical education of women, the improvement of the conditions of working women in general, and the passage of women's suffrage. She joined the Women's Provident and Protective League, becoming its president in 1902 when it had been renamed the Women's Trade Union League, and joined the Woman's Suffrage Society at Oxford. She also became an important promoter of trade unions.

Dodd, George (1808–1881) Dodd did much of his writing for Charles Knight, the publisher who specialized in popular instruction. His writings for Knight include articles, primarily but not exclusively on industrial art, in the *Penny Magazine* (1832–1845), *Penny Cyclopædia* (1833–1844), *London* (1841–1844), *The Land We Live In* (1847) and the *English Cyclopædia* (1853–1861). Dodd edited and wrote most of the *Cyclopædia of the Industry of all Nations* (1851) and *The Textile Manufactures of Great Britain* (1844–46) and wrote the *Dictionary of Manufactures, Mining, Machinery, and the Industrial Arts* (1871). Some of his articles were collected in *Days at the Factories* (1843) and *Curiosities of Industry* (1852).

Engels, Friedrich (1820–1895) Engels's father owned textile factories, both in the family's native Germany and in Manchester, England. Young Engels spent 1838 to 1841 learning the export business in Bremen, living a middle-class life at the same time that he was reading revolutionary texts. He published articles under a pseudonym and first met Marx when he joined the Young Hegelians, the followers of Hegel's philosophy who combined atheism with political activism. After a year in military service, Engels went to England and published *The Condition of the Working Classes in England in 1844* (1845). His partnership with Marx grew out of his contributions to *The German-French Yearbooks,* which Marx edited. See entry for Karl Marx for an account of their joint publications.

Gandhi, Mohandas Karamchand (1869–1948) Gandhi was eventually called Mahatma, which means "great-souled," as the leader of Indian independence from

Great Britain. He studied law in England, practiced briefly without much success in India, and then went to South Africa. There he became involved in, and then the leader of, the campaign for the rights of Indian settlers, adopting passive resistance or nonviolence, which he called Satyagraha ("truth-force"), as a political tool. He also assumed an ascetic lifestyle that celebrated manual labor, the renunciation of material goods, and celibacy. After achieving a compromise on Indian rights in South Africa, Gandhi returned to India in 1915 where he led the Indian National Congress with five main goals: Indian self-rule, the emancipation of Indian peasants, Hindu-Muslim unity, abolition of untouchability, and a return to hand-spinning.

Gaskell, Peter (1806?–1841) A surgeon and Liberal social reformer. Author of *Artisans and Machinery* (1836), *The Manufacturing Population of England* (1833).

Kay-Shuttleworth, Sir James Phillips (1804–1877) Kay-Shuttleworth was best known for envisioning the structure of what became the English system of public education, with trained teachers, public inspection, religious instruction alongside secular teaching, liberty of religious consciousness, and funding from both local and public sources. He began his career, however, as a doctor in Manchester, devoting himself to the cholera hospital and a dispensary in a poor district. His 1832 book *The Moral and Physical Condition of the Working Classes Employed in the Cotton Manufacture in Manchester* led to sanitary and educational reforms, which he continued to make as an assistant poor-law commissioner after 1835.

Macaulay, Baron Thomas Babington (1800–1859) In 1825, Macaulay started writing regularly for the *Edinburgh Review.* He entered the House of Commons as a Whig in 1830 and won praise for his frequent speeches. He spent 1834 to 1838 in India, accompanied by one of his sisters; as a member of the Supreme Council in India, he set up a Western system of education and drafted the penal code practically by himself. After returning to England, and returning to Parliament representing Edinburgh, he was made Secretary of War, from 1839 to 1841. Macaulay lost his seat in 1847. Two years later the first volumes of his *History of England,* which he had been writing for ten years, were published. The *History* was extraordinarily popular, and Macaulay was reelected to Parliament without even running in 1852. His health broke down soon after, however, and he resigned from Parliament in 1856.

Martineau, Harriet (1802–1876) Martineau, who began to go deaf as a child and whose health was never good, first started to write for the Unitarian periodical, the *Monthly Repository,* in 1821. By 1829, her father had died and her family had lost what little money they had, forcing Martineau to do needlework to survive. She was also writing regularly for the Unitarians when, in 1832, she found success with *Illustrations of Political Economy* (1832–1834). That series of a story a month for twenty-five months was joined by *Poor Laws and Paupers Illustrated* (1833) and *Illustrations of Taxation* (1834). Martineau's popularity and her place in literary society were secured with those three popularizations of economic theory. Her later books include two works critical of America, *Society in America* (1837) and *A Ret-*

rospect of Western Travel (1838); *Deerbrook* (1839), a novel; *The Hour and the Man* (1841) with Toussaint L'Ouverture as hero; *The Philosophy of Comte, freely translated and condensed* (1853), which Comte admired; and *The Factory Controversy, a Warning against "Meddling Legislation"* (1855). She also wrote for periodicals and produced three to six articles a week for the *Daily News* for many years. Martineau first wrote her autobiography in 1855, but it was not published until after she died in 1876.

Marx, Karl (1818–1883)   Marx, born in Prussia, came from a long line of rabbis, though his father had converted to Christianity. As a student at the University of Berlin, Marx was introduced to Hegel's philosophy, which he later was to critique, and he was part of a group called the Young Hegelians, who combined atheism with political action. Moving to Paris in 1843, Marx first became associated with communist workingmen's societies and became friends with Friedrich Engels. The two men both moved to Brussels when Marx was expelled from France in 1845. There, they wrote *The Holy Family* (1845), criticizing Hegelian idealism, and *The German Ideology* (written 1845–1846, published 1932). They wrote the *Communist Manifesto* (1848) at the request of the Communist League, a London organization of immigrant German handicraftsmen. From 1850 to 1864, Marx and his family were poverty-stricken. They were mostly supported by Engels, though Marx also wrote regularly for the *New York Tribune* and published *The Eighteenth Brumaire of Louis Bonaparte* (1852) and *A Contribution to the Critique of Political Economy* (1859). Marx took on a public role when the International Working Men's Association was founded in 1864. He became famous throughout Europe with his support, in *Civil War in France* (1871), of the short-lived revolutionary government, the Paris Commune, and with his leadership of the First International. Only the first volume of his masterwork, *Das Kapital,* was published in his lifetime (in 1867). The last two volumes were published by Engels from Marx's notes in 1885 and 1894. Marx's other important works include *Economic and Philosophic Manuscripts of 1844* (not published until 1859), *The Poverty of Philosophy* (1847), and *The Class Struggles in France, 1848 to 1850* (1850). It is important to note that most of these works were not translated into English until the 1880s or later.

Morley, Henry (1822–1894)   After training as an apothecary, Morley abandoned that profession and set up a school in Manchester. He did some journalistic writing that Dickens admired and he was invited to take part in the management of *Household Words* in 1850. He wrote for that journal and for *All the Year Round* until 1865. He published biographies, satires, and fairy tales in addition to numerous articles. In 1857 he became a lecturer in English at King's College, London.

Morris, William (1834–1896)   After leaving Oxford, where he formed a lifelong friendship with the painter Edward Burne-Jones and became fascinated by the Middle Ages, Morris trained to be an architect. As part of the Pre-Raphaelite Brotherhood, under the influence of Dante Gabriel Rossetti, Morris then began to paint. He was already writing poetry and stories, publishing them in the Pre-Raphaelites' *Ox-*

ford and Cambridge Magazine. His books of poetry include *The Defence of Guenevere and other Poems* (1858), *The Life and Death of Jason* (1867), *Earthly Paradise* (1868–1870), *Sigurd the Volsung and the Fall of Niblungs* (1876), and *Poems by the Way* (1891). In 1861, Morris founded a remarkably influential firm of decorators that made everything from stained-glass windows to wallpaper, tapestries to furniture, all with the purpose of returning the decorative arts to the field of fine arts. Morris helped found the Socialist League in 1885.

O'Neil, John Ward (1810–1876)   O'Neil's diary, written in fourteen pages of a cash-book and covering the years of the cotton famine from 1860 to 1864, was found in a trash heap in 1947. What has been discovered of his life was that he was born in Carlisle and was married in the mid-1830s. In 1854, because he was unemployed, O'Neil left Carlisle and found work as a power-loom weaver in Garnett and Horsfall's factory Low Moor in Clitheroe. He was a supporter of reading-rooms, mechanic institutes, and trade unions; in fact, he was often a delegate or committee member of the latter.

Oastler, Richard (1789–1861)   Oastler was articled to an architect as a boy, but took over his father's job as steward to the Fixby estates, which had over 1,000 tenants. Starting in 1830, he became known as the "factory king" when he devoted his energies to improving the lives of laborers, particularly by campaigning for a ten-hour day bill and child-protection legislation. Oastler traveled throughout England, lecturing, organizing, and writing to promote factory reforms. He also opposed the Poor Law Amendment Act of 1834 because he thought it would harm church and land interests. In refusing to enforce the new poor law on the Fixby estates, he lost his position and spent 1840–1844 in prison for debt to his former employer. From prison, he published a weekly paper, *The Fleet Papers*, which inspired working men to form Oastler Committees and hold Oastler Festivals to raise money to free him.

Owen, Robert (1771–1858)   Owen's first experiment in social reform was in the management of the cotton mills of New Lanark starting in 1799. He modified children's working conditions, improved housing, opened a company store and schools, and tried to influence the morality of his employees—all while running the business successfully. New Lanark attracted thousands of visitors, and Owen's vision of socialist villages spread widely. After withdrawing from New Lanark, partially because his partners disapproved of his antireligious views, Owen founded a cooperative community in the United States called New Harmony which failed rather quickly. He wrote several works on manufacturing, including *A Statement regarding the New Lanark Establishment* (1812); *Observations on the Effect of the Manufacturing System* (1815); and *Address to Master-Manufacturers of Great Britain* (1819).

Place, Francis (1771–1854)   A leather-breeches maker and son of a bailiff, Place took his first public role when he helped organize an unsuccessful strike in 1793, a role which he continued as a central member of the radical working-class group, the London Corresponding Society. He opened his own, quite successful, tailor's shop in 1799, withdrawing from politics for about ten years. As he became friends with important political thinkers like James Mill and Jeremy Bentham, his involvement in social issues grew; in 1817 he turned his business over to his son in order to devote himself to politics. The library behind his shop became a central meeting place for reformers, and Place was noted for gathering the facts used by his friends in Parliament, particularly in the campaign for the repeal of the anticombination laws. While Place helped draft the *People's Charter* (1838), he was not central to the Chartist movement.

Ricardo, David (1772–1823)   Ricardo was a successful stockbroker before he published a series of letters in the *Morning Chronicle* responding to Adam Smith's *Wealth of Nations* during a currency crisis in 1809. These letters were followed by a number of pamphlets and tracts, and finally, with the support of his friends Thomas Malthus and James Mill, Ricardo published a systematic elucidation of his views in *Principles of Political Economy and Taxation* (1817). This work quickly became one of the central texts of classic political economy. Having retired from business in 1814, he entered Parliament in 1819 as a radical, often supporting the utilitarians.

Ruskin, John (1819–1900)   Ruskin's first major work was the first volume of *Modern Painters* (1843, second volume 1846, third and fourth volumes 1856, fifth volume 1860), which he started as a defense of the painting of J. M. W. Turner, but expanded into a general treatise on the principles of art. The book was both a popular success and an influential work of criticism. By the third volume, Ruskin had added the subtitle "Of Many Things," since it now covered everything from botanical classification to political economy. Ruskin's other important works on art and architecture from this period include *The Seven Lamps of Architecture* (1849), *Stones of Venice* (1851–1853), *The Elements of Drawing* (1856), *The Political Economy of Art* (1856), and *The Elements of Perspective* (1859). He established a utopian society, St. George's, whose projects, whether farming or reviving handmade linen, mostly failed. These ventures were only the last in a life of philanthropy and patronage through which Ruskin gave away most of the fortune he had inherited and earned.

Smith, Adam (1723–1790)   Smith was born in Kirkcaldy and studied at Glasgow and Oxford. He returned to Glasgow, lectured on English literature, briefly occupied the chair of logic, and then became a professor of moral philosophy in 1752. He made his reputation as an important thinker with the publication of *Theory of Moral Sentiments* (1759). Smith's *Wealth of Nations* (1776) founded the field of political economy; its account of the marketplace was influential from the moment the book was published.

Ure, Andrew (1778–1857)   Born in Glasgow, Ure received his M.D. from Glasgow University in 1801 and was appointed professor of chemistry and natural philosophy at Andersonian University in 1804. The popular scientific lectures he started in Glasgow are thought to be the first of their kind and were widely imitated. In 1830, he left for London to work as an analytical and commercial chemist for the board of customs on such problems as estimating the quantity of sugar in sugar-cane juice. In addition to the fifty-three papers on physics and pure and applied chemistry listed in the Royal Society's Catalogue, Ure published *A New Systematic Table of The Materia Medica* (1813), the *Dictionary of Chemistry* (1821), *New System of Geology* (1829), *Philosophy of Manufactures* (1835), *The Cotton Manufactures of Great Britain* (1836), *Dictionary of Arts, Manufactures, and Mines* (1839), *The Revenue in Jeopardy from Spurious Chemistry* (1843), and *The General Malaria of London* (1850).

Wing, Charles (dates unknown)   Author of *Evils of the Factory System,* First ed Published in 1837. Surgeon to the Royal Metropolitan Hospital for Children.

Suggestions for Further Reading

LOOKING INSIDE

Nineteenth-Century Sources

Aitken, W. C. *The Early History of Brass and the Brass Manufactures of Birmingham.* Birmingham: Martin Billing, 1866.

Felkin, William. *Felkin's History of the Machine-wrought Hosiery and Lace Manufactures.* (1867) Devon: Newton Abbot, 1967.

Head, George. *A Home Tour through the Manufacturing Districts of England in the Summer of 1835.* New York: Harper & Brothers, 1836.

James, John. *History of the Worsted Manufacture in England.* London: Longman, Brown, 1857.

Shaw, Simeon. *History of the Staffordshire Potteries.* Handley: The Author, 1829.

Taylor, W. C. *Notes of a Tour in the Manufacturing Districts of Lancashire.* London: Duncan and Malcolm, 1842.

Taylor, W. C. *Factories and the Factory System: from Parliamentary Documents and Personal Examination.* London: J. How, 1844.

Ure, Andrew. *The Cotton Manufacture in Great Britain.* London: Knight, 1835.

Modern Sources

Ashton, T. S. *Iron and Steel in the Industrial Revolution.* Manchester: Manchester Univ. Press, 1924.

Chapman, Stanley D. *The Cotton Industry in the Industrial Revolution.* 2nd ed. Basingstoke: MacMillan Education. Ltd. 1987.

Coleman, D. C. *The British Paper Industry, 1495–1860.* Oxford: Clarendon Press, 1958.

Flinn, Michael W. *The History of the British Coal Industry.* Vol. 2, 1700–1830. Oxford: Clarendon Press, 1984.

Haber, L. F. *The Chemical Industry during the Nineteenth Century.* Oxford: Clarendon Press, 1958.

Harris, J. R. *The British Iron Industry, 1700–1850.* Houndsmill and London: Mac Milan Education Ltd., 1988.

Malmgreen, Gail. *Silk Town: Industry and Culture in Macclesfield 1750–1835.* Hull: Hull Univ. Press, 1985.

Unwin, George. *Samuel Oldknow and the Arkwrights.* 1924. Reprint, New York: Augustus Kelly, 1968.

MACHINES AND MANAGEMENT

Eighteenth- and Nineteenth-Century Sources

Dodd, William. *The Factory System Illustrated.* 1841. Reprint, London: F. Cass, 1968.

Malthus, Thomas. *Principles of Political Economy.* London: J Murray, 1820.

Mandeville, Bernard. *The Fable of the Bees.* 1732. Reprint, Oxford: Oxford Univ. Press, 1924.

Mill, John Stuart. *The Principles of Political Economy.* 1848. Reprint, New York: Colonial Press, 1900.

Modern Sources

Keynes, John Maynard. *General Theory of Employment, Interest, and Money.* New York: Harcourt, Brace, 1936.

CALCULATING LOSSES

Nineteenth-Century Sources

Irish University Press. *Index to British Parliamentary Papers on Children's Employment.* Dublin: The Press, 1973.

Modern Sources

Johnson, Richard. "Notes on the Schooling of the English Working Class, 1780–1850." In Roger Dale, Geoff Esland, and Madeleine MacDonald, eds., *Schooling and Capitalism: A Sociological Reader.* London: Routledge & Kegan Paul in association with the Open Univ. Press, 1976.

Laqueur, Thomas. *Religion and Respectability: Sunday Schools and Working Class Culture, 1780–1850.* New Haven: Yale Univ. Press, 1976.

Nardinelli, Clark. *Child Labor and the Industrial Revolution.* Bloomington, Ind.: Indiana Univ. Press, 1990.

Nicholas, Stephen J., and Deborah Oxley. "The Living Standards of Women during the Industrial Revolution." *Economic History Review* (1993) 46:723–749.

———. "The Industrial Revolution and the Genesis of the Male Breadwinner." In Graeme Donald Snooks, ed., *Was the Industrial Revolution Necessary?* London: Routledge, 1994.

Pinchbeck, Ivy. *Women Workers and the Industrial Revolution 1750–1850.* London: Routledge, 1930.

Rackham, Clara D. *Factory Law.* London: T. Nelson, 1938.

Smelser, Neil J. *Social Change in the Industrial Revolution.* Chicago: Univ. of Chicago Press, 1959.

Ward, J. T. *The Factory Movement, 1830–1855.* London: Macmillan, 1962

BY HAND

Nineteenth-Century Sources

Arts and Crafts Exhibition Society. *Arts and Crafts Essays by Members of the Arts and Crafts Exhibition Society.* London: Rivington, Percival, & Co., 1893.

Eastlake, Charles. *Hints on Household Taste.* London: Longmans, Green, 1878.

Pugin, A. W. N. *An Apology for the Revival of Christian Architecture in England.* London: J. Weale, 1843.

Modern Sources

Clark, Kenneth. *The Gothic Revival: [An Essay on the History of Taste.]* London: John Murray, 1995.

Gandhi, M. K. *Hind Swaraj: or Indian Home rule.* Ahmedebad: Navajvan Pub. House, 1938.

Parel, Anthony. *Gandhi, Freedom, and Self-Rule.* Lanham, Md: Lexington Books, 2000.

Stansky, Peter. *Redesigning the World: William Morris, the 1880s and the Arts and Crafts Movement.* Princeton: Princeton Univ. Press, 1985.

Index